COMPARATIVE AND CRITICAL STUDY OF EKĀVALĪ

COMPARATIVE AND CRITICAL STUDY

OF

EKĀVALĪ

(CONTRIBUTION OF VIDYĀDHARA TO SANSKRIT POETICS)

BY

DR. (MRS.) SAVITRI GUPTA
Department of Sanskrit
Lakshmi Bai College
University of Delhi

With a Foreword by

DR. SATYA VRAT SHASTRI
Professor Sanskrit Department
University of Delhi
Ex-Vice-Chancellor
Shri Jagannath Sanskrit University
Puri, Orissa

EASTERN BOOK LINKERS
DELHI : : (INDIA)

Publisher :
EASTERN BOOK LINKERS
5825, New Chandrawal, Jawahar Nagar,
DELHI-110007.

First Edition : 1992

Price EASTERN BOOK LINKERS EBL RS. 500-

ISBN : 81-85133-57-3

Printed at :
R. R. Printers
X-3A, X Block, G. N. 2,
Brahmpuri, DELHI-110053.

Dedicated

To

DR. KRISHNA LAL
Professor & Head
Department of Sanskrit,
University of Delhi, Delhi-110007

एकामेकावलीमेव कण्ठे धत्त कवीश्वराः ।
आः किमन्यैरलङ्कारैरसारैर्भारदायिभिः ।।

FOREWORD

I have great pleasure in introducing to the world of scholars Dr. (Mrs.) Savitri Gupta's work, "Contribution of Vidyādhara to Sanskrit Poetics", which had got her the degree of Ph.D. from the University of Delhi.

The work 'Comparative and Critical Study of Ekāvalī' makes a complete, critical and comparative study of each topic discussed in the *Ekāvalī* of Vidyādhara, who though not a torch-bearer, has made a significant contribution to the field of Sanskrit-Poetics. His work is written on the pattern of Kāvyaprakāśa. What Mammaṭa presents in ten Ullāsas, Vidhyādhara has presented in eight Unmeṣas.

A speciality of the Ekāvalī lies in the fact that Vidyādhara composed all the illustrative verses in praise of his patron Narasiṁha. He has set a tradition, not existent till his time, which was enthusiastically espoused by his successors in Pratāparudrayaśobhūṣaṇa, Nañrājayaśobhūṣaṇa, Raghunāthabhūpālīya, Alaṁkāramañjuṣā and other works of this kind.

The Ekāvalī is fortunate enough to have a Sanskrit commentary 'Taralā' by a well-known Sanskrit commentator Mallinātha. This commetary has added much to the value and importance of the Ekāvalī.

In the Ekāvalī the nature of Kāvya, three powers viz. Śabdaśaktis namely Abhidhā, Lakṣaṇā and Vyañjanā, the types of Dhvani, Rasa, Guṇa, Doṣa, Śabdālaṁkāras and Arthālaṁkāras are discussed in detail.

Each of the eight unmeṣas of the *Ekāvalī* consists of three parts viz; kārikās in verse which define and classify the technical terms; the vṛtti or the explanation of the kārikas in prose and the examples given to illustrate the kārikās. It is important to note here that *all these three parts are the creations of Vidyādhara himself.* This is something generally not to be met within other ācāryas of Sanskrit-Poetics. Moreover, the illustrative verses of the *Ekāvalī* make a complete kāvya as they are composed in praise of king Narsiṁha. Vidhyādhara is thus, both, an ācārya and a kavi.

The *present work* has been divided into nine chapters and ends with the summary of the topics discussed in the main body. In the concluding chapter, the author has tried to trace the original ideas of Vidyādhara as given in the *Ekāvalī* which are not found in any work on Sanskrit-Poetics and which are the original contribution of Vidyādhara only.

Thus, our author has presented a thorough critique on the work under study, highlighting at every stage the original contribution of Vidhyādhara. Her work shows her capacity for critical examinations of facts and her ability to arrive at sound judgement on their basis. She has worked hard to bring to light the contribution of Vidhyādhara to Sanskrit-Poetics and has, thus, laid the scholarly community under deep debt of gratitude.

Vidhyādhara's work, apart from being full scale and indepth analysis of the principles of literary criticism, is also an original and independent kāvya containing as it does through a large corpus of illustrations dotting it his creative composition. Since this composition pertains to one central figure, the patron of the poet, it required of him all the ingenuity to appear innovative, a feat by all standards, considering the limit that he has set before himself in picking up the range of his description. It was this feat which must have aroused the interest of later writers who thought of repeating it, leading in course of time, to the emergence of a whole class of literature which has few parallels elsewhere. Our author has done full justice in the present work to the pioneer of this literature even while concentrating on his contribution to Sanskrit-Poetics. She has put the spotlight on a writer, who believing as he did in the commingling of theory and practice and illustrating the theory through his own illustrations, stood out as a class in himself. I am pretty sure that her work presented so diligently and meticulously will meet with full approbation of discerning critics.

SATYAVRAT SHASTRI

31.1.92

Professor, Department of Sanskrit
University of Delhi
Ex-Vice-Chancellor
Shri Jagannath Sanskrit University
Puri, Orissa

PREFACE

The present work is the doctoral thesis submitted by the undersigned to the University of Delhi, for a Ph.D. degree in Sanskrit. This is an attempt to trace, as its name denotes, a comparative and a critical study of each and every topic of Ekāvalī of Vidyādhara, who occupies a dominant place in Sanskrit-Poetics.

Inspite of discussing all the topics of poetics, a very peculiar feature of Ekāvalī needs special mention i.e., Vidyādhara composed all the illustrative verses in praise of his patron Narasiṁha of Orissa. This originality of Vidhyādhara designates him a kavi also. The tradition is followed by many ācāryas in Sanskrit.

The subject-matter of Ekāvalī is critically examined in nine chapters of this work. It opens with the introductory-chapter, covering briefly the nature, characteristics, history and different schools of Sanskrit-poetics with life, date and works of Vidhyādhara and culminates in the original contributions of Vidhyādhara as found in Ekāvalī. References from Sanskrit-works consulted have been given in the foot-notes and original-quotations in Sanskrit have been incorporated at the end of the work.

I have not come across with any such work, devoted to the study of either Vidhyādhara or his magnumopus Ekāvalī. I have recently seen an edition of Ekāvalī with a Hindi translation.

I would gratefully welcome any suggestion from scholars regarding the work. I am definite that this would add a drop in the ocean of the vast literary—criticism available in Sanskrit.

It gives me great pleasure in expressing my heart-felt thanks to all those who have helped me. Some of the works, I have taken help from, have been referred to in the bibliography. But I owe more to the scholars, whose works could not be referred to but who have helped me in formulating my thoughts.

Above all I record my deep sense of gratitude to my mentor

Dr. C. B. Gupta, without whose kind help, valuable suggestions, constant guidance and blessings, this work would not have seen the light of the day. I pray Him for his early recovery and a healthy long life.

I wish to express my deep sense of gratitude to my revered teacher, Professor Dr. Satya Vrat, a distinguised scholar; former Vice-chancellor Shri Jagannatha Sanskrit University, Puri-Orissa and presently the seniormost Professor in the Sanskrit Department. He was kind enough to write a foreword of this work by sparing his precious time. His blessings will always enlighten my path, I am sure.

I owe an irredeemable sense of gratitute to Dr. Krishan Lal, Professor and Head Sanskrit Department, University of Delhi for encouraging me always with affection.

My grateful thanks are due to my husband and my children for their ungrudging support to me in giving the present shape to the undertaken work.

I shall be failing in my duties if I do not remember my parents who even at this stage, always encourage me to do always better creative work. May He grant them a very healthy and happy long life.

I offer my thankful regrads to Dr. (Mrs.) B. Nangia, Principal Lakshmi Bai College, University of Delhi, whose constant encouragement provides a new zeal to work hard.

I offer my sincere thanks to Shri Sham Lal Malhotra, Proprietor, Eastern Book Linkers, for speedy and encouraging publication.

16th Feb. 1992 **SAVITRI GUPTA**

SCHEME OF TRANSLITERATION

Vowels	—a ā i ī u ū ṛ lṛ e o ai au
Anusvāra	—ṁ
Visarga	—ḥ
Consonants—	
Gutterals	— k kh g gh ṅ
Palatals	— c ch j jh ñ
Cerebrals	— ṭ ṭh ḍ ḍh ṇ
Dentals	—t th d dh n
Labials	— p ph b bh m
Semi-vowels	—y r l v
Sibilants	—ś (palatal)
	ṣ (cerebral)
	s (dental)
Aspirate	—h

LIST OF ABBREVIATIONS

Sanskrit-original books

AS	...	Alaṁkārasarvasva
Ekā	...	Ekāvalī
KAB	...	Kāvyālaṁkāra of Bhāmaha
KP	...	Kāvyaprakāśa
KASV	...	Kāvyālaṁkārasūtravṛtti
KD	...	Kāvyādarśa
KM	...	Kāvyamīmāṁsā
KAR	...	Kāvyālaṁkāra of Rudraṭa
KAnu	...	Kāvyānuśāsana
KASS	...	Kāvyālaṁkārasārasaṅgraha
DR	...	Daśarūpaka
DhL	...	Dhvanyāloka
NS	...	Nāṭyaśāstra
RG	...	Rasagaṅgādhara
VJ	...	Vakroktijīvita
VV	...	Vyaktiviveka
SKBh	...	Sarasvatīkaṇṭhābharaṇa
SD	...	Sāhityadarpaṇa

Sanskrit Journals

ABORJ	...	Annals of the Bhandarkar Oriental Research Journal.
JASB	...	Journal—Asiatic Society of Bengal.
OHRJ	...	Orissa Historical Research Journal.
PO	...	Poona Orientalist.

....

CONTENTS

INTRODUCTION

Sanskrit-Poetics : Its Nature and Characteristics

The science which examines poetic-charm is called poetics. It presents a picture of the complete form and soul of poetry. It is variously named as Alaṁkāraśāstra, Sāhityavidyā, Sāhityaśāstra, Saundaryaśāstra and Kāvyaśātra. Out of these names, the name alaṁkāraśastra is the most common and the oldest one. The history of poetics may be divided into three periods on the following bases :

(i) predhvani age,
(ii) dhvani age,
(iii) post dhvani age.

The oldest name i.e. alaṁkāraśāstra was employed according to the predominence of various alaṁkāras in the pre-dhvani-age. Alaṁkāras are assigned the prominent place in the works of old ācāryas like Bharata, Daṇḍin, Udbhaṭa, Vāmana and Rudraṭa. Rasa is not given an independent place in their works and is recognised as a form of alaṁkāra. Moreover, rasa and bhāva are included under Rasavat, Preya, Ūrjasvi and Samāhita alaṁkāras. So, the alaṁkāras are treated here as the very life and breath of poetry.

Gradually, poetics made progress and other constituents like rīti, vakrokti, dhvani and rasa were given important places.

In dhvani-age, i.e. in the time of Ānandavardhana, Kuntaka and Mahimabhaṭṭa, the alaṁkāras were not paid importance rather they were employed to heighten the charm of rasa and dhvani. So, in the middle age, the alaṁkāras lost their predominence but again in post-dhvani-age they occupied a prime-position Mammaṭa, Ruyyaka, Vidyādhara, Viśvanātha and Jagannātha were influenced by dhvani-age and Jayadeva, Keśavamiśra and Appayya Dīkṣita follow the ācāryas of predhvani-age.

The concept 'Alaṁkāra' had such a dominating influence throughout the entire history of Sanskrit-poetics that it came to be generally used to denote the theory of poetics, alaṁkāraśāstra.

Śabdārtha-sāhitya occupies an important place in poetry. This is why most of the ācāryas like Bhāmaha, Rudraṭa, Bhoja and Mammaṭa accept Kāvya to be the Sāhitya[1] of śabda and artha. A famous poet Bhartṛhari[2] also uses it as a synonym of kāvya. Kuntaka[3] gives the name vakra-kavi-vyāpāra to śabdārthasāhitya.

In course of time, the term 'Kāvya' was applied for that particular composition where *ātman* was established in the form of *rasādidhvani*; rīti in the form of Saṁghaṭanā; *guṇa* in the form of *ātmagatadharma* and the alaṁkāras as outer form. At that time the name alaṁkāraśāstra or sāhityaśāstra seemed to be incomplete for this *śāstra* and it came to be called kāvyaśāstra.

In this manner, the names alaṁkāraśāstra, sāhityaśāstra or sāhityavidyā and kāvyaśāstra echo the history of the development of this śāstra.

History of Sanskrit-Poetics

The history of Sanskrit-poetics can be traced only from the NS of Bharata (approximately 200-300 B.C.), but in Vedic as well as in classical literature, the seeds of alaṁkāraśāstra can be traced.

Kāvya is said to have started from one of the two great epics, i.e. the Rāmāyaṇa.[4] The ādikāvya Rāmāyaṇa is called the

---

1. In the beginning the word sāhitya was employed for śāstra but afterwards it was used for poetry. It is derived variously as :

 (i) हितेन सह-सहितम्, तस्य भाव: ।

 (ii) सहितयो: (शब्दार्थयो:) भाव: ।

 (iii) Vikramāṅkadevacarita, I. 11.

2. Nītiśataka 12.
3. VJ-vṛtti on I. 7.
4. DhL, I. 5.

producer of Karuṇarasa. All the eight rasas are mentioned in the Bālakāṇḍa of the Rāmāyaṇa.[1]

Yāska has discussed four nipātas in the sense of Upamā.[2] In Aṣṭādhyāyī[3] also the words, upamāna, sāmānyavacana, upameya and upamita are discussed.

Poetics started with the earliest known literature i.e. Vedas. But in a formal wayBharata is the oldest writer of Sanskrit poetics and Jagannātha is the last one.

Schools of Sanskrit-Poetics

Giving prominence to different elements as alaṁkāra, rīti, rasa, dhvani, vakrokti and aucitya, there existed different schools of Sanskrit-poetics. *Alaṁakāra-school* is the oldest school and the alaṁkāra is the oldest element of Sanskrit-poetics. It is realised as the soul of poetry by Bhāmaha, Daṇḍin, Udbhaṭa, Rudraṭa and Jayadeva. An alaṁkāra was realised as the most important element at that time and the poetry was not belived in its absence.[4]

Vāmana called rīti to be the soul of poetry and originated the *Rīti-School.* He believed rīti to be the most prominent element of poetry. Defining guṇa and alaṁkāra he assigned the first place to guṇa and established rīti as the soul. It consists in the particular arrangement of words only according to Vāmana.[5]

But this theory of rīti was criticised by the later ācāryas calling it an outer element of poetry. It was realised as a part of the body of poetry. Bharata assigned rasa the highest place and propounded the *Rasa-school.* Though rasa-theory was first discussed by Bharata, yet the credit of dealing it with complete elaboration and upgrading rasa as the soul of poetry goes to Abhinavagupta. Certain permanent properties or basic moods are called sthāyibhāvas which are roused by appropriate stimuli as

1. Bālakāṇḍa of Rāmāyaṇa, 4.9.
2. Nirukta I. 2.
3. Aṣṭādhyāyī, II. 1.55 and 56.
4. (a) KAB, II. 85.
   (b) KD, II. 220.
5. KASV, I. 2.7.

songs, acting and music. They evolve a pleasurable state of mind called rasa. The fundamental determining and exciting moods are called ālambanavibhāvas and uddīpanavibhāvas respectively. The external manifestations as the movements of eye, eye-brows and glances are called anubhāvas. The secondary moods which serve the purpose of manifesting the permanent mood such as nirveda, glāni or śaṅkā are called vyabhicāribhāvas or sañcāribhāvas. The resultant aesthetic enjoyment is called rasa.

Ānandavardhana realised dhvani as the soul of poetry and included alaṁkāra and rasa even under dhvani. Actually rasa was properly realised in dhvani-school. Ānandavardhana is the propounder of *Dhvani-school.* Dhvani is only an extension of rasa-theory. Rasa is always suggested. It comes under Asaṁlakṣya-kramavyaṅgya-dhvani.

Kuntaka, the establisher of *Vakrokti-school* did not realise the importance of dhvani. He considered the extent of vakrokti from varṇa, the smallest form of kāvya to prabandha. Even abhidhā, lakṣaṇā and vyañjanā were not realised out of vaktokti. Thus Kuntāka believes that vakrokti exists in each and every part of kāvya.

Then Kṣemendra originated *Aucitya-school.* He did not oppose any prevalent previous school but considered the presence of aucitya necessary everywhere i.e. in rasa, guṇa, alaṁkāra or rīti. The scope of aucitya was extended from poetics to social and other fields also.

Vidyādhara : His life, date and works :

Vidyādhara is credited with two works namely Ekāvalī and Kelirahasya. In his Kelirahasya, establishing various parts of rasarāja śṛṅgāra, the element of rasa is properly explained. In Ekāvalī, the nature of kāvya, abhidhā, lakṣaṇā, vyañjanā, the kinds of suggestion, rasa, guṇa and doṣa as well as śabdālaṁkāras and arthālaṁkāras are discussed in detail. The Ekāvalī is a valuable treatise covering all the topics of Sanskrit-poetics.

There are only very brief reports on Vidyādhara, his personal life, his date and works in Histories of Sanskrit-poetics. He does not say anything about himself in his works.

The benedictory verse of the Ekāvalī and the title Mahāmāheśvara mentioned in the colophon of each chapter of Ekāvalī seem to show that he was a great devotee of lord Śiva.[1] He remained a staunch Śaiva in that age, when Vaiṣṇavism was becoming predominant in Orissa. His patron Narasiṁha I had strong leanings towards Śaivism and calls himself 'parama māheśvara' in Kapilāsa temple-inscription. Vidyādhara is silent about his parents and gotra.

There is no doubt that he belonged to Orissa as he had sung the eulogy of his patron Narasiṁha Deva, King of Utkala, The controversy regarding the identity of Narasiṁha, however, remained unresolved to this day as there have been at least four rulers of this name in Gaṅga family of Orissa.

From the copper-plate inscriptions of Narasiṁha Deva IV and Narasiṁha Deva II of Orissa, which are the important source of information regarding kings of Utkala, these four dates are available :

Narasiṁha I—1238 to 1264 A.D.
Narasiṁha II—1278 to 1307 A.D.
Narasiṁha III—1327 to 1352 A.D.
Narasrṁha IV—1378 to 1407 A.D.

Vidyādhara has not eulogised Narasiṁha IV because the Ekāvalī has been criticised in the Rasārṇavasudhākara of Siṁha Bhūpāla, the date for whom has been fixed at 1330 A.D. by Mm. H.P. Śāstrī, Dr. De and Dr. Rāghavan.[2]

Even Narasiṁha III cannot be taken as the patron of Vidyādhara because it was impossible in that age for any work written

---

1. Ekā. I. 1. (Benedictory verse).
2. The date of Siṁha Bhūpāla has been fixed at c. 1330 A. D. by Mm.
   (i) Sri H.P. Śāstrī in Descripiive Catalogue of Sanskrit manuscripts in collection of ASB, Vol. VI=Preface, pp. ccxciii-ccxciv.
   (ii) Dr. S.K. De, History of Skt. Lit. p. 525.
   (iii) Dr. V. Rāghavan, A.B.O.R.J. Vol. XVI, p. 189.

in Orissa to gain circulation outside the state within three years (1327-1330 A.D.). Therefore he must be taken as a centemporary of Narasiṁha II.

The period during which Vidyādhara lived can be correctly ascertained by certain references to well-known classical poets of Sanskrit. In the first unmeṣa Śrīharṣa, Harihara, Arjuna and the king of Malaya are mentioned.[1] Prof. Trivedi suggested that Vidyādhara was patronised by either Kesarī Narasiṁha (1282-1307 A.D.) or Pratāpa Narasiṁha (1307-1327 A.D.).[2]

According to Śri Satyanārāyaṇa Rājaguru,[3] Vidyādhara must have lived between 1327 A.D. and 1377 A.D. during which time Narasiṁha Deva III ruled over Orissa. Śrī Satyanārāyaṇa believes that in several verses of the Ekāvalī[4] Vidyādhara hints allegorically that this patron Narasiṁhadeva's queen was Kamalā. Except Narasiṁha III (1327-52 A.D.) no other king of the Gaṅga dynasty of Orissa, bearing the name Narasiṁha, had a queen of this name.

Śri Kedāranātha Mahāpātra[5] has criticised the above date saying that "the word Kamalā denotes Lakṣmī, the goddess of fortune in those verses and not specifically Kamalā, the queen of Narasiṁha III." According to Kedāranātha Mahāpātra, the patron of Vidyādhara can convincingly be identified as Narasiṁha I and not as Narasiṁha II since former is not mentioned in aṅy of his own copper plate grants. He cannot be Narasiṁha IV, who fought with the Muslims of Bengal or with the army of the Hammīr (Amīr) of Delhi. So, according to Kedāranātha, Vidyādhara adorned the court of Narasiṁha I.

In a verse in 8th Unmeṣa, King Narasiṁha is called Yavanāvanivallabha and there is a reference to war in Bengal.[6] From

1. Ekā. I. 11.
2. Introduction to Ekā.
3. OHRJ. 1954, Vol. IV='Date of Vidyādhara, the author of Ekāvalī', Śri Satya Nārāyaṅa Rājaguru, pp. 89-98.
4. Ekā. example under 8-2, 8-3, 8-48 etc. etc.
5. OHRJ=1959 (vol. 8) 'King Narasiṁha eulogised in the Ekāvalī of Vidyādhara' Śrī Kedāranātha Mahāpātra, p. 118.
6. Ekā. Example under 8-2.

contemporary epigraphic records, it is known that the war reached its climax in 1243 A.D. during the reign of Narasiṁha I.

In Ekāvalī, Vidyādhara refers to Bilhaṇakavi, Pāṇini, Śrīharsa, Harihara, Cārvāka in first unmeṣa, Bhartṛhari in II unmeṣa Bhoja, Vāmana and Alaṅkārasarvasvakāra in fifth unmeṣa and Abhinavaguptācārya in the eighth one. Of the poets and ācāryas mentioned by Vidyādhara, Bilhaṇa is the latest and his date is 1085 A.D. So, Vidyādhara cannot have lived earlier than 1085 A.D.

Dr. Bhandarkar[1] identifies Vidyādhara with Narasiṁha Deva II, while M.M. Cakravartī[2] identifies Vidyādhara with Narasiṁha Deva I. Accepting the opinion of Prof. Trivedi, Dr. P.V. Kane[3] gives the period 1285-1325 A.D. as the time of composition of Ekāvalī.

Mm. H. P. Śāstrī[4] attributes the time of Vidyāhara to be about the second quarter of the 13th cent. A.D. He does not seem to have consulted the paper of M.M. Cakravartī on the Gaṅga chronology of Orissa for the correct date of Narasiṁha I (1238-1264 A.D.).

Since Mallinātha has quoted verses from the Ekāvalī in his commentary on Meghadūta, Śiśupālavadha and other Kāvyas, and has written Taralā, lucid and learned commentary on the Ekāvalī, Vidyādhara can safely be assigned a period between the end of 13th and beginning of 14th eentury.

According to Baladeva Upādhyāya[5] Vidyādhara lived at the time of Narasiṁha II of Kaliṅga who reigned in the period between 1280 and 1314. Hence Vidyādhara belonged probably to the end of the 13th and the beginning of the 14th century.

---

1. Reports on Sanskrit MSS., 1887-91, pp. lxv-lxix.
2. JASB Vol. 72-73. 'Chronology of Eastern Gaṅga Kings of Orissa', Babu M.M. Cakravartī, p. 97.
3. History of Sanskrit Poetics, p. 282.
4. Descriptive catalogue of the Sanskrit Mss. in the collection of the ASB, Vol. VI, Preface, pp. ccxciii-ccxciv.
5. PO. 1936, I, p. 13. Royal Patronage and Sanskrit Poetics—Baladeva Upādhyāya.

From the above discussion, it can be concluded that Vidyādhara must have lived between middle of the 13th and beginning of the 14th century.

Besides the Ekāvalī and Kelirahasya, Vidyādhara has also written various commentaries—e.g. ṭīkā on Naiṣadhacaritaṁ, known as Sāhityavidyādhara;[1] ṭīkās on Śiśupālavadha, Rāghavapāṇḍavīya and Raghuvaṁśa and eommentary Śiśuhitaiṣiṇī on Kumārasambhava. But these commentaries unfortunately are lost to us.

Ekāvalī—its importance

In ordinary usage the word 'Ekāvalī' is used for a particular kind of necklace in which various flowers or jewels are intermingled and connected in a well-arranged order. People are proud to wear this Ekāvalī on their breasts on account of its extra-ordinary beauty. Bearing this well-known but simple idea in mind, Vidyādhara named this particular work on poetics '*Ekāvalī*', Since according to him a reader who keeps it in his heart becomes an object of special interest.

As in the necklace, so in Ekāvalī, too, various poetic-constituents are kept together in eight parts (i.e. in eight unmeṣas). The Ekāvalī can give special charm to the readers of poetics. There is also a figure of speech called Ekāvalī; so the title Ekāvalī at once shows that this is a work on alaṁkāra.

Each unmeṣa consists of three parts : kārikās in verses, which define and classify the technical terms; the vṛtti or the explanation of the kārikās in prose and the examples given to illustrate the kārikās. It is important to note here that all these three parts are created by Vidyādhara himself.

The illustrative verses of Ekāvalī make a complete kāvya as they are composed in praise of Narasiṁha. Thus Vidyādhara is both an ācārya and a kavi.

The striking feature of the examples given in verses of the Ekāvalī is that they all panegyrise Narasiṁha, the king of Utkala or Kaliṅga.[2]

---

1. JASB. 1903, p. 49.
2. Ekā., I. 7.

So Vidyāhara has proved his extra-ordinary poetical-excellence by composing himself all the verses in praise of his patron.

Vidyādhara originated this type of tradition. The Ekāvalī served as a model for Pratāparudrayaśobhūṣaṇa of Vidyānātha, who like Vidyādhara, composed all the illustrative verses in praise of his patron Pratāparudradeva. Other works e.g. Nañrājayaśobhūṣaṇa of Narasiṁha, Raghunāthabhūpālīya of Kṛṣṇadīksita and Alaṁkāramañjuā of Devaśaṁkarabhaṭṭa also are modelled on the Ekāvalī.[1]

So, one cannot oppose the impartial critcism of a poet in respect to the Ekāvalī.

एकामेकावलीमेव कण्ठे धत्त कवीश्वराः ।
आः किमन्यैरलङ्कारैरसारैभारदायिभिः ।।

The Ekāvalī is fortunate enough to have got a Sanskrit commentary viz. Taralā, written by Mallinātha. Taralā is quoted several times in the commentaries on Meghadūta, Kirātārjunīya and Śiśupālavadha and also in Ratnāpaṇa, a Sanskrit commentary on Pratāparudrayaśobhūṣaṇa.

Editions of the Ekāvalī

Bombay Sanskrit Series edition of Ekāvalī, available for the present study, is based upon the following manuscripts existing in different libraries of India :

1. This is a transcript of a manuscript of the Ekāvalī which belongs to Govinda Śāstrī Nirantar of Nāsik. It was published by Dr. Bhandarkar in 1893 and was deposited in the Deccan College Library. This manuscript generally agrees with the commentary Taralā of Mallinātha.

2. A manuscript from Conjeveram, is in grantha character on plain palm-leaf which is now in a damaged condition. It was writtcn by Tirumalacangar. The manuscript was in the possession

---

1. OHRJ, April 1959, Vol. 8, p. 118. King Narasiṁha eulogised in the Ekāvalī of Vidyādhara Mahāpātra (Śrī Kedāra Nātha).

of the late Mr. Viralācārya, a great Paṇḍit of Conjeveram and is now in his grand son's possession. It appears to be fairly old.

3. A manuscript in charge of the Oriental Library of Madras is in Devanāgarī characters.

4. A manuscript in charge of the Oriental Library of Mysore is a transcript of a Grantha manuscript containing the first six unmeṣas and of an Andhra manuscript containing the last two unmeṣas.

5. A copy af a manuscript in charge of the Library of Mahārāja's Sanskrit College, Trivandrum, is in Dreviḍa Grantha characters. It is a palm-leaf manuscript and appears to be more than a hundred years old.

6. A eopy of a manuscript in charge of the Tanjore Palace Library is in Telugn characters.

7. A manuscript belongs to Pandit Balamukund Karmakāṇḍa of Gayāghāṭ, Benares. It is in Nāgarī character.

The text of the commentary, Taralā, is based upon two manuscripts, one a transcript of a manuscript in charge of the Deccan College Library and the other a copy of a manuscript secured through T. Gaṇapati Śāstrī, Principal Mahārāja's Sanskrit College, Trivandrum.

CHAPTER I

KĀVYA

Purposes of Kāvya

Vidyādhara enumerates the following as the purposes of kāvya viz. world-wide fame, immense wealth, relief from evils due to worries, cherishing of sentiments, aesthetic pleasure and expansion of peace by removing mental fickleness.[1] In the exposition of these purposes, Vidyādhara owes much to Bhāmaha[2] and Mammaṭa.[3] Worldly-knowledge is accepted by Mammaṭa as one of the purposes of kāvya but it is not mentioned by Vidyādhara and in its place the removal of mental fickleness is placed.

Of the purposes discussed above, pleasure is recognised as the chief purpose of kāvya but in the Nāṭyaśāstra,[4] the Viṣṇupurāṇa[5] and the Dhvanyāloka,[6] pleasure is considered to be the only purpose. Vāmana[7] and Bhoja[8] accept only two purposes, namely pleasure and fame.

These purposes are to be appreciated by the poet and Sahṛdaya (enlightened) according to their individual position. Two of these purposes viz. fame and wealth can be achieved by the composer only. All the poets are not fortunate enough to adhieve fame like Śrīharṣa.[9]

---

1. Ekā. I.9.
2. KAB. I.2.
3. KP. I.2.
4. NS. I. 113-115.
5. Viṣṇupurāṇa, 6.5.54.
6. DhL. vṛtti on I.1.
7. KASV. I. 1.5.
8. SKBh, I. 2.
9. Ekā. I. 11,

Poetry imparts instruction in the pleasing manner of a beloved and is, therefore, called kāntāsammita. Here dhvani or rasa is predominant and word and sense are subordinate.[1] Thus kāntāsammitakāvya is different from :

(i) śabdapradhāna or prabhusammitakāvya; where word in the form of a master's command predominates. and (ii) arthapradhāna or mitrasammitakāvya; where friendly-counsel is the predominant element.

The prabhusammitakāvya is mostly based on expression.[2] The mitrasammitakāvya consists of histories, purāṇas and legends dealing mainly with descriptive matter and is full of anecdotes and morals. Like a friend, it advises but does not command.[3] A kāntāsammitakāvya, however, gives both pleasure and advice. Hence, it possesses a significant charm.

Definition of Kāvya

Though Vidyādhara does not give any specific definition of poetry but while discussing its purposes, he says that one who composes poetry is a kavi and kāvya is the work of a poet.[4] Thus, he attaches importance to kavikarma in defining poetry. It is not a mere arrangement of words but a charming composition. The selected words should be properly arranged and the sense should always carry significance as well as pleasant humour.[5] Properly used words fulfil all desires,[6] but even a single word improperly used is an offence. Thus, a poet should be very careful while composing poetry and arranging the words properly.

The definitions propounded by scholars are diverse. Some of them give importance to śabdārtha (word and sense) or to śabda only, while others connect śabdārtha with a sahṛdaya or with a kavi. Bhāmaha, Vāmana, Rudraṭa, Rājaśekhara, Kuntaka,

---

1. Ekā. I. 6.
2. *Ibid.* I. 4.
3. *Ibid.* I. 5.
4. *Ibid.*, vṛtti on I. 9.
5. *Ibid.*, I. 10.
6. KD. I. 6.

Mammaṭa and Hemacandra give prominence to śabdārtha while defining poetry.[1]

In the definition of poetry given in the Agnipurāṇa[2] and the Kāvyādarśa,[3] only śabda is important. According to this group, poetry consists of a group of words which give pleasing sense.

Ānandavardnana[4] defines poetry as the word and sense which please the hearts of the sahṛdayas and according to Bhoja,[5] a poet attains fame and happiness in creating poetry which is full of guṇas, alaṁkāras and rasa and which is also free from faults. Thus Ānandavardhana lays stress on sahṛdaya and Bhoja on kavi while defining poetry.

Causes of Kāvya

Pratibhā, vyutpatti and abhyāsa are considered as the conjoint cause of poetry by Vidyādhara[6] and also by Daṇḍin[7], Rudraṭa[8] and Mammaṭa.[9] Vidyādhara has discussed these causes separately also. Though all the three causes are considered as the conjoint cause of poetry, still pratibhā has been given a position of unique significance.

According to Vidyādhara, pratibhā is that power by which śabda, artha, guṇa and alaṁkāra (all the essentials of poetry)

---

1. (i) KAB, I. 16,
   (ii) KASV on I. 1.1.
   (iii) KAR, II. 1.
   (iv) KM, p. 24.
   (v) VJ, I. 7.
   (vi) KP, I. 4.
   (vii) K Anu. I. 11.
2. Agnipurāṇa 337, 6-7.
3. KD, I. 10.
4. supra, 1.6 on p. 11.
5. supra, I.8 on p. 11.
6. Ekā, I. 12.
7. KD, I. 103.
8. KAR, I. 14.
9. KP, I. 3.

arise. If a poet, devoid of pratibhā, tries to create poetry, he is doomed to a ridiculous failure. It is better to refrain from poetry than to compose bad poetry.[1] Like Vidyādhara Bhāmaha[2] also believes that bad composition is death itself. Pratibhā is more significant than vyutpatti according to Vidyādhara.[3] Here Vidyādhara is influenced by Ānandavardhana[4] in propounding this idea. One observes the title 'poet' only by virtue of pratibhā, according to Bhaṭṭatauta, (writer of Kāvyakautuka).[5] Vāmana[6] opines that it is the very seed out of which poetry blossoms. According to Rudraṭa,[7] several senses of the sentence and words capable of manifesting the meaning immediately arise by pratibhā. It is descrided as an innate natural (sahajā) and cultivable quality by Rudraṭa[8] and sahajā and aupādhikī (due to external agencies like mantras, the grace of God) by Hemacandra.[9]

Vyutpatti is the knowledge and skill in various śāstras and kāvyas. According to Vidyādhara[10] and Mammaṭa[11] abhyāsa or the constant practice in composition enables a poet to create poetry.

There has, however, been a theory that abhyāsas and śikṣā hardly contibute anything to the element of pratibhā which supersedes them. This view was held by Rājaśekhara,[12] Vāgbhaṭṭa II[13]

1. Ekā. vṛtti on I. 12.
2. KAB, I. 12.
3. Ekā. vṛtti on I. 12.
4. DhL. Parikaraśloka under III. 6.
5. Quoted by Hemacandra in KAnu under I. 3, also quoted by Dr. Kane in History of Sanskrit Poetics, p. 335.
6. KASV, I. 3.16.
7. KAR, I. 15.
8. KAR, I. 16.
9. KAnu, I.4 and its vṛtti.
10. Ekā. vṛtti on I. 12.
11 KP, vṛtti on I. 3.
12. KM, p. 21.
13. Quoted by Dr. Kane in History of Sanskrit Poetics, p. 324.

(Alaṁkāratilaka) and Jagannātha.[1] Rājaśekhara conceives pratibhā as the sole cause of poetry.

Though pratibhā is indispensible in creating poetry, vyutpatti and abhyāsa polish, brighten and sharpen pratibhā. Hence, all the three causes together constitute the cause of poetry, according to Vidyāhara.

Nature of Dhvani

Vidyādhara[2] calls dhvani to be the soul of poetry and word and sense are considered as its body. It is defined as that 'wherein a primary meaning is subordinated or a word connotes a suggested meaning'.[3] Dhvani has three kinds namely Vastu-dhvani, alaṁkāra dhvani and rasadhvani. In vastu-dhvani mere fact is suggested by words that express another sense. By alaṁkāra-dhvani is meant that what is suggested is imaginative (not a matter of fact). In alaṁkāra-dhvani, the suggested sense constitutes a figure of speech. The expressed sense, howeve, does not do so.

Under rasa-dhvani, all the nine rasas, all the bhāvas and their ābhāsas also are included. By rasa-dhvani it is implied that rasa is always suggested and is not directly expressed. Rasa-dhvani occurs where rasa, bhāva, rasābhāsa, bhāvābhāsa, bhāvodaya, bhāva-sandhi, bhāvaśānti and bhāvaśabalatā are the principal elements and the words, the expressed-sense and the figures of speech are dependent upon them. Vastu and alaṁkāra-dhvani also suggest rasa.

An example of dhvani is found in the very first (benedictory) verse of the Ekāvalī.[4] All the three kinds of dhvani are presented here in one verse. The first line of this benedictory verse describes God Śiva as a lover (Kāmī). In the second, He is portrayed as an enemy of the God of Love (Kāmaripu). These contradictory emotions of love and anger are present in the same person at the

---

1. RG, p. 8.
2. Ekā. I. 13.
3. DhL. I. 13.
4. Ekā. I. 1.

same time, suggesting His inconceivable greatness. Here exists vastu-dhvani which resolves the apparent paradoxical sentiments of love and anger. In discussing this rasavirodha-parihāra (absence of contradiction of emotions), Vidyādhara is influenced by Ānandavardhana.[1] The two opposite sentiments namely śṛṅgāra and raudra suggest Virodhālaṁkāra thus causing alaṁkāra-dhvani here.

The discussion of rati-sthāyibhāva gives place to rasa-dhvani. There is also a suggestion of emotion (bhāvadhvani) here since the poet's subject is God. This is helped by the threefold suggestion of vastu, alaṁkāra and rasa. Thus, this verse is a lucide example of dhvani.

Vinyādhara[2] and previously Ānandavardhana[3] have tried to establish dhvani by refuting various anti-dhvani views of those who believe in the non-existence of dhvani, or include it under some other head or accepting its existence call it indescribable.

Refutation of Abhāvavādins

(a) The abhāvavādins (cārvākas)[4] maintain that there is no such thing as dhvani and the suggested sense is merely the expressed sense, since it simply adorns it.

Refuting the abhāvavādins, Vidyādhara argues that whether dhvani is denied being apprehended or it is denied being unapprehended ? Does it exist in some places or it is not found anywhere ?

It cannot be said that dhvani does not exist in some places for then the argument would be open to the fault siddhasādhana (proving what is already proved), because if it does not exist in some places, it does exist in some other places. It cannot be said that it is denied being apprehended and is not found anywhere. It would be a contradictory statement, for on one hand,

1. DhL. III. 22.
2. supra, I. 2. on p. 15.
3. DhL. I. 1.
4. Ekā. vṛtti on I. 13.

we accept its apprehension, still, on the other hand, say that it is not found anywhere. Again, if it is denied and does not exist, then, too, it is not correct, for a thing cannot be denied unless it is first conceived in the mind.

Thus dhvani does exist for it is apprehended and conceived in the mind.

(b) According to Bhāmaha, dhvani is the cause of poetical charm, hence it is similar to guṇas and alaṁkāras.[1] Rītis and vṛttis are also the causes of poetical beauty. There is no use of giving different names, e.g. dhvani, guṇa or alaṁkāra. Dhvani may be included under either guṇa or alaṁkāra.

In the opinion of Vidyādhara,[2] dhvani cannot be included under guṇas because they are the properties of rasa. Just as the human qualities bravery and enthusiasm reside in the soul, so mādhurya and other guṇas reside in sentiment which is the soul of poetry. Properties cannot be identified with the substance in which they reside. So, guṇas cannot be identified with the guṇī i.e. dhvani. Nor can dhvani be placed under alaṁkāras because alaṁkāras like Śleṣa have no relation with the suggested sense. Dhvani can not be included under Samāsokti and such other alaṁkāras which have clear apprehension of the suggested sense, because the term dhvani is applicable only where the suggested sense is predominant. In Samāsokti, the suggested sense is subordinated to the expressed sense.

Thus, dhvani is undoubtedly different from the above stated guṇas and alaṁkāras.

(c) Mahimabhaṭṭa accepts only one function for words namely abhidhā.[3] He considers dhvani inseparable from anumāna.[4] Vyāpti is a constitument part (aṅga) of anumāna. It is the concomitance of sādhana (middle-term) with sādhya (major-term). Vyāpti is established in two ways :

1. Ekā. vṛtti on I. 13.
2. *Ibid.* vṛtti on I. 13.
3. VV, I. 27.
4. *Ibid.*, vṛtti on I. 20.

(i) kāryakāraṇabhāva and
(ii) tādātmyabāva

A man can infer fire on a mountain by the hetu of smoke, by relating it to the smoke in a kitchen. He establishes vpāpti by acknowledging the inevitable concomitance of smoke and fire after analysing the kāryakāraṇabhāva between them.

When we infer that śiṁśapā is a tree by the hetu of śiṁśapātva, the vyāpti between śiṁśapātva and vṛkṣatva is ascertained by tādātmya.

Refuting Mahimbhaṭṭa Vidyādhara[1] says that dhvani can not be included under anumāna. Here dhvani is sādhya and śabdārthau sādhana. The absence of dhvani cannot be proved from the non-cognition of words and their sense. Therefore, the non-cognition of words and their sense also cannot prove the absence of dhvani. Thus anupalabdhi (non-cognition) cannot establish the vyāpti between dhvani and śabdārtha. Words and their sense are not produced from the suggested-sense, because they manifest themselves from their generating cause even before the suggested sense arises. Thus as neither anupalabdhi, nor tādātmya, nor tadutpatti can establish the vyāpali between śabdārtha and dhvani, there is no vyāpti and consequently, dhvani cannot be included under anumāna.

(d) Abhihitānvayavādins[2] hold that there is no vyañjanāvṛtti and the suggested sense is conveyed by abhidhā itself. Words have a general meaning. The logical connection of words that form a sentence, is not known from the import of those words but from ākāṅkṣā, yogyatā and sannidhi and when this conneetion is known, a special sense arises through tātparyavṛtti. This sense is tātparyārtha or vākyārtha.

Refuting Abhihitānvayavādins, Vidyādhara[3] saya that when words can convey only a general meaning and cannot express the

1. Ekā. vṛtti on I.13.
2. (a) Ekā. vṛtti on I. 13.
   (b) KP. vṛtti on V. 47.
3. Ekā. vṛtti on I. 13.

exact sense of the sentence or we can say that when abhidhāvṛtti is not capable to explain the meaning of the sentence, it cannot be expected that it can convey pratīyamānārtha (the suggested sense) of a sentence which arises only after the sentence is understood.

(e) Anvitābhidhānavādins[1] also believe in the existence of abhidhā only and hold that the suggested sense is arrived by abhidhā itself. They maintain that a single arrow, shot by a strong man, rapidly destroys the armour of the enemy, pierces his vitals and takes away his life, similarly a single word used by a good poet, brings before us, through abhidhā, the sense of a word. It teaches us its syntactical connection and makes us understand the suggested meaning. In other words, according to them, abhidhā is capable of expressing whatever sense is understood after hearing a word.

But this view does not hold good. Vidyādhara[2] states that when a sentence expresses the collective notion of words and is unable to express the sense which is not connected by ākāṅkṣā, yogyatā and sannidhi, then the suggested sense, which is altogether different from the sense which is first conveyed by a sentence, cannot be conveyed by abhidhā. Thus, suggestion cannot be discarded.

Moreover, if there is no other power than abhidhā, the question of accepting lakṣaṇā by them also does not arise at all. The lakṣyārtha also should appear through abhidhā.

Again, to prove the existence of dhvani, Vidyādhara points out that if suggestion is not accepted, the relation of vyañjaka (suggester) and vyaṅgya (suggested) will also not stand. In the absence of this relation, the doṣas cannot be classified into nitya (permanent) and anitya (temporary).[3] Then in the absence of the suggested sense, a word that denotes something indecorous cannot be avoided in the absence of its connection with the sense given

1. Ekā. vṛtti on I. 13.
2. *Ibid.*, vṛtti on I. 13.
3. *Ibid.*, vṛtti on I. 13.

to it by context.[1]

Again, if contradictory objects with different causes are present, the difference between the expressed and the suggested sense is not observed, and then the difference should not exist anywhere.[2] Yet the difference between the nature of expressed and suggested sense is quite apparent due to the difference between kāla, āśraya, kāraṇa, kārya and viṣaya.

The difference between the expressed and the suggested sense exists due to the difference of subjects, for example in 'Kassa va ṇa...eṇhim',[3] their difference is shown because of the difference of various subjects, e.g. svairiṇī, priyatamā, prativeśī and sapatnī.

Even Mammaṭa does not clarify this kind of difference, while Vidyādhara explains it clearly and properly. Mammaṭa simply says 'ādi' mentioning the friend and the beloved, i.e. two subjects.[4] Since dhvani can never be indescribable, its presence cannot be opposed on these grounds.[5]

(f) The opponents of dhvani believe that the suggested sense can be arrived at by lakṣaṇā.[6] Therefore, these two are not different.

This view cannot stand[7] because lakṣaṇā is based upon barring the principal sense, while dhvani is based upon the particular nature of the speaker, the person to be informed, context and such other factors.[8] Hence two can never be identical. Moreover, as lakṣaṇā does not exist in abhidhāmūlādhvani, the hetu is bhāgā-

---

1. (a) Ekā. vṛtti on I. 13.
   (b) KP. vṛtti on V. 47.
2. Ekā. vṛtti on I. 13.
3. *Ibid.* example under I. 13.
4. KP. example V. 135 and vṛtti on V. 47.
5. Ekā. vṛtti on I. 13.
6. *Ibid.*, vṛtti on I. 13.
7. *Ibid.*, vṛtti on I. 13.
8. (a) KP. III. 21-22.
   (b) SD. V. 2.

siddha (non-existent in a part of the pakṣa). Lakṣaṇā is found in conventional words like Kuśala but suggestion does not exist here. So, here the hetu is contrary. Dhvani can exist without lakṣaṇā also.

Thus Vidyādhara has refuted above the views of Cārvākas, Bhāmaha, Mahimabhaṭṭa, Abhihitānavayavādins and Anvitābhidhānavādins and has proved the existance of dhvani as a separate power. In this context Vidyādhara follows Ānandavardhana and Mammaṭa.

From the above discussion, it is clear that dhvani does exist separately and cannot be included under any head like guṇa, alaṁkāra, anumāna or rīti etc. Thus Dhvani is an independent entity.

———

CHAPTER II

ŚAKTIS, ŚABDAS AND ARTHAS

Vidyādhara has discussed three powers viz. abhidhā (denotation), lakṣaṇā (indication) and vyañjanā (suggestion).

Abhidhā

Abhidhā is a primary power because it conveys the conventional meaning of the word according to Vidyādhara[1] and Mammaṭa.[2] The conventional sense itself is known as the 'primary-sense', because it comes to the mind immediately on hearing a word. K. Kunjuni Rājā[3] thinks that the primary meaning of a word is the universal which is the essential quality common to the particular instances of the class.

While dealing with abhidhā a question arises, as to where the convention (saṁketa) is to be understood. There are different views on this question. According to Vidyādhara,[4] saṁketa is to be placed on jāti alone. Now an examination of the different views about the placement of saṁketa is called for here.

First of all, saṁketa cannot be placed on vyakti (individual). Although, on account of its capacity of performing an action for a purpose, a vyakti alone is the subject of action or inaction, yet it is not possible to place saṁketa on vyakti.[5] If it is to be placed on vyakti, a question arises whether it is to be placed on each or some vyaktis. Since vyakti is endless, each cannot be seen. As

---

1. Ekā. II. 2.
2. KP. II. 8.
3. The Primary meaning of a word, p. 72.
4. Ekā. vṛtti on II. 1.
5. (a) Ekā. vṛtti on II. 1.
   (b) KP. vṛtti on II. 7.

long as all are not seen, there is no saṁketa and consequently, here is no comprehension of the meaning. If we accept saṁketita on vyakti alone, the objects cannot be divided into jāti, guṇa, kriyā and dravya. On seeing a white ox moving, we say, 'gauḥśuklaś-calodittha̱ḥ'. If 'go' (cow) denotes a vyakti and śukla, cala and ḍittha, the same vyakti, these would be synonymous. If, to avoid this doṣa, saṁketa is to be placed on a certain number of vyaktis, there will be vyabhicāradoṣa, e.g., if 'go' is to signify a certain number of cows, that are saṁketita, it cannot signify asaṁketita or those which are not seen. If the word 'go' signifies asaṁketita cow it can signify other things, e.g., jar. If it indicates a cow and not a jar then it cannot signify asaṁketita cows.

Vidyādhara does not prefer to place saṁketa on the properties of vyakti namely jāti, guṇa, kriyā and dravya. This jātyādivāda is generally accepted by the rhetoricians and grammarians. There is only one guṇa, kriyā and dravya but owing to many things in wnich it can exist, it appears variously.

A quality which exists in different objects in a similar form, does not remain a guṇa but assumes the form of jāti, e.g. whiteness which exists variously in ice, milk, conch and such other white things does not remain a guṇa but becomes jāti due to its common attributes. Similarly, in kriyā, the act of cooking of different things is similar, i.e. cooking. So, the general name 'cooking' is given to the cooking of either potato or rice etc. Thus the titie 'jāti' is given again due to this common feature. Similar is the case with dravya. So, jāti should not be thus divided. These jāti, guṇa, kriyā or dravya are not to be so named. These should be called jāti due to their common qualities.

Similarly saṁketa cannot be placed on jātiviśiṣṭavyakti, as all the individuals cannot be signified by that. Some special characteristics shall be required then, to place saṁketa.

Apohavāda is also not an accepted theory. According to this theory, there is no positive entity in the world and the import of all words is 'apoha' or the negation of the contrary, e.g., the word 'ox' denotes the negation of 'non-ox'. This theory could not be accepted because here the positive nature of the objects cannot be known. It is known that a particular thing is different from its opposite one, but its own form and nature cannot be understood. This theory has its approach only in a negative way.

To remove the above difficulties Vidyādhara thinks it proper to place *saṁketa on jāti alone*. Words can be understood with reference to group only. The form of objects can be understood only when they are arıanged in groups and only by making their groups. A particular group of objects is given one name only because of similarity or some common qualities (i.e. sāmānyatvaṁ which is another name of jāti). Thus saṁketa can be understood only with referenee to jāti.

Lakṣaṇā

The second power of words is called lakṣaṇā. When the primary meaning is barred, the secondary meaning connected intentionally (phalāt) or through usage (rūḍhitaḥ) with the primary one is called the lakṣya-sense and the power by which this sense is indicated is called lakṣaṇa according to Vidyādhara[1] and Mammaṭa.[2] 'Rūḍhito athavāpi phalāt' is one of the requisites of lakṣaṇā but the commentator Mallinātha[3] takes it to divide lakṣaṇā into rūḍhi-lakṣaṇā and prayojanavatī-lakṣaṇā. He does not accept it to form a part of the definition.

Vidyādhara examplifies lakṣaṇā by giving the illustrations, 'kuśalaḥ' and 'Gaṅgāyāṁ ghoṣaḥ'. Here, the primary sense of kuśalaḥ and Gaṅgāyāṁ are barred. 'Kuśalaḥ' actually means 'Kuśān latīti' (one who takes up kuśa or darbha grass), but this sense is inapplicable in 'kuśalaḥ'. Here it denotes 'clever' since a person who collects darbha grass knows the distinction between darbha and ordinary grass. So the meaning 'clever' is linked to the primary meaning. In general usage too, kuśala means 'clever' hence, the meaning clever is understood by rūḍhi. We find all the three requisites of lakṣaṇā fulfilled here in 'kuśala'. Conse-

1. Ekā. II. 5.
2. KP. II.9.
3. TaralāSanskrit Commentary on Ekā. II. 5.

quently, the lakṣyārtha 'clever' comes out through lakṣaṇā.

In 'Gaṅgāyāṁ ghoṣaḥ', the primary sense of 'Gaṅgā' viz. current is inapplicable, because the cow-herds can have no village on the current of water. It conveys the secondary sense, 'its bank'. Both the primary and the secondary senses are joined by their nearness. The purpose in saying 'Gaṅgāyāṃ ghosaḥ', instead of 'Gaṅgā taṭe ghoṣaḥ', is to emphasize its purity and coolness. Here also all the three essentials are fulfilled and the lakṣyārtha 'bank of Gaṅgā', arises through lakṣaṇā.

Kinds of Lakṣaṇā

Vidyādhara divides lakṣaṇā into seven kinds namely jahatsvārthā, ajahatsvārthā, jahadajahatsvārthā, sāropāgauṇī, sāropāśuddhā, sādhyavasānā-gauṇī and sādhyavasānā-śuddhā.

Lakṣaṇā

I	II	III	IV	V	VI	VII
Jahad lakṣaṇā	Ajahad lakṣaṇā	Jahada-jahad lakṣaṇā	Gauṇa sāropā	Śuddha sāropā	Gauṇa sādhya-vasānā	Śuddha sādhya-vasānā

These seven kinds increase to twenty-one each getting three kinds of Saṁkara namely Aṅgāṅgibhāva saṁkara, Saṁśaya saṁkara and Ekalakṣakāṇupraveśa saṁkara (7×3 kinds of Saṁkara). Each of these seven also gets one form of Saṁsṛṣṭi, thus making the number twenty-eight. Taking into account the seven forms of śuddhabheda, too, the final number goes to thirty-five according to Vidyādara.[1]

Vidyādhara stands singular in accepting these kinds of lakṣaṇa. While discussing each kind of lakṣaṇā, Vidyādhara also states that a particular lakṣaṇā is the basis of a particular alaṁkāra. Before him, Hemacandra[2] and Jayadeva[3] also hold this idea.

---

1. Ekā. II. 10-11.
2. K. Anu. vṛtti on I. 17.
3. Candrāloka, IX. 16.

Mammaṭa[1] accepts six divisions namely upādānalakṣaṇā, lakṣaṇalakṣaṇā, śuddhasāropā, śuddha-sādhyavasānā, gauṇīsāropā and gauṇīsādhyavasānā. The number of the subdivisions of lakṣaṇā given by Viśvanātha[2] goes upto eighty. Jagannātha[3] also deals with the similar divisions which were proviously discussed by Mammaṭa.

Annamabhaṭṭa[4] and Dharmarāja Adhvarīndra[5] accept three divisions of lakṣaṇā namely jahallakṣaṇā, ajahallakṣaṇā and jahadajahallakṣaṇā but jahadajahallakṣaṇā is not accopted by any rhetorician except Vidyādara.

Now it is proposed to take up, one by one, the divisions of lakṣaṇā as discussed in the Ekāvalī.

Jahatsvṣṇārthā is that type of lakṣaṇā where the primary meaning is subjugated by the secondary meaning.[6] Before Vidyādhara, Mammaṭa[7] had defined it similarly calling it lakṣaṇalakṣaṇā and Vidyādhara[8] himself refers to this nomenclature. Anoter type of jahallakṣaṇā is defined as where the opposite meaning to the denoted one is expressed through lakṣaṇā.[9] The verse 'Tvatkhaḍga... Suradīrghikāyām'[10], illustrates jahatsvārthālakṣaṇā. Here the word Suradīrghikāyā originally meant 'stream', but here it indicates 'its bank', suggesting śaitya and pāvanatva.

When a word maintains its own sense while conveying an

1. KP. II. 12.
2. SD. vṛtti on II. 23.
3. RG. page 146.
4. Tarkadīpikā, p. 128.
5. Vedāntaparibhāṣā, p. 204.
6. Ekā. II. 6.
7. KP. II. 10.
8. Ekā. vṛtti on II. 6. This jahatsvārthā is the basis of the alaṁkāras like Aprastutapraśaṁsā.
9. *Ibid.*, II. 6 and vṛtti on it also. This kind of lakṣaṇā is the seed of vyājastuti alaṁkāra.
10. *Ibid.*, example under II. 6.

additional sense, it is called *ajahatsvārthā lakṣaṇā.*[1] Mammaṭa[2] names it upādānalakṣaṇā accepting its similar nature. In the verse 'Kāvyalaṁkāramīmāṁsā......Narasiṁha nareśvara',[3] the words kāvya, alaṁkāra, mīmāṁsā, tarka and vyākaraṇa give up their primary meanings and express 'the scholars' connected with these śāstras.

When a word gives up its meaning only partly, the power is called *jahadajahatsvārthā,*[4] since it gives up only some of its peculiarities and not all, it is called jahadajahallakṣaṇā. This type of lakṣaṇā is not accepted by any rhetorician. In the verse 'Yatkarṇatāla prabhavaiḥ......vīrakareṇurājaḥ',[5] 'soayaṁ kareṇurājaḥ', being the same Kareṇurājaḥ, it gives up its connection with the particular time and place which is denoted by the word 'saḥ'.

In *sāropā lakṣaṇā* both āropyamāṇa and āropa-viṣaya are directly exprerassed as existing in the same person or place.[6] The purpose here is the suggestion of the similarity between different objects.[7] Sāropālakṣaṇā is twofold viz. gauṇī (qualitative) or śuddhā (pure). *Gauṇī sāropā lakṣaṇā* arises from the comparison of similarities[8] e.g. in 'Vīra śrīsvara...kārttāntikaḥ',[9] the qualities of an astrologer, e.g. suggesting an auspicious hour for expedition are associated with the object denoted by the lakṣya-sense. But these eommon attributes link the word Kārttāntika to its lakṣya-sense i.e. khaḍga. Though by the expression of kārttāntika and khaḍga the difference between the āropyamāṇa and āropavisaya is shown, yet the viṣya is coloured with the form of the viṣayin.

1. Ekā. II. 7 and also vṛtti on it. This lakṣaṇā is the seed of samāsokti and such other alaṁkāras.
2. KP. II. 10.
3. Ekā. example under II. 7.
4. *Ibid.*, II. 8.
5. *Ibid.*, example under II. 8.
6. *Ibid.*, II. 9.
7. *Ibid.*, vṛtti on II.9.
8. *Ibid.*, vṛtti on II.9.
9. *Ibid.*, example under II. 9.

Śuddhā-sāropā-lakṣaṇā[1] is one possessed of upacāra. Vidyādhara[2] and Mallinātha[3] explain the word upacāra in the sense of attributing to an object a property which does not belong to it due to extreme similarity. Similarly, before Vidyādhara, Mammaṭa[4] uses the word upacāra in two senses :—

(i) the relation of similarity and

(ii) setting one thing against another.

Śuddha-sāropā-lakṣaṇā is illustrated in the verse 'Madakṣība ...dorutkalapate'.[5] Here, the arms of the king of Kaliṅga are called trilokikalyāṇa which bring happiness to the whole world. Here the noun kalyāṇa becomes the adjective to the arms of the king of Kaliṅga. The āropaviṣaya is swallowed up by the āropyamāṇa in *sādhyavasānā-lakṣaṇā*.[6] It is again twofold, viz. gauṇī and śuddhā. *Gauṇī-sādhyavasānā* is illustrated in 'ayaṁ pārijātaḥ'. Here, the qualities of Pārijāta, attributed to vīra Narasiṁha, are not expressed. *Śuddhā-sāddya-vasānā* is cited in 'ayamānandaḥ'. Here, viṣaya namely that which causes joy is not stated and so it is swallowed up in the viṣyain. The purpose in this lakṣaṇā is complete identity between the viṣaya and the viṣayin.[7]

The difference between sāropālakṣaṇā and sādhyavasīnālakṣaṇā may be considered now. In sāropālakṣaṇā viṣaya and the viṣayin are used together in a sentence while in sādhyavasānā viṣaya is swallowed up by the viṣayin.

Now the examples of lakṣaṇā through three kinds of saṁkara and one kind of saṁsṛṣṭi are being cited. Vidyādhara has considered the combination of two lakṣaṇā as saṁkara and saṁsṛṣṭi

1. Ekā.vṛtti on II. 9.
2. *Ibid.*, vṭtti on II. 9.
3. Taralā (Sanskrit commentary) on Ekā. II. 9.
4. K.P. vṛtti on II. 11-12.
5. Ekā. example under II. 9. This saropā lakṣaṇā is the basis of the alaṁkāras like Rūpaka and others.
6. *Ibid.*, II. 9.
7. *Ibid.*, vṛtti on II. 9. This sādhyavasānā lakṣaṇā is the basis of Atisayokti alaṁkāra.

just as the combination of different alaṁkāras is called saṁkara and saṁsṛṣṭi alaṁkāras.

In 'Ākramya......pañcānanam',[1] in 'tathāhaṁkārabhāroddhura-stvatkīrttirpa-saraḥ śakrasya dantāvalaṁ hasti', there is *aṅgāṅgi-bhāvasaṁkara* of two lakṣaṇās. Alaṁkāra and hāsa are the properties which belong to a sentient being and not to a lifeless object like kīrttiprasara. So, the word ahaṁkārabhāraḥ is to be taken as 'one who produces it', similarly, hāsa is to mean its 'producer' by lakṣaṇā. This is śuddhā-sāropā-lakṣaṇā. There are two lakṣaṇās present here. 'Tathāhaṁkārabhāroddhuraḥ kīrttiprasaraḥ' is the principal lakṣaṇā and 'Kīrttiprasaraḥ hasti' is the subordinate one thus causing saṁkara.

In the śloka 'Eṣaḥ cintāmaṇiḥ...kimīdṛśaḥ',[2] there is *sandeha-saṁkara* (fusion of lakṣaṇā due to uncertainty). If eṣaḥ, ayaṁ and asau are taken for the viṣaya rājan, it will be sāropā-gauṇīlakṣaṇā If these are taken as adjectives qualifying Cintāmaṇiḥ, Kalpapādapaḥ and Kāmadhenu respectively, there will be Sādhyavasānā-gauṇī-lakṣaṇā, because in that case viṣaya will be enveloped in the viṣayin. Thus there arises a doubt in accepting or rejecting a particular lakṣaṇā.

The verse 'Rākātārakarājamaṇḍalam...tāpicchayoḥ'[3] illustrates the third kind of saṁkara which arises when the same word becomes subject to two or more lakṣaṇās. (*ekalakṣakānupraveśena-saṁkara*). In 'pāṇḍityavaitaṇḍikīkīrttiḥ' pāṇḍitya is attributed to whiteness of fame (śubhratva). Śubhratva is here viṣaya and pāṇḍitya, viṣayin. This is an example of sādhyavasānā-gauṇī-lakṣaṇā because viṣaya is swallowed up by the viṣayin. Vaitaṇḍikī-kīrtti is an example of sāropā-gauṇī-lakṣaṇā. Here kīrtti is viṣaya vaitaṇḍikī, viṣayin. Thus there are two lakṣaṇās here, sādhya-vasānā-gauṇī and sāropā-gauṇī-lakṣaṇā. Here two different words pāṇḍitya and vaitaṇḍikī form a compound and are there-fore regarded as one. Thus here arises ekalakṣakānupraveśasaṁkara.

1. Ekā. example under II. 12.
2. *Ibid.*, example under II. 12.
3. *Ibid.* example under II. 12.

The verse 'Dvirbhāvaḥ puṣpaketoḥ...Śrī Narasiṁhaḥ',[1] contains *saṁsṛṣṭi* of gauṇī-sāropā-lakṣaṇā. Here dvirbhāvaḥ has the sense of dvirbhāvasadṛśaḥ and the viṣaya, bhūpati and the viṣaya dwirbhāvaḥ are both stated. Thus, here exists saṁsṛṣṭi of many sajātīya (of the same kind) lakṣaṇās.

In 'Ayurdānamahot-savasya......Kaliṅgeśvaraḥ',[2] there is *saṁsṛṣṭi* of sajātīya-śuddhasāropā lakṣaṇā. Here 'āyuḥ' is used in the sense of āyurjanaka i.e. producer of ayu.

In all the above examples the purose is suggested. The indicated sense cannot include the purpose as the subject of knowledge and the fruit of knowledge cannot be identified. When a Nīlagau is seen, it is the object of perception and comprehending is the fruit of knowledge. Thus the object known is different from the fruit of knowledge. In 'Gaṅgāyāṁ ghoṣaḥ' the object known from lakṣaṇā is pāvanatvādiviśiṣṭataṭa and the fruit of knowledge is pāvanatvādi. Though the object and the fruit of knowledge are pāvanaṭvādi, the lakṣyārtha here cannot include the purpose because the word 'Gaṅgā' in the example 'Gaṅgāyaṁ ghoṣaḥ' gives the sense of 'its bank' and the idea of 'sanctity'. This is accomplished by vyañjanāvyāpāra only.

Vyañjanā

Vyañjanā is used, according to Vidyādhara[3] and Mammaṭa[4] where the scope of abhidhā is restricted by saṁyoga etc. given by Bhartṛhari[5] in two kārikās, i.e., connection, disjunction, association, enmity, purpose, context, peculiarity, proximity of another word, capacity, compatibility, place, time, gender, accent etc...... these conditions help to convey an idea of the particular meaning of a word, when there is an uncertainty regarding its actual meaning, in a particular meaning e.g. in 'Hari with conch and discus', Hari is restricted to mean Viṣṇu through connection, similarly Rāma is restricted to mean Rāma, son of Daśaratha

1. Ekā. example under II. 12.
2. *Ibid.*, example under II. 12.
3. *Ibie..* II. 3.
4. KP. II. 14-15.
5. Vākyapadīya, II. 315-316.

through disjunction in 'Sītaā entered the forest Daṇḍaka without Rāma', Rāma and Lakṣmaṇa are restricted to mean the two sons of Daśaratha, Rāma and Lakṣmaṇa only in 'Rāmalakṣmaṇau' on account of their association. In 'the behaviour of these two fighters is like that of Rāma and Arjuna', the meaning of Rāma and Arjuna are restricted to Paraśurāma and the son of Kṛttavīrya through enmity; in the instance, 'worship Sthāṇu for removing the shackles of the world', the meaning of 'Sthāṇu' is restricted to 'Śiva' through purpose; in the example, 'deva knows everything', the word 'deva' is restricted to 'you' only, through context; in 'Makaradhvaja is angry', Makaradhvaja is restricted to mean only the 'Love-god', through peculiarity; in 'Devasya śṛṅgāriṇa', 'Deva' is restricted to mean 'Śiva' through the proximity of the word 'śṛṅgāriṇ'; in 'cuckoo is intoxicated by spring', 'madhu' is restricted to mean 'spring' through capacity; in the example 'pātu vo dayitāmukham', 'pātu' is restricted to confrontation through compatibility; in 'Parameśvara shines here', the word 'Parameśvara' is restricted to mean 'king' only through the place referred to being king's capital; in 'citrabhānu is shining', citrabhānu means sun if mentioned during the day time and fire only at night through time and in 'friend, look at......', mitra' means 'friend' when used in neuter gender and 'sun' only in masculine gender, through gender. Accent restricts the meaning to particular sense only in Veda. Thus the intended meaning should be so understood.

Though the meaning of the words is restricted in the above manner, there are some words with several meanings and the only power to restrict their significance is vyañjanā.

The śloka, 'Ācchāditāyatadigambaram...nageśam',[1] describes Raivataka mountain. Māgha in this verse intends to convey two meanings one applicable to Raivataka mountain and the other to 'Śiva, the lord of Kailāsa. The second sense Śiva cannot arise from abhidhā where there is a limitation of context. The tātparyārtha, which is possible in the case of the sense of words actually expressed, cannot take us to the other sense. There is no province of lakṣaṇā as the primary sense is not barred here. This other

1. Ekā. example under II. 3.

sense cannot be convyed through Śleṣa where the two meanings are either connected or unconnected with the context.[1] In the present example a meaning applicable to the mountain is connected with the context while that applicable to Śiva is not so connected. Hence the sense applicable to Śiva arises through Vyañjanā or dhvanana. Through vyañjanā the verse implies similarity between the mountain and Śiva. Mallinātha also thinks that these two meanings arise through dhvani. These cannot come through Tulyayogitā, Samāsokti, Śleṣa or Abhidhā.[2]

Vyañjanā alone is the power by which vācya, lakṣya or vyaṅgya senses convey another sense comprehended through the peculiar character of the speaker and the audience, i.e. the person spoken to.

Vidyādhara has thus discussed śābdī-vyañjanā though he does not mention the name śābdī or ārthī. In the above manner the words restrict themselves to a particular meaning. Thus vyañjanā depends upon words here.

Without discussing ārthīvyañjanā Vidyādhara quotes a verse from Kāvyaprakāśa saying that 'Kāvyaprakāśakāra has discussed the suggestiveness of meanings also. Ārthī Vyañjanā is that power of the meaning which suggests another meaning to the sahṛdayas through the peculiarities of the speaker, the person spoken to, intonation, the sentence, the expressed meaning, the presence of another context, place, time etc.'[3] Thus, where another meaning is suggested through any these conditions, there exists ārthī-vyañjanā.

Śabdas

Vidyādhara has accepted three types of words namely vācaks (denotative), lākṣaṇika (indicative) and vyañjaka (suggestive). According to him, a vācaka-śabda is that which directly expresses

1. Ekā. vṛtti on II. 3.
2. Śiśupālavadha-vyākyāna of Mallinātha on IV. 19.
3. KP. III. 21-22. Also quoted by Vidyādhara in Ekā. under II. 13.

its conventional meaning.[1] A lakṣaka-śabda gives a meaning connected with but different from the primary one, hence, it depends upon the vācaka-śabda. A vyañjaka-śabda depends on both vācaka and lakṣaka-śabdas but expresses a new and inderpendent meaning.

The above division of words does not mean that a particular word is always vācaka, lakṣaka or vyañjaka. On the other hand, the same word can be vācaka, lakṣaka or vyañjaka according to the context and the conditions of its use.

Arthas

According to Vidyādhara a word has three meanings viz. vācya (expressed), lakṣya (indicated) and vyaṅgya (suggested),[2] which belong to abhidhā, lakṣaṇā and vyañjanā respectively. So, vācya is conveyed by abhidhā, lakṣya by lakṣaṇā and vyaṅgya by vyañjanā.[3] Hemacandra[4] has accepted four kinds of meanings namely mukhya, gauṇa, lakṣya and vyaṅgya.

Vidyādhara divides the suggested-sense into two gūḍha (concealed) and agūḍha (not-concealed). In 'Krīḍāsaudhaṁ...yasya kīrttiḥ',[5] the desire of praising is implied by the itchy irritation of their tongues (kaṇḍū-latva). Here the actual sense of praising is suggested but being conealed. Thus the verse illustrates gūḍha-vyaṅgya.

In 'Bhagnadvārā...Śrī Nṛsiṁha bruvanti',[6] the suggested sense in 'they say' is expressed directly. Thus, vyaṅgya is not conealed here.

Tātparyārtha

Tātparyārtha or vākyārtha arises from the logical connection

---

1. Ekā. II. 1.
2. *Ibid.*, II. 13.
3. SD. II. 11.
4. K. Anu. I. 15.
5. Ekā. example under II. 13.
6. *Ibid.*, example under II. 12.

between several senses implied by words.[1] Vidyādhara[2] does not accept tātparya but simpiy quotes others.

According to Abhihitānvayavādins, a sentence as a whole conveys tātprayārtha through the power tātparya. It conveys the related meaning of several words and so differs from other powers that convey the meaning of a particular word. The opposite-school namely Anvitā-bhidhānavāda[3] believes that words do not express their meanings separately bnt unitedly as parts of a sentence. In ordinary life, the meanings of sentences are first understood.

Among the ālaṁkārikas, Abhinavagupta, for the first time, refers to tātparya as a separate vṛtti. He speaks of four distinct functions of words viz. abhidhā, tātparya, lakṣaṇā and vyañjanā and arranges them under four separate classes.[4] Bhoja has a unique way of treating tātparya. It is divided into three types : expressed, implied and suggested (abhidhīyamānā, pratīyamānā and dhvanirūpa).[5] The term is used as equivalent to the intended meaning or suggestion. These have nothing to do with the conveying of the syntactic-relation of word-meanings.

Before Vidyādhara, Mammaṭa also refers to Tātparya in many places. But he does not entirely approve this view since he uses the word 'keṣucit'.[6] Like the other three powers, he does not declare Tātparya as a power.

In the verse 'Umāṁ sa paśyan...anujjhitakramaḥ',[7] the eye is always the instrument for the action of seeing. Cakṣuṣā, therefore, is already known, it is qualified here by the adjective ṛjunā.

1. (a) Ekā. vṛtti on II. 2.
   (b) Kāvya Pradīpa on KP. II. 1.
2. Ekā. vṛtti on II. 2.
3. KP. vṛtti on II. 6.
4. DhL. Locana on DhL. I. 4.
5. Dr. Rāghavan in Bhoja's Śṛṅgāraprakāśa, p. 19.
6. KP. II. 6.
7. Ekā. example under II. 2.

But it is a mere repetition here. Therefore, there is no need to accept tātparyārtha as a separate vṛtti as tātparya does not exist in all the sentences.

Thus, Vidyādhara believes in the existence of there śaktis, three śabdas and three arthas.

He stands singular in dividing lakṣaṇā into seven kinds. No other rhetorician has accepted the jahadajahatsvārthā kind of lakṣaṇā. Moreover, each kind of lakṣaṇā is said to be the basis in originating one alaṁkāra or the other.

— — — —

CAPTER III

DIVISIONS OF KĀVYA

Kinds of Dhvani

According to Vidyādhara dhvani is twofold namely avivakṣitavācya and vivakṣitānya-paravācya. Avivakṣitavācya dhvani is based on lakṣaṇa and is called lakṣaṇāmūlādhvani. Vivakṣitānyaparavācya is based on abhidhā and is, hence, named abhidhāmūlādhvani,[1]

In *avivakṣitavācyadhvani*, the concealed vyaṅgyārtha is predominant and vācyārtha is subordinate.[2] It is of two types viz. arthāntara-saṁkramita-vācya and atyantatiraskṛtavācya. In arthāntarasaṁkramitavācya, vācyārtha is compatible but is altered to convey another sense by vyañjanā.[3] This type of dhvani is again twofold, the vyaṅgyārtha being conveyed either by a word or by a sentence.[4] The verse 'Śrī ramaṇaḥ śrīramaṇaḥ ...tritaye',[5] illustrates padaprakāśya dhvani. Here vācyārtha of the second words Śrīramaṇa, Suddhāṁśumauli and Narasiṁha, is compatible but being a mere repetition, is taken in the sense of possessing the properties of Śrīramaṇa, Sudhāṁśumauli and Narsiṁha. Vākyaprakāśya arthāntarasaṁkramitavācyadhvani is illustrated by the verse 'Eṣā te kathayāmi...abhūdānataḥ.'[6] Here too, vācyārtha of kathayāmi is purposeless and is barred. The sense 'I say' is superfluous and so means 'upadiśāmi', 'Jadvise'. Being a predicate, kathayāmi is a sentence and not a word.

In the second kind of avivakṣitavācyadhvani i.e. atyantatiras-

1. Ekā. III. 1.
2. *Ibid.*, vṛtti on III. 1.
3. *Ibid.*, vṛtti on III. 1.
4. *Ibid.*, vṛtti on III. 1.
5. *Ibid.*, Example under III. 1.
6. *Ibid.* Example under III. 1.

kṛtavācya, vācyārtha is incompatible and hence is eliminated.[1] It is also of two kinds namely padaprakāśya and vākyaprakāśya.[2] The verse 'Jāyeta tvāṁ...kaṇḍūlajihvaḥ',[3] illustrates the kind of padaprakāśya. Here the word 'kaṇḍūla', cannot convey the vācyārtha of 'having an itching sensation'. This meaning is inapplicable and so develops into the lakṣyārtha of 'desiring to praise'. Dhvani is called padarakāśya here for 'kaṇḍūla' is pada i.e. word. The verse 'Bāṇaiḥ pañjaritā...vairistriyaḥ',[4] contains vākyaprakāśyadhvani. Here the kings returning defeated from the battlefield, are questioned as to how many elephants fell to their arrows ? This and similar questions do not convey any meaning in vācyārtha.

In *vivakṣitānyaparavācyadhvani*, vācyārtha is the desired sense but is subordinated to the vyaṅgyārtha.[5] This kind of dhvani is also twofold namely asaṁlakṣyakramavyaṅgya and saṁlakṣyakramavyaṅgya. Asaṁlakṣyakramavyaṅgya is considered first, because rasa, a prominent feature, is discussed here.

In *asalṁakṣyakramavyaṅgya* the order of vācyārtha with vyaṅgyārtha is not observed. *Rasa* is asaṁlakṣyakramavyaṅgya. Rasa is entirely different from vibhāva, anubhāva and vyabhicāribhāva. They are vyañjakas (efficient—causes) because they suggest rasa and therefore precede it. Rasa is suggested by them. But this order of vyaṅgya and vyañjaka cannot be perceived because vibhāvas etc. very quickly lead to the perception of rasa. For example, when a hundred petals of a lotus are pierced by a needle, all are not pierced simultaneously, but are said to be so since the difference of time is too small to be observed. In this way, the suggestion of vyaṅgya and vyañjaka occurs so suddenly that the order of precedence is not perceived.[6] Asaṁlakṣyākramavyaṅgya has eight varieties namely rasa, bhāva, rasābhāsa, bhāvābhāsa,

1. Ekā. vṛtti on III. 1.
2. *Ibid.* vṛtti on III. 1.
3. *Ibid.* example under III. 1.
4. *Ibid.* example under III. 1.
5. *Ibid.* vṛtti on III. 1.
6. *Ibid.* vṛtti on III. 1.

bhāvaśānti, bhāvodaya, bhāvasandhi and bhāvaśabalatā. When any one of these is predominant in a composition, there exists dhvani. When these are subordinate, they constitute Rasavad and other alaṁkāras. Their predominace makes them fit to be adorned (alaṁkārya), but suppression makes them constitute alaṁkāras and adorn the principal idea in a poem.[1]

When a permanent feeling (sthāyibhāva) is brought to a relishable condition by vibhāvas, anubhāvas and vyabhicāribhāvas, it constitutes rasa.[2] It is necessary to explain the terms sthāyibhāva, vibhāva, anubhāva and vyabhicāribhāva here.

Certain permanant states of the mind are called sthāyibhāvas. They are eight or nine, according to the number of rasas. Bharata enumerates eight sthāyibhāvas namely rati (love), hāsa (smile), śoka (grief), krodha (anger). utsāha (energy), bhaya (fear), jugupsā (disgust) and vismaya (wonder).[3]

The causes of the sthāyibhāvas are called *vibhāvas*. These vibhāvas are of two kinds namely ālambana-vibhāvas and uddīpanavibhāvas. A person or a thing that produces rasa is known as ālambana e.g. a woman for whom love is aroused. Actions that make the feelings stronger are known as uddīpanavibhāvas e.g. cooing of cuckoo. *Anubhāvas* are the effects of the sthāyibhāvas e.g. smiling, casting sidelong glances. Vyabhicāribhāvas are transcient subordinate feelings which rise and fall like waves in the ocean of sthāyibhāvas. These appear with the suggestion of rasa and disappear just after it. There are thirty-three vyabhicāribhāvas.[4] There are also eight sāttvikabhāvas which are external indications of emotions.[5]

---

1. (a) Ekā. vṛtti on III. 1.
   (b) DhL. II. 5.
   (c) Kāvya Pradīpa on KP. IV. 3.
2. (a) Ekā. vṛtti on III. 1.
   (b) NS. vṛtti on VI. 32.
3. NS. VI. 18.
4. NS. VI. 19-22.
5. *Ibid.* VI. 23.

Of the four famous views namely utpattivāda of Bhaṭṭalollaṭa, anumitivāda of Śrī Śaṅkua, bhuktivāda of Bhaṭṭa Nāyaka and abhivyaktivāda of Abhinavagupta, the last one namely abhivyaktivāda is generally accepted by the ālaṁkārikas. According to Abhinavagupta rasa is suggested by the union of sthāyibhāva with the vibhāvas, anubhāvas and vyabhicāribhāvas. It is neither produced nor inferred.

Vidyādhara[1] also makes it clear that rasa does not come under abhidhā, tātparya, lakṣaṇā, pratyakṣa, anumāna or smaraṇa. To him it is an exclusive relish. It is found in the subtle form of impressions in the hearts of the sahṛdayas who generally understand the beauty of poetry. Rasa is like the bliss of contemplation of God. Poetry is relished by the investigation of vibhāvas, anubhāvas and vyabhicāribhāvas and Brahmavāda is relished by the meditation of God. The pleasure in both the cases is supernatural.

Rasa cannot be called vācya as it is completely apart from vācaka words as śṛṅgāra. It can be realized by vibhāvas even without using the word 'rasa' or vice versa and is always suggested.[2]

Rasa cannot be realized in tātparyārtha. Tātparya conveys only that sense which is not known from other sources. If Tātparya conveys any sense arising from a word, the sentence, 'pūrvodhāvati' can convey the meaning of 'aparo dhāvati' but this is not true.[3] Rasa cannot be lakṣya, for it is suggested by vibhāvas etc. and the principal idea is not obscured.[4] Rasa cannot be realized by pratyakṣapramāṇa (perception). Pratyakṣa is of two kinds namely nirvikalpa (indeterminate) and savikalpa (determinate). The knowledge of the object itself without distinction of its attributes is nirvikalpaka. The realization of rasa

1. Ekā. vṛtti on III. 1.
2. *Ibid.* vṛtti on III. 1.
3. *Ibid.* vṛtti on III. 1.
4. *Ibid.* vṛtti on III. 1.

cannot be nirvikalpaka because it is based on the investigation of the vibhāvas etc. of rasa. Likewise it cannot be realized through savikalpaka for it is concerned with the object and its distinguishing properties and follows its nirvikalpaka. Hence nirvikalpaka is the cause of savikalpa and, as there can be no effect without a cause, so rasa cannot be savikalpa, it is not nirvikalpa even.[1]

Rasa cannot be inferred as produced through Sītā, which cause pleasure or sorrow from saṁyoga or viyoga. The vibhāvas simply suggest the sthāyibhāva of love and others. They are not the well-known causes which show that the liṅga (middle-term) is pervaded by the sādhya (major-term). The vibhāvas, anubhāvas and vyabhicāribhāvas cannot be taken as liṅga in proving the sthāyibhāvas of love. They also cannot be taken as liṅga in inferring sthāyibhāva. In poetics these causes etc. are known as vibhāva, anubhāva and vyabhicāribhāva.[2]

Rasa is also beyond the limits of rememberance (smaraṇa). An object is realized only when it comes into contact with the sense organs and impresses the mind. When this impression is recalled later, rememberance is produced. Rasa is never apprehended, but when vibhāvas etc. are apprehended, apprehension is attributed to it by lakṣaṇā. Moreover, if rasa is considered as apprehended, it cannot be suggested. Since there is no rememberance without apprehension, rasa can only be suggested.[3]

Rasa cannot be an effect because the vibhāvas etc. which suggest it are not produced in an actor. Though rasa can be realized, but the enjoyment of rasa is eliminated by the disappearance of vibhāvas etc. Rasa, also, cannot be realized by ordinary means of knowledge e.g. Rāma's permanent emotions are of the remote past and cannot contact the sense-organs, at the present time and place.[4]

---

1. Ekā. vṛtti on III. 1.
2. *Ibid.* vṛtti on III. 1.
3. *Ibid.* vṛtti on III. 1.
4. *Ibid.* vṛtti on III. 1.

The vibhāvas etc. are neither an efficient (kārakatva) nor a logical (jñāpaktva) cause of rasa. They help in the enjoyment of rasa, but are extraordinary causes and depict the extra-ordinary character of rasa.[1] The enjoyment of rasa is said to be extra-ordinary.[2] Mammaṭa,[3] also, accepted this nature of rasa previously.

There may arise a question as to how Karuṇa, Bībhatsa, Bhayānaka and other rasas which cause grief and horror, are called rasas ? The enjoyment of rasa is an extraordinary bliss. The mind is so lost in its enjoyment that when a poem is heard where the vibhāvas, anubhāvas and vyabhicāribhāvas are arran. ged, pain is not felt even in karuṇa and such other rasas.[4] In Nāṭyadarpaṇa, Rāmacandra and Guṇacandra consider karuṇa rasa to be full of sorrow while Vidyādhara, Ānandavardhana and Dhanañjaya consider it to be pleasure-giving when enjoyed in the heart.

Thus, enjoyment of rasa which arises from poetry and is suggested by vibhāvas etc. is like the bliss of Ātman. This enjoyment is of four types namely blooming (vikāsa), expansion (vistāra), agitation (kṣobha)and distraction (vikṣepa) of the mind.[5] These four mental states are like the blooming of a flower, expansion of tree, the agitation of an ocean and the distraction of wind.[6] The four basic rasas namely śṛṅgāra, vīra, raudra and bībhatsa are based on the properties of vikāsa, vistāra, kṣobha and vikṣepa respectively. These four rasas are the causes of the origin of four other rasas namely hāsya, karuṇa, adbhuta and bhayānaka.

Vidyādhara and before him Bharata and Mammaṭa accept

---

1. Ekā. vṛtti on III. 1.
2. *Ibid.* quoted in Ekā. vṛtti on III. 1.
3. KP. vṛtti on IV. 28.
4. Ekā. vṛtti on III.1 .
5. (a) *Ibid.* quoted in vṛtti on III. 1.
   (b) DR. IV. 43.
6. Ekā. quoted in vṛtti on III. 1.

śāntarasa also. To show its exitence Bharata[1] mentions the sthāyibhāva nirveda first of all the vyabhicāribhāvas. Though its mention in the beginning is inauspicious, yet it serves some purpose. Its mention immediately after the sthāyibhāvas indicates that Bharata mentioned it both as a sthāyibhāva as well as vyabhicāribhāva.[2] Like Bharata,[3] Vidyādhara,[4] Mammaṭa[5] and Jagannātha[6] believe in the existence of nine rasas accepting śānta as the ninth rasa.

Bhoja[7] accepts only one rasa namely śṛṅgārarasa. Dhanañjaya[8] believes in the existence of eight rasas and does not accept nirveda as a sthāyibhāva.

Vidyādhara has defined and illustrated all the nine rasas. Even Ānandavardhana and Mammaṭa do not define them individually.

Śṛṅgāra rasa is enjoyed in the form of the sthāyibhāva rati through the vibhāvas strī, puṁsa, mālya; anubhāvas stambha, sveda and all the vyabhicāribhāvas except jugupsā, ālasya (indolence) and augrya (irascibility). Śṛṅgārarasa is of two kinds namely sambhoga and vipralambha. Sambhoga-śṛṅgāra rasa is illustrated in 'Mamāsanārdhe...katarttavāsanam',[9] and pūrvarāga, one of the four kinds of vipralambhaśṛṅgāra is cited in the verse 'Vīra Narasiṁha...bharamadhurā'.[10]

The sthāyibhāva hāsa gives rise to *hāsyarasa* through the vibhāvas as abnormally awkward dresses; anubhāvas like expansion of eye, falling of tears and sahakāribhāvas like lajjā

1. NS. VI. 19.
2. Ekā. vṛtti on III. 1.
3. NS. VI. 84.
4. Ekā. vṛtti on III. 1.
5. KP. IV. 35.
6. RG. pp. 29-30.
7. SKBh. V. 1 & 3.
8. DR. IV. 36.
9. Ekā. example under *III*. 1.
10. *Ibid.* example under III. 1.

(shame). The verse 'Utkāse...jantuketuḥ',[1] illustrates hāsyarasa.

The sthāyibhāva śoka assumes the form of *karuṇarasa* through vibhāvas like misery, distresses, trouble of the father; anubhāvas like daivopālambha, tears and sahakāribhāvas like depression (dainya), Karuṇarasa is exemplified in the verse, 'Hṛdaye vasatīti...ratiḥ'.[2] It does not seem to be a proper example of karuṇarasa as death or destruction of anyone is not mentioned here.

Vīrarasa attains its position when the sthāyibhāva utsāha has vibhāvas like witnessing heroic deeds; anubhāvas like romāñca, kṛpāṇa, kampana and vyabhicāribhāvas like harṣa (joy). Vīrarasa is cited in 'Kṣudrāḥ saṁtrāsamenaṁ...anveṣayāmi'.[4]

The sthāyibhāva bhaya gives rise to *bhayānakarasa* through vibhāvas like the look of an enemy soldier; anubhāvas like glaring in a frightening manner and vyabhicāribhāvas like dainya. The verse 'Grīvābhaṅgābhirāmaṁ......prayāti',[5] illustrates bhayānakarasa.

Sthāyibhāva jugupsā assumes the form of *bībhatsarasa* through vibhāvas like seeing pus, dead body; anubhāvas like closing nose, turning pale and vyabhicāribhāvas like moha (fainting). This rasa is cited in 'Dasamāṇuśa...bhavīyadu'.[6]

The sthāyibhāva vismaya gives rise to *adbhutarasa* through vibhāvas like observing strange things; anubhāvas like looking with curiosity and vyabhicāribhāvas like vitarka. 'Paśya kañcana ...carācaram',[7] examplifies adbhutarasa.

The sthāyibhāva nirveda attains the state of *śānta*, the ninth rasa when there are vibhāvas like analysing the temporal nature

1. Ekā. example under III. 1.
2. *Ibid.* example under III. 1.
3. *Ibid.* example under III. 1.
4. *Ibid.* example under III. 1.
5. *Ibid.* example under III. 1.
6. *Ibid.* example under III. 1.
7. *Ibid.* example under III. 1.

of world; anubhāvas like horripilation and vyabhicāribhāvas like dhṛti. Śāntarasa is citedin the verse 'Kadā Vārāṇasyāṁ...divasān'.[1] Of its two kinds, vairāgya and śama, vairāgya is illustrated here.

Śṛṅgārarasa pleases people and hence is given primary position in the discussion. Then hāsyarasa is discussed for it follows śṛṅgārarasa. Karuṇarasa does not require any particular anubhāva to represent it. Raudra rasa is based on the feeling of objects (artha pradhāna). Then comes vīrarasa; based on religious spirit (dharma pradhana), for dharma is the basis of both artha and kāma. After vīra, bhayānaka rasa is discussed because vīrarasa removes fear. Bhayānaka is closely allied to the next rasa i.e. bībhatsa. Vīra ultimately produces marvellous exploits so adbhuta is discussed last of all the rasas.

All the above eight rasas are based on the first three puruṣārthas. Śānta rasa which comes at the end, is, however, not related with these three puruṣārthas. It is characterized by passivity (nirveda) and concerns mokṣa. Vidyādhara does not deal with the kinds of rasas exhaustively as he himself believes that these are easily available in other works also.[2]

Rati of which the subject is Deva (God), dvija (brāhmaṇa), guru (teacher), putra (son) and mitra (friend) and vyabhicāribhāva which is nourished by vibhāvas and anubhāvas becomes bhāva, but rati of which the subject is a beloved, becomes śṛṅgāra rasa. The verse 'Chintte brahmaśiro...eveśvaraḥ',[3] illustrates bhāva where the suject is Deva, and where love for God is suggested. Love of which the subject is brāhmaṇa, guru, putra or mitra may also be so illustrated.

Though rasa is the very life and beauty of kāvya, yet in some instances vyabhicāribhāvas are more beautiful; so the name bhāva is given when they are expressed through vibhāvas and anubhāvas.

---

1. Ekā. example under III 1.
2. *Ibid.* vṛtti on III. 1.
3. *Ibid.* example under III. 1.

In the verse 'Kimasubhiḥ...smaraḥ',[1] jealousy of Damayantī towards Śaśī is suggested through vyabhicāribhāva.

According to Vidyādhara,[2] when the sthāyibhāvas arise from one side but there is no response from the other side, there is rasābhāsa (semblance of rasa) and bhāvā-bhāsa. But Bhoja,[3] Vidyānātha[4] and Viśvanātha[5] describe rasa in animals as rasābhāsa and not rasa, but Vidyādhara[6] believes that even lower beings can experience rasa, e.g. in 'Dadau...rathāṅganāmā,'[7] rati of even an elephant attains the state of sambhoga-Śṛṅgārarasa.

The śloka 'Brahmannadhyayanasya...Laṅkeśvaraḥ',[8] illustrates rasābhāsa. Here only Rāma can enjoy the love of the daughter of the king of Mithilā. Her love of Rāvaṇa is regarded as an impropriety. So, there occurs rasābhāsa of vipralambha-śṛṅgāra. The verse 'Asmadvikrama...spṛhācañcalam',[9] illustrates bhāvābhāsa, where autsukyabhāva of Rāvaṇa is improper.

Though rasa is prominent in kāvya, sometimes even bhāvas, bhāvaśānti etc. become predominant; just as sometimes a king may follow his own attendants on the eve of their marriage. Bhāvaśānti is illustrated in 'Paśyāmaḥ...muktastayā.'[10] The anger of the jealous nāyikā is pacified here. The verse 'Tadadya...... matpriyaḥ';[11] is illustrated for bhāvodaya where there is rise of autsukya-bhāva of Damayantī towards Nala. When two opposite

1. Ekā. example under III. 1.
2. (a) Ekā. vṛtti on III. 1.
   (b) KP. IV. 36.
3. SKBh. V. 20.
4. Pratāparudrayaśobhūṣaṇa—Rasaprakaraṇa, pp. 162-63.
5. SD. III. 219-220.
6. Ekā. vṛtti on III. 1.
7. *Ibid.* example under III. 1.
8. *Ibid.* example under III. 1.
9. *Ibid.* example under III. 1.
10. *Ibid.* example uhder III. 1.
11. *Ibid.* example under III. 1.

emotions striving for supremacy are experienced at the same place and time, they constitute bhāvasandhi (mixture of emotions). In the example 'Ardhe cetasi...karīṣāgninā',[1] there is mixture of rati and krodha. A series of emotions in which each supresses preceding one and all are not relished simultaneously, constitute bhāvaśabalatā (variegation of emotions). Jagannātha[2] disagrees with Vidyadhara in thinking that to constitute bhāvaśablatā each successive emotion should overcome the previous one. The verse 'Kvākāryaṁ śaśalakṣmaṇaḥ...dhāsyati',[3] contains variegation of vitarka, autsukya, mati, smaraṇa, śaṅkā, dainya, dhṛti and cintā emotions. Vidyādhara discusses these eight kinds of asaṁlakṣyakramavyaṅgya on the lines of Ānandavardhana.

Saṁlakṣyakramavyāṅgya is so named because the sequence between vyaṅgya and vyañjaka is perceptible.[4] It is of three types namely—

i. Śabdasaktimūlānuraṇanarūpavyaṅgya,

ii. Arthaśaktimūlānuraṇanarūpavyaṅgya, and

iii. Ubhayaśaktimūlānuraṇanarūpavyaṅgya.

Vidyādhara and Mammaṭa accept these three kinds while Ānandavardhana accepts only the first two kinds.[5] When vyaṅgyārtha depends on a particular word and disappears with its replacement, it is known as śabdaśaktimūlānuraṇanarūpavyaṅgya. It is sub-divided into two classes according to whether a figure or matter is suggested. Each of these two is again classified into two depending on whether they are manifested by a word or a

---

1. Ekā. example under III. 1.
2. (a) *Ibid.* vṛtti on III. 1.
   (b) RG., p. 103.
3. Ekā. example under III. 1
4. DhL. vṛtti on II. 20.
5. (a) Ekā. vṛtti on III. 1.
   (b) KP. IV. 37, 38.
   (c) DhL. II. 20.

sentence. In the instance 'Narasiṁha dharāpāla...vijṛmbhate',[1] Rājan is taken as viṣaya and conquering is taken as the prakṛtakārya. Here the word rājānaṁ principally suggests Pariṇāmālaṁkāra. The verse 'Ākramya smaravairi...pañcānanam',[2] also illustrates pariṇāmadhvani. Here the glory of the king Narasiṁha is said to surpass that of the moon and other white objects. The word 'musalāyudha' suggests 'cleverness in battles'. The figure Upamā is suggested in the verse 'Hiraṇyakaśipu...jagatpate'.[3] Hence it is an example of alaṁkāradhvani. A word uttered once can denote only one meaning. When a second meaning is taken, the first one does not remain. So śliṣṭa words (having more than one sense) do not remain.[4] Abhidhā restricts the word rājan to the sense applicable in the context. Similarly in the verse 'Gauḍagurjara...karahāṭakāḥ',[5] Virodhālaṁkāra is suggested. Here the power of śabdaśakti suggests virodha through a sentence. The alaṁkāras, which are suggested here and in other places of alaṁkāradhvani, are present where rasa is vyaṅgya. Though in the example of alaṁkāradhvani they are not alaṁkāras but have become alaṁkārya, yet the name alaṁkāradhvani is employed only because they are recognised as alaṁkāras in other instances, as a Brāhmaṇa, even though he becomes a Śramaṇa or Baudhasanyāsin, is called a Brāhmaṇa.

Where there is alaṁkāratva, there arises vastudhvani, e.g. in 'Sattvasāgara ..tvayi',[6] the matter, 'the enemies are killed quickly in the battle fields as soon as he takes up the bow', is suggested through a sentence by the śabdaśakti.

The second kind of saṁlakṣyakramavyaṅgya is *arthaśaktimūlānuraṇanavyaṅgya.* It is of three kinds—

---

1. Ekā. example under III. 1.
2. *Ibid.* example under III. 1.
3. *Ibid.* example under III. 1.
4. (a) *Ibid.* vṛtti on III. 1.
   (b) DhL. vṛtti on II. 21.
5. Ekā. example under III. 1.
6. *Ibid.* example under III. 1.

(i) Self-possible (svataḥ-samdhavī),

(ii) established by the poet's bold assertion though not exciting in the outer world (kavipraudhoktimātraniṣpannaśarīra) and

(iii) established by the bold assertion of some character drawn by the poet (kavinibaddhavaktṛpraudhoktimātraniṣpannaśarīra).

In each of these three kinds, vastu and alaṁkāra may suggest themselves or each other. Thus there are twelve kinds. The total becomes thirty-six, since each of the latter may be of three types depending on whether a word, a sentence or a passage makes the suggestion. Just as an ornament decorates a lady, speech appears graceful to sahṛdayas through vyaṅgya manifested by a word.[1] The verse 'Nṛsiṁha vasudhādhipa...dwipāḥ',[2] illustrates first kind of arthaśaktimūlānuraṇanayaṅgya where matter is suggested through the word 'cirād'. In the verse 'Nṛsiṁha Kṣmāpāla...pakṣmaladṛśām',[3] Parisaṁkhyālaṁkāra is suggested by matter through the word. In the śloka 'Samaravasundharāsu...ādadhate',[4] vastu is suggested by Nidarśanālaṁkāra through the force of a word while Atiśayokti alaṁkāra is suggested by Paryāyālaṁkāra through the force of aword in the example 'Pūrvaṁ payodherudare...tavābhirāmam'.[5] All these examples illustrate the suggestion of sense of svataḥsambhavī type.

In the verse 'Hemādreḥ...kṣitīndra',[6] where the matter, viz. that his fame shone even in darkness, is suggested by the matter that it caused happiness, through the word 'mudam'. This is an example for kavipraudhoktimātraniṣpannaśarīraḥ. In the example 'Ambhojabhū...Nṛsiṁhadeva',[7] the matter, that your fame spreads every where, suggests through the force of word 'mahimā'

1. Ekā. vṛtti on III. 1.
2. *Ibid.* example under III. 1.
3. *Ibid.* example under III. 1.
4. *Ibid.* example under III. 1.
5. *Ibid.* example under III. 1.
6. *Ibid.* example under III. 1.
7. *Ibid.* example under III. 1.

Sāmānyālaṁkāra, which is brought about by sayings that lotus etc. cannot be recognised in a world dazzled by your glory. In 'Tanau dattvā...śriyamapi',[1] the matter is suggested by Parivṛttyālaṁkāra through the word 'pākonmukhaśarasakhī'. Vyatirakālaṁkāra is suggested by Asṅgati-alaṁkāra through the force of a word 'vilokyatām'. In these examples there is a suggestion of the sense of kavipraudhoktimātraniṣpannaśarīra.

Now kavinibaddhavaktṛpraudhoktimātraniṣpannaśarīra type is being illustrated. In the verse 'Bhuvaḥ kelitalpaṁ...*bhajatiyaḥ*'[2] the matter is suggested by matter through a word 'navapreyolābha'. In the verse 'Dhūrttādhoraṇa...camūreṇavaḥ',[3] Atiśayokti alaṁkāra is suggested by matter by the force of a word 'sphāyanta'. In 'Āyodhaneṣu...vipakṣān',[4] a question 'were the enemies left alive by Nṛsiṁha ?' is effect and the answer 'the arm of Nṛsiṁha is never able to kill those who submit to him', is the cause. There is Aprastutapraśaṁsālaṁkāra, the question being prastuta and the cause aprastuta. There is Hetūtprakṣā also because the cause of not killing those who fall prostrated at his feet is given here as 'vīraśriyaḥ stananitambabharātibhārāt', which is not real. There is Vyājaṣtuti alaṁkāra also because the king is extremely merciful and conscious of the duties of kṣatriya, sparing who seek his shelter. The Vyājastuti alaṁkāra is strengthened by Utprekṣā which also suggests that the king is always careful in fulfilling the duties of a kṣatriya, through the word 'pādopakaṇṭhapatitān'. In 'Bāhuste Narasiṁha...hā vidhim',[5] the prowess of Nṛsiṁha's arms is described as the cause of the plight of the wives of enemies. Thus it becomes Aprastutapraśaṁsālaṁkāra. Aprastutapraśaṁsā suggests Kāvyaliṅgālaṁkāra which again suggests, through the force of the words 'hā hā hā vidhim', Ākṣepālaṁkāra. Thus here alaṁkāra is suggested by alaṁkāra and these verses contain suggestion of the sense of kavinibaddhavaktṛpraudhoktimātraniṣpannaśarīra.

---

1. Ekā. example under III. 1.
2. *Ibid.* example under III. 1.
3. *Ibid.* example under III. 1.
4. *Ibid.* example under III. 1.
5. *Ibid.* example under III. 1.

In the following examples the force of a sentence is shown and there is suggestion of the sense of svataḥsambhavī type. In the example 'Etāstārāḥ...rājñaḥ',[1] through the affirmative use of 'etāstārāḥ sphurantu', the negative matter 'na sphurantu' is suggested. Both the senses are vācya simultaneously. They cannot be denoted by abhidhā one after another because abhidhā ceases after denoting onething. So here vastu is suggeted by vastu while alaṁkāra Rūpaka is suggested by matter 'you constructed the bridge over the ocean to kill Rāvaṇa' in the example 'Saṅgharṣotkarṣa...candrakāntaiḥ'.[2] In the example 'Pṛthvībhārāvatāraṁ...kṣitīndra',[3] the matter, 'your sword cannot be seen by your enemies', is suggested by Apahnuti alaṁkāra. In the verse 'Senārajobhistava...malinaprakāśaḥ'[4] Asaṅgati alaṁkāra suggests Atiśayokti that is 'the enemies ran away as soon as they looked at the sky darkened by the dust raised by Nṛsiṁha's army, Asaṅgati may suggest Aprastutapraśaṁsālaṁkāra by the cause which is aprastuta that is the immensity of the army inferred from their looking at the dark, dust-laden sky, suggesting the routing of the enemies which is prastuta. On the other hand, the suggested alaṁkāra may be Paryāyokta because here the effect is the darkness of the faces of the enemie's wives which is represented here as an anubhāva of vyabhicāribhāva viṣāda (grief). Consequently, it is prastuta and the cause, i.e. 'running away of the enemies from the battlefield' is also prastuta.

In the verse 'Surāṅganābhyo...nāgāḥ',[5] the matter, 'your fame has made lotus-stalks milky to both elephants and serpents' of Bhrāntimadalaṁkāra, is suggested by the matter 'rasanāñcalollolana'. In the śloka 'Viyogino...pakṣe',[6] Bhrāntimadalaṁkāra is suggested by the matter. In 'Udgīyamānamaniśaṁ...vataṁsaḥ',[7]

1. Ekā. example under III. 1.
2. *Ibid.* example under III. 1.
3. *Ibid.* example under III. 1.
4. *Ibid.* example under III. 1.
5. *Ibid.* example under III. 1.
6. *Ibid.* example under III. 1.
7. *Ibid.* example under III. 1.

the matter, 'your charity is extra-ordinary', is suggested by Pariṇāmālāṁkāra. Upameyopamā is suggested by Anyonālaṁkāra in the example 'Pṛthvi pūrvāpara...vidhātuḥ'.[1] These examples illustrate suggestion of the sense kavipraudhoktimātraniṣpanna-śarīra.

In the verse 'kastvaṁ...vīravrate',[2] matter is suggested by matter. In the example 'Yuktā vipakṣeṣu...sapatnāḥ',[3] the matter viz. 'we are not enemies', suggests Ākṣepālaṁkāra. The enemies deny being so suggesting themselves as faithful well-wishers. Thus Ākṣepālaṁkāra is uktaviṣaya. In the verse 'Prāgāsīnmakaranda ...netrāñcale',[4] the matter is suggested by Paryāyālṁkāra. In 'Kātvaṁ bhīru...kaṣāyaṁ payaḥ',[5] Vyatirekālaṁkāra is suggested by Atiśayokti. These examples represent suggestion of the sense of kavinibaddhavaktṛprauḍhoktimātraniṣpannaśarīra.

When suggestion depends on words it is connected with the sense too. When it depends on sense, a connection of words is invariably present. The suggestion in each ls discussed separately.

Suggestion through the force of a passage is illustrated by 'Alaṁ sthitvā...gatirīdṛśī',[6] where matter is suggested by matter. Similarly in 'Ādityoayaṁ...aviśaṅkitāḥ',[7] also, matter is suggested by matter. Other examples of this type of Arthaśaktimūlādhvani may be similarly cited.

When Vyaṅgyārtha depends on both words and sense; that is when some words can or cannot be changed, it is known as ubhayaśaktimūlānuraṇanarūpavyaṅgya. This type of dhvani can only be manifested by a sentence, e.g. in 'Saccakrānandakaḥ...na sevyase'[8], Upamālaṁkāra is suggested by a sentence, King Nara-

1. Ekā. example under III. 1.
2. *Ibid.* example under III. 1.
3. *Ibid.* example under III. 1.
4. *Ibid.* example under III. 1.
5. *Ibid.* example under III. 1.
6. *Ibid.* example under III. 1.
7. *Ibid.* example under III. 1.
8. *Ibid.* example under III. 1.

siṁha being like Narasiṁha. Here 'saccakra' word is śabdaśktimūla and mahānubhāva is arthaśaktimūla. All the above kinds of dhvani are subdivided by one type of Saṁsṛṣṭi and three types of Saṁkara, but these are not examplified in the Ekāvalī.

Vidyādhara accepts asaṁlakṣyakramavyaṅgya in pada and vākya only while Mammaṭa accepts its six kinds namely those of pada, vākya, padāṁśa, varṇa, racanā and prabandha. Ānandavardhana accepts these kinds leaving only one that is padāṁśa.

Śabdaśaktyudbhava is not divided according to vastu and alaṁkāra and ubhayaśaktyudbhava kind of saṁlakṣyakramavyaṅgya also is not accepted by Ānandavardhana. These are discussed by Vidyādhara and Mammaṭa.

The divisions of dhvani, according to Vidyādhara, can be thus shown by making a chart—

- Dhvanikāvya
  - Avivakṣitavācya
    - Arthāntarasaṅkramitavācya
      - Padaprakāśya (1)
      - Vākyaprakāśya (2)
    - Atyantatiraskṛtavācya
      - Padaprakāśya (3)
      - Vākyaprakāśya (4)
  - Vivakṣitānyaparavācya
    - Saṁlakṣyakramavyaṅgya
      - Śabda śaktyuttha
        - Suggested through matter (vastu)
          - Pada prakāśya (5)
          - Vākya prakāśya (6)
        - Suggested through alaṁkāra
          - Pada (7)
          - Vākya (8)
      - artha śaktyuttha
        - Svataḥ sambhavi (4)
        - Kavipraudhoktimātraniṣpannaśarīra (4)
        - Kavinibadhavaktṛ-praudhoktimātra-niṣpannaśarīra (4)
          1. Matter suggested by matter (vastu)
          2. Matter suggested by alaṁkāra
          3. Alaṁkāra suggested by alaṁkāra
          4. Alaṁkāra suggested by matter

          { —Padaprakāśya / —Vākyaprakāśya / —Prabandhaprakāśya }
      - ubhaya śaktyuttha—only in vākya (9)
    - Asaṁlakṣyakramavyaṅgya
      - Padaprakāśya (10)
      - Vākyaprakāśya (11)

All these twelve kinds having pada, vākya and prabandhaprakāśya kinds, thus 36 kinds (12×3).

Total=47 kinds of dhvani (36+11).

All these kinds are further subdivided on the basis of three kinds of Saṁkara and one kind of Saṁsṛṣṭi, thus resulting in its many-many subdivisions.

Guṇībhūtavyaṅgya

Guṇībhūtavyaṅgya, as its name denotes, is that division of kāvya where the vyaṅgyārtha is considered as secondary to the vākyārtha.[1] So here vācyārtha is more or equally charming to vyaṅgyārtha.

It has been divided into agūḍhaṁ, aparāṅgaṁ, vācyasiddhyaṅgaṁ, asphuṭaṁ, sandigdhaprādhānyaṁ, tulyaprādhānyaṁ, kākvākṣiptaṁ and asundaraṁ.

In agūḍhaṁ, lakṣyārtha is so clear that it appears as vācyārtha,[2] e.g. in 'Gaṇḍairasthirapatrakhaṇḍaracanaiḥ...pratyarthivāmabhruvaḥ',[3] the sense has been suggested to be atyantatiraskṛtavācya. Since this is well-known, it is a case of guṇībhūtavyaṅgya of agūḍha type.

Aparāṅga arises when the vyaṅgya such as rasa, bhāva, rasābhāsa, bhāvābhāsa, bhāvodaya, bhāvaśānti, bhāvasandhi and bhāvaśabalatā become subsidiary to another rasa etc.,[4] In 'Tattadvira...cābhāṣate',[5] there is Samāsokti alaṁkāra which arises when aprastuta (which is not desired to be described) is inferred from the description of the prastuta (desired to be described) through adjectives common to both prastuta and aprastuta.[6] Here through the common attributes aśleṣa, rāgapuṣṭi smitavīrabhāva and ābhāṣaṇa, the prastuta attribute of nāyaka and nāyikā is inferred. Here kalpadruma is the nāyaka and latā, nāyikā. The vācyārtha i.e. the wishing tree is not embraced by the creeper etc. is predominant and vyaṅgyārtha, which is understood through Samāsokti viz. 'the action of the lover towards his beloved', is sub-ordinate to the vācyārtha merely and heightens its beauty.

1. (a) DhL. III. 34.
   (b) KP. I. 5.
2. Ekā. IV. 1.
3. *Ibid.* example under IV. 1.
4. *Ibid.* IV. 2.
5. *Ibid.* example under IV. 2.
6. *Ibid.* VIII. 23.

In the example 'Narasiṁha...vṛjatu',[1] there is Ākṣepālaṁkāra. After composing a poem on Narasiṁha, Vidyādhara states that—he is not a poet. The denial suggests that the kāvya composed by him simply repeats the qualities of the king and it is not possible to attribute to him more qualities than he already possesses. Hence vyaṅgyārthā heightens the charm of vācyārtha only. The śloka 'Brūmaḥ kiṁ padmanābhaṁ...Gāṅgavaṁśāvataṁsa',[2] also illustrates aparāṅga-guṇībhūtavyaṅgya. Here adbhutarasa is subordinate to the rati bhāva (devotion) to God.

In 'Tvatpratyarthi...lolairapāṅgairapi'[3] rasābhāsa is subordinate to the rati bhāva to God.

In 'Tvayi locanagocaraṁ...*dwiṣāṁgaṇaḥ*',[4] bhāvābhāsa is subservient to the rati-bhāva to God.

In 'Nṛsiṁha bhavato...rājakuñjarāḥ',[5] Śānti of the emotion of mada (madness or intoxication) is subordinate to the rati-bhāva to God.

In 'Samālokyālekhya...*vīravipine*',[6] bhāvodaya, the emotions to the fear of the wives of the enemy-kings are subservient to the emotion of rati to the king Narasiṁha.

In 'Ekābhūt...prauḍhāhavāḍambaram'[7] a linking of the anxiety of love and courage with women rolling their eyes, has been subordinated to the rati-bhāva to God.

In 'Saubhāgyaṁ ..kṣitīndra',[8] Śabalatā of the bhāvas smṛti, nirveda, mati and cintā of the enemy, who has run away, from the battlefield, is subordinate to the rati-bhāva to the king.

---

1. Ekā. example under IV. 2.
2. *Ibid.* example under IV. 2.
3. *Ibid.* example under IV. 2.
4. *Ibid.* example under IV. 2.
5. *Ibid.* example under IV. 2.
6. *Ibid.* example under IV. 2.
7. *Ibid.* example under IV. 2.
8. *Ibid.* example under IV. 2.

Thus Vidyādhara has given examples of rasavadalaṁkāras, which arise when any one of the rasa, bhāva, rasā-bhāsa, bhāvābhāsa, bhāva-śānti, bhāva-sandhi, bhāvodaya and bhāva-śabalatā are made subordinate to some other rasa, bhāva, rasā-bhāsa etc.[1] Vidyādhara has not dealt with them separately.[2]

Vācyasiddhyaṅga-guṇībhūta-vyaṅgya occurs when vyaṅgya becomes the cause of the accomplishment of vācya.[3] In the instance 'Patrāvalī...*tavāsidhenuḥ*',[4] the word asidhenu (the sword) suggests a cow and the vyaṅgyārtha of the cow becomes subordinate in accomplishing the vācyārtha of the Rūpaka, milk of glory (yaśaḥ-payāṁsi). In the verse 'Dhārāviṣaṁ...varṇabhedam'[5] a doubt arises, whether 'Dhārāviṣaṁ tvadasikalā bhujaṅgamasya' is Paramparitarūpaka or Upamā or Śleṣa or vācyasiddhyaṅga. The identification of viṣa (water) with viṣa (poison) is not the cause of identification of asi with kālabhujaṅgama, for even before the former that of the latter is established from the sword possessing the property of being powerful. Consequently, it cannot be Paramparitarūpaka. Moreover, the context restricts the sense of viṣa to water. Water is possible only on a sword and not on a serpent. Upamā, again, is not possible here because the upameya and the upamāna as water is not possible on a serpent. If the word 'viṣa' be śliṣṭa conveying the two senses water with sword and poison with serpent, then Śleṣālaṁkāra becomes the cause of Upamā. But this is improper because, according to the context, when the sword is the principal sense of the sentence and abhidhā restricts the sense of viṣa to water, Śleṣālaṁkāra is not possible. So the suggested sense 'poison' accomplishes the expressed sense of Rūpaka in asikalābhujaṅgama (asireva kalābhujaṅgama).

Asphuṭaguṇībhūtavyaṅgya occurs when the vyaṅgya is very

1. DhL. II. 5.
2. (a) Ekā. vṛtti on IV. 2.
   (b) DhL. vṛtti on II. 5.
3. Ekā. IV. 3.
4. *Ibid.* example under IV. 3.
5. *Ibid.* example under IV. 3.

subtle and hidden even to the sahṛdayas.[1] In 'Nṛsiṁha bhūpa... jagattrayam'[2], innumerous qualities cannot exist in the world measured on the footsteps of God Trivikrama...; this suggested sense does not appear immediately.

When the vācya or vyaṅgya is not definite, it is a case of Sandigdhaprādhānya.[3] Here the importance of either is doubtful. In 'Tvāmārūḍha...sapatnaḥ',[4] it is doubtful whether the vyaṅgya, viz., 'you started running on seeing the fast-running horse', is predominant or vācya namely bhayānubhāva 'he looks at the horse' is predominant. So this verse exemplifies Sandigdhaprādhānyaṁ.

When both vācyārtha and vyaṅgyārtha are equally predominant, then it is known as tulyaprādhānyam.[5] There is Paryāyoktālaṁkāra in 'Aspṛṣṭāñjanasampadaḥ...pṛthvībhujām[6]'. Here, 'the absence of the touch of collyrium of the wives of the enemies' is the effect expressed and 'the death of the enemy king' is the cause which is suggested. Both the effect and the cause, or the expressed and suggested senses are equally predominant here.

Where vyaṅgyārtha is known simultaneously with Vācya through kāku i.e. a speciality in pronunciation, it is a case of kākvākṣiptaguṇībhūtavyaṅgya.[7] In the śloka 'Sarvārthinām... pārijātaḥ',[8] 'Definitely feels shame' is the vyaṅgya, but it is realised simultaneously with the negative idea.

In asundara type of guṇībhūtavyaṅgya, vyaṅgya is not charming,[9] e,g. in 'Ayajñaḥ svarlokaḥ...asmākamagamat',[10] svarlokaḥ,

1. Ekā. IV. 3.
2. *Ibid.* example under IV. 3.
3. *Ibid.* IV. 4.
4. *Ibid.* example under IV. 4.
5. *Ibid.* IV. 5.
6. *Ibid.* example under IV. 5.
7. *Ibid.* IV. 5.
8. *Ibid.* example underIV. 5.
9. *Ibid.* IV. 6.
10. *Ibid.* example under IV. 6.

sukṛta, sudhāsāra, phala, sāmrājya and nidhi are represented as effects and causes, i.e. what generates extreme pleasure is suggested, it does not convey any charm. In the example 'Uttiṣṭha... darīmariste'[1], also, only fear of Nṛsiṁha caused by rememberance of the power of his bow, is implied. However, as there is no charm, these two verses illustrate asundara i.e. last type of guṇībhūtavyaṅgyakāvya.

Previously Mammaṭa[2] also accepted these kinds similarly.

Adhamakāvya

Vidyādhara has not mentioned the name adhamakāvya or citrakāvya. The reason here may be that he does not think the presence of kāvya where rasa or bhāva is not clear or which is based on the charm of words or sense only as in citrakāvya. Dhvanikāra[3] calls citrakāvya to be only a copy of poetry. Later scholars like Viśvanātha[4] hold that this citra is not a kāvya, but a mere collection of sentences. Therefore, a good poet's efforts should be in the direction of composing dhvanikāvya only.[5]

Thus, in this chapter various divisions and subdivisions of dhvāni have been discussed. Then rasa, a kind of asaṁlakṣya-kramavyaṅgya, is discussed in full details. Each rasa is defined individually.

As far as the divisions of asaṁlakṣyakramavyaṅgyadhvani are concerned, Vidyādhara does not follow Ānandavardhana or Mammaṭa totally. He has given up its four divisions, thinking that this type of dhvani cannot be possible in varṇa or padāṁśa and it's also of no use to accept it in racanā or prabandha separately.

---

1. Ekā. example under IV. 6.
2. KP. V. 45-46.
3. DhL. vṛtti on III. 42.
4. SD. vṛtti on IV. 17.
5. DhL. vṛtti on III. 42.

CHAPTER IV

CONCEPTS OF GUṆA, RĪTI AND VṚTTI

Definition of Guṇa

According to Vidyādhara[1], guṇas are those properties which belong to the soul of poetry. Just as heroism, bravery and other qualities belong to the soul and adorn it, similarly guṇas belong to rasa and are the cause of its excellence. They cannot be imagined in the absence of rasa. Prior to him, Ānandavardhana[2] and Mammaṭa[3] have also defined them similarly.

Without defining guṇa, Bharata[4] states that guṇas are antonyms of doṣas. However, there used to arise a difference of opinion among the rhetoricians regarding the presence of guṇa, doṣa or alaṁkāra accepting guṇa as the opposite of doṣa. For example, according to Bhāmaha, the verse 'Vyālavanto...pramādinām',[5] contains Sasaṁśayadoṣa[6] because a doubt arises here as which of the two objects is meant here, but this very verse is cited by Hemacandra[7] to illustrate Sandehālaṁkāra as the doubt here arises regarding Parvatarāja, though the word Himālaya is not mentioned. The doubt here arises whether this verse refers to a king or to a mountain. The word 'bhūbhṛtaḥ' denotes 'the kings' and 'the mountains' as well. Thus the same verse is treated as the illustration of a doṣa and an alaṁkāra also.

Dr. Lahiri, in his work, 'Concepts of Rīti and Guṇa in Sanskrit Poetics',[8] surmises that, "it will be seen from the enumeration

---

1. Ekā. V. 1.
2. DhL. vṛtti on II. 6.
3. KP. VIII. 66.
4. NS. 16.96.
5. KAB. IV. 19.
6. *Ibid.* IV. 17-18.
7. Sanskrit Commentary Viveka of Hemacandra on KA nu. VI.20.
8. p. 48.

of Bharata's guṇas, both by themselves and with reference to the interpretation of later writers, that in spite of attempts made by Abhinavagupta and others, a great deal of obscurity still remains and it is difficult to understand what Bharata sometimes means exactly by a particular guṇa".

Bhāmaha has mentioned three guṇas namely Mādhurya, Ojas and Prasāda, but he has used the term 'Guṇa' only in connection with Bhāvikālaṁkāra. He has not defined a guṇa and the alaṁkāra is primary for him.

Daṇḍin, too, does not define guṇa. He accepts all the ten guṇas of Bharata and calls them the soul of Vaidarbhī-rīti,[1] yet he regards them as mere alaṁkāras because they embellish poetry. According to Vāmana, the attributes that create beauty in poetry are called guṇas.[2] These are permanent.[3] He establishes the intimate link between rīti and guṇa and shows how guṇas are indirectly essential in poetry. It is to be noted that Vāmana lays emphasis on the aviodance of doṣas,[4] and the utilization of guṇas and alaṁkāras[5] in creating poetic-beauty.

While defining kāvya, Kuntaka has neither mentioned the word 'Guṇa' nor considered them as the soul of kāvya. Guṇas are not classified on the basis of śabda or artha, but are treated as pervading the composition as a whole.

Without defining guṇa, Bhoja states that though kāvya is embellished with alaṁkāra it should not be devoid of guṇas, because, of the two, the latter is more important.[6] He also opines that since certain alaṁkāras themselves are made up of guṇas, one or the other is prominent at different times.

In the Agnipurāṇa,[7] guṇas are stated as imparting lustre to kāvya and increasing its descriptive beauty.

1. KD. I. 41-42.
2. KASV. III. 1.1.
3. *Ibid.* III. 1.3.
4. *Ibid.* vṛtti on I. 1.3.
5. *Ibid*, vṛtti on I. 1.3.
6. SKBh. I. 72.
7. 346.3,

Difference between guṇa and alaṁkāra

An alaṁkāra is that element which enhances the poetic-charm. Alaṁkāra belong to poetry as throat and limbs belong to the body. They heighten rasa[1] and consequently Mādhurya, Prasāda and Ojas guṇas, which are expressed by proper letters, are the properties of rasa. The alaṁkāras enrich the soul indirectly and heighten the beauty of kāvya. However, if rasa is absent, they produce only a variety of expressions.

There are three views regarding the difference between guṇā and alaṁkāra :

(i) Bhaṭṭodbhaṭṭa believes in the similarity of the guṇa and alaṁkāra. He believes that these two reside by intimate relation in poetry.[2] Just as the adjective 'brave' is used for a tall, well-built person, even though he might not be courageous, similarly soft letters, that express the properties of Mādhurya-rasa, are called as such.

However, this cannot really be a differentiating property. Actually, guṇas are the properties of rasa. Therefore, guṇa and alaṁkāra cannot reside by intimate relation in poetry.[3]

(ii) Vāmana has drawn a clear distinction between guṇa and alaṁkāra. According to him, guṇas are the properties which create charm in poetry while alaṁkāras enhance the charm. Alaṁkāras cannot produce charm and so depend completely on guṇas. It can be concluded from Vāmana's view that alaṁkāras but not guṇas are dispensible.

It is again improper to differentiate the two on the basis that alaṁkāras are fully dependent on guṇas.

Daṇḍin also opines that guṇas are of primary importance as

1. Ekā. vṛtti on V. 1.
2. (a) KP. vṛtti on VIII. 67.
   (b) Bhāmaha vivaraṇa—Bhaṭṭodbhaṭṭa—Quoted by Ācārya Viśveśvara in the Kāvyaprakāśadīpika on KP. VIII chapter (Introduction) (p. 378). Also quoted by Jhalakīkara in his ṭikā on KP. VIII. 67 (p. 470).
3. Ekā. vṛtti on V. 1.

essentials of a good diction and the alaṁkāras as secondary constituents of diction. Bhoja thinks that a poem is enjoyed only if it contains guṇas. Even in the presence of beautiful alaṁkāras, poetry is harsh if devoid of guṇas, just like an old woman even if adorned with excellent alaṁkāras.[1] The two verses quoted by Vidyādhara from Bhoja's SKBh also belong to Vāmana.[2] In reality, Bhoja quotes these verses of Vāmana and makes them part of his own text. On the differentiation of guṇa and alaṁkāra, too, Bhoja follows Vāmana.

(iii) Ānandavardhana[3] thinks that guṇas are based on the principal part of kāvya i.e. rasa, while alaṁkāras are based on its secondary part in the form of śabda and artha. In this way, he has drawn a distinction between the guṇas and the alaṁkāras.

Ānandavardhana, Mammṭa and Vidyādhara are justified in their view that guṇas belong to the soul and that they coordinate rasa in kāvya, while alaṁkāras belong to the body and are subordinate.

Refuting Vāmana's view, Vidyādhara questions whether some or all guṇas can be the cause of a poetical composition. If it is accepted that all the guṇas are required for a particular composition, then the Gauḍīyā and Pāñcālī styles which lack some of them cannot be termed kāvya. On the other hand, if one or two guṇas can produce poetical charm, then a passage, devoid of many guṇas can also be regarded as poetry and the mere existence of guṇas will also cause a composition to be named as poetry.

Thus, Vidyādhara believes that actually alaṁkāras alone are the causes in poetical composition i.e. the presence of alaṁkāras is compulsory in composing poetry. Guṇas exist there as they are the properties of rasa which is the very life of poetry but the existence of alaṁkāras do not depend upon them. If guṇas cannot bring charm, alaṁkāras cannot add to it or be the cause of its excess.[4]

1. SKBh. I. 193-194.
2. KASV. examples I. 2 under III. 1.2.
3. DhL. II. 7.
4. Ekā. vṛtti on V. 1.

Three guṇas

After thus differentiating between guṇa and alaṁkāra, Vidyādhara explains three guṇas namely Mādhurya (sweetness), Ojas (floridity) and Prasāda (lucidity).

Mādhurya guṇa is that property which delights and softens the heart. It has increasing force in Sambhoga-Śṛṅgārarasa (Erotic Sentiment), Karuṇa (Pathetic), Vipralambha (Love-grief) and Śānta (Quietistic).[1] Here Vidyādhara agrees with Ānandavardhana[2] and Mammaṭa.[3] Bharata[4] also says that it consists of sweetness.

Ojas is described as the cause of the brilliant expansion of the heart. It is a peculiar state where the mind is luminous and the heart is expanded. It's excessiveness rises in Vīrarasa (Heroic-sentiment), Bībhatsa (Abhorrent) and Raudra (Furious). It is highly developed in Bhayānakarasa (Dreadful sentiment) even though, here mind is plunged in fear. This is by virtue of the lustrous vibhāvas (generating-causes) of the rasa.[5] Before Vidyādhara, Mammaṭa[6] gave a similar definition of Ojas guṇa.

Prasāda-guṇa is that property which pervades the mind as fire spreading through dry fuel. It is characterized by its lucidity and captures the heart. It is present in all the rasas and in all the compositions.[7]

While defining Mādhurya-guṇa Bhāmaha,[8] Vāmana[9] and Kuntaka[10] think the absence of long-compounds there. According to Bharata,[11] Ojas guṇa is characterized by the use of varied,

1. Ekā. V. 2-3.
2. DhL. II. 8.
3. KP. VIII. 68-69.
4. NS. 16-103.
5. Ekā. V. 4-5.
6. KP. VIII. 69-70.
7. Ekā. V. 6.
8. KAB. II. 3.
9. KASV. vṛtti on III. 1.21.
10. VJ. vṛtti on I. 30.
11. NS. 16-104.

striking and dignified compound-words that are in concord with each other. Daṇḍin[1] also accepts the abundance of compound-words in Ojas. According to Vāmana,[2] Ojas guṇa is the compactness of word-structure produced by the frequent use of conjunct-consonants. Vidyādhara has not given place to either presence or absence of compound-words while defining Mādhurya or Ojas guṇa like these scholars.

All the earlier and the later scholars accept the similar nature of Prasādaguṇa albeit in different words. They all agree on the chief character of this guṇa, that is easy-comprehension.

Number and classification of guṇas

Number of guṇas varies from scholar to scholar. Vidyādhara, as it had been seen, has accepted three guṇas only. Bharata has mentioned ten doṣas and ten guṇas making them subsidiary to rasa.[3] Rājaśekhara[4] has mentioned five guṇas viz. Sāmya, Prasāda, Mādhurya, Audārya and Ojas. Like the Kāvyamīmāṁsā, rasa is considered as the life of poetry in the Agni purāṇa also.[5] However, guṇas are not considered as attributes of rasas though Rājaśekhara considers the former as attributes of śabdaracanā. In the Agnipuraṇa, the guṇas are considered as attributes of style in a wide sense. Guṇas here, are subdivided into Sāmānya and Vaiśeṣika.[6] Sāmānya is further divided into śabda. artha and śabdārtha.

For the first time, Bhāmaha mentions three guṇas i.e. Mādhurya, Ojas and Prasāda. A fourth guṇa, Bhāvika is mentioned as being the quality of the whole composition.[7] The three guṇas mentioned by him were accepted by the followers of the Dhvani-school.

1. KD. I. 80.
2. KASV. III. 1.5.
3. NS. 16-89 and 16-97.
4. KM. p. 6.
5. Agnipurāṇa, 339-9.
6. *Ibid.*, 346-3-7.
7. KAB. III. 53-54.

Daṇḍin, somewhat changes Bharata's order and definitions and when dealing with the same guṇas, like his successor Vāman, he makes no precise distinction between śabdaguṇas and artha-guṇas. Vāmana is the first rhetorician to classify guṇas as śabda-guṇas and artha guṇas. Theoretically, he follows his predecessors in the number and nomenclature of guṇas but practically he doubles the number by splitting each guṇa on the basis of relation to śabda or artha. Bhoja[1] lists twenty-four technical guṇas, each of which belongs to śabda and artha. All of these guṇas are, however, included in the guṇa of Vāmana. Bhoja actually, deals with two sets of guṇas—

(i) a set of nine guṇas in connection with rītis, and

(ii) an independent set of twenty-four guṇas.

He classifies the guṇas thus—bāhya, ābhyāntara and vaiśeṣika. The first set corresponds to the śabda-guṇas of earlier writers and the second to artha-guṇas. Those of the last category have not been treated by orthodox writers as a class of technical guṇas. They were originally doṣas but do not remain so owing to some special circumstances. Hence they are called vaiśesika-guṇas.

Like Vidyādhara, Ānandavardhana and Mammaṭa also consider only three guṇas viz. Mādhurya, Ojas and Prasāda. Some of the ten guṇas discussed by previous scholars are included in them. Some are negations of doṣas and do not constitute guṇas while still others sometimes become doṣas.[2] Thus, all other guṇas can be included under these three alone.

Śleṣa, Samādhi and Audārya guṇas accepted by Bharata, Daṇḍin and Vāmana are included under Ojas and they do not exist separately.[3] Arthavyakti is not at all different from Prasāda.[4] Samatā is merely an absence of doṣa while Saukumārya and Kānti are contrary to Pāruṣya and Grāmyatva doṣas respectively. So,

1. SKBh. I. 72.
2. KP. VIII. 72.
3. Ekā. vṛtti on V. 8.
4. *Ibid.* vṛtti on V. 8.

these cannot be regarded as guṇas.[1] Thus, there exist these three guṇas only.

The three rītis : their Nature and definition

Rīti means a style of composition.[2] According to Daṇḍin[3] these styles are numerous, but critics on poetics, generally, define only a few of the most prevalent ones. The name rīti is not found before Vāmana. Ānandavardhana calls it Saṅghaṭanā.[4]

Vidyādhara[5] has accepted three rītis viz. Vaidarbhī, Pāñcālī and Gauḍīyā and has defined Vaidarbhī-rīti as devoid of compounds and sparśa letters but endowed with all the guṇas. It is full of beauty like the tone of a vīṇā.[6]

Before Vidyādhara, Mahimabhaṭṭa[7] also describes Vaidarbhī rīti similarly and later Bilhaṇa[8] agrees too. Kuntaka's Sukumāra-mārga[9] corresponds to Vaidarbhī rīti.

Daṇḍin describes ten guṇas as the very essentials of Vaidarbha-mārga. Prof. S.P. Bhaṭṭācārya[10] remarks in his article 'The Gauḍī rīti in Theory and Practice', "In—Iti Vaidarbha mārgasya prāṇā daśaguṇāḥ smṛt h—the term Vaidarbha mārga is an upalakṣaṇa." If the term Vaidarbha mārga is accepted to be upalakṣaṇa representing a good diction, as Prof. S.P. Bhaṭṭācārya has suggested, these excellences are essential in any good composition.

Pāñcālī rīti is defined by Vidyādhara[11] as deviod of Ojas and Kānti and contains beautiful and simple compounds. Vāmana is

1. Ekā. vṛtti on V. 8.
2. KASV. I. II.7.
3. KD. I. 40.
4. DhL. III. 5-6.
5. Ekā. V. 9.
6. *Ibid.* V. 10.
7. VV. II. 16.
8. Vikramāṅkadevacarita, I. 9.
9. VJ. vṛtti on I. 24.
10. IHQJ. June, 1927.
11. Ekā. V. 11.

the first to define it and points out that it is marked by the presence of Mādhurya and Saukumārya guṇas.[1] According to Bhoja[2] also, Mādhurya and Saukumārya guṇas should predominate in this rīti. There is no difference of opinion about the nature of this rīti.

Gauḍīyā rīti is described by Vidyādhara[3] as consisting of Ojas and Kānti guṇas. It contains harsh letters too. Vāmana[4] and Bhoja[5] have also defined it similarly.

Other rītis like Āvantikā and Lāṭīyā are a combination of the above mentioned rītis,[6] and hence are not discussed separately.

It is interesting to note here that Vidyādhara does not accept Kānti as a separate guṇa. He thinks it to be the opposite of grāmyatvadoṣa but he has mentioned it while discussing Pāñcālī and Gauḍīyā rītis.

Vicitra-mārga of Kuntaka[7] corresponds to Gauḍīyā rīti. There is yet another class i.e. Madhyama-mārga, where, according to Kuntaka, the composition is an admixture of the former two classes of poetry.[8]

While assessing the contribution of Vidyādhara, Dr. Lahiri[9] remarks that 'Vidyādhara enumetates and defines three rītis after Vāmana remarking that Āvantikā and other rītis are not separately mentioned in view of the fact that they constitute special cases only by the admixture of the three orthodox rītis. He accepts and defines three guṇas and explains away the ten guṇa-theory of the rīti-school after the manner of Mammaṭa. But

1. KASV. I. 2.13.
2. SKBh. II. 54.
3. Ekā. V. 12.
4. KASV. I. II. 12.
5. SKBh. II. 55.
6. (a) Ekā. V. 13.
   (b) SKBh. II. 56-57.
7. VJ. I. 34-43.
8. *Ibid.* I. 49-50.
9. Concepts of Rīti and Guṇa, p. 235.

although Vidyādhra accepts only three guṇas and does not admit Kānti as a separate guṇa, it is strange that he defines Pāñcālī and Gauḍīyārītis in terms of Kānti'.

Of the three rītis Vāmana assigns chief importance to Vaidarbhī as it contains all the guṇas that enrich poetry. The other two varieties have been relegated to an inferior position;[1] for they lack some aspect of guṇa;—the Gauḍīyā lacks Mādhurya and Saukumārya, and the Pāñcālī is devoid of Ojas and Kānti. In KAR,[2] Agnipurāṇa[3] and SD[4] four rītis are enumerated one Lāṭīyā being added to Vāmana's enumeration.

Bhoja's[5] treatment of the rītis is somewhat unique. He does not treat rīti as a separate element of poetry but includes it under the Śabdālaṁkāras. He takes rīti to be synonymous with mārga which he describes as the manner of composition followed by the people of Vaidarbha and other lands. He deals with the largest number of rītis viz. six. Vaidarbhī rīti, according to him, is marked by a presence of all the guṇas but only a few compound-words.

Mammaṭa[6] gives the name Upanāgarikā, Paruṣā and Komalā corresponding to Vaidarbhī, Gauḍīyā and Pañcālī.

It may be said now that Vāmana classifies rītis on the basis of guṇas, while later writers discuss three distinguishable types of rītis. The inseparable relationship of these elements viz. guṇa, rīti and vṛtti, may be noted from the definition and nature of the rītis. A particular rīti is based on the existence or absence of particular guṇas.

Enumerating three entities, Bhāmaha thinks that particular guṇas constitute the characteristics of particular classes of kāvya

1. KASV. I.II. 14-15.
2. KAR. II. 3, 4 & 6.
3. Agnipurāṇa, 340. 1-4.
4. IX. 1.2.
5. SKBh. II. 51 and 53.
6. (a) KP. IX. 80.
   (b) Vāmanācārya Jhalakīkara on KP. IX. 80.

namely gauḍa and vaidarbha. However, he opines that these three entities should be present in good kāvyas. His guṇas are absolute entities, bearing no relation to any other poetic element. Daṇḍin treats guṇas in connection with mārga (which is equivalent to rīti) and not with rasa.

Three vṛttis

In accordance with three rītis, there are three vṛttis called madhurā, madhyamā and paruṣā. They are based on the use of soft; medium and harsh letters in accordance with rasa respectively.[1] Vidyādhara has himself said that these rītis are given the name vṛttis in other works as they are the properties of rasa. Hence the names rīti and vṛtti may be synonymous. These three vṛttis were first recognised by Udbhaṭa[2] but his three vṛttis, which he comprehends under Vṛttyanuprāsa, are really equivalent to the three rītis of Vāmana and the three guṇas of Ānandavardhana and his followers.

Bharata recognises four vṛttis—Bhāratī, Sāttvatī, Kaiśikī and Ārabhaṭī, and their aṅgas. He states that Kaiśikī vṛtti should be employed in Śṛṅgāra and Hāsya rasas; Sāttvatī in Vīra, Raudra and Adbhuta ; Ārabhaṭī in Bhayānaka, Bībhatsa and Raudra and Bhāratī in Karuṇa and Adbhuta rasas.[3] According to Dhanañjaya,[4] Kaiśikī should be employed in Śṛṅgāra; Sātīvatī in Vīra; Ārabhaṭī in Raudra and Bībhatsa while Bhāratī may be employed in any rasa.

Rudraṭa[5] speaks of five vṛttis of Anuprāsa viz. Madhurā, Prauḍhā, Paruṣā, Lalitā and Bhadrā, all of which are based on the employment of certain letters and conjunct consonants. His Madhurā and Paruṣā are like Upanāgarikā and Paruṣā of Mammaṭa; but he uses them only in relation to Anuprāsa while

---

1. (a) Ekā. vṛtti on V. 13.
   (b) AS. vṛtti on 5.
2. KASS. 1.4.
3. NS. 20-62-63.
4. Dr. II. 62.
5. KAR. II. 19.

Mammaṭa and Ruyyaka consider them from the point of view of rasa.

According to Ānandavardhana[1] the appropriate words and meanings that are favourable to rasa are known as various vṛttis, These vṛttis refer primarily to Anuprāsa and are separate from the four dramatic vṛttis mentioned by Bharata. Ānandavardhana clearly distinguishes between dramatic vṛtti and poetical vṛtti by saying that the former is dependent on sense and the latter on expression.[2] Bhoja[3] includes rīti and vṛtti among the twenty-four śabdālaṁkāras.

Some assign the name rīti while some call them vṛtti. The name vṛtti was employed only in the works which are concerned with drama and the title rīti was used in the works on poetics. Mammaṭa has used rīti and vṛtti as synonymous. According to him, the three vṛttis namely Upanāgarikā, Paruṣā and Komalā are accepted as three rītis namely Vaidarbhī, Gauḍīyā and Pāñcālī[4]

In this chapter, guṇa has been discussed in three ways :

(i) as doṣābhāva i.e. absence of doṣa results in guṇa,

(ii) as doṣaviparyaya i.e. the opposite of doṣa is guṇa and

(iii) in connection with rasa.

The older ācāryās, like Bharata, accept the existence of the first type. Later scholars like Ānandavardhana, Mammaṭa and Vidyādhara accept guṇa as connected with rasa.

There are various theories regarding the number of guṇas :

(i) Ten-guṇa-theory—accepted by Bharata and Daṇḍin.

(ii) Ten-guṇas of śabda and ten of artha—accepted by Vāmana.

(iii) Twenty-four-guṇas—accepted by Bhoja.

(iv) Nine-guṇas—discussed by Rudraṭa.

---

1. DhL. III. 33.
2. DhL. vṛtti on III. 33.
3. SKBh. II. 3-5.
4. KP. vṛtti on IX. 81.

(v) Three-guṇa-theory—accepted by Bhāmaha, Ānandavardhana, Mammaṭa, Hemacandra and Vidyādhara.

Three rītis viz. Vaidarbhī; Gauḍīyā and Pāñcālī are accepted by Vāmana. Mammaṭa and Vidyādhara. Three corresponding vṛttis namely Madhurā, Madhyamā and Paruṣā do not occupy an important place in poetics but are significant in nāṭya. Like Ānandavardhana and Mammaṭā, whose works mainly concern poetics, Vidyādhara, also, does not attach any importance to these vṛttis. However, he states that vṛttis are concerned with sentiments.

CHAPTER V

DOṢĀS

Definition of a Doṣa

Vidyādhara does not define a doṣa by which his commentator Mallinātha[1] infers that Vidyādhara accepts its traditional nature, that is, doṣa (blemish) is that aspect which diminishes the beauty of poetry.

Doṣas have been discussed in two ways :

(i) as the cause of hinderance in poetic-beauty or rasa-pratīti. This view is held by Mahimabhaṭṭa,[2] Ānandavardhana,[3] Mammaṭa[4] and Viśvanātha.[5]

(ii) they are considered as negative qualities, i.e. opposite of guṇas...This view is held by Bharata,[6] Bhāmaha,[7] Vāmana[8] and Rudraṭa.[9]

These are the three views on whether doṣas always are to be avoided :

(i) Vidyādhara accepts and discusses only four principal doṣas by which he believes that Avimṛṣṭavidheyāṁśa, Prakramabhaṅga, Avācyavacana and Prarūḍha doṣas shouid be avoided but minor

1. Taralā Sanskrit commentary on Ekā. beginning of VI unmeṣa.
2. VV. beginning of II vimarśa.
3. DhL.—under vṛtti on III. 14.
4. KP. VII. 49.
5. SD.—a. I. 4 and vṛtti on it.
   b. VII. 1.
6. NS. 16-96.
7. KAB. I. 11.
8. KASV. I. 1.3.
9. KAR. II. 8.

doṣas may be overlooked. Kālidāsa[1] also opines that some minor doṣa does not appear due to the existence of guṇas. Mammaṭa[2] also repeated the same idea by accepting the sense 'alpadoṣau' in the nañ particle in 'adoṣau'. Out of the six meanings of the particle 'nañ', the idea of alpatva (meagre) suits most here. Viśvanātha[3] also admits 'kāvyatva' in the presence of some minor doṣa as for example a jewel does not lose its proper name even when scratched by insects. Hence a doṣa may be overlooked if it does not mar the main sense.

(ii) Bhāmaha,[4] Daṇḍin,[5] Rudraṭa,[6] Kuntaka,[7] and Keśavamiśra[8] do not allow any doṣa in a composition.

(iii) Doṣa does not mar poetic-beauty, it rather adds to its charm, just as a spot increases the beauty of the moon.

Principal Doṣas—

i. *Avimṛṣṭavidheyāṁśa Doṣa*

The word Avimṛṣṭavidheyāṁśa doṣa means that the predicate, which should be principal in a sentence, is not stated as such. However it should not be subordinate, nor should it precede the subject in which case there will arise padagata Avimṛṣṭavidheyāṁṣa doṣa according to Vidyādhara.[9]

A sentence has two parts—the principal part, called vidhi (predicate) and the subordinate one called anuvāda (subject). By vidhi the unknown is known. Anuvāda means mentioning a known thing for a particular object in view. In 'gaurayaṁ padā na spraṣṭavyaḥ', 'gaurayaṁ', is anuvāda and the rest of the sentence is vidhi.

---

1. Kumārsambhava—I. 3.
2. KP. Jhalakīkara's Sanskrit commentary on KP. I.4.
3. SD. vṛtti on I. 2.
4. KAB. I. 12.
5. KD. I. 7.
6. KAR. VI. 40.
7. VJ. vṛtti on I. 57.
8. Alaṁkāraśekhara, p. 14.
9. Ekā. VI. 1.

In 'Nyañcadbhūtala...adhīśvare', Samāsa, in 'Jāte vīra... giraḥ',[1] uragādhīśvara is predominant i.e. anuvādya, and the adjective 'nyañcadbhūtala bhārabhaṅgurafaṇotsaṅga' is subordinate, i.e. vidheya. Vidheya should predominate in a sentence but here it is subordinate; since it is the first member of a Karmadhāraya Samāsa, thus here exists Avimṛṣṭavidheyāṁśa doṣa. The reading 'Faṇotsaṅge bhujaṅgeśvare' removes this doṣa.

If in the śloka 'Vidhuntuda...vidyotate',[2] trijagatyāṁ were read instead of 'triṣu jagatsu', Avimṛṣṭavidheyāṁśa doṣa would have arisen in a Dvigu samāsa. The poet here wants to say that Narasiṁha's brilliant glory is so great that the moon shines fearless of Rāhu in all the three worlds. Here the word 'jagatsu' conveys a plural sense, but the use of 'triṣu' with it indicates that there is no place where the Moon does not shine or is not secured from the fear of Rāhu. Triṣu is predominant here but it would have been subordinate if used in a Dvigu-samāsa.

In the verse 'Yadiha kakubhāṁ...kaviḥ',[3] the limitation of glory is denied by 'amitaṁ yaśaḥ'. Therefore denial is the predominant idea while limitation is the subordinate one. The compound of the two words 'a' and 'mitaṁ' is not proper because in a compound what should be subordinate becomes predominant. The compound-word, amitaṁ yaśaḥ, therefore, contains Avimṛṣṭavidheyāṁśa doṣa.

The poet shows the relation of the lion (pañcānana) with Devī Pārvatī, to express the extra-ordinary qualities of her lion in the example, 'Ākramya smaravairi...pañcānanam'.[4] The greatness of the lion appears when it is not compounded with Devī. If compounded as 'taṁ Devī pañcānanam', the word Devī loses its greatness ; hence it is not subordinated by compounding it (Tatpuruṣa), to give rise to Avimṛṣṭavidheyāṁśa doṣa.

---

1. Ekā. example under VI. 1.
2. *Ibid.* example under VI. 1.
3. *Ibid.* example under VI. 1.
4. *Ibid.* example under VI. 1.

In the verse 'Sarvaṁ-kaṣati...pāṇau',[1] the word Sarvaṁkaṣā in Upapada samāsa loses the prominence of 'sarva'. Thus kṛpāṇī loses the virtues desired by the poet. To show the greatness of kṛpāṇī, therefore, he does not compound it.

In 'Na kasya karṇayoḥ...bhūpateḥ',[2] the Nṛsiṁha's greatness of speech is expressed. The poetry on him brings joy to all listeners. Here vidheya i.e. the king's greatness of speech is predominant. It would have become subordinate if the word 'Narasiṁhasya' were to be replaced by 'Nārasiṁhī'. A Taddhita-pratyaya, 'aṇ', is added to the word Narasimha in Nārasiṁhī in the sense of 'tasyedam'. So, the Vibhakti keeps the sense predominant while Taddhita pratyaya makes it subordinate.

Likewise, in other compounds also, e.g. in Avyayībhāva, where the first member is predominant, words become subordinate.

The verse 'Nāthaḥ kākodarāṇāṁ...kṣitīndra',[3] conveys the greatness of Nṛsiṁha who is of exceptional talents. Saṅkhyā is the anuvādya and parārdhātivarttinī or 'dūre parārdhāt' is vidheya. Here in Avyayībhāva-samāsa as 'pāreparārdhaṁ' the relation of principal and subordinate is not maintained. This doṣa is removed by making the script 'Saṅkhyā-dūre parārdhāt'.

In Dvandva samāsa, both members are equally important. There is no relation of the vīśeṣya and viśeṣaṇa; yet when each member of the compound is to be connected with a verb prominently, the compound should not be used. The words should be used separately. In 'Garjjaddurjaya...cābhavat',[4] abhavat is used in singular and Mandāraḥ, Surataruḥ and Sarpādhipaḥ are each connected with it to show that these become useless. If these words are compounded, their relation with the vidheya, vyarthi-

1. Ekā. example under VI. 1.
2. *Ibid.* example under VI. 1.
3. *Ibid.* example under VI. 1.
4. *Ibid.* example under VI. 1.

bhāva is not expressed prominently and there, arises Avimṛṣṭavidheyāṁśa doṣa.

The example 'Tyāgaśrī...Kaliṅgeśvara',[1] conveys the prowess of Narasiṁha which transcends that of the celestial-wishing-tree, the moonlight (Indumahīṣī) and the destructive fire (Kalpānala). Here predominant components become subordinate because they are used as parts of a Bahubrīhi, in which the members are subordinate and another object is predominant. A flawless reading may be 'Tyāgenopahasana...kalpānalam', iti.[2]

When the predicate is subordinate, the Avimṛṣṭa-vidheyāṁśa doṣa is pada-doṣa. Vākyagata arises when the predicate is used before the subject.[3]

Use of Candrāvatāra (vidheya) before tvaṁ (anuvādya) would have caused a doṣa in '*Kalānidhevīra*...kavikairvāṇām.'[4]

In 'Utkaṇṭhābhāra...kṣitīndraḥ',[5] the poet wants to describe Śrīnṛsiṁha as bhānu, nakṣatranātha and kambhodbhava. The word 'yoasau' for king Nṛsiṁha, being anuvādya, should be used before. Bhānu, nakṣatranātha and kambodbhava are vidheyas. Use of yoasau afterwards causes a doṣa.

Vidyādhara believes that adas or etad or tad immediately following yad mean 'well-known'. Thus a combination of yad with etad, tad or adas requires the correlative tad. This correlated tad is the predicate and if it is not mentioned, there arises Avimṛṣṭavidheyāṁśa doṣa.

Vidyādhara establishes it by arguing thus—

'In 'Utkaṇṭhābhāra...kṣitīndraḥ', the use of yad in yoasau is incorrect, for when yad or tad are used in the first clause of a sentence, the correlatives tad or yad should be used in the second

1. Ekā. example under VI. 1.
2. *Ibid.* expmple under VI. 1.
3. *Ibid.* VI. 2.
4. *Ibid.* example under VI. 2.
5. *Ibid.* example under VI. 2.

clause. They are considered as anuvādya and vidheya, and the relation between them is constant. Either may be used as subject or predicate; or one may be used and the other implied, or both may be implied.[1]

In the verse 'Himakara...yaśaḥ śriyaḥ',[2] yad is used in the beginning and tad is used as a correlative in the later clause of the sentence. When both are used their relation is expressed. If one or neither of the two are used, the relation is implied.[3]

When tad is used alone, yad should be implied in the context (prakrānta) or should be well-known (prasiddha) or experienced (anubhūta viṣaya). Therefore tad is connected with yad.[4]

In 'Loke asmin...no vākpatiḥ',[5] yad is implied because it is used and saḥ is prakrānta, i.e. the king Narasiṁha is understood by reference to the context.

In 'Sā kiṁ dattavatī...samastāḥ amī,[6] yad is used and yad appears through implication because it is prasiddha. Hence the well-known Cintāmaṇi tree stands for Kalpavṛkṣa and cow for Kāmadhenu.

In 'Tvatpratyarthī...kṣitīndra',[7]—tattad is apparent from experience. In all the three examples, the senses of yad are implied being prakrānta, prasiddha and anubhūta respectively and tad has been used. The sense arises as yad prakrāntaṁ tad, yat prasiddhaṁ tat and yadanubhūtaṁ tad.

When yad alone is used in the second (or last) clause of a sentence, tad may be understood by implication in the first clause. Its

---

1. Ekā. vṛtti on VI. 2.
2. *Ibid.* example under VI. 2.
3. (a) Ekā. vṛtti on VI. 2.
   (b) VV. vṛtti on II. 5.
4. (a) Ekā. vṛtti on VI. 2.
   (b) VV. vṛtti on II. 5.
   (c) KP. vṛtti on VII. 52.
5. Ekā. example under VI. 2.
6. *Ibid.* example under VI. 2.
7. *Ibid.* example under VI. 2.

use is not necessary,[1] as in the example 'Śrīmannṛsiṁha...ca romarājiḥ',[2] yad is used in the later part of the sentence and tad is implied in first clause. However if yad is used in the first clause of a sentence tad cannot be implied simultaneously in the first clause. Tad must be used, otherwise yad is open to Sākāṅṣatā doṣa. This mars the meaning arising from a word having Sākāṅkṣatā (expectancy) for the sense of another word not expressed. In the example 'Yatradwīpas...kṣitīndra',[3] and 'Yāsāmambudhi... kīrttayovīrudhaḥ'[4] if 'Sa jayati' and 'tāḥ prītiṁ dadhati' were not used in the later clauses, the word 'yad' would be sākāṅkṣa for 'tad' and would be incomplete without it. There may thus arise a doṣa.

Sometimes both yad and tad may be comprehended by implication.[5] In 'Na bhavasi kathaṁkāraṁ...api',[6] both yad and tad are implied. In the śloka 'Utkṇṭhābhāra...kṣitīndraḥ', yoasau used in the first clause is sākāṅkṣa tad being not used in the later clause. Asau, according to Vidyādhara does not express the sense of tad, since in the verse 'Kavi kuvalaya...lajjitaḥ',[7] adas does not do so.

There would be Paunaruktya doṣa (repetition) if adas conveys the sense of tad in 'Kati kati......Nṛsiṁhanareśvaraḥ'[8] where tad and adas both are used in the last clause. Moreover, when tad immediately follows yad, it suggests 'well-known,,[9] as in the verses 'Yattaduttīrṇa...mukhe'[10], and 'Yattadvairi...mahī'.[11] Here another

1. Ekā. vṛtti on VI. 2.
2. *Ibid.* example under VI. 2.
3. *Ibid.* example under VI. 2.
4. *Ibid.* example under VI 2.
5. (a) *Ibid.* vṛtti on VI. 2.
   (b) VV. vṛtti on II. 5.
6. Ekā. example under VI. 2.
7. *Ibid.* example under VI. 2.
8. *Ibid.* example under VI. 2.
9. *Ibid.* vṛtti on VI. 2.
10. *Ibid.* example under VI. 2.
11. *Ibid.* example under VI. 2.

tad is used after yattad. If tad used immediately after yad, does not possess the sense of prasiddha, another tad in the later clause need not be used. Similarly idaṁ, etad and adas when used in proximity with yad, mean well-known. Without yad these words imply only that which is visible. Thus in 'Utkaṇṭhābhāra...... kṣitīndraḥ', adas, used in proximity with yad, conveys the sense of well-known. Tad must be used for expectancy, in the absence of which there would arise Avimṛṣṭavidheyāṁśa doṣa. A correct expression, therefore, would be 'jagati sa jayati' instead of 'jagati vijayate', so that saḥ may be correlative of 'yoasau'.

Avimṛṣṭavidheyāṁśa doṣa, being a grammatical one, is shown in all the compounds. This doṣa, therefore, should never be overlooked.

Bhoja does not discuss this doṣa, but Asādhu, Śabdahīna and Vyartha[1] doṣas dealt by him are similar to Avimṛṣṭavidheyāṁśa doṣa.

ii. *Prakramabhaṅga doṣa*

Bhagnaprakrama or Prakramabhaṅga doṣa is then discussed in the Ekāvalī. It means violation of expression. Uddeśya means to mention for the first time a base, an affix, prefix, word, expression etc. Its repetition with some purpose is called pratinirdeśa. When repeating it, the form should be similar. If its synonyms were to be used, there would be delay in comprehending the sense and there would thus arise Bhagnaprakramatā doṣa.[2]

Violation of the uniformity of expression affects either a base (prakṛti), affix, suffix, vibhkati (Sup or case-termination or tiṅ or a tense-termination) number, tense, case-ending and gender; or a pronoun, adjective, synonym, sentence, compound and a figure. Bhagnaprakramatā doṣa therefore has a variety of forms.[3]

1. SK. Bh. I. 4, 25, 49.
2. (a) Ekā. VI. 3.
   (b) Quoted in VV. II. 31.
3. (a) Ekā. vṛtti on VI. 3.
   (b) VV. vṛtti on II. 29.

In the example 'Jīyāt' pārvaṇarohiṇīśa...srotasi',[1] if the word nipatya were used instead of nimajya, prakṛtaprakramabhaṅga doṣa would have arisen, for afterwards, too, the same prakṛti in pronmajjanti is employed.

In 'Loke vikramituṁ......antareṇādhikaḥ',[2] the expression 'dānāya kalpadrumāt' instead of 'dātuṁ surakṣmāruhāt' would have caused Pratyaya prakramabhaṅga doṣa, because other forms also with tumunpratyaya are used here.

Use of the word pradeyaṁ after the word prattā in the verse 'Dayāyaidṛk...kṣitipate'[3] does not give rise to upasarga prakrama-bhaṅga doṣa. This would have arisen by the use of any other upasarga instead of pra.

The use of liṭ lakāra in both the forms viz. jagṛhire and daduḥ in 'Madāndhāstvannāgāḥ......gīrvāṇanagaram'[4] does not cause vibhakti prakrama doṣa. This would have arisen if aduḥ (luṅlakāra) were used instead of daduḥ (liṭ).

Vacanaprakramabhaṅga doṣa does not arise in 'Vīra Nṛsiṁha ...mānyam',[5] the singular number being used everywhere in kavitvaṁ and campakasaurabhyaṁ.

The verse 'Sūtrāmā gotrabhedaṁ......*naivopamānam*'[6] is free from Kālaprakramabhaṅga doṣa because everywhere the forms are used in the present tense. This doṣa would have arisen if the forms in different tense are used in the same verse.

In Sanskrit, tṛtīyā vibhakti is used in the sense of karttṛ (agency) and karaṇa (instrumentality),[7] In the example 'Tava kriyante...guṇavarṇāni',[8] the form kriyante is passive and denotes

1. Ekā. example under VI. 3.
2. *Ibid.* example under VI. 3.
3. *Ibid.* example under VI. 3.
4. *Ibid.* example nnder VI. 3.
5. *Ibid.* example under VI. 3.
6. *Ibid.* example under VI. 3.
7. Aṣṭādhyāyī, II. 3.18.
8. Ekā. example under VI. 3.

the sense of its objects only, viz. kaṭākṣa, śrī, vikāsa and sūkta. These subjects are, therefore, used in the instrumental case. No Kārakaprakramabhaṅga exists here, for the instrumental-case-relation is maintained throughout.

In 'Bimbaṁ candramasaḥ...yaśaḥ',[1] the neuter gender is employed in every subject (karttā); so it is free from Liṅgaprakramabhaṅga doṣa.

In 'Prāgāsīnmakaranda...netrāñcale',[2] every locative qualified word (viśeṣya) is used with its qualifier (viśeṣaṇa), thus there is no Viśeṣaṇa-prakramabhṅga doṣa here.

In 'Kimetāsāmantaḥpura...kimidam,[3] the same word asūrayaṁpaśyatvaṁ is employed in both the places. If its synonym anarkālokitvam were to be used there, Paryāyaprakramabhaṅga doṣa would have taken place.

In 'Santyajya puṣpasamayaṁ...Kaliṅganātha',[4] the whole subject is expressed by a sentence: so it is free from Vākyaprakramabhaṅgadoṣa.

The poet begins with the compound words and maintains it upto the end in 'Kāśmīrapāṁsu...sūtraiḥ'.[5] This does not give a chance to Samāsaprakramabhaṅgadoṣa. Alaṁkāra-prakramabhaṅga doṣa does not arise in 'Tyāgastāvat...kṣitīndra'[6] where Rūpakālaṁkāra is employed from the beginning to the end.

Vidyādhara explains only prakṛti, pratyaya, upasarga, vibhakti vacana, kāla, kāraka, paryāya and alaṁkāra kinds of Prakramabhaṅga doṣa.

iii. *Avācyavacana*

Avācyavacanadoṣa arises by expression of that which in not

1. Ekā. example under VI. 3.
2. *Ibid.* example under VI. 3.
3. *Ibid.* example under VI. 3.
4. *Ibid.* example under VI 3.
5. *Ibid.* example under VI. 3.
6. *Ibid.* example under VI. 3.

included to be expressed.[1]

This doṣa also arises when a word signifying a cause, a place of residence or relation, is used, though that word with which instrumentality, the place of residence or the relation is invariably connected, is expressed.[2] Sometimes this doṣa arises when the desired connection between two words is not brought out. According to Vidyādhara it may be called Vācyāvacana.[3] This Vācyāvacanadoṣa of Vidyādhara corresponds to Abhavanmatyogadoṣa of Mammaṭa[4] which is devoid of desired connection. Mahimabhaṭṭa considers both Avācyavacana and Vācyāvacana as one doṣa.[5]

In the lines 'Niśśeṣa...*Nṛsimhadeva*'[6] Nīlapūrvaṁ lohitam is given as constituting Avācayavacana doṣa. It is incorrect to express the well-known name Nīlalohita in two parts...nīlapūrva and lohita, corresponding to viśeṣya. A name qualifies the person and not itself. Thus in nīlapūrvaṁ lohitam, nīla qualifies lohita. Moreover, it imitates the name and this imitation is either śābda or ārtha. In Śābda 'iti' is not combined with the name, e.g. 'yaṁ nīlapūrva lohita iti sfuṭamāmananti'. In ārthī, the meaning of the object is not expressed by 'iti'; for example 'yaṁ nīlalohitamami sfuṭamāmananti'. In the verse, the name is Nīlalohita and not Nīlapūrvalohita. Avācyavacana doṣa arises here, for something other than a name is imitated here and this is avācya (i.e. not desired to be expressed).

In 'Camatkāraṁ...kalayati'[7] the words tanu, taṭaruha and sthita are avācya because they do not convey any meaning. The sense is expressed by Gaurīsahacaraspardhi, Kālindī tamāladyuti and Sudhābhānukroḍahariṇakelim. So, Avācyavacana doṣa exists here.

1. Ekā. VI. 3.
2. *Ibid.* VI. 4.
3. *Ibid.* VI. 5.
4. KP. vṛtti on VII. 54.
5. VV. Vṛtti on II. 99.
6. Ekā. example under VI. 3.
7. *Ibid.* example under VI. 3.

In 'Dikkukṣiṁbharibhiḥ...unmīlitam'[1] the hooves of horses are said to raise dust. The relation between utkīrṇa or khura is constant, so whenever words like karaṇa, ādhāra etc. are used they cause Avācyavacanadoṣa. Hence, there is Sambandhavyabhicāra here.

In 'Hṛda hṛṣyati...śṛṇoti ca'[2] delight, knowledge, meditation, study and sorrow are said to be always experienced by the heart. The acts of seeing and hearing are done by the eyes and ears respectively without any other Karaṇa. As Karaṇa has been used here, there arises Avācyavacanadoṣa, Karaṇavyabhicāra.

In 'Citraṁ cetasi......madātyayāḥ'[3] feelings like anxiety and jealousy exist in the mind, so the words cetasi and manasi are superfluous; since there is ādhāra-vyabhicāra. Avācyavacanadoṣa is caused here. This Avācyavacandoṣa of Vidyādhara corresponds to Apuṣṭārtha doṣa of Mammaṭa[4] and Vyartha of Bhoja.[5] Apuṣṭārthadoṣa of Mammaṭa consists in where the adjectives are irrelevant, thus no harm is done by dropping them. Vyarthadoṣa of Bhoja, as the name suggests, arises where the suggested sense serves no purpose.

Another kind of Avācyavacanadoṣa may be seen in 'Dāridryasya...adarśayat'[6], where the subject of the verbs implying knowledge in the primitive, is used in the accusative case (karma) in causative construction (ṇijanta). When dṛś is used as a parasmaipadadhātu, the subject of the primitive verb becomes the object of the causative form. Asmābhiḥ undesirably expresses Karttṛtva. Karmattva is vācya and Karttṛtva avācya; so there arises Avācyavacanadoṣa. The proper form may be 'māṁ bhavantamadarśayat' instead of 'asmābhistvamadarśayat; in which

1. Ekā. evample under VI. 4.
2. *Ibid.* example under VI. 4.
3. *Ibid.* example under VI. 4.
4. KP. vṛtti on VII. 57.
5. SKBh. I. 49.
6. Ekā. example under VI. 4.

case the verse would not contain another doṣa i.e. Vacanaprakramabhaṅga doṣa. Here 'stuve' is singular while asmābhiḥ is plural giving rise to Vacanaprakramabhaṅga.

According to Mahimabhaṭṭa, the three examples (Camatkāraṁ ...kalayati, Hṛdā...śṛṇotica, Citraṁ...madātyayāḥ) are included under Paunaruktya doṣa. According to him whenever some sense appears through some implied words, use of other words for the same sense would be redundant and would cause Paunaruktya doṣa.[1] For the same reason general verbs like asti, bhavati and karoti etc. probably may not be used by poets.[2] In the instance 'Nijacaraṇa...khaḍgaḥ',[3] nija is connected grammatically with khaḍga. It is connected with the principal word in a sentence (though desired to be construed with Nṛsiṁha). The doṣa therefore is Vācyāvacana or Abhavanmatyoga according to Mammaṭa. 'Ṭava' reading may be better than nija.

Another case of this doṣa arises when one alaṁkāra is used in place of another;[4] e.g. in 'Mṛgyāparibhavo...kṛtam'.[5] Dṛṣṭānta is used in the province of Nidarśanālaṁkāra. Alaṁkāras are used for their sake to help in suggesting kāvyārtha (rasa). They (alaṁkāras) are subordinate to rasas and sometimes they may be avoided for the sake of poetic-charm. 'Dṛḍhataranibadhamuṣṭeḥ...bhedaḥ',[6] Vyatirekālṁkāra exists due to the difference of 'a' in the words Kṛpaṇa and Kṛpāṇa.[7]

iv. *Prarūḍha artha-paunaruktya*

A poetic blemish arthapaunaruktya is caused by the repetition

1. (a) VV. I. 18.
   (b) *Ibid.* II. 58.
2. VV. I. 19.
3. Ekā. example under VI. 5.
4. (a) *Ibid.* vṛtti on VI. 5.
   (b) VV. vṛtti on II. 72.
5. Raghuvaṁśa—XII. 37.
6. VV. example under II. 102.
7. *Ibid.* vṛtti on II. 102.

of sense. When the apparent sense and the final sense are the same, it is called Prarūḍha.[1]

Repetition of a word is a kind of Anuprāsālaṁkāra and not a doṣa. The reading 'Varṇapaunaruktya' is better than 'Śabda-paunaruktya', since Śabdapaunaruktya', creates doubt about padapaunaruktya and this is a doṣa.

This doṣa corresponds to Apuṣṭārtha of Mammaṭa, according to whom paunaruktya is the unnecessary repetition of a word which is irrelevant.[2]

Owing to prakṛti and pratyaya there are many varieties of this doṣa.[3] In 'Karaṭaviluṭha...gajatāgaṇaḥ'[4] the word 'gajatā', with the suffix 'tā' denotes a group. The use of gaṇa results in paunaruktya doṣa. So 'kariṇāṁ gaṇaḥ' may be more correct than 'gajatāgaṇaḥ'.

In 'Ardhamaṅgaṁ......virāgiṇāmapi',[5] the possessive termination 'iṇ' in virāgiṇām is a mere repetition, for the Bahubrīhi Samāsa, virāga expresses that sense, 'vigato rāgo yeṣāṁ te virāgāḥ', means the same as virāgiṇaḥ. It is better to use the Bahubrīhi form virāgāḥ than to take virāgaḥ as a Karmadhāraya Samāsa and affix the possessive termination 'iṇ' to it (vigataścāsau rāgaśca virāgaḥ; virāgo asti eṣāmiti virāgiṇaḥ). It cannot be argued that Bahubrīhi samāsa means asti (the possessive sense) and the possessive terminations, in, mat and others, represent abundance, censure, praise, constant—union, excellence or relation in general; and that there is therefore no paunaruktya doṣa. Expression of abundance, censure etc. is in addition to that of possession. Matup and other possessive terminations are added in the sense of tadasyāsti or tadasminn-

1. (a) Ekā. VI. 5.
   (b) AS. 2.
2. Kāvya Pradīpa on KP. VII. 57.
3. (a) Ekā. vṛtti on VI. 5.
   (b) VV. II. 49.
4. Ekā. example under VI. 5.
5. *Ibid.* example under VI. 5.

asti.[1] These possessive terminations also mean Bhūmādi[2] without giving up the sense of tadastyasya or tadastyasmin.

Sometimes both prakṛti-paunaruktya and pratyayapaunaruktya are present together; as in the verse 'Durvāraiste...dwāradeśopakaṇṭham',[3] there is repetition of prakṛti gajatā denoting a collection. The proper reading may be 'prāptāḥ pratyantaśaila iva madakariṇaḥ'.

The word ālocya causes paunaruktya in 'Devasyāsya...jagajjāṅghikī',[4] because 'iti' conveys the sense of ālocya too; so here arises padapaunaruktya. The śloka 'Palāyanaparasya......pṛthvīpate'[5] is free from Padapaunaruktya doṣa, for here ālocya is not used after iti.

A verb should not be denoted in mentioning a well-known karttā, related with that verb. Therefore, in the verse 'Utaṇṭhābhāra...kṣitīndraḥ',[6] the verb 'to blossom' is not mentioned. In 'Vīrāḥ prāk...Kaliṅgeśvara',[7] the word Śāsana is a repetition for the intended sense can be conveyed by the word arāti. Kaṁsapurārāti will mean Kaṁsārāti and Purārāti, for Kaṁsa and pura should be first formed into a Dwanda-Samāsa, Kaṁsapurau and then arāti should be compounded with Kaṁsapurau. It will thus mean Kaṁsārāti and Purārāti. This is explained by a prevalent maxim.[8] It is improper to take Dwandvasamāsa of Kaṁsaśāsana and purārāti; however when there is no inconsistency, Kaṁsa and pura are first united into Dwandva and arāti is joined to the Samāsa so-formed, thus creating a Tatpurṣa, samāsa. Owing to the brevity of process the sense is grasped sooner in this case. Thus, whether a doṣa is present or not should not be decided by grammatical rules only. According to Vidyā

1. Aṣṭādhyāyī, V. 2.94.
2. Vārttika on Aṣṭādhyāyī, V. 2.94.
3. Ekā. example under VI. 5.
4. *Ibid.* example under VI. 5.
5. *Ibid.* example under VI. 5
6. *Ibid.* example under VI. 5.
7. *Ibid.* example under VI. 5.
8. Maxim in Skt.

dhara, the same sentence free from Paunaruktya doṣa may be 'Ambhojāsanakaiṭabhārigiriśāneṣā Kaliṅgeśvara'. Actually this line is not free from doṣa, for letters ka, ṭa used together, cause a doṣa.[1]

The verse 'Vīrāḥ prāk...Kaliṅgeśvara', stated by Vidyādhara as containing a Paunaruktya doṣa is flawless. The repetition here is helpful from the point of view of guṇa, dhvani etc. Moreover, it contains Anuprāsa in āsana and śāsana.

Where a single iva is competent to show that the subject, the object and other words stand in relation of upamāna and upameya the use of another iva is redundant,[2] e.g. in 'Tataḥ pratasthe... rasāniva',[3] iva is repeated three times. Raghu being compared to Bhāsvat, Śara and Udīcya, can represent Usra and rasa respectively without using iva. An extra iva is improper.

Adjcctives are used properly when the poet qualifies an object, when he indicates the object by adjective-words only, use of qualified–denoting words cause repetition,[4] e.g. when the words Meru, Śvāsa and Candana are used, it is unnecessary to mention Giri, Marut and Pādapa with them.

To avoid Paunaruktyadoṣa in, 'Saṅgītādivicāravārdhitaraṇe ......ujjṛmbhate',[5] the word 'vyāpāra' does not accompany the word 'taraṇa'.

The Paunaruktya and Prakramabhaṅga doṣas differ in that the first is caused when a word which ought to have been repeated with a special object is not repeated, but its synonym is used and uniformity of expression, so, is violated. The other arises when a word is repeated without any purpose.

In discussing only these four principal doṣas, Vidyādhara

1. RG. p. 69.
2. Ekā. vṛtti on VI. 5.
3. Raghuvaṁśa. IV. 66.
4. Ekā. VI. 6.
5. *Ibid.* example under VI. 8.

does not follow the tradition. From this it may be concluded that he believes in completely avoiding these four doṣas.

The Number and divisions of doṣas.

Without strict classification Vidyādhara discusses four principal doṣas, namely Avimṛṣṭavidheyāṁśa, Prakramabhaṅga, Avācyavacana and Prarūḍha (or Paunaruktya) and Mahimabhaṭṭa adds Kramabheda to this list.[1] Later first divides doṣas into two categories namely antaraṅga and bahiraṅga. The first one directly hinders rasa.[2] Bhiraṅga ones sometimes become guṇas by helping in the suggestion of rasa. Hence they are called temporary doṣas.[3] Permanent doṣas must be avoided, though temporary doṣas may be overlooked.

(i) Vidyādhara follows Mahimabhaṭṭa and accepts four principal doṣas.

(ii) Bharata[4] and Daṇḍin[5] accept ten kāvya-doṣas.

(iii) Vāman[6] classifies twenty doṣas under four main heads namely pada, padārtha, vākya and vākyārtha. Discussing the anyārtha sub-class of padārthadoṣa of Vāmana, Prof. Bechan Jha opines that, 'Vāmana here draws attention to the fundamental rule of meaning. There are words whose meaning is determined only by component parts analysed in etymological derivation' (p. 76). Rudraṭa[7] discusses twenty-five doṣas under the groups—Śabda doṣas, vākya doṣas, artha doṣas and upamā doṣa. Bhoja[8]

1. VV. I.93-94.
2. *Ibid.* Beginning of II Vimarśa.
3. (a) DhL. II. 11.
   (b) KD. III. 179.
4. NS. 16.89.
5. KD. III. 125-126.
6. KASV. (i) II. 1. 4. (ii) II. 1. 10. (iii) II. 11. 1.
   (iv) II. 11. 9.
7. KAR. (i) II.8 & VI. 1-2. (ii) VI. 40. (iii) XI.2.
   (iv) XI. 24.
8. SKBh. I.3.

deals with sixteen doṣas all belonging to pada, vākya and vākyārtha. Mammaṭa[1] enumerates thirteen pada-doṣas, eleven vākya-doṣas, ten artha doṣas and fourteen rasa-doṣas.

(iv) Anaucitya is regarded as the basis of all doṣas by Ānandavardhan[2] and Kuntaka[3]. Doṣas discussed by Ānandavardhana may be called rasa-doṣas because when discussing rasa, he deals mostly with the nature of anaucitya. According to Prof. Bechan Jha[4] also Ānandavardhana deals with rasa-doṣas only.

Besides these four views, Bhāmaha enumerates two sets of doṣas—

(i) concerning the inner nature of Kāvya i.e. Vakrokti, and

(ii) which mentions external doṣas.

Acoording to him, doṣas belong to both śabda and artha. Seven doṣas of Upamā, quoted from Medhāvin, are also mentioned.

In total, therefore, thirty-two doṣas are enumerated here.

Inclusion of all other doṣas in these four

Doṣas mentioned by various ācāryas may be included in the four doṣas discussed by Vidyādhara e.g. gūḍhārtha, arthāntara, bhinnārtha, abhiluptārtha, nyayādapeta and śabdacyuta accepted by Bharata; neyārtha, kliṣṭa, anyārtha, avācaka, ayuktimat, gūḍhaśabdābhidhā and śrutikaṭutva doṣas of Bhāmaha which do not give pleasant sense: apārtha, vyartha, sasaṁśaya, śabdahīna, deśaviruddha and kālaviruddha doṣas of Daṇḍin which arise due to denoting unpleasant meaning; asādhu, kaṣṭa, grāmya, apratīta and anekārthapadadoṣas; neyārtha, gūḍhārtha, aślīla and kaṣṭa-

---

1. KP. VII. 50-52, VII. 55-57 and VII. 60-62.
2. DhL. under vṛtti on III. 14, III. 18-19.
3. VJ. vṛtti on I.57.
4. Concepts of Poetic Blemishes in Sanskrit Poetics, p. 124.

padārthadoṣas; vyartha, sandigdha, aprayukta and lokavidhā viruddha-vākyārthadoṣas of Vāmana and asamartha, apratīta, visandhi, viparīta-kalpatā, grāmya, deśya, saṅkīrṇa and garbhita doṣas accepted by Rudraṭa—in these doṣas either what is desired to be stated is not mentioned or what is not desirable is mentioned; thus all of these doṣas may have their inclusion under Vācyāvacana and Avācyavacanadoṣas.

Upakramadoṣa of Bhāmaha, Daṇḍin and Vāmana may be accepted under Kramadoṣa. Their ekārthadoṣa may be included in Paunaruktya. Avimṛṣṭavidheyāṁśa of Mammaṭa may come under Vidheyāvimarśa. The absence of uniformity of Vāmana may be included under Prakramabhaṅga. Most of the remaining doṣas may be included under Vācyāvacana and Avācyavacana.

Some doṣas as Visandhi and Viṣama of Bharata, Yatibhraṣṭa, Bhinnārtha and Visandhi of Daṇḍin and Vāmana do not have any direct relation to kāvyārtha. Their presence or absence do not affect kāvyārtha. So, they may not be regarded as doṣas.

Thus there are only these four doṣas and all the other doṣas can be included under these four alone. The first type of doṣa arises when the part that should be prominent is less so (i.e. Vidheyāvimarśadoṣa). If it is given proper importance, it creates the best kind of poetry.

The second kind of doṣa namely Prakramabhaṅgadoṣa arises where the style is not maintained upto the end (the causes may be various as prakṛti, pratyaya, paryāya, upasarga, pada ātmanepada parasmaipada etc.).

The third variety of doṣa is based on unpleasant repetition but if this repetition is with some purpose it does not remain a doṣa (Punaruktadoṣa).

The last kind of doṣa arises where that which should be discussed is not mentioned and vice-versa. (Vācyāvacanda and Avācyavacana doṣa).

These last two doṣas, namely Vācyāvacana and Avācyavacana,

should not be thought as separate, for, if one is present, the other is naturally present, too.

While citing the examples of these doṣas Vidyādhara mostly gives the faultless verses and then shows that this particular doṣa arises by changing these words. So, he has not cited, mostly, the verses containing doṣas. The reason here may be that he believes in absolute avoidance of these four doṣas.

———

CHAPTER VI

ŚABDĀLAMKĀRAS

Nature and importance of the Alaṁkāras

According to Vidyādhara[1], alaṁkāras are those factors which enhance the beauty of poetry just as a necklace enhances the beauty of a lady. This is a traditional mode of defining an alaṁkāra. Daṇḍin[2], Vāmana[3], Ānandavardhana[4] and Mammata[5] define an alaṁkāra similarly.

The scholars of the Alaṁkāra-school namely Bhāmaha, Daṇḍin, Udbhaṭa, Vāmana and Rudraṭa call alaṁkāra to be the soul of poetry and consider the alaṁkāras to be the most important element of poetry.

An alaṁkāra is a very old element, the presence of which can be traced in ancient works like the Upaniṣads, the Brāhmaṇas and as far back as even the Vedic Saṁhitās. The opening stanza of the Ṛgveda contains Parikarālaṁkāra. Yāska[6] has given many divisions of Upamā as Karmopamā, Bhūtopamā, Rūpopamā, Siddhopamā, Arthopamā and Luptopamā. Alaṁkāras have also been mentioned in the Aṣṭādhyāyī of Pāṇini, Vārttikas of Kātyāyana and the Mahābhāṣya of Pātañjali. All the four factors ot Upamā namely—Upamā, upamāna, upamita and sāmānya—are mentioned in the Aṣṭādhāyī.[7] It is obvious then that alaṁkāras, in some form or other had already been set during the earliest recorded stage of vedic literature.

---

1. Ekā. vṛtti on V.1.
2. KD. II.1.
3. KASV. III. 1.1-2.
4. DhL. vṛtti on II.5 and II.17.
5. KP. VIII. 67.
6. Nirukta—III-III-14. pp. 142-149.
7. Aṣṭādhyāyī—II-III-72, II.I.55, 56.

Misuse of the alaṁkāras often make the language stereo-typed and defective. Anaucityapūrṇālaṁkāras are useless in poetry as ornaments are useless on a corpse.[1] In the absence of rasa, alaṁkāras are merely fanciful expressions i.e. uktivaicitryamātra.[2] Their excessive use sometimes mars the delicacy and beauty of rasa. So they do not occupy an independent place in poetry and are known as the delightful helpers of the main theme.

Number of Alaṁkāras

The number of alaṁkāras increases from Bharata to Panditarāja Jagannātha. Seventeen alaṁkaras are found in Viṣṇudharmottarapurāṇa and thirty-eight in Bhaṭṭikāvya, but as these works do not deal mainly with poetics, they are not considered here.

Vidyādhara has discussed seventy-six alaṁkāras of which five are śabdālaṁkāras, sixty-nine arthālaṁkāras and two ubhayālaṁkāras. Omitting Śabdaśleṣa and Vakrokti śabdālaṁkāras discussed by Mammaṭa ; Parikarāṅkura, Pariṇāma, Ullekha, Arthāpatti, Vikalpa, Tatkara, Praśnottarikā and Arthavakroti alaṁkāras are added. Other alaṁkāras are accepted by previous Ācāryas like Vāmana, Bhoja, Jayadeva and Ruyyaka. In agreement with Mammaṭa, rasavadādi alaṁkāras are not discussed along with other ones. No new alaṁkāra is originated by Vidyādhara.

The later Ācāryas like Viśvanātha, Appayyadīkṣita and others have discussed a large number of alaṁkāras. If all alaṁkāras discussed by various ācāryas are counted together, the number would have exceeded two-hundred while in the beginning only four alaṁkāras were discussed by Bharata.

Classification of alaṁkāras

The figures are divided into three heads viz. the figures pertaining to words, to sense and to both words and sense. Śabdālaṁkāra arises where the poetical charm depends only on words but is destroyed by synonyms. In arthālaṁkāra beauty depends

---

1. (a) DhL Locana on II.5.
   (b) DhL vṛtti on II.17.
2. KP vṛtti on VIII.67.

on the sense alone and disappears if the meaning is changed.[1] A combination of śabdālaṁkāra and arthālaṁkāra is called an ubhayālaṁkāra.

Bhāmaha has, for the first time, divided the figures on the basis of word and sense. Daṇḍin, Vāmana, Bhoja, Mammaṭa and Agnipurāṇakāra have discussed ubhayālṁkāras also.

Udbhaṭa has divided the arthālaṁkāras into six groups, for the first time. He has not named the groups. Then Rudraṭa has divided them into four groups namely vāstava, aupamya, atiśaya and śleṣa. Uttara, Samuccya, Virodha, Adhika, Utprekṣā and Viṣama have been discussed twice under two groups. Ruyyaka has given five groups of arthālṁakāras viz. sādṛśyagarbha, virodhagarbha, śṛṅkhlābaddha, nyāyamūla (tarkanyāyamūla, kāvyanyāyamūla or vākyanyāyamūla and lokanyāyamūla) and gūḍhārthapratītimūla. Sādṛśyagarbha group is again divided into bhedabhedatulyapradhāna, abhedapradhāna and gamyamāna-upamya. Thus Ruyyaka has made a complete classification.

Vidyāhara divides the arthālaṁkāras into seven main heads thus—

1. Kāvyapradīpa on KP. IX. 8.

- **Arthālaṁkāras**
  - 1 Sādṛśyagarbha
    - Bhedābheda pradhāna
      - Upamā
      - Upameyopamā
      - Ananvaya
      - Smaraṇa
    - Abhedapradhāna
      - Āropamūla
        - 1 Rūpaka
        - 2 Pariṇāma
        - 3 Sandeha
        - 4 Bhrāntimat
        - 5 Ullekha
        - 6 Apahnuti
      - Adhyavasāyamūla
        - 7 Utprekṣā
        - 8 Atiśayokti
    - Gamyaupamyāśraya
      - 1 Padārthagata
        - Tulya-Yogitā
        - Dīpaka
      - 2 Vākyārthagata
        - Prativastūpamā
        - Dṛṣṭānta
        - Nidarśanā
      - 3 Bhedapradhāna
        - Vyatireka
        - Sahokti
      - 4 Vinokti
      - 5 Viśeṣaṇa Vicchityāśraya
        - Samāsokti
        - Parikara
      - 6 Viśeṣa-Vicchityāśraya
        - Parikaraṅkura
      - 7 Viśeṣaṇa-viśeṣya-vicchityāśraya
        - Śleṣa
      - 8 Aprastutapraśaṁsā
      - 9 Arthāntaranyāsa
      - 10 Paryāyokta
      - 11 Vyājastuti
      - 12 Ākṣepa
  - 2 Virodhagarbha
  - 3 Śṛṅkhlābandha
  - 4 Tarkanyāyamūla
  - 5 Vākyanyāyamūla
  - 6 Lokanyāyamūla
  - 7 Gūḍhārthapratītimūla

2
Virodhagarbha

- Virodha
- Vibhāvanā
- Viśeṣokti
- Atiśayokti
- Asaṅgati
- Viṣama
- Sama
- Vicitra
- Adhika
- Anyonya
- Viśeṣa
- Vyāghāta

3
Śṛṅkhlābandha

- Kāraṇamālā
- Ekāvalī
- Māladīpaka
- Sāra

4
Tarkanyāyamūla

- Kāvyaliṅga
- Anumāna

5
Vākyanyāyamūla

- Yathā saṅkhya
- Paryāya
- Parivṛtti
- Parisaṅkhyā
- Arthāpatti
- Vikalpa
- Samuccaya
- Tatkara
- Samādhi

6
Lokanyāyamūla

- Pratyanīka
- Pratīpa
- Mīlita
- Sāmānya
- Tadguṇa
- Atadguṇa
- Uttara
- Praśnottarikā

7
Gūḍhārthapratītimūla

- Sūkṣma
- Vyājokti
- Vakrokti
- Svabhāvokti
- Bhāvika
- Udātta
- Saṁsṛṣṭi
- Saṅkara

Vidyādhara deals with five Śabdālaṁkāras namely Chekanuprāsa, Vṛttyanuprāsa, Yamaka, Lāṭānuprāsa and Citra. Though the Seventh chapter of the Ekāvalī deals with the Śabdālaṁkāras yet it starts with an arthaṁkāra namely Punaruktavadabhāsa. The reason may be that in its previous chapter Kavyadoṣas are discussed and the opposite of the Paunaruktyadoṣa[1] results in an arthaṁkāra i.e. Punaruktavadābhāsa. All other alaṁkāras discussed here are śabdālaṁkāras. It is again important to note here that all the alaṁkāras discussed here depend on repetition except Citrālaṁkāra.

1. *Punaruktavadābhāsa*

Vidyādhara has named the figure in the masculine gender. According to him, when the sense, though different seems repeated, the figure is called Punaruktavadābhāsa.[2] Repetition of the sense must be apparent and not actual, for, otherwise, the two words would be synonymous. Thc figure was accepted similarly by the previous ācāryas namely Udbhaṭa,[3] Mammaṭa,[4] Ruyyaka,[5] Hemacandra[6] and Jayadeva.[7]

Divergent views exist on whether the figure is śabdālaṁkāra or arthālaṁkāra. Vidyādhara[8] like Ruyyaka[9] and his commentator Jayaratha[10] call the figure arthālaṁkāra because the sense is repeated as it is and not the word. Mammaṭa[11] calls it a śabdālaṁkāra and an ubhayālaṁkāra both.

Actually, it is proper to call it an arthālaṁkāra only, for

---

1. Ekā. VI. 5.
2. *Ibid.* VII. 1.
3. KASS. I. 3.
4. KP. IX. 86.
5. AS. 3.
6. KAnu. V. 8.
7. Candrāloka, V. 7.
8. Ekā. VII. 2.
9. AS. vṛtti on 3.
10. Vimarśinī Sanskrit ṭikā on AS. 3.
11. KP. IX. 86.

beauty lies where the sense appears similar. It should be considered neither as a śabdālaṁkāra nor an ubhhyālaṁkāra. Here, there is actually no repetition of words or sense, hence it is not reasonable to assume it to be dependent on words. But considering that only repetition can be found in the meaning and the meaning itself depends on words, all the arthālaṁkāras cannot be regarded as śabdālaṁkāras.

This figure is divided into two classes according to whether the repetition affects nouns and verbs.

In the example 'Abhyastāśeṣa...kṣitīndra',[1] the nouns guru and dhiṣaṇam nistriṁśa and khaḍga, yakṣa and vibhūti and āloka and prabhāva appear to have the same sense in the beginning only. Actually there is no repetition of the meaning. Similarly, in the next instance 'Tān nirmāti...Kaliṅgeśvara',[2] the verbs nirmāti and karoti, bharate and bibhartti and śamayasi and ākarṇayasi having different meanings appear to convey the same sense. Again the repetition is apparent only and not real. This, therefore, constitutes the figure Punaruktavadābhāsa.

2. *Chekānuprāsa*

Vidyādhara[3] says that the word 'cheka' means 'scholar' while according to Udbhaṭa, 'it denotes the birds approaching towards the nest'.[4] Chekānuprāsa is so termed for it is liked by the scholars and implies the single repetition of several consonants.[5] Before Vidyādhara, Udbhaṭa,,[6] Mammaṭa,[7] Ruyyaka,[8] and Jayadeva[9] give almost similar definitions.

---

1. Ekā. example under VII. 1.
2. *Ibid.* example under VII. 1.
3. *Ibid.* vṛtti on VII. 3.
4. KASS. vṛtti on I. 4.
5. Ekā. VII. 3.
6. KASS. I. 4.
7. KP. IX. 79.
8. AS. 4.
9. Candrāloka, V. 2.

In the verse 'Kalākalāpaṁ...bhūpatiḥ',[1] a single repetition of many consonants viz. 'jva' and 'jva', 'sta' and 'sto' and 'karaḥ' and 'karo' illustrate Chekānuprāsa. Here the same pair of consonants is repeated only once, resulting thus in Chekanuprasālaṁkāra.

3. *Vṛttyanuprāsa*

Vṛttyanuprāsa is so termed because the arrangement of letters in it is favourable to the development of a particular rasa.[2]

According to Vidyādhara,[3] Mammaṭa[4] and Jayadeva[5] it is the single or manifold repetition of one or more consonants but Udbhaṭa,[6] Bhoja[7] and Ruyyaka[8] have given importance to the placing of letters in accordance with the vṛttis.

The following are the cases under which vṛttyanuprāsa arises according to Vidyādhara[9] and Ruyyaka—

(i) when only a single consonant is repeated more than once,

(ii) when two consonants are repeated once, or

(iii) when three or more consonants are repeated once.

In the example 'Śrīmannṛsiṁha...āsīt',[10] n, k, r, d and m etc. are repeated several times. There is thus Vṛttyanuprāsa of first case namely 'asakṛdekaikavyañjana-paunaruktyaṁ'.

In the next instance 'Yuktā vipakṣeṣu...sapatnāḥ',[11] two consonants 'n' and 'jh' are repeated once in 'nātha', and 'nāthaṁ' and

---

1. Ekā. example under VII. 3.
2. AS. vṛtti on 5.
3. Ekā. VII. 4.
4. KP. IX. 79 and vṛtti on it.
5. Candrāloka, V. 3.
6. Laghuvṛtti ṭīkā on KASS I. 4.
7. SKBh. II. 230-231.
8. AS. 5 and vṛtti on it also.
9. Ekā. vṛtti on VII. 4.
10. *Ibid.* example under VII. 4.
11. *Ibid.* example under VII. 4.

in the last verse 'Jagati gajagti...Śrīnṛsiṁhaḥ',[1] three consonants j, g and t are repeated once in jagati and jagati.

The last two verses are really instances of Yamaka, because in 'nāthaṁ' and 'nātha' and 'jagati' and 'jagati' there is not only the similarity of consonants but also that of vowels. According to Vidyādhara, aunsvāra and visarga do not make any difference in the combinations of consonants with vowels, provided they are similar in other respects.[2]

4. *Yamaka*

This is one of the four oldest alaṁkāras, discussed by the ancient ācārya Bharata.

Vidyādhara[3] defines Yamaka as the repetition of a number of letters (two or more) in the same order either without meaning or with different meanings, or of one group of letters without meaning and one having meaning. The definitions given previously by Daṇḍin,[4] Vāmana,[5] Bhoja,[6] Mammaṭa,[7] Hemacandra,[8] Jayadeva[9] and others echo the same idea. Bharata[10] has called it Śabdābhyāsa. According to Bhāmaha[11] and Rudraṭa[12] the repetition of letters which sound similar but have different meanings, constitutes Yamakālaṁkāra.

In all the above definitions, the difference in meaning is mentioned as an important factor of Yamakālaṁkāra. Ruyyaka[13]

1. Ekā. example under VII. 4.
2. *Ibid.* VII. 6-7.
3. *Ibid.* VII. 4. & vṛtti on it.
4. KD. III. 3.
5. KASV. IV. I.1.
6. SKBh. II. 146.
7. KP. IX. 83.
8. KAnu. V. 3.
9. Candrāloka, V. 8.
10. NS. 16-62.
11. KAB. II. 17.
12. KAR. III. 1.
13. AS. 6.

does not mention this difference in the definition, but divides the figure on this basis viz. the repetition of letters with different meanings; of letters without any meaning and of letters which were formerly meaningless but are meaningful later.

In the examples 'Kalinganātha...nāpare[1]' and 'Bhāgya-subhāgya...pālane,[2] given in the Ekāvalī 'prabhavaḥ', and 'prabhavaḥ' have different senses, the first meaning 'source' and the second 'able'; 'bhāgyasau' and 'bhāgyasau', have no meaning because these are only parts of words. Of 'caturaṁ' and 'caturaṁ', the only first has a meaning.

Prior to Vidyādhara,[3] these three varieties of Yamaka were accepted by Ruyyaka also. Ācāryas like Mammaṭa and others have not mentioned the divisions of Yamakālaṁkāra and the reason may be that this particular alaṁkāra delays the comprehension of a rasa. No sentiment is expressed in Yamaka,[4] yet poets resort to it for the sake of variety. Mallinātha quoted a half verse of Vidyādharā about Yamaka in his commentary on the Kirātārjunīyam.[5]

Vidyādhara opines that Yamaka should not be used as tripādavṛtti.[6] In other words, the first, second and the third quarters of a verse should not be the same.

5. *Citra*

The name Citrālaṁkāra may be explained in three ways :

(i) Citrālaṁkāra is so termed for it causes a surprise; in that

---

1. Ekā. example under VII. 4.
2. *Ibid.* example under VII. 4.
3. (a) *Ibid.* vṛtti on VII. 4.
   (b) AS. vṛtti on 6.
4. Ekā. VII. 5.
5. (a) *Ibid.* VII.5.
   (b) Commentary of Mallinātha on Kirātārjunīyam, V. 7.
6. (a) Ekā. VII. 7.
   (b) K. Pradīpa on KP. IX. 6.

the order of the letters used once in a portion of a verse is the same as is found again in later portion of it.[1]

(ii) The name 'Citra' is given for letters written in the form of a lotus etc. or looking like a picture.[2]

(iii) Poetry must suggest some rasas, otherwise it is not a real poetry. Citra prevents the relish of sentiment. Hence it is not a real poetry but merely an imitation of it according to Dhvanikāra.[3] It has not suggested sense and is simply based on the charm of words or meanings.

These are, generally, the ways in which the critics explain this figure.

There may be another (fourth) way to explain the word Citra. It protects and develops knowledge by attentively observing and musing on the sense arising from new words.[4]

According to Vidyādhara, Citrālaṁkāra arises when the letters of a poem can be arranged in the form of a lotus etc. It is the contraction of letters by taking them repeatedly from different places as the pericarp of a lotus kamalabandhacitra.[5] Similar definitions have previously been given by Mammaṭa,[6] Ruyyaka[7], Hemacandra[8] and Jayadeva.[9]

The name Citra is given, according to the Agnipurāṇa,[10] to a

---

1. (a) KAR. V. 1-3.
   (b) Ekā. vṛtti on VII. 8.
2. (a) *Ibid.* vṛtti on VII. 8.
   (b) KP. vṛtti on IX. 85.
   (c) AS. 10.
3. DhL. vṛtti on III. 42.
4. Ekā. vṛtti on VII. 8.
5. *Ibid.* vṛtti on VII. 8.
6. KP. IX. 85.
7. AS. 10.
8. KAnu. V. 4.
9. Candrāloka, V. 9.
10. Agnipurāṇa, 343-22.

special type of arrangement of words used in the assemblies which causes anxiety (kutuhala) in the minds of hearers. Rudraṭa[1] very simply says that the wonderful description of things, in poetry is called Citrālamkāra.

Vidyādhara has not mentioned its kinds for according to him gatapratyāgata, ardhabhrama, sarvatobhadra, dhenu and other classes of gaticitra can be included under Citra itself. It will be applicable to these, if we take it to arise from the arrangement of letters. The alaṁkāra Citra causes surprise that the order of letters in coming and returning is the same.[2]

In its etymological sense, citra means that which protects knowledge. As those of lesser intellect protect their knowledge by observing the sense arising from new words in which letters belong to one organ of pronunciation, the poem is significantly called citra. This explanation of citra includes in its significance naiṣkaṇṭya, niroṣṭhya, nistālavya and other varieties of sthāna-citra.[3]

Bhoja[4] has discussed varṇacitra as arising from the similarity of consonants without vowels. This is, however, Vṛttyanuprāsa[5]

Vidyādhara quotes a verse given by Bhoja, who accepts svaracitra and cites an example for the same, where the short vowel alone is repeated.[6] But Vidyādhara does not accept it, because it causes looseness of construction and is, therefore, a doṣa not an alamkāra.[7]

Mammaṭa does not deal with the kinds of Citrālamkāra. He accepts the possibilities of other varieties but considers them

---

1. KAR. V. 1-3.
2. Ekā. vṛtti on VII. 8.
3. *Ibid.* vṛtti on VII. 8.
4. SKBh. vṛtti on II. 359.
5. Ekā. vṛtti on VII. 8.
6. (a) SKBh. II. 359 and 377.
   (b) Ekā. quoted under VII. 5.
7. Ekā. vṛtti on VII. 5.

merely to show the poet's power. Such compositions are not poetry as they cannot create extra-ordinary charm.[1] Ruyyaka[2] accepts many kinds as khaḍga, padma etc. Vidyādhara[3] does not deal with this alaṁkāra in detail because it does not create charm in poetry. Criticising various kinds of Citrālaṁkāra as ākāracitra and bandhacitra, Vidyādhara says that these simply present a particular arrangement. Letters when arranged in the form of a lotus and a mountain which have only one creator, the lord, constitute ākāracitra. The arrangement of letters in the form of a plough, a pestle, a drum, gomūtrikā, a bow and a wheel, which are created by both the lord and man constitutes bandhacitra. Though it is possible to distinguish the two in this way, in both ākāracitra and bandhacitra, letters present a particular arrangement.[4]

6. *Lāṭānuprāsa*

Lāṭānuprāsa is named so because it is liked by the people of Lāṭa country.[5]

Vidyādhara and prior to him Udbhaṭa, Ruyyaka and his followers have considered it as an independent alaṁkāra while other writers like it as a kind of Anuprāsa.

According to Vidyādhara,[6] if words are differently construed, the repetition of words having the same sense constitutes Lāṭānuprāsa. Tātparya is explained as Anyaparatva ṁ or difference of import.

Previous scholars like Udbhaṭa,[7] Bhoja,[8] Mammaṭa,[9]

1. KP. vṛtti on IX. 85.
2. AS. 10 & vṛtti on it.
3. Ekā. vṛtti on VII. 8.
4. *Ibid.* vṛtti on VII. 8.
5. KP. vṛtti on IX. 81.
6. Ekā. VII. 9.
7. KASS. I. 5.
8. SKBh. II. 355.
9. KP. IX. 81.

Ruyyaka,[1] Hemacandra,[2] and Jayadeva[3] define it almost similarly. Ruyyaka[4] calls it an Ubhayālaṁkāra. Bhāmaha mentions it as a kind of anuprāsa but does not explain its nature. He says, 'Others agree to Lāṭānuprāsa in the context of Anuprāsa'.[5]

Difference in import is the life of Lāṭānuprāsa.[6] Tātparya is explained by Pradīpakāra as the difference of syntactical construction.[7] The verse 'Tālā jānti guṇā...kamalāi'[8] is cited as the example of Lāṭānuprāsa. Here the two words kamalāi and kamalā resemble in form and sense but differ in import. The first is jātipara, meaning lotuses, while the second implies fragrance, beauty, delicacy and other qualities found in a lotus. Here, Vidyādhara follows Ruyyaka[9] who explains tātparyam as anyaparatvam.

Difference between Lāṭānuprāsa, Ananyaya and Paunaruktya doṣa

In Ananvaya, a synonym is repeated as upamāna and upameya. Repetition of words and sense throughout, constitutes paunaruktya doṣa.[10] When the repetition has some poetic purpose, it results in an alamkāra and does not cause a dosa.

In bringing about Lāṭānuprāsa the object of the poet is to use words having the same form and same sense, the difference between the two words lying only in their construction or import. The object of the poet in bringing about Ananvaya is to show that upamāna and upameya are the same.[11] Thus in Lāṭānuprāsa the poet aims at Śabdārtha-paunaruktya, while in Ananvaya, he only aims at arthapaunaruktya, though in the latter case, the same

1. AS. 8.
2. KAnu. V. 2.
3. Candrāloka, V. 4.
4. AS. vṛtti on 8.
5. KAB. II. 8.
6. AS. Vimarśinī on AS. 8.
7. Kāvya Pradīpa on KP. IX. 4.
8. Ekā. example under VII. 9.
9. AS. vṛtti on 8.
10. Ekā. VII. 8.
11. *Ibid.* VIII. 4.

words may have used.[1]

Lāṭānuprasa is thus different from Ananvaya. However, sometimes there may be an admixture of both, either being conveyed by the same expression e.g. in 'Pratibhaṭakāntā...jayati'.[2]

All these śabdālamkāras are based on similarity (Sādṛśya). In Yamaka, similar words are repeated. In Chekānuprāsa similar letters are repeated twice. In Vṛttyanuprāsa the repetition is more than two times while in Lāṭānuprāsa similar words and sense are repeated. So arthālamkāras may not necessarily depend on artha only and Śabdālamkāras need not be based on Śabdas only. They primarily depend on one subject (of which they are the alamkāras) and secondarily on another.

In conclusion it may be said that in the beginning there was only one Śabdalamkāra i.e. Yamaka. Bhāmaha added Anuprāsa but it was accepted by him under vṛttis only not separately in the alamkāras. Daṇḍin added Citra also but Anuprāsa was considered by him in discussing guṇas. In Agnipurāṇa only three Śabdālamkāras are discussed namely Yamaka, Citra and Anuprāsa. Anuprāsa is considered a guṇa there and it is based on vṛttis. Udbhaṭa explained only Anuprāsa Śabdālamkāra and it is dealt through various vṛttis like Bhāmaha. Vāmana discussed Yamaka and Anuprāsa Śabdālamkāras also. In the discourse on Anuprāsalamkāra, Vāmana does not deal with the vṛttis. Yamaka, Citra and Anuprāsa Śabdālamkāras are dealt with by Rudraṭa. Almost all the later writers upto Viśvanātha have accepted these Śabdālam kāras. Appayyadīkṣita and Jagannātha, however, do not accept Śabdālamkāras. In neither of his two works namely Citramīmānsā and Kuvalayānanda, Appayyadīkṣita has dealt with the Śabdālamkāras.

In this way, it is seen that in the beginning the Śabdālamkāras occupied an important place and were discussed elaborately with their divisions and subdivisions. But at the time of Ānandavardhana their place was examined and by and by they were neglected. Being inspired by him, Vidyādhara has discussed only Yamaka, Citra and Anuprāsa Śabdālamkāras.

---

1. AS. vītti on 8.
2. Ekā. example under VII. 9.

CHAPTER VII

ARTHĀLAMKĀRAS : VĀCYASĀDṚŚYAMŪLAKA

In the Ekāvalī, sixty-nine arthālamkāras are discussed by Vidyādhara which may be divided under three main heads :

(i) Vācyasādṛśyamūlaka—where sādṛśya is expressed directly and is very clear and apparent.

(ii) Gamyasādṛśyamūlaka—where sādṛśya is suggested. Here sādṛśya appears through deep study only.

(iii) Sādṛśyetaramūlaka—where sādṛśya does not exist. These alamkāras are devoid of sādṛśya but other causes do exist.

In this chapter Vācyasādṛśyamūlakārthālamkāras are discussed. Under this head come Upamā, Upameyopamā, Ananvaya, Smaraṇa, Rūpaka, Pariṇāma, Sandeha, Bhrāntimān, Ullekha, Apahnuti, Utprekṣā and Atiśayokti alamkāras.

1. *Upamā*

Vidyādhara[1] defines Upamā as the similarity and dissimilarity of upamāna and upameya. So, when mukha is compared with candra, both the similarity and difference between them are known.

The common property of upamāna and upameya may be an attribute or an action. It may be expressed by the same word, which can be construed with the words signifying an upamāna and upameya in one (aśliṣṭa) or in different senses (śliṣṭa).[2]

---

1. Ekā. VIII. 2 and vṛtti on it also.
2. *Ibid.* vṛtti on VIII. 2.

Kinds of Upamā

Upamā is first divided into pūrṇā and luptā in the Ekāvalī. Pūrṇopamā requires that all the four constitutents—upameya, upamāna, sādhāraṇadharma and upamāvācaka words—be stated directly. Where any of these constiutents is dropped, there arises luptopamā. Pūrṇopamā is divided into śrautī and ārthī. When the words iva, vā, yathā and vat, added in the sense of 'tatra tasyeva',[1] are used, it is known as Śrautī Upamā.[2] Here the connection of upamāna and upameya through common property is comprehended directly from the words themselves. Ārthī occurs[3] when the words tulya, sadṛśa, sanābhi and vat, suffixed in the sense of 'tena tulyam kriyā cedavatiḥ',[4] are used. Here the connection of upamāna and upameya with a common property is implied (lakṣya) and not expressed (vācya). It should be noted, too, that the division śrautī and ārthī is based on the meanings of iva, vat etc. in the sense of 'tatra tasyeva', vā, iva, yathā, tulya, sadṛśa etc. and vat in the sense of 'tena tulyam kriyā'.

Both śrautī and ārthī are possible in a sentence, (vākya), compound (samāsa), or taddhita. Each is thus of three kinds giving rise to six kinds of Pūrṇopamā.

Śrautī

A Śrautī Upamā in a sentence is called so because it is embodied in a sentence. In the śloka 'Mahīmaṇḍalamandāra...vapuryathā',[5] the word yathā is used and there is no possibility of its being compounded.

The stanza 'Kṛpāṇastava...iva rājate',[6] is an instance of Śrautī Upamā resting on a compound. By a vārttika,[7] iva is supposed

1. Aṣṭādhyāyī, V. I. 116.
2. Ekā. vṛtti on VIII. 2.
3. *Ibid.* vṛtti on VIII. 2.
4. Aṣṭādhyāyī, V. I. 115.
5. Ekā. example under VIII. 2.
6. *Ibid.* example under VIII. 2.
7. vārttika on Aṣṭādhyāyi—II. I. 4.

to form a compound with the word which precedes it, so 'Vaśiṣṭha iva' must be taken as a samāsa by this vārttika. In this example 'Vaśiṣṭha iva' is a compound even though it does not appear to be so.

There are two kinds of suffixes in Sanskrit grammar viz. Kṛta and Taddhita. Kṛta affixes are added to verbs and Taddhita are secondary affixes added to substantives. So Taddhitagā Śrautī Pūrṇā occurs when the affix vat is added to nouns by the sūtra 'tatra tasyeva'. In the verse 'Vāhinīśvaratā...nṛpate tava'[1] in akūpāravad, the affix vat is added in the sense of 'iva' the genetive case (ṣaṣṭhi vibhakti) being used.

Another example of Śrautī Pūrṇā with taddhita affix is in 'Nṛsimha bhūpa bhavataḥ...sadā'.[2] Here in 'sāgaravat', the affix vat is added in the sense of iva, the locative case (saptami vibhakti) being used.

Ārthī pūrṇā

Ārthī Pūrṇopamā is also of three kinds. The verse 'Helayaiva vinidhūrtatārāpati...nareśvara',[3] illustrates Ārthī pūrṇopamā in a sentence.

In samāsagā, sadṛśa, tulya etc. are used, without being compounded. In 'Narasimha mahīpāla...svapadacyutaḥ';[4] the word 'pārāvārasamānatvam' is in compound-form.

Taddhitagā Ārthī Pūrṇopamā is illustrated in the verse 'Ayam tava yaśorāśir...mahīpate'.[5] Here 'vat' is affixed in 'Rāmavad', meaning 'Rāmeṇa tulyam'. Thus, according to Vidyādhara,[6] Pūrṇopamā has six divisions.

Luptopamā

Luptopamā arises if one, two or three of the four constituents

---

1. Ekā. example under VIII. 2.
2. *Ibid.* example under VIII. 2.
3. *Ibid.* example under VIII. 2.
4. *Ibid.* example under VIII. 2.
5. *Ibid.* example under VIII. 2.
6. *Ibid.* vṛtti on VIII. 2.

are not mentioned but implied. It also has two kinds viz. śrautī and ārthī.

Śrautī luptopamā again is of two kinds, i.e. vākyagā and samāsagā. When the common attribute is not mentioned Śrautī luptopamā is found in a sentence and a compound. Śrautī luptopamā is not possible in taddhita;[1] for the affix vat is impossible in the sense of 'iva' but the affix (employed according to 'tatra tasyeva') necessarily requires statement of 'sādhāraṇadharma'.

The taddhita affixes kalpa, deśīya, deśya give rise to ārthī Upamā for they do not possess the sense of iva and convey sādharmya by implication.

Ārthī luptopamā is threefold, viz., vākyagā, samāsagā and taddhitagā. Thus luptopamā has five subdivisions.

The verse 'Khaḍgo yathoragapatis...Sumerukalpaḥ',[2] cites Śrautī luptopamā, the sādhāraṇadharma 'krūratva' (cruelty) not being mentioned. In this verse, in the sub-clause 'tava khaḍgaḥ yathā uragapatiḥ' and 'Kaumudīva kīrttiḥ', Śrautī vākyagata and samāsagata are seen and in 'yugānta tapanena samaḥ pratāpa', 'vākyam pacelimarasāla-phalānukārī' and 'bāhustu vīra Narasimha Sumeru kalpaḥ', Ārthī vākyagata, Samāsagata and Taddhitagata respectively may be seen. All five kinds are cited here in a single śloka.

Upamānaluptā can only be ārthī. Śrautī upamānaluptā is not possible, because iva, vā, yathā and vat in the sense of 'tatra tasyeva' are always used after upamāna. When the latter is not expressed, they, too, cannot be used; upamānaluptā can consequently be ārthī only. It may be possible in a vākya or in a samāsa. Taddhitagā ārthī upamānaluptā is not possible, because the taddhita suffixes vat and kalpa are affixed to an upamāna alone.

In the verse 'Sāhityārṇavakarṇadhāra...na prāpnumaḥ',[3] the

1. Ekā. vṛtti on VIII. 2.
2. *Ibid.* example under VIII. 2.
3. *Ibid.* example under VIII. 2.

word 'tulya' is not compounded. Moreover, the word is mentioned so it is an instance of arthi upamānaluptā Upamā in a sentence. The word 'tvattulyam' can convert it to upamānaluptā, Samāsagā.

Vācakaluptopamā : Upamā where words like iva, tulya etc. which signify similarity, are omitted, cannot be Śrautī, for it requires the use of iva, vā, yathā or vat in the sense of 'tatra tasyeva'. It cannot also be expressed in a sentence, because 'mukham candro ramaṇīyam', conveys no sense without any word like iva which expresses Upamā. So, this type of Upamā is possible in a samāsa only, when kyac is affixed to a word that signifies an object of a verb or a place where the action denoted by a verb occurs. It can also occur when kyaṁ is affixed to a word signifying the subject of a verb; or when ṇamul is added to word which has the sense of the subject/object of a verb.[1]

In the verse 'Samasamayasamudyad......dugdhavīcīsamīcī',[2] 'dugdhavīcīsamīcī' is Samāsagāvādiluptopamā. In 'Pṛthulakuca-bhāraṁ...Nṛsiṁha nṛpa',[3] antaḥpurīyati vanaṁ (antaḥ-puramivācarati) is an instance of vādiluptā by 'karmakyac' according to Pāṇini.[4]

'Tava vīra......payāyate',[5] 'kṛpaṇaḥ pannagāyate' (pannaga ivācarati) and 'payāyate' (paya ivācarati) is an instance of vādiluptā by kyaṅ according to Pāṇini.[6] In the verse 'Paśyannava-ghanadarśaṁ...marālasaṁcāram',[7] 'navaghanadarśaṁ saṁcarti' (navaghanamiva dṛṣṭvā) and 'Marālasaṁcāraṁ saṁcarti' (Marāla iva saṁcarti) illustrates vādiluptā with ṇamula added to a root. The form is used in conjunction with Upāmanavācākaśabda and is the object and the subject of an action respectively denoted by the verb to which ṇamul is suffixed by the sūtra of Pāṇini.[8]

---

1. KP. X. 89.
2. Ekā. example under VII1. 2.
3. *Ibid.* example under VIII. 2.
4. Aṣṭādhyāyī, III. I. 10.
5. Ekā. example under VIII. 2.
6. Aṣṭādhyāyī, III. I. 11.
7. Ekā. example under VIII. 2.
8. Aṣṭādhyāyī, III-IV. 45.

Dviluptā : Vidyādhara has cited only the second kind of Dvilopi-upamā in 'Tulāmālambate...mahītale'.[1] Here upamāna 'yasya' and dharma 'sūrya' are suppressed, giving rise to Dharmopamānaluptopamā. It is not in a samāsa or taddhita and so is an example in a vākya.

Triluptā : When three viz. vācakaśabdas, dharma and upamāna are dropped, there can be samāsagā Upamā only. In the stanza, 'Samālokyālekyasthitamapi...vipine',[2] mṛgākṣyaḥ is the instance. The compound is thus dissolved 'mṛgasyākṣiṇī iva āyate akṣiṇī yāsāṁ tāḥ'. Thus this compound is considered as bahubrīhi.[3]

In the instance mṛgākṣya, mṛgākṣī is unamāna and mṛga being its part and the property of the whole being attributed to its part, mṛga also is upamāna. Mṛgākṣī is thus a compounded word which has upamānavācaka word as its first member. When compounded with akṣī, the compound is bahubrīhi and the latter member of the first compounded word, viz., akṣi of ṣaṣthi tatpurṣa mṛgākṣī, is dropped.

When the same sādhāraṇadharma is sometimes denoted by different words in different sentences[4] it is known as vastuprativastubhāva.[5] When two similar dharmas are mentioned differently for different objects in the upameya sentences, it is known as bimbapratibimbahāva.[6]

In 'Parārghyamaṇikeyūras...Śriyam,'[7] one common property 'slāghyatva' is expressed by two different words viz. parārghyatvaṁ and ślaghyatvaṁ. Thus here is cited vastuprativastubhāva.

The purpose of using synonyms is to avoid the kāvya-doṣa Kathitapadatā which arises by repetition of words.

1. Ekā. example under VIII. 2.
2. *Ibid.* example under VIII. 2.
3. Aṣṭādyāyī, II. II. 24.
4. AS. vṛtti on 11.
5. Ekā. vṛtti on VIII. 2.
6. *Ibid.* vṛtti on VIII. 2.
7. *Ibid*, example under VIII. 2.

The śloka 'Vakṣasthalī...viṭaṅkitaśrīḥ',[1] illustrates bimbapratibimbabhāva. Here vinyasta—hāratva, Mandākinī—śrītva, are two similar dharmas but are mentioned separately.

When the relation of upamāna with the various properties of upameya is desired, then the sādhāraṇadharma and vācaka-śabdas should always be expressed and not suggested by mentioning the words sādhāraṇa-dharma.[2] When it is apprehended through śabdaśaktimūlānuraṇanarūpadhvani, it is not to be expressed in order to avoid Paunaruktya doṣa.[3]

The earlier writers like Bharata,[4] Bhāmaha,[5] Daṇḍin,[6] Udbhaṭa,[7] Vāmana,[8] Rudraṭa,[9] Kuntaka,[10] and Bhoja[11] emphasize on similarity only while defining Upamā but in the definitions, given by other scholars, both the similarity and dissimilarity are given importance.

2. *Upameyopamā*

The word Upameyopamā is significant being equivalent to Upameyenopamā.

Vidhyādhara[12] defines it as that which is created when both upameya and upamāna exchange places and come in turn. Thus upamāna takes the place of upameya and vice versa. Here upameya and upamāna are mutually similar and there is no third object like them.

---

1. Ekā. example under VIII. 2.
2. *Ibid.* vṛtti on VIII. 2.
3. *Ibid.* vṛtti on VIII. 2.
4. NS. 16-43.
5. KAB. II. 30.
6. KD. II. 14.
7. KASS. I. 15.
8. KASV. IV-II. 1.
9. KAR. VIII. 4.
10. VJ. III. 30-31.
11. SKBh. IV. 5.
12. Ekā. VIII. 3.

Kinds : Vidyādhara accepts its two divisions viz., the sādhāraṇadharma being mentioned through vastuprativastubhāva and ordinarily i.e. by one word (anugamitayā ekarupeṇa).[1] In 'Locanamadhukaramadhuraṁ...vīra Narasiṁha',[2] when the compound is dissolved as 'locanaṁ madhukaraḥ iva' it is called 'upamitasamāsa' locana being upamita or upameya. When dissolved as 'locanamiva madhukaraḥ' or 'locanasadṛśaḥ madhukaraḥ', it is 'madhyamapadalopin' or upamāsamāsa, locana being upamāna. So when there is difference in meaning, there is no difference in dharma. The different dharma is described as similar owing to the power of Atiśayokti alaṁkāra.[3] The common property is vastuprativastubhāvāpanna. In vastuprativastubhāva, the same dharma is mentioned twice to show the difference which in turn is due to difference of sentences. Purity etc. is the common property suggested here. In 'Vīra Narsiṁha...kīrttiriva',[4] the common property vimalatvādi (purity etc.) is not mentioned by two words, but suggested. This exemplifies dharmasādhāraṇya.

3. *Ananvaya*

'Na anvaya itī' Ananvaya means 'the absence of connection'. According to Vidyādhara,[5] Ananvayālaṁkāra is constituted when the same object becomes both upameya and upamāna in the same sentence.

In the example, 'Pratibhaṭakāntā...jayati',[6] here there is a description of being extraordinary, so to make the upamāna of upameya, there is no upamāna for it.

Vidyādhara treats Upameyopamā first and then Ananavaya while Mammaṭa, Ruyyaka, Jayadeva and Viśvanātha discuss Upameyopamā after explaining Ananvaya. Here Vidyādhara

---

1. (a) Ekā. vṛtti on VIII. 3.
   (b) AS. vṛtti on 13.
2. Ekā. example under VIII. 3.
3. *Ibid.* VIII. 13.
4. *Ibid.* example under VIII. 3.
5. *Ibid.* VIII. 4.
6. *Ibid.* example under VIII. 4.

differs from Ruyyaka though elsewhere he follows him in maintaining the order of the alaṁkāras. The reason for discussing Upameyopamā prior to Ananvaya may have been to remove the difference between upameya and upamāna gradually.

In Ananvaya and Upameyopamā, the difference between upamāna and upameya is lesser than that in Upamālaṁkāra. Thus, the two should be treated after Upamā. Even in these two, Upameyopamā consists of more difference between upamāna and upameya because these two are different there, while in Ananvaya only one object is treated as both upamāna and upameya. So, in Ananvaya, the two are not different and it is appropriate to discuss Upameyopamā first and then Ananvaya.

4. *Smaraṇa*

Smaraṇa is sometimes called Smṛti, which is a philosophic term and is defined as 'the knowledge which arises only from saṁskāra'.[1]

On seeing a similar object, when some other similar object is remembered, it is called Smaraṇālaṁkāra. according to Vidyādhara.[2] In the example 'Tvatpratyarthī...kṣitīndra',[3] a similar thing 'pīnastanataṭādi' is remembered. In 'Aho sa raṇadundubhiḥ...Kaliṅgeśvara',[4] the Smṛti arising by separation from the army is only a vyabhicāra and does not constitute Smaraṇālaṁkāra. Hence, Smṛti may be due to any cause, while Smaraṇālaṁkāra arises only by Sadṛśānubhava.

Besides Sādṛśya, Bhoja[5] accepts adṛṣṭacintā, paraprayatna, svapna and pratyabhijñāna also as the causes of Smaraṇālaṁkāra.

This alaṁkāra does not find a place among the figures discussed by Bhāmaha, Daṇḍin, Udbhaṭa and Vāmana.

---

1. (a) Tarkasaṅgraha, p. 68.
   (b) Vaiśeṣikadarśana, 9.2.6.
   (c) Praśastapādabhāṣya, p. 128.
2. Ekā. VIII. 5.
3. *Ibid.* example under VIII. 5.
4. *Ibid.* example under VIII. 5.
5. SKBh. III. 169 and vṛtti on III. 175.

5. *Rupaka*

Having explained bhedābhedapradhāna Sādṛśyamūlakālaṁkāras, Vidyādhara discusses abhedapradhāna Sādṛśyamūlakālaṁkāras of which Rūpaka is the first. According to him,[1] there is superimposition of viṣayin on viṣaya and the subject of superimposition is not denied here. There is difference between āropa and adhyavasāya. Viṣaya and viṣayin both are expressed in āropa while in adhyavasāya viṣaya is lost in the viṣayin. The former leads to Rūpaka and the latter to Atiśayokti. In Rūpaka the viṣayin colours the viṣaya with its own properties.

Kinds : Vidyādhara[2] accepts eight divisions of Rūpaka. It is first divided into Niravayava, Sāvayava and Paramparita. Niravayava is again subdivided into Kevalaṁ and Mālārūpakaṁ, of which the former is categorized as Samastavastuviṣayaṁ and Ekadeśavivartti, Paramparita is first divided into Śliṣṭa and Aśliṣṭa and each of these is subdivided into Kevala and Mālārūpaka.

Kevala niravayava : The word 'Niravayava' means that which does not consist of parts.[3] The word kīrttijyotsanā (kīrtti eva jyotsanā) is Kevala niravayava in 'Hemādreḥ...kṣitīndra'.[4] This word is not related to another unit.

Niravayava mālā : In the example 'Kalānāmālambaḥ...Narasiṁhakṣitipatiḥ',[5] one 'āropaviṣaya kṣitipati' is identified with eight āropyamāṇas, viz., ālambaḥ, pratinidhiḥ, kṣema, śaraṇa, araṇiḥ, vilāsaḥ, sukṛtaparipākaḥ, and khalūrī.

Samastavastuviṣaya : When one avayavī having avayavas is superimposed on another avayavī, it is called Sāvayavarūpaka. When all the objects superimposed are expressed in words and not merely implied, this is called Samastavastuviṣaya.[6] The verse

1. Ekā. VIII. 6.
2. *Ibid.* vṛtti on VIII. 6.
3. *Ibid.* vītti on VIII. 6.
4. *Ibid.* example under VIII. 6.
5. *Ibid.* example under VIII. 6.
6. *Ibid.* vṛtti on VIII. 6.

'Yatra dwīpastuṣāra...kṣitīndra',[1] exemplifies Samastavastuviṣayasāvayava Rūpaka. Here on the kīrtti of Narasiṁha kṣīravārdhi is superimposed having avayavas like dwīpa, mauktika, śaivāla, pravāla etc.

Ekadeśavivartti : In Ekadeśavivartti sāvayava Rūpaka, some of the objects superimposed are expressed and some are implied. It is called Ekadeśavivartti as it is present in an explicit form in a part of the description.[2] Here the superimposition of nāyikā on 'bhūḥ' is implied from the superimposition of a pillow on the hand which is expressed. It may be explained from the feminine gender of 'bhū', as the earth is described by the poets as thc wife of kings (kings being called bhūpati, mahībhuj etc.), it does not require the superimposition of kelītalpa on bhuj for its support.

Paramparita : Paramparita is named owing to the presence here of the paramparā of kāryarūpaka and kāraṇarūpaka. It is either based on śliṣta words known as Śliṣtaparamparita or on aśliṣṭa words viz. Aśliṣṭaparamparita. The āropa which supports another āropa is generally expressed by śliṣṭa words.[3]

In the example 'Kiṁ varṇyase vīra...Nalakūbarādyāḥ',[4] the superimposition of the king Narasiṁha on rājahaṁsa is the cause of the superimposition of Mānasarovara on Mānasa (mind of vilāsinī). The word Mānasa which expresses the āropyamāṇa and āropaviṣaya is Śliṣṭa and the verse is an example of Śliṣṭaśabdanibandhena kevalaparamparitarūpaka. Here the superimposition of haṁsa or rāja requires for its support that of Mānasa (the lake) or manasa (the mind).

Śliṣṭa paramparita mūlārūpaka : The verse 'Raviḥ padmollāse ...bhavān',[5] exemplifies Śliṣṭaparamparitarūpaka as there is Ślesa in Kāraṇarūpakas viz. in padmollāsa (padmasya ullāsa or padmāyāḥ ullāsa), kuvalayavikāsa (ku valaya vikāsa or kuvalaya vikāsa),

1. Ekā. example under VIII. 6.
2. *Ibid.* vṛtti on VIII. 6.
3. *Ibid.* vṛtti on VIII. 6.
4. *Ibid.* exampie under VIII. 6.
5. *Ibid.* example under VIII. 6.

kṣamābhṛtapakṣālī (sides of the kings and wings of the mountains) etc. and āropa of many on one viz. the king.

Aśliṣṭa paramparitakevalarūpaka : In the verse 'Vīra Narasiṁha...bhagavān',[1] the superimposition of viṣadharatva of pratibhaṭas is the Kāraṇarūpaka on which depends the superimposition of garutmatva of the king Narasiṁha. It is aśliṣṭa. It is kevala as only one thing, garutmatva, is superimposed. Thus Aśliṣṭa paramparitarūpaka occurs here.

Aśliṣṭaparamparitamālārūpaka : Some Rūpakas are causes of certain others in 'Yaśaḥ...Kaliṅgeśvaraḥ'.[2] It is aśliṣṭa and himagiritva, bhūdharatva, Mandācalatva and Vindhyatva are superimposed on one āropaviṣaya Kaliṅgeśvara. These cause the superimposition of Tridaśavāhinī on Yaśa, ātapaprathā on pratāpa, abdhi on pratibala and mahāmadadvirada on parākrama respectively. Thus there exists Aśliṣṭa paramparitamālārūpaka here.

It can be created by negative qualities (vaidharmya). In the instance 'Tyāgastāvat...kṣitīndra',[3] the charity of a king is identified with a destructive cloud, because it dispels the moonlight from the heavenly tree.

Sometimes there may arise a doubt between Upamā and Rūpaka alaṁakāras where the sentence-construction is in compound e.g. pādāmbhujaṁ, can be resolved in two ways viz., 'pādau ambuje iva' (feet like lotuses) and 'pādau iva ambuje' (lotus feet). In first Upamā is clear, because feet are compared to lotuses and in second there is Rūpakālaṁkāra because lotuses are superimposed on feet. Whenever the sādhaka or bādhaka pramāṇas are used for Rūpaka or Upamā, there must be certainty of Upamā or Rūpaka alaṁkāras. When the pramāṇas are not found, due to uncertainty, there will be sandehasaṁkara instead of Upamā or Rūpaka. Where the sentence construction is not in compound, there is no doubt of Upamā and Rūpakālaṁkāra.

---

1. Ekā. example under VIII. 6.
2. *Ibid.* example under VIII. 6.
3. *Ibid.* example under VIII. 6.

In the example 'Śarāsanamidaṁ...pādāmbujām',[1] in the word pādāmbujām there is Upamālaṁkāra certainly because the relation of ratnavirudāṅgada is possible in feet only. In 'Śositāśesa...tava'[2] 'Śoṣitāśeṣadurvāravairistrījanamānasaḥ' removes doubts of Upamā and there is Rūpaka in the word pratāpatapana.

In 'Yasyāniśaṁ...Narasiṁhadeva',[3] there is Rūpakālaṁkāra in the word caraṇārvinda because there is no possibility of uttaṁsana with caraṇa but with arvinda only.

Some differences are seen in the definition of Rūpaka given by various scholars, e.g., Udbhaṭa[4] defines Rūpaka as that where a noun is connected to another in a subsidiary manner, their direct relation being impossible. Kuntaka[5] included 'upacāravakratā', also in the definition of Rūpaka. While defining it, Bhoja[6] believes in the importance of lakṣaṇā. According to Jayadeva[7] when the upameya is coloured by upamācitra, it is called Rūpaka.

6. *Pariṇāma*

According to Vidyādhara[8] when the viṣayin makes the viṣaya accomplish the purpose by assuming its form, it is Pariṇāmālaṁkāra. So the identification of the viṣaya with the viṣayin constitutes Rūpaka. When this identification serves some purpose it constitutes Pariṇāma.[9]

The figure may be divided into Samānādhikaraṇa and Vaiyadhikaraṇa.[10] In the example 'Amaranagarī...Kaliṅgapurandara',[11]

---

1. Ekā. example under VIII. 6.
2. *Ibid.* example under VIII. 6.
3. *Ibid.* example under VIII. 6.
4. KASS. I. 11.
5. VJ. III. 20.
6. SKBh. IV. 48.
7. Candrāloka. V. 18.
8. Ekā. VIII. 7.
9. *Ibid.* vṛtti onVIII. 7.
10. (a) AS. vṛtti on 16.
    (b) Ekā. vṛtti on VIII. 7.
11. *Ibid.* example under VIII. 7.

the āropaviṣaya Kṛpāṇalatā assumes the form of āropyamāṇa Niśreṇi to accomplish the purpose i.e. Amaranagarīsaudhotsaṅgādhirohaṇam. Here āropaviṣaya and āropyamāṇa are used in nominative case.

The verse 'Rājan Nṛsiṁha...śātravāṇām',[1] exemplifies Vaiyadhikaraṇya Pariṇāma. Here āropaviṣaya 'dhūli' (dhūlibhiḥ) assumes the form of āropyamāṇa—andhatamas to fulfil the purpose viz. making the atmosphere for Svargāṅgaṇa Suratakeli. Here āropaviṣaya dhūli is used in instrumental case and āropyamāṇa andhatamasa is in accusative case.

(7) *Sandeha*

Saṁśaya and Sasandeha are also applied for Sandehālaṁkāra. Saṁśaya is a philosophical term also which is defined as looking at two similar objects or finding many properties in one object, when a doubt arises to find out the reality.[2]

Vidyādhara says that it is different from Sandehālaṁkāra where prakṛtārtha is suspected by the poet to be another and when the suspicion is based upon similarity between these two and is set up by his genius.[3] According to Vidyādhara, the doubt must be poetical, so mere 'sthāṇurvā puruṣo vā' which expresses a doubt and is set up by one's own will but not by poetic genius cannot be an alaṁkāra.[4]

Kinds : According to Vidyādhara, it has three kinds as the doubt is described as pure, without certainty (śuddha) or with certainty in the middle (niścayagarbha) or with certainty at the end (niścayānta).

The verse 'Kāntaḥ kiṁ...vicitraiścaritraiḥ',[5] illustrates Niścayāntasandeha. Here various doubts are raised regarding king

1. Ekā. example under VIII. 7.
2. (a) Vātsyāyanasūtra I.I.23.
   (b) Bhāṣya on Vātsyāyanasūtra I.I.23.
3. Ekā. VIII. 8.
4. *Ibid.* vṛtti on VIII. 8.
5. *Ibid.* example under VIII. 8.

Narasiṁha. The properties do not enable us to arrive at the real character of the object. If the description had stopped here, it would have been an example of Niścayagarbhasandeha.

The particular character peculiar to the king alone and not to any of three upamānas i.e. Moon, Sun, and Viṣṇu, makes it certain that he is Nṛsiṁha. So, the verse contains Niścayānta-sandeha.

(8) *Bhrāntimān*

The figure Bhrāntimān is treated immediately after Sandehālaṁkāra as both depend on false apprehension. According to Vidyādhara[1] Bhrāntimān exists when something is mistaken charmingly as another on account of their resemblance.

The verse 'Surāṅganābhyomalaye......nāgāḥ',[2] exemplifies Bhrāntimān. Bhrānti arises here due to similarity between fame and milk and mṛṇāla (i.e. whiteness).

Thus Bhrāntimān alaṁkāra is different from bhrānti which arises from kāma, krodha, śoka, bhaya and unmāda. The figure Bhrāntimān arises from the causes as sādṛśya only. So, bhrānti, which arises from causes other than sādṛśya does not come under this alaṁkāra. In 'Kalpānta...Kṣitīndra',[3] bhrānti arises from the embarrassment of the mind caused by blows on the vital parts of the body. So, the figure does not exist here.

This figure is also different from Smaraṇa which is accepted as knowledge that concerns itself with a distant impression. Bhrāntimān is also different from Sandehālaṁkāra which is accepted to be knowledge concerning two opposed properties, their opposition first flashing on the mind as superimposed upon an object. Bhrāntimān takes the form 'idameva' and not 'idam vā idaṁ vā' as Sandeha nor 'tat jānāmi', as smaraṇa.

In both Rūpaka and Bhrāntimān, one thing is known as another i.e. prakṛta as aprakṛta, but in Rūpaka the certitude is volutary

1. Ekā. VIII. 9.
2. *Ibid.* example under VIII. 9.
3. *Ibid.* example under VIII. 9.

while in Bhrāntimān it is caused by some adventitious circumstances.

Bhrāntimān alaṁkāra is not found in the works of Bhāmaha, Udbhaṭa and Vāmana.

(9) *Ullekha*

The word 'Ullekha' means 'to mention'. This figure is not treated by the old ācāryas. Vidyādhara[1] defines it as when an object is apprehended in different ways by different persons, it is called Ullekha. e.g. in 'Na bhavasi kathaṁkāraṁ...api',[2] only one king of Kaliṅga is understood in many forms e.g. Cupid (Smara), Mukunda, Surataru and Bharatamuni, due to appropriate qualities like beauty etc. possessed by him.

Ullekhālaṁkāra cannot be comprehended under Rūpaka, which simply requires aprakṛta to be superimposed on prakṛta while Ullekha requires an object to be grasped differently by different persons through different causes. *It cannot be included under Bhrāntimān also*, though in both the cases there is an idea of a thing being different from what it is, still Ullekha is based on additional charm of an object being apprehended in various ways. *Ullekhālaṁkāra cannot be a kind of Atiśayoki* which consists in considering different objects to be identical.

(10) *Apahnuti*

The word 'Apahnuti' is derived from the root 'Hnūñ' with the prefix 'apa' and suffix 'ktin' and it means 'to conceal'.

Vidyādhara[3] defines the figure as that when the subject of superimposition is latent and the object super-imposed shines out prominently.

Kinds : Vidyādhara[4] divides it into three kinds; in some cases the subject of superimposition is expressed; in others this order is

1. Ekā. VIII. 10.
2. *Ibid.* example under VIII. 10.
4. *Ibid.* VIII. 11.
4. *Ibid.* vṛtti on VIII. 11.

reversed; while in some others the denial of the subject of superimposition is expressed by words signifying falsity, such as chala. The first two varieties require different sentences for the denial of the subject of superimposition and the superimposition of another object, the third requires only one sentence.[1] All the three varieties are illustrated in order. In 'Aśrāntasyandamānoddhura......svahastān',[2] cañcarīkaprakara is denied and then nīlapaṭāvaguṇṭharūpa is superimposed. In the verse 'Pṛthvī-bhārāvatāraṁ......kṣitīdra',[3] śeṣeṇa preṣitaṁ is superimposed and then kṛpāṇa is denied. Here through denial 'you will bring widowhood at once in the battle to all the wives of the enemies', the matter is suggested.

Denial is expressed by the word 'apadeśa' in the śloka, 'Vīraśrīsiṁha......tvadripūṇām'.[4] When the words like chala, vyāja, kapaṭa, misa, chadma, vapus and ātman are used, it is śābdī Apahnuti.

(11) *Utprekṣā*

The name Utprekṣā (ut+pra+īkṣā) is explained as 'utkaṭā prakṛṣṭasyopamānasyekṣā jñānaṁ utprekṣā'.[5]

Vidyādhara[6] has defined Utprekṣā as when the identification of prakṛta with aprakṛta is to be accomplished on account of common properties.

According to him[7] Utprekṣā is treated here because identification causes greater charm than superimposition on account of the relation of the prakṛta with the properties and actions of the aprakṛta. When the viṣaya is engulfed by the viṣayin it is called adhyavasāya.[8] Here, either the viṣayin actually conceals the

---

1. Ekā. vṛtti on VIII. 11.
2. *Ibid.* example under VIII. 11.
3. *Ibid.* example under VIII. 11.
4. *Ibid.* example under VIII. 11.
5. Udyota on KP. X. 92.
6. Ekā. VIII. 12.
7. *Ibid.* vṛtti on VIII. 12.
8. (a) *Ibid.* vṛtti on VIII. 12.
   (b) As vṛtti on 21.

viṣaya which is consequently not expressed or the viṣayin, as it were, swallows up the viṣayin. Here the resemblance between them is understood by suggestion. In the first case, the adhyavasāya is called siddha and in the second it is sādhya.[1] In siddhādhyavasāya, viṣaya is swallowed up by the viṣayin and is consequently not expressed. It is different from āropa where both viṣaya and viṣayin are expressed. In sādhyādhyavasāna viṣaya may not be expressed; when expressed, it is, as it were, swallowed up by viṣayin, since viṣaya is conceived as identical with viṣayin. Siddhādhyavasāya is the basis of Atiśayokti. Utprekṣā is based on sādhyādhyavaṣāya which is equivalent to sambhāvanā and is designated by different synonyms like sambhāvana, abhimāna, tarka and ūha.[2]

Though Vidyādhara does not point out any sort of division, still there are the following examples of various *kinds* of Utprekṣā discussed by him :

(i) anupāttaguṇanimittā vācyajāti svarūpotprekṣā
(ii) guṇa hetūtprekṣā
(iii) kriyā hetūtprekṣā
(iv) kriyā phalotprekṣā
(v) guṇarūpa hetūtprekṣā (Śleṣa and abhedātiśayokti)
(vi) kriyānimittaguṇa hetūtprekṣā
(vii) kriyānimittaguṇa hetūtprekṣā (Śleṣa and abhedātiśayokti)
(viii) kriyānimittakriyāphalotprekṣā (abhedātiśayokti) and
(ix) upamopakrama Utprekṣā.

The examples are examined here one by one—

(i) The verse 'Śrīmannṛsiṁha......tadātmajasya'[3] illustrates anupāttanimitta (not expressed) vācyajāti svarūpotprekṣā. Here

1. Ekā. vṛtti on VIII. 12.
2. (a) *Ibid.* vṛtti on VIII. 12.
   (b) AS. vṛtti on 21.
3. Ekā. example under VIII. 12.

the deer is conceived to be smoke due to the property 'blackness', which is common to both. The property is not expressed and 'iva' expresses the sense of Utprekṣa. By lakṣaṇā smoke expresses the sense of 'deer' and the object of lakṣaṇā, which is conveyed by vyañjanā, is the apprehension of the identity of the two. It may be an example of dharmyutprekṣā because conceived śokāgnidhūma is a dharmī and not dharma.

(ii) Guṇa hetūtprekṣā is illustrated in 'Kailāsān kīrttireṣā... Nṛsiṁha kṣitīndra'.[1] Here excess of shame and anxiety has made brāhmaṇa lose his senses before the fame and the liberality of Nṛsiṁha, which generates many Kailāsa and Meru mountains respectively. In this example this state of brāhmaṇa is conceived to be the cause of his concealing himself in the hollow of the lotus in the navel of Viṣṇu. Here the property vidhuradhītva is the hetu when an attribute is superimposed on an object, Utprekṣā is pratiyamānā and not vācyā. Dharma consists of guṇa or kriyā and guṇa is conceived as hetu while kriyā as both hetu and phala.

(iii) Similarly, the verse 'Tvattaḥ koapyaparaḥ......nijām'[2] is an instance of Kriyā hetūtprekṣā. Here pratyāyanakaraṇaṁ is the hetu of śuddhiprakāśana.

(iv) The śloka 'Trailokyaprathamānavīra...budhāḥ',[3] exemplifies Kriyāphalotprekṣā. Here śiraḥ kampana is the hetu of prabhraṁśana of avataṁsita parayaśaḥ and this prabhraṁśana is the hetu to make avataṁsa, the fame of Śrīnṛsiṁha which is phala.

(v) When a property residing in an animate object is conceived as found in an inanimate one, the similarity between them both is apprehended. Therefore words like iva, which signify it, should not be used, otherwise there will be the fault of repetition. In 'Nanumṛgāṅkamṛgasyā...yaśaḥ',[4] there is Guṇarūpahetutprekṣā. Here the property mercy, which belongs to animate beings is

1. Ekā. example under VIII. 12.
2. *Ibid.* example under VIII. 12.
3. *Ibid.* example under VIII. 12.
4. *Ibid.* example under VIII. 12.

conceived as existing in the inanimate object, glory and the basis of, Utprekṣā is tṛṇa karaṇa to the moon. The word 'tṛṇa-karaṇa', has two meanings namely supplying grass and regarding worthless. These two senses are conveyed by the force of Śleṣa and are identified by abhedhādhyavasāya or abhedātiśayokti.

(vi) In 'Kāntyānayā...yathārthā',[1] shame, which is a property of animate objects is conceived of as gold, an inanimate object. The basis for this conception is the belittling (avāñcana) of gold when compared with the beauty of Nṛsiṁha. This then is an example of kriyānimittaguṇa Hetūtprekṣā. The sense of 'iva' is implied, as the sense of lajjā is impossible in an inanimate being, and 'iva' is not used consequently.

(vii) Kriyānimittaguṇahetūtprekṣā is exemplified in 'Marutpāthovahni...vasatim'.[2] Here disgust is conceived as gold and the basis of conception is tīrthavasati which has two senses, i.e., living with worthy persons and living in holy places, conveyed by Śleṣa. These senses are identified by abhedātiśayokti.

(viii) The verse 'Diṅgamātaṅgaiḥ...nṛpate tava'[3] illustrates Kriyānimitta-kriyāphalotprekṣā. Here the purport of purification is conceived as fame. The reason of the concept is puṣkaragāhana which conveys two senses, viz., entering puṣkaratīrtha for ablution and crossing the sky. These senses are identified by abhedātiśayokti. As phala does not exist in an inanimate object, iva is implied. If iva were used, the fault of repetition would have arisen.

(ix) Some instances first appear to be of Upamā but are later found to be of Utprekṣā. In 'Svaḥ Sindhau...hāranti ca',[4] diṇḍīraprakaranti etc. are denominatives and diṇḍīraprakara etc. are upamānas. At first sight, the figure appears to be Upamā. The splendours of fame are conceived to be identical with the foam of the heavenly Ganges etc. and what appears to be Upamā eventually turns out to be Utprekṣā. If this is taken as Upamā, the

1. Ekā. example under VIII. 12.
2. *Ibid.* example under VIII. 12.
3. *Ibid.* example under VIII. 12.
4. *Ibid.* example under VIII. 12.

attributes of diṇḍīraprakara etc., denoted by svaḥasindhau etc. would be useless, because the similarity of kīrtti and diṇḍīraprakara etc. can be established by the latter existing anywhere and not in svaḥsindhu etc. This may be an instance of Dharmyutprekṣā here. Kīrtti is conceived to be diṇḍīraprakara. This last type namely 'Upamopakramotprekṣā' is exemplified for the first time by Vidyādhara. Here Upamā is found in the beginning of Utprekṣā.

(12) *Atiśayokti*

As the name itself shows, Atiśayokti means 'the statement of something supernatural'.[1] Vidyādhara[2] defines Atiśayokti alaṁkāra in two ways :

(i) on the basis of adhyavasitaprādhānya which may be included in sādṛśyamūlakāṁkāras and

(ii) based on the simultaneity of cause and effect or the inversion of the order of cause and effect.

The first type of Atiśayokti arises under any one of the four conditions, e.g., when different things are described as similar or vice versa, when connection is described between unrelated objects and when disparity is put forth between objects where there is connection. It is called Atiśayokti as the excellence of the object described is spoken of in each case.

The other type of Atiśayokti consists in the simultaneity of cause and effect and in the inversion of the order of their precedence.

Kinds : Vidyādhara discusses four kinds of the Sādṛśyamūlā Atiśayokti—

(i) Bhede apyabhedaḥ is illustrated in 'Pallavataḥ kalpataroreṣa....tiraskurute',[3] the excellence of the king's hand is shown by describing two different karṇas as one. Its superiority is also conveyed over a leaf of the kalpa tree. Thus there is Saṅkara of Vyatireka and Atiśayokti alaṁkāras based upon Śleṣa.

1. Jhalakīkara on KP. X. 100.
2. Ekā. VIII. 13 and 37.
3. *Ibid.* example under VIII. 13.

The first kind is illustrated in the verse 'Aśeṣabhogādhāraṁ... puruṣotamam',[1] too. The meanings conveyed by puruṣottama, though different are represented as one and the king is represented as a new puruṣottama, superior to the old one, i.e. Viṣṇu. Here Utprekṣā is set up by Atiśayokti which is based upon Śleṣa, and Vyatireka.

(ii) 'Idamanyat sārasvataṁ...sṛṣṭiḥ'.[2] illustrates abhede api bhedaḥ kind of Atiśayokti. The king's learning gravity and liberality are shown to be superior to those of others by identifying them with another sort of learning, gravity and liberality. Though similar, they are represented as different by the word anyat.

(iii) Asambandhe Sambandhaḥ variety is illustrated in the śloka 'Sthāne sthāne...kṣitīndra'.[3] Here the connection between malaya breezes and the king's vehicle is described, though there is none.

(iv) The last variety namely sambandhe asambandhaḥ is exemplified in 'Tvayīitthaṁ sarvebhyo...vyatikaraiḥ'.[4] Here though there is connection between divine trees and liberality, absence of connection is described to express the extreme liberality of the king Nṛsiṁha.

The second type of Atiśayokti is divided into two on the basis of the simultaneity and perversion of the order of the cause and effect.

In the verse 'Koṣagṛhaciraniṣaṇṇā......samākṛṣṭā'[5], the cause namely pulling out asilatikā and effect, namely pulling out ripunṛpalakṣmī are mentioned simultaneously (yugapat).

In 'Kavīndrāṇāṁ...sahacarāḥ'.[6] the effect, viz., the wealth of the poets is stated first and then its cause, namely, kaṭākṣapatana of king Narendra. So, this verse is an example of the perversion of the order of cause and effect.

---

1. Ekā. example under VIII. 13.
2. *Iibd.* example under VIII. 13.
3. *Ibid.* example under VIII. 13.
4. *Ibid.* example under VIII. 13.
5. *Ibid.* example under VIII. 37.
6. *Ibid.* example under VIII. 37.

No doubt, Vidyādhara is greatly influenced by Mammaṭa and Ruyyaka in dealing with the figures; yet he has his own way and style to adopt. He discusses the figure Upameyopamā prior to Ananvaya. The reason here may be that in Upameyopamālaṁkāra, the difference between upamāna and upameya is more than it is in Ananvayālaṁkāra. Upameyopamā has separate upamāna and upameya while in Ananvaya the same thing is treated as both. From this point of view he deals with Upameyopamā before Ananvaya and this seems to be quite appropriate.

From the above discussion, it is quite clear that in Upamālaṁkāra, upameya and upamāna are linked on the basis of similarity. In Rūpaka, two different things appear as similar through super-imposition. So in Rūpaka, Pariṇāma, Sandeha and Ullekha, āropaviṣaya is not concealed while it is concealed in Apahnuti. This different upameya is called upamāna, denying its own characteristics by the words signifying falsity, such as chala, vyāja, kapaṭa, miṣa etc. In Utprekṣā abheda becomes deeper and the poet wants to say that āropaviṣaya is āropyamāṇa. The way of adhyavasāya (certainty) is proved by using the words sambhāvana, abhimāna, tarka and ūha and manye, śaṅke, dhruvaṁ, nūnaṁ, iva, vā etc. while in Atiśayokti prominence of adhyavasāna comes with its perfection. Thus the difference between prakṛta totally disappears in Atiśayokti.

Thus the difference between the two, which exists in its full form in Upamālaṁkāra goes on decreasing slowly in these alaṁkāras. In Atiśayokti, it disappears totally as is evident from the study of the eighth chapter of the Ekāvalī.

CHAPTER VIII

ARTHĀLAMKĀRAS: GAMYASĀDṚŚYAMŪLAKA

In Gamyasādṛśyamūlakārthālaṁkāras[1] similarity is suggested. These alaṁkāras are Tulyayogitā, Dīpaka, Prativastūpamā, Dṛṣṭānta, Nidarśanā, Vyatireka, Sahokti, Vinokti, Samāsokti, Parikara, Parikarāṁkura, Śleṣa, Aprastutapraśaṁsā, Arthāntaranyāsa, Paryāyokta, Vyājastuti and Ākṣepa.

1. *Tulyayogitā*

The name 'Tulyayogitā' in itself is significant as it means 'connection (of prakṛta or aprakṛta) with the same property'.[2] The beauty of this figure depends on this connection.[3]

According to Vidyādhara,[4] when prakṛta or aprakṛta objects are connected with the same property (i.e. an attribute or an action) or when their similarity is implied, the figure is Tulyayogitā.

Kinds : Vidyādhara accepts its five divisions namely :

(i) all the prastuta attributes construed with guṇa;
(ii) all aprastuta with guṇa;
(iii) all prastuta with kriyā;
(iv) all aprastua with kriyā and
(v) śleṣapratibhotthāpitā.

In 'Pratyarthipṛthvīpatimānamardanaṁ...bhūpate',[5] crushing the pride of hostile kings who surrender themselves and worshipping the feet of Durgā, are all prakṛta. They are the attributes of

1. Ekā. VIII. 14.
2. *Ibid.* vṛtti on VIII. 15.
3. Udyota on KP. X. 104.
4. Ekā. VIII. 15.
5. *Ibid.* example under VIII. 15.

the king described and are construed with the property 'natural'. If 'vidyotate' (kriyāväckapada) were the reading instead of 'naisargikaṁ', the verse would have been an example of 'kriyātulyayogitā'.

In 'Garjaddurjaya...abhavat'[1] Mandāra, Kalpatree and Śeṣa are aprakṛta and with these objects the hand of the king is compared. They are connected with the property 'futile'.

If kriyāvācakapada 'nindyaḥ' is to be substituted for 'vyarthaḥ', the verse would have illustrated aprakṛta Tulyayogit ā.

Sometimes the figure is set up by Śleṣa, e.g. in 'Alaṁkārāvabaddhāni...pallavayanti te',[2] the two prakṛta objects, kāvyāni and arikulāni are construed with the same pada, alaṁkārāvabaddhāni or with the senses of alaṁkārāvabaddhāni. Though different, the letters are taken as one by the indentification of the two meanings 'full of figures' (in the case of property) and 'thrown into external confinement' (in the case of enemies).

Accepting the similar nature of Tulyayogitā, Mammaṭa[3] illustrates its two types viz. śuddhāprākaraṇika and śuddhāaprākaraṇika. Daṇḍin[4] and Bhoja[5] accept the figure in a little different way. They consider Tulyayogitā to occur where for the sake of praise or blame, a statement is made equating a thing with others possessing the particular quality prominently.

2. *Dīpaka*

This name has been given on the analogy of dīpaka, i.e. a lamp which throws light on many sides when kept on the threshold.[6]

---

1. Ekā. example under VIII. 15.
2. *Ibid.* example under VIII. 15.
3. K.P. vṛtti on X. 104.
4. KD. II. 330.
5. SKBh. IV. 166.
6. (a) Kāvyapradīpa on K.P. X. 103.
   (b) Sañjīvinī on AS. 24.
   (c) Jhalakīkara on KP. X. 103.

This is one of the four oldest alāṁkāras and is defined by Vidyādhara[1] as that where prakṛta and aprakṛta objects are grammatically connected with the same word denoting property. Similarity may be implied between an attribute or an action.

Kinds : Vidyādhara[2] first divides it into two kinds through use of dharma with prakṛta and aprakṛta. These two again may be subdivided into three through the use of dharma in the beginning, middle or at the end of a sentence. Thus it has six varieties. He also implies division of these three through kriyā and guṇa.

In 'Karoti na mudaṁ......yaśastava',[3] Ādiprakṛtadīpaka is illustrated. Here bimbaṁ, puṇḍarīkaṁ and yaśaḥ (of which the first two denote aprakṛta objects and the last prakṛta objects, because the king's glory is decribed and compared with the moon or a lotus) are connected with karoti, which stands in the beginning of a sentence nearer to aprakṛta.

In 'Kṣīrodavīcī......tvayā ca',[4] 'prakāśate' which expresses common property is in the middle near to bhānumatā, dinaśrīḥ that is aprakṛta. Thus this exemplifies Madhyāprakṛtadīpaka.

In 'Vīra Nṛsiṁha......mānyaṁ',[5] mānyaṁ, expressive of common property is in the end nearer to Gaṅgājalamādhuryaṁ i.e. aprakṛta. This illustrates Antaprakṛtadīpaka.

In the last two examples many aprakṛta and one prakṛta are connected with the action. In the first one aprakṛta and one prakṛta are connected with the same.

Thus the common property denotes action in all these three instances. Without citing the examples for those kinds where the common property consists of an attribute, he simply says that, in this way, the common property which denotes attribute may be cited.

---

1. Ekā. VIII. 16.
2. *Ibid*. vṛtti on VIII. 16.
3. *Ibid*. example under VIII. 16.
4. *Ibid*. example under VIII. 16.
5. *Ibid*. example under VIII. 16.

Some ācāryas accept Dīpakālṁkāra slightly in a different way. Daṇḍin[1] and Bhoja[2] opine that if by remaining in one place, a word indicating jāti (genus), kriyā (action), guṇa (quality) or dravya (the subject-matter) can help the entire sentence, then it is called Dīpaka. According to Rudraṭa[3] when there is one Kriyāpada for many vākyārthas, it is called Dīpakālṁkāra. Kuntaka[4] says that the matter which throws light upon the suggested property of the objects, which are appropriate to aucitya, beautiful and charming to the sahṛdayas is called Dīpaka. Mammaṭa,[5] Hemacandra[6] and Jayadeva[7] define it as that where the property of prastuta and aprastuta is presented only once in place of a word standing in case-relation to many actions.

Upamā is suggested in Dīpaka and Tulyayogitā alaṁkāras as there are no upamāvācaka words as īva and such others. In this way, one may say that here there is Upamādhvani, but there is no question of dhvanikāvya because the charm consists not in the suggested Upamā but rather in the expressed Dīpaka.

Dīpaka is distinct from Tulyayogitā, for in Dīpaka, ekadharmābhisambandha, connection with one dharma, exists between prakṛta and aprakṛta but in Tulyayogitā that connection exists only in Prastuta or aprastuta but not in both.

3. *Prativastūpamā*

Prativastu+Upamā means the similarity in the meaning of every sentence, vastu there meaning the sense of a sentence.[8] According to Vidyādhara,[9] the figure arises when the same

1. KD. II. 97.
2. SKBh. IV. 264.
3. KAR. VII. 64.
4. VJ. III. 17.
5. KP. X. 103.
6. KAnu. VI. 7.
7. Candrāloka. V. 53.
8. (a) Ekā. vṛtti on VIII. 17.
   (b) AS. vṛtti on 25.
9. Ekā. VIII. 17.

common property is expressed by different synonyms in sentences conveying the senses of upameya and upamāna.

Kinds : Vidyādhara[1] accepts two kinds of the figure which are through Sādharmya and vaidharmya and again divides it into two, the sādharmya being mentioned through the same and synonymous words.

In the example, 'Dātāraḥ kati na......Kailāsahelāmapi',[2] 'Nṛsiṁha ārohati', is upameyavākya and 'Cintāmaṇiprakriyāṁ kaścanamaṇi, kṣīrapayodhibhaṅgiṁ kaścana abdhi and Kailāsahelāṁ kaścana acalaḥ na adhyāste' are upamāvākyas. The sādhāraṇadharma is mentioned by two different synonyms tulāṁ nārohati and nādhyāste due to sādharmya.

In some cases the common characteristic is expressed in one sentence and implied in another e.g., 'Yāñcādainya...vṛkṣairapai.[3] Here in upameyavākya, sevyatāṁ expresses the common property, while in upamāvakya, the same property is implied by the words, 'when Mandāra stands before us, what is the use of thousands of other trees ?', which implies that one can resort to Mandāra alone. In both these sentences the comparison is positive.

In the verse 'Santoṣa kāraṇanipuṇo...koapyasti'[4] comparison is expressed by vaidharmya. So here is a contrast, the common property in the sentence expressive of the upameya being santoṣakaraṇanipuṇaḥ and of the upamāna being nānandadānacaturaḥ. It should be noted that similarity in this alaṁkārā is implied and not expressed by iva or other such words.

Prativastūpamā differs from Tulyayogitā and Dīpaka. Its chief characteristic is similarity in two vākyārthas, while in Tulyayogitā and Dīpaka, similarity exists only in padārtha.

1. Ekā. vṛtti on VIII. 17.
2. *Ibid.* example under VIII. 17.
3. *Ibid.* example under VIII. 17.
4. *Ibid.* example under VIII. 17.

4. *Dṛṣṭānta*

The figure Dṛṣṭānta is significantly named so because illustration in the sentence definitely clarifies the sense of the sentence.[1] Vidyādhara[2] opines that Dṛṣṭānta consists in the reflection of upamāna, upameya, their adjectives and sādhāraṇadharma through bimba-pratibimbabhāva. In bimbapratibimbabhāva characteristics of the objects and not the objects themselves are similar.

Kinds : Vidyādhara[3] explains two kinds of Dṛṣṭānta on the basis of sādharmya and vaidharmya. There is bimbapratibimbabhāva between the king and the lion, the destruction of enemies and elephants and arms and nails in the verse 'Tvamasi ripu...mṛgendraḥ'.[4] Tvamasi...Nṛsiṁhaḥ is an upameyavākya or one for which an illustration is given, while madakaraṭi...mṛgendraḥ, containing an illustration is called an upamānavākya. Here Nṛsiṁha and mṛgendra do not have one sādhāraṇadharma by which similarity may be expressed in the two but the quality of Nṛsiṁha ripunarādhinātha prakaṭabhujārgalavikramaḥ is quite similar to the quality of mṛgendra i.e. madakaraṭikaṭhorakumbhapīṭhīdalanadurantanakhāṅkuraḥ. Thus here similarity is based on bimbapratibimbabhāva in the two sentences. This is an example of sādharmyamūladṛṣṭānta.

'Api sahajamanoharaṁ...durbhagatvam',[5] illustrates Dṛṣṭānta by contrast. Here there is bimbapratibimbabhāva between poetry and pearl-necklace and 'marked by the merits of Nṛsiṁha' and 'united with large breasts' and a contrast between manojñaṁ bhavati and durbhagatva kalayati.

---

1. (a) Ekā, vṛtti on VIII. 18.
   (b) KP. vṛtti on X. 102.
   (c) Udyota on KP. X. 102.
2. Ekā. VIII. 18.
3. *Ibid.* vṛtti on VIII. 18.
4. *Ibid.* example under VIII. 18.
5. *Ibid.* example under VIII. 18.

Difference between Prativastūpamā, Dṛṣṭānta, Tulyayogitā and Dīpaka

Dṛṣṭānta and Prativastūpamā are quite similar both having vākyārthasādṛśya, yet the two differ on the nature of their similarity. Dṛṣṭānta consists of bimbapratibimbabhāva while Prativastūpamā is vastuprativastubhāvamūlaka.

In Dṛṣṭānta, Tulyayogitā and Dīpaka similarity is suggested but these differ from each other. Dṛṣṭānta has vākyārtha sādṛśya and so differs from Tulyayogitā and Dīpaka. The two latters have padārthasādṛśya. In this way all the three differ from Upamā also.

5. *Nidarśanā*

Nidarśanā means to give an illustration.[1] Vidyādhara[2] defines it as that when the possible or impossible relation between two objects implies similarity.

Nidarśanā has *two divisions* according to Vidyādhara,[3] namely, where the relation is possible and where it is impossible. The verse 'Yadapyekākinyo......kṣitipate',[4] cites padārthavṛttiḥ sambhavadvastusambandhaḥ Nidarśanā. Here the glory which remains pure even among serpents is compared to woman who though single and attractive is chaste, implying thus a relationship between glory and a chaste woman.

In 'Dṛpyaddurvāra...līlām',[5] the connection between the sky and the sportive charm of Kṛṣṇa is not possible. One thing can not bear the charm of another and the sentence simply implies a resemblance between the two qualities. It is not proper to resort to lakṣaṇā here to remove anvayānupapattiḥ, for it can be removed even by the superimposition of onething upon the other. Similarity is suggested here not by lakṣaṇā but by the force of sense, so this is

1. KP. vṛtti on X. 97.
2. Ekā. VIII. 19.
3. *Ibid.* vṛtti on VIII. 19.
4. *Ibid.* example under VIII. 19.
5. *Ibtd.* example under VIII. 19.

an example of padārthavṛttiḥ asambhavadvastusambandha Nidarśanā.

In 'Vīra Narasiṁhatejaḥ...vaḍa vāgnim',[1] the connection between one who wishes to glorify the Nṛsiṁha's greatness and one who throws submarine fire into the hollow of a fresh lotus is not possible and implies resemblance between them. This is an instance of vākyārthavṛtti Nidarśanā, because the verse implies a resemblance between the sense of two sentences.

In 'Yā caṇḍāṁśu...vidviṣaḥ',[2] the impropriety of the greatness of Nṛsiṁha's valour i.e. prakṛta as existing the forest fire, which is aprakṛta, is shown. It implies resemblance between pratāpa and dāvānala and is an example of asambhavadprakṛtadharmāropa on aprakṛta.

In the next instance 'Yaḥ Kailāsanivāsa......prekṣyate',[3] the greatness of the splendid waves of the heavenly Ganges is apratuta, but its glorious existence which is prastuta is impossible. Resemblance is consequently implied between the splendour of the waves of the Ganges and glory. This verse, therefore, exemplifies asambhavadaprakṛtadharmāropa on prakṛta.

The charm of this figure consists in the apprehension of identity between the senses of two words or two sentences, ending in conceiving resemblance between two things.

The earlier ācāryas define Nidarśanā in a different way. According to Bhāmana[4] it is employed to show through action only the specific meaning in the absence of the words yathā, iva and vati. Daṇḍin[5] says that in Nidarśanā a similar good or bad consequence is exhibited by connecting a thing with another object. Following Bhāmaha, Vāmana[6] says that it is the setting

1. Ekā. example under VIII. 19.
2. *Ibid.* example under VIII. 19.
3. *Ibid.* example under VIII. 19.
4. KAB. III. 33.
5. KD. II. 348.
6. KASV. IV-III. 20.

of a relation between the meaning and the word itself by pure kriyā. Bhoja[1] and Hemacandra[2] define it as when Dṛṣṭānta is given for the certainty of Prākaraṇika.

In Dṛṣṭānta, two sentences between which resemblance is implied are independent of each other, while in Nidarśanā they depend on each other.[3] Bimbapratibimbabhāva exists in both of them.

6. *Vyatireka*

According to Vidyādhara,[4] Vyatireka exists when upameya is described as superior to upamāna and when the distinction between them is predominant.

Kinds : Vidyādhara does not give any basis for its divisions, but his commentator, Mallinātha[5] accepts its twenty-four kinds.

In the verse 'Śrīmannutkalabhūmipāla...prāgiva',[6] the river of the king's charity is implied to be superior to other rivers (Śiprā, Narmadā, Godāvarī, Kālindī and Gaṅgā). This is because after having seen the former, the sea (the lord of rivers) dislikes others.

In 'Pavitra sadgotraṁ......apārijātaḥ',[7] the lord of Utkala, Nṛsiṁha, is upameya. Indra is upamāna and the last line shows that the latter is superior to the former. Indra is described as 'na apārijāta', one whose enemies are not destroyed or one who is not without pārijāta and the king as apārijāta (one whose enemies are destroyed). Here both the causes of Vyatireka, viz., the superiority of upameya over upamāna and the inferiority of

1. SKBh. III. 111.
2. KAnu. VI. 6.
3. (a) Ekā. vṛtti on VIII. 19.
   (b) AS. vṛtti on 27.
4. Ekā. VIII. 20.
5. Taralā on Ekā. VIII. 20.
6. Ekā. example under VIII. 20.
7. *Ibid.* example under VIII. 20.

upamāna to upameya, are expressed, the former by tvamapārijātaḥ and the latter by eṣa nāpārijātaḥ. The similarity between upamāna and upameya is implied in the first two lines. These contain the śliṣṭa word pavitrasadgotra. The king is pavitrasadgotra in the sense one who has good and holy family and Indra is pavitrasadgotra in the sense of one whose thunderbolt is feared by mountains.

Vyatireka differs from Upamā and Upameyopamā having bhedaprādhānya between both upamāna and upmeya. Upamā and Upameyopamā have the prādhānya of bheda and abheda both. *It differs from Rūpaka and Pariṇāma also* because they have only abhedaprādhānya.

7. *Sahokti*

Saha+ukti, i.e. Sahokti literally means 'to say connectedly'. Vidyādhara[1] defines Sahokti as that when the prominence of either upameya or upamāna is mentioned the other being related as 'sahārtha—together with'. The connection of a verb with upameya is direct and expressed while that with upamāna is implied through the force of the word 'saha'. Here what is connected with 'saha' is 'apradhāna' by a Pāṇini Sūtra[2] and that is upamāna while the other is pradhāna i.e. upameya.

Kinds : Based on Atiśayokti, Vidyādhara divides it into three. Adhyavasāyamūlā may have two subdivisions through existence or absence of Śleṣa.

In 'Saṅgrāmāṅgaṇabhūṣaṇasya...ullaṅghitam',[3] hostile kings are described as fleeing in different directions along with Nṛsiṁha's arrows. Though the arrows are the causes of their flight, their discharge is described as contemporaneous with the flight of enemies which is the effect. The figure is thus based on Atiśayokti in which the order of the precedence of cause and effect is left. The connection of bhūmipatibhiḥ with dikcakramullaṅghitaṁ is

1. Ekā. VIII. 21.
2. Aṣṭādhyāyī, II-III. 19.
3. Ekā. example under VIII. 21.

expressed and direct, while that of mārgaṇaiḥ with it is implied through the force of the sense of 'saha'.

In 'Raṇe vīra Nṛsiṁhasya......paripanthinaḥ',[1] the figure is based on the identification (caused by śleṣa) of the two different words pride (mada, in case of enemies) and ichoral juice (in case of elephants).

The previous ācāryas define Sahokti in a different way. According to Bhāmaha,[2] Udbhaṭa[3] and Vāmana,[4] Sahokti occurs when two actions are simultaneously connected with two things but are mentioned by a single word. In Agnipurāṇa[5] and according to Daṇḍin[6] and Hemacandra,[7] it is the statement, conjunctly, of the qualities and actions of things. Rudraṭa[8] defines in vāstava and aupamya categories and in both places it is generally the same. When upameya is similar to upamāna, which is well-known and has many verbs with the word saha or its synonym, it is called Sahokti.[9] It also arises where a verb is described which has one karttā and many karma.[10] According to Kuntaka,[11] Sahokti is to mention a meaning twice in order to portray the proper sense through only one sentence. Bhoja takes it as ubhayālaṁkāra. According to him, to mention many subjects etc. with others in one Kriyā etc. which are different or not different is called Sahokti[12]. Mammaṭa[13] defines it as where one expression,

---

1. Ekā. example under VIII. 21.
2. KAB. III. 39.
3. KASS. V. 15.
4. KASV. IV-III. 21.
5. Agnipurāṇa, 344-23.
6. KD. II. 351.
7. KAnu. VI. 13.
8. KAR. VII. 13.
9. *Ibid.* VIII. 99.
10. *Ibid.* VIII. 101.
11. VJ. III. 37.
12. SKBh. IV. 181.
13. KP. X. 112.

on the strength of a word signifying 'together with', conveys two senses. Jayadeva[1] opines that it exists when Sahabhāva is very charming.

8. *Vinokti*

Vidyādhara[2] defines Vinokti as that when even without a certain good or bad object, another one is described as its reverse. The two kinds of the figure are discussed in the very definition, namely, the thing which is sometimes bad and sometimes good.

In 'Na tvadvairivadhūvaktraṁ......kṣitimaṇḍana',[3] the face is described as not shining without beauty and the moon without light. In 'Vinā padmākaro......sabhā',[4] a lake is described as shining without crocodiles, sandal without serpents and the council of Nṛsiṁha-rogues.

There is no divergence of opinion with regard to its nature or kinds.

9. *Samāsokti*

The name Samāsokti is called so because it conveys two ideas in brief.[5] According to Vidyādhara[6] when from the force of adjectives common to prakṛta and aprakṛta, aprakṛta is inferred from prakṛta, the figure is called Samāsokti. Āropviṣaya appears with the padārtha-dharma of aropyamāṇa.[7] It means that through dharmasamāropa (vyavahārasamāropa) aprastuta is suggested through prastuta.

Kinds : Vidyādhara cites three kinds or Sāmāsokti viz., the adjectives may be śliṣṭa, aupamyagarbha or sādhāraṇa. In the

1. Candrāloka. V. 60.
2. Ekā. VIII. 22.
3. *Ibid.* example under VIII. 22.
4. *Ibid.* example under VIII. 22.
5. (a) Ekā. vṛtti on VIII. 22.
   (b) KAB. II. 79.
   (c) KD. II. 205.
6. Ekā. VIII. 23.
7. *Ibid.* vṛtti on VIII. 23.

verse 'Guṇapraṇayinī...mudam',[1] through the force of the common property. i.e. property found in prastuta and aprastuta, dhanurvallī is apprehended. It is characterized by the attributes of a woman, without giving up its own nature. The common property consists of an attribute viz., guṇapraṇayitva, muṣṭigrāhyamadhyātva and suvaṁśajātva which have two meanings, one connected with dhanurvallī and the other with strī. In this example the adjectives are śliṣṭa.

In 'Viśālavalabhībhujān......vipinapāvakajvālikā',[2] they are aupamyagarbha. Here, through the force of the similarity of attributes arising from the power of compounds showing resemblance (upamāsamāsa) viz., viśālavalbhībhujān and others, houses, and flames are apprehended as characterized by the attributes of a nāyaka and a nāyikā.

The śloka 'Viśrāṇanaistaiḥ......ca puṣpaiḥ',[3] illustrates the implication of aprastuta from prastuta which consists of an action. Here kalpadruma and latā are apprehended as nāyaka and nāyikā since they have the common property of the action of speaking etc.

In 'Dhāṭīṁ vīra......muhuḥ',[4] adjectives are sādhāraṇa, i.e., they apply both to trees and to a lover. Here Samāsokti alaṁkāra is set up by the samāsa 'śākhābhujaiḥ', which may be dissolved either as śākhā eva bhujāḥ taiḥ or śākhā bhujāḥ iva taiḥ, for ākarṣaṇa and other actions can be performed either by branches or hands. As there is neither sādhaka nor bādhaka pramāṇa in favour of Upamāsamāsa or Rūpakasamāsa or of Upamā or Rūpaka, there is a Saṁkara of Upamā and Rūpaka caused by the uncertainty about them.

However, where there is a certainty about Rūkapa even though it is possible to arrive at a common property by disolving the samāsa (containing the Rūpaka) in another way, it does not

1. Ekā. example under VIII. 23.
2. *Ibid.* example under VIII. 23.
3. *Ibid.* example under VIII. 23.
4. *Ibid.* example under VIII. 23.

become a ground for Samāsokti. Samāsokti is useless as the second sense is suggested by Ekadeśavivarttirūpaka.

In 'Dhāvantīr-Narasiṁha...puṣpandhayānāṁrutaiḥ',[1] creepers are described as consoling the wives of enemies by mercy. Mercy, a quality of animate objects, is conceived as existing in creepers. To establish its existence, it is quite proper that they should be described as friends. If Rūpaka and Samāsokti both suit the description, one should accept Rūpaka and not Samāsokti. The compound prasūnekṣaṇaiḥ must be dissolved as prasūnānyeva ikṣaṇāni taiḥ and not prasūnāni ikṣaṇānīva taiḥ for the act of seeing can be accomplished by eyes and not by flowers. So the compound must be taken as favouring Rūpaka. It is Ekadeśavivarttirūpaka, because the superimposition of ikṣaṇa on prastuta which is expressed suggests that of sakhī on latā. The apprehension of this Rūpaka also becomes a ground for Utprekṣā, which consists in conceiving of mercy in creepers.

Through the very force of adjectives common to prastuta and aprastuta, Samāsokti brings out the idea of the aprastuta or upamāna which is not expressed. Upamāna therefore should not be expressed. In the instance 'Vidhurīkurvan...te khaḍgaḥ',[2] the idea of the lover, which is aprastuta, is implied through the very power of common properties, such as opening the braid of hair, rubbing out pointed marks on cheeks and so on. If, therefore, Upamā is used as in kām iva, there would be a repetition of sense. Upamā, therefore, should not be employed where Samāsokti has scope.

Daṇḍin,[3] Vāmana,[4] Bhoja[5] and Jayadeva[6] do not give prominence to 'adjective'. According to them in order to define something the poet defines another similar thing briefly. According

1. Ekā. example under VIII. 23.
2. *Ibid.* example under VIII. 23.
3. KD. II. 205.
4. KASV. IV-III. 3.
5. SKBh. IV. 133.
6. Candrāloka. V. 62.

to Kuntaka,[1] Samāsokti exists when something is said with Śleṣa but other alaṁkāras constitute no charm. It is to be noted that whenever Śleṣa is used generally there should be other alaṁkāras like Upamā. According to Hemacandra[2] Samāsokti arises when viśeṣaṇas having Śleṣa give the idea of upamāna.

Superimposition is common in Samāsokti, Pariṇāma and Rūpakālaṁkāras. But in Rūpaka there is only uparañjaktva. In Pariṇāma, there is superimposition of actions but there āropaviṣaya becomes subordinate, while in Samāsokti there is prominence of āropaviṣaya having vyavahārasamāropa.[3] As in Samāsokti, upamānārtha is suggested through upameya, thus it has the vyaṅgyārtha which however is not prominent. If prominent, it is called Dhvani by Dhvanivādis, but where subordinate, it is called guṇībhūtavyaṅgya by them. In this way, Samāsokti may be similar to guṇībhūtavyaṅgya.

10. *Parikara*

According to Vidyādhara[4] significant adjectives suggest another meaning than the one expressed in Parikarālaṁkāra. The suggested sense is to help the expressed sense in this alaṁkāra.

Vidyādhara has not divided the figure and has given the following example only, i.e. 'Narasiṁha narendreṇa......kṛtā'.[5] Here the adjectives nandanadrumabāhunā and dhaneśāṁśāvatāreṇa suggest the king's generosity and opulence.

11. *Parikarāṁkura*

According to Vidyādhara,[6] Parikarāṁkura is found when the viśeṣyas are significant. It is thus the opposite of Parikara and therefore follows it.

1. VJ. III. 147 Antarśloka.
2. KAnu. VI. 14.
3. Ekā. vṛtti on VIII. 23.
4. *Ibid.* VIII. 24.
5. *Ibid.* example under VIII. 24.
6. *Ibid.* VIII. 25.

In 'Narasiṁhamahīpāla...bhuvanatrayam',[1] the substantive tripathagā is significant. It suggests the idea of fitness for the purification of the three worlds. Suggesting this sense it assists and beautifies the expressed sense. The suggested sense being thus subordinate to the expressed sense, this is not dhvani, but comes under guṇībhūtavyaṅgya. The substantive in this verse suggests a meaning by its etymological sense yoga (as trībhiḥ pathibhirgachatīti tripathagā). Sometimes it may suggets a meaning by convention. Here the substantive, though not used to suggest the meaning directly, does so by convention.

In 'Nāthaḥ kākodarāṇāṁ......kṣitīndra',[2] the substantives kākodaranātha and kārttavīrya suggest the idea of sahasramukhatva and sahasrakaratva by prasiddhi. This suggested sense helps in the development and embellishment of the expressed sense.

12. *Śleṣa*

The word 'śleṣa' is derived from the root śliṣ, that means where more than one meaning is cling together. Bharata[3] places it under guṇa. The same śleṣa then came into the province of alaṁkāra according to śabda and artha. So, it has been discussed as both śabdālaṁkāra and arthālaṁkāra. According to Mammaṭa if an alaṁkāra disappears with the change of words, it is śabdālaṁkāra and if it remains as it is, even by changing the words, it is arthālaṁkāra.[4] He holds that not āśrayāśrayibhāva but anvaya and vyatireka must be worked upon as a test for deciding whether a guṇa, a doṣa or an alaṁkāra belongs to words and sense. One shall have to resort to anvaya and vyatireka finally, since āśrayāśrayibhāva does not exist independent of anvaya and vyatireka.[5]

Vidyādhara[6] accepts śleṣa only as an arthālaṁkāra. According to him, when the resemblance between two objects is only verbal

1. Ekā. example under VIII. 25.
2. *Ibid.* example under VIII. 25.
3. NS. 16-96.
4. Ekā. vṛtti on VIII. 26.
5. KP. vṛtti on X. 141.
6. Ekā. VIII. 26.

and pertains to both adjectives and noun qualified by them and when they convey two meanings both applicable to prakṛta or to aprakṛta, the figure is Śleṣa.

Kinds : Vidyādhara, gives two varieties of Śleṣa, for the objects may both be prakṛta or aprakṛta. Here the noun qualified by attributes expresses two meanings referring to similar objects, i.e. to objects that are both prakṛta or both aprakṛta. In 'Kandarpodayaṁ...parābhūtayaḥ',[1] both the liberality and bravery of Narasiṁha have to be described. The meanings of friends and enemies are therefore both connected with the context. Bhavatomitraiḥ is thus equal to bhavatomitraiḥ, or bhavato amitraiḥ. Mitra or amitra are both prakṛta and the adjectives kandarpodayamāśrayadbhiḥ etc. convey two meanings, one referring to mitraiḥ and the other to amitraiḥ. This is, therefore, an instance of kevalaprakṛtagocaraḥ Śleṣaḥ.

'Nijakarakalitasvāhaṁ......jayati'[2] is an instance of kevalāprakṛtagocaraḥ Śleṣaḥ. Here vibhāvasu means both fire and sun; its attributes also nijakarakalitasvāhaṁ etc. convey two senses, one connected with fire and the other with the sun. It is thus represented as the upamāna of tejas and is therefore aprakṛta.

Where the expressive power of words is restricted to the sense of the described object by context or other restricting causes,[3] and where though aprakṛta cannot be expressed but is apprehended, there is dhvani,[4] as in—

hiraṇyakaśipukṣetradānadarśitavismayaḥ/
na kasya ślāghanīyo asi Narasiṁha jagatpate//[5]

To remove the confusion between Śabdāśaktimūlādhvani and Śleṣa, Ānandavardhana clearly distinguished them. When the vastu and alaṁkāra both appear through the śabdaśakti, there

1. Ekā. example under VIII. 26.
2. *Ibid.* example under VIII. 26.
3. Vākyapadīya (Bhartṛhari)—Quoted in KP. under II. 19.
4. Ekā. vītti on VIII. 26.
5. *Ibid.* example under VIII. 26.

must be dhvani. When only two vastus appear through śabda-śakti there would be Śleṣa. Śleṣa may also appear when the alaṁkāras are denoted directly through śabdaśakti. When they do not appear through śabdaśakti but are guessed, there should be dhvani.[1]

The earlier ācāryas Bhāmaha[2] and Vāmana[3] opine that Śliṣṭa occurs where there is similarity of upameya with upamāna through guṇa, kriyā and saṁjñā.

Śleṣa differs from Samāsokti in as much as here the resemblance pertains to both the noun and its adjectives. Samāsokti concerns only adjectives. It is also different from Tulyayogitā since there, the noun does not convey two meanings.

13. *Aprastutapraśaṁsā*

The very name 'Aprastutapraśaṁsā' suggests statement of aprastuta. Here praśaṁsā does not mean 'praise', but is only equivalent to description.

Vidyādhara[4] defines Aprastutapraśaṁsā as that where prastuta is suggested from the description of aprastuta through sāmyaviśeṣabhāva, sārūpyabhāva and kāryakāraṇabhāva. Here the description of aprastuta is improper, because it is aprastuta (for what is aprastuta cannot be described). To bring about propriety in it, therefore, it must be taken to be implying prastuta. Prastuta, which is suggested, brings about the accomplishment of the aprastuta. which is expressed. It is, therefore, an instance of vācyasiddhyaṅgaguṇībhūtavyaṅgya where the suggested is subordinate to the expressed sense. Dhvani does not exist here.

Kinds : Vidyādhara[5] accepts its five divisions; the matter under consideration being the effect or the cause or a general fact or a particular one, a statement of the other (correlate) and the

1. DhL. vṛtti on II. 21.
2. KAB. III. 14-15.
3. KASV. IV-III. 7.
4. Ekā. VIII. 27.
5. *Ibid.* vṛtti on VIII. 27.

statement of an equal (the matter under consideration being its equal).

The verse 'Dayāyaiḥ dṛk karṇaḥ......kṣitipate',[1] is an instance of the viśeṣa being implied from the sāmānya. Here 'I have been obliged by your excessive distribution' etc., is viśeṣaprastuta which is implied and 'what is not to be given to whom by you ?', is sāmānya aprastuta and also expressed.

'Nṛsiṁha vasudhādhipa......dvipāḥ',[2] illustrates the sāmānya being implied from the viśeṣa. Here the idea—which kings do not experience woe from the king Narasiṁha who lusts for battle—being sāmānya prastuta is implied from viśeṣa aprastuta, of the hostile kings.

'Kṣīrodo lavaṇodavat...sfurantyagrataḥ',[3] exemplifies kāryāt kāraṇapratīti. Here kṣīroda, Kumudinī etc. being the upamānas are aprastuta and kīrtti being the upameya is prastuta. From the aprastuta kārya kṣīrasāgara etc. and the possibility being of lavaṇārṇava etc., the kāraṇa extra-ordinary kīrtti being prastuta is implied.

In the verse 'Bāhuste Narasiṁha......vidhim',[4] the implied kāraṇa suggested kārya. The king is asked about the condition of the wives of the hostile kings. This is kārya suggested through the stated kāraṇa.

In 'Eṇaśreṇī...karīndraḥ',[5] the similar tree being aprastuta and vācya, the similarity being prastuta it is implied that the king Narasiṁha is capable of protecting even the great. So here no superimposition of the suggested on the expressed sense is necessary. This is necessary where inanimate objects are addressed or represented as animate objects.

---

1. Ekā. example. under VIII. 27.
2. *Ibid.* example under VIII. 27.
3. *Ibid.* example under VIII. 27.
4. *Ibid.* example under VIII. 27.
5. *Ibid.* example under VIII. 27.

The nature of Aprastutapraśaṁsā was accepted variously by various ācāryas. Daṇḍin[1] opines that where redundant praise of an object is made there occurs Aprastutapraśaṁsā. Vāmana[2] defines it as consisting in any statement of upameya only through liṅgamātra. Terming it as Anyokti, Rudraṭa[3] defines it as when such an upameya is suggested through the upamāna described, which (upameya) though different from the adjectives of the upamāna, still has the same form (actions). According to Kuntaka[4] when aprastuta suggests prastuta through simile or any other connection or the suggested prastuta vākyārtha does not exist, it is called Aprastutapraśaṁsā. Bhoja[5] defines it as the statement of aprastuta (astotavya) owing to any hetu denoted or suggested. Mammaṭa[6] very simply believes it to be the statement of something not considered on the basis of that under consideration. According to Ānandavardhana and Abhinavagupta in Aprastutapraśaṁsā, the expressed sense and the suggested sense are equally prominent.[7]

14. *Arthāntaranyāsa*

The word Arthāntaranyāsa literally means 'to place some other sense'. This figure follows Aprastutapraśaṁsā in its treatment because here, too, aprastuta is mentioned.

According to Vidyādhara,[8] where a particular statement which is prastuta is strengthened by a general statement, or a general statement which is prastuta by a particular statement, the figure is Arthāntaranyāsa. It is represented here as supporting the prastuta. The prastuta must be regarded by the speaker to require, strengthening and the aprastuta can support the prastuta.

---

1. KD. II. 340.
2. KASV. IV-III. 4.
3. KAR, VIII. 74.
4. VJ. III. 23.
5. SKBh. IV. 158.
6. KP. X. 98.
7. DhL. vṛtti on I. 13.
8. Ekā. VIII. 28.

Kinds : Vidyādhara stands singular in accepting two divisions of Arthāntaranyāsa in the definition, namely, the general corroborated by the particular or vice versa, by similarity only.

In the verse 'Lakṣmīste paricārikā...striyaḥ',[1] the particular 'Lakṣmī embraces you' is strengthened by the general 'mantraśakti' by resemblance.

In 'Vīraḥ sarvānapi...Utkalakṣoṇipālaḥ',[2] the general sakalavīravṛttāntaḥ is strengthened by the particular 'Narasiṁha narapativṛttānta' by resemblance.

Vidyādhara has not accepted Arthāntaranyāsa through dissimilarity which is accepted by Rudraṭa, Mammaṭa and Ruyyaka.

The difference between Arthāntaranyāsa and Dṛṣṭānta lies in the fact that in the former the sāmarthya and samarthaka statements are respectively general and particular or vice-versa, while in Dṛṣṭānta, both are general or both particular. The use of the plural number for a noun serves the same purpose as its repetition. In Arthāntaranyāsa the noun in the general statement must be used in the plural number qualified by an adjective like sarva. So that, vyāpti which shows invariable connection of the vyāpya and the vyāpaka may be suggested. Otherwise there would be Vācyāvacanadoṣa.

15. *Paryāyokta*

According to Vidyādhara,[3] when the cause, though suggeted is expressed in another way as effect, the figure is Paryāyokta.

In the instance 'Aspṛṣṭāñjanasampadaḥ......pṛthvībujām'[4] the destruction of enemies is the cause of their having discarded collyrium and ornaments. The cause is suggested and the effect expressed. In fact, the cause is suggested through the expression of the effect. Moreover, the greatness of the power of king

---

1. Ekā. example under VIII. 28.
2. *Ibid.* example under VIII. 28.
3. *Ibid.* VIII. 29.
4. *Ibid.* example under VIII. 29.

Nṛsiṁha is the subject of description and it is equally described through the cause i.e. the destruction of enemies and the effect i.e. the actions indicative of the mourning of their widows. Both the cause and effect, therefore, being the result of the greatness of Nṛsiṁha's power, are prastuta or subjects of description. Such description of the cause through its effect is more charming than if it were described directly.

Kuntaka[1] defines Paryāyokta in a different manner. He says that it exists there where is, in a sentence, corroboration with a sense other than the one which should be stated.

The difference betwcen Paryāyokta and Aprastutapraśaṁsā is that in Aprastutapraśaṁsā Prastutakāraṇa is suggested from aprastutakārya. In other words, of the cause and the effect, one is prastuta and the other is aprastuta, while in Paryāyokta, both kārya and kāraṇa are prastuta. In Paryāyokta, though there is vyaṅgya, it is not predominant. It is subordimate to the vācya which is more charming than the vyaṅgya. So it is guṇībhūta-vyaṅgya and not dhvani.

16. *Vyājastuti*

According to Vidyādhara,[2] if when the praise of an object is begun, censure is implied in some way or when the censure of an object is begun, praise is somehow implied, the figure is Vyājastuti. The particular nature of the speaker, the person addressed, the context etc. are important in this figure.[3] When an object is to be censured and its praise is refuted by the context, it ends in censure or conveys the ultimate idea of censure. Similarly, when an object is desired to be praised, its censure being disapproved by the context, ends in praise.

Kinds : Vidyādhara accepts two divisions of the figure in the very definition. In 'Prāṇeśvara...induḥ',[4] there is outward praise

1. VJ. III. 24.
2. Ekā. VIII. 30.
3. (a) Ekā. vṛtti on VIII. 30.
   (b) Skt. commentary Vimarśinī on AS. 37.
4. Ekā example under VIII. 30.

and final censure. 'You are happy like the persons of your category' is stuti which implies censure, that is, 'You are attached with other'.

In 'Diṅgamātaṅgāḥ...avalepaḥ',[1] there is outward censure and final praise. 'The elephants of the quarters, Sumeru (mountain of gold) etc. were not given to the beggers', contains censure which implies praise that everything, except these, have been given to them (yācakas).

In both these varieties, the suggested sense is not predominant, but simply goes to enrich the expressed sense. This is therefore, guṇībhūtavyaṅgya and not dhvani.

Vyājastuti is different from Aprastutapraśaṁsā; though in both prastuta is implied from the description of aprastuta but in Vyājastuti, something additional viz. Prastutanindā is implied from apratutastuti or vice versa. Moreover, in Vyājastuti, there is no relation of general and particular or of similarity between prastuta and aprastuta as there is in Aprastuta-praśaṁsā.

17. *Ākṣepa*

According to Vidyādhara,[2] Ākṣepa is the semblance of denial or suppression of what has been said or will be said, in order to express something particular about it. Another sort of Ākṣepa consists in the semblance of affirmation of what is not desired to be expressed ending in its denial.[3] The word 'Ākṣepa' meaning that which implies or suggests something is thus significant in both varieties of the figures.

Kinds : Vidyādhara divides it first into two i.e. pertaining to what has already been said and to what is to be said. In the first variety sometimes the object itself is denied and sometimes it is not mentioned. In the second variety, the mention of the object is denied and not the object itself. But here also sometimes the

1. Ekā. example under VIII. 30.
2. *Ibid.* VIII. 31.
3. *Ibid.* VIII. 32.

mention of what is desired to be expressed generally is denied and sometimes it is partly denied. Thus Ākṣepa has four varieties.

In 'Nāhaṁ dūtī bhavāmi...sūryakāntaiḥ',[1] which is said by a dūti, the object dūtitva which has already been mentioned is denied. The denial implies affirmation suggesting a particular meaning, viz.. not in the habit of telling lies like a dūti. This suggested meaning simply develops the expressed sense, confirming the truth of the opening of sun-lotuses, the losing of moon-lotuses, the delight of Cakravāka birds and the shining of sun-gems caused by the heat of the bodies of the wives of your enemies.

The mention of the object is denied in 'Kiṁ tvāṁ brūmaḥ... Śrīnṛsiṁha'.[2] Here the mention of king Nṛsiṁha as merciful, wellbehaved, free from the desire of slaughter and obeyed by his people, which is put forth in the words kṛpāluṁ, sadvṛttaṁ, hiṁsāśūnyaṁ manaḥ and ājñā is denied and suggests a particular meaning namely the extraordinary heroism and generosity of the king.

In denying what is about to be said, the denial of the mention of what is generally accepted is illustrated by 'Kṣaṇaṁ pratīkṣasva...kim'.[3] Here the mention of vakṣyamāṇārtha, generally accepted in the words 'ayaṁ janaḥ kiñcidudīrayiṣyati' is denied in the words 'udiraṇena kiṁ'. Thus here the denial of the mention of what is desired to be expressed generally, is objectionable and ends in affirmation, suggesting the particular sense of the beloved having resolved to put an end to her life.

The last variety of particular denial is illustrated in 'Kāntaḥ kiṁ kairaviṇyāḥ...vicitraiḥ'.[4] Here the poet says to king Nṛsiṁha, 'your glory is difficult to be imitated by others how much of it can I describe then !' Hence a part is described by comparing him to the moon, the sun and Kṛṣṇa and a part is denied and it suggests the particular sense of the praise of indescribable glory.

---

1. Ekā. example under VIII. 31.
2. *Ibid.* example under VIII. 31.
3. *Ibid.* example under VIII. 31.
4. *Ibid.* example under VIII. 31.

In 'Tvaṁ cedgacchasi gaccha...āseduṣaḥ',[1] the departure of the lover is disliked by his beloved. When therefore it is outwardly approved, then there is apparent affirmation of what is not desired to be affirmed. Moreover it suggests the denial of his going forth by showing that Nṛsiṁha kills those enemies who face him on the battle-field. This variety is represented here, because in it also as in the first variety something is suggested. In this figure also the suggested sense is not so charming as the expressed and is therefore subordinate to it. This again is therefore guṇībhūta-vyaṅgya but not dhvani.

It is thus noted that to constitute this figure denial must be apparent and must not end in affirmation. So, in Ākṣepa, affirmation is implied from negation. This figure does not exist where denial is final.

In Tulyayogitā, Dīpaka, Prativastūpamā, Dṛṣṭānta and Nidarśanā sādṛśya being suggested appears clearly. These names are synonymous to sādṛśya. In Vyatireka, the upamāna is changed into upameya and vice versa. The sādṛśya does not disappear but the idea that upameya is similar to upamāna, is suggested and not expressed. Due to the opposite use of upamāna and upameya, the similarity becomes more concealed here than in previous alaṁkāras.

In Sahokti, similarity with others is suggested through the word 'saha'. In ordinary sentences, when it is said that 'Devadatta goes with his brother' similarity is not found there, but in poetry, with the word saha, the poet conveys the idea of similarity between the two, although it is more concealed than it was in previous alaṁkāras.

In Samāsokti, there is not a single sign for similarity between prakṛta and aprakṛta but to only adjectives (having double meaning), readers have a shadow of aprakṛta and then upamānopameyabhāva arises. In Arthāntaranyāsa, the use of adjectives with double meaning also disappears. Only the use of two

1. Ekā. example under VIII. 32.

sentences, in which one expresses the general idea and the other the particular one, connected with sāmarthya-samarthakabhāva, suggests similarity. In Paryāyokti, Vyājastuti and Ākṣepa, similarity is totally concealed and the charm of these alaṁkāras depend only on suggestion.

In this way, in these alaṁkāras, the concealment of the suggested similarity goes on increasing gradually and in Arthāntaranyāsa, it becomes more and more concealed. In other alaṁkāras like Paryāyokti, Vyājastuti and Ākṣepa tbe similarity is so concealed that it is not possible for a reader of general poetry to find it but it may only be inferred.

CHAPTER IX

ARTHĀLAṀKĀRAS

(a) Sādṛśyetaramūlaka
(b) Ubhayālaṁkāras

Sādṛśyetaramūlakārthālaṁkāras

As the name denotes, these alaṁkāras depend on any reason other than Sādṛśya.

(1) *Virodha*

Virodha is the first of Sādṛśyetaramūlakārthālaṁkāras. Virodha actually represents virodhābhāsa i.e. semblance of conflict since genuine Virodha is a negation of yogyatā; it has no place in poetry.

Vidyādhara[1] defines it as where opposition between two objects is apparent.

Kinds : Vidyādhara[2] states its ten divisions namely virodha exists between jātis; jāti and guṇa; jāti and kriyā and jāti and dravya, similarly between guṇas; guṇa and krīyā and guṇa and dravya; so on and so forth. In the verse 'Yaśonidhe......eṣaḥ',[3] Virodha exists between the jātis namely kara and karṇa in the previous half and between jāti and guṇa, dhārādharatva and tāpakārītva in the later half.

The verse 'Aśrāntaviśrāṇanakelikautukaḥ......vāmanīkṛtāḥ',[4] contains Virodha between digdanti and vāmanīkaraṇa, i.e. jāti and kriyā.

---

1. Ekā. VIII. 33.
2. *Ibid.* VIII. 34-35.
3. *Ibid.* example under VIII. 35.
4. *Ibid.* example under VIII. 35.

In the example 'Śailāḥ sarvepi...kīrttibhiḥ'.[1] Virodha is found between jāti, namely śaila and sindhu and dravya, i.e. Kailāsa and Surasindhu.

'Paradāraparopi...bhavān'[2] contains virodha between guṇas namely paradāraparatva and paradāraparāṅmukhatva.

In 'Cāpasthitaguṇasya...nareśvara',[3] there is virodha between guṇa, viz., cāpasthitaguṇasya and kriyā vyāpti.

In 'Karpūrahāra...abhavat'[4] virodha exists between guṇa, viz., viśadatva and dravya i.e., pitāmbaratva.

The example 'Sa jayati vīra...rañjayati',[5] contains virodha between kriyās namely rañjana and arañjana.

'Vismayamasau...sarvatodikkam',[6] contains Virodha between kumudodañcana kriyā and tapanadravya.

In 'Āyodhana...deva',[7] there is virodha between dravyas viz., ugra and Kṛṣṇa. It should be noted that this figure requires that the object in which two things (jāti, guṇa, kriyā or dravya) are represented as apparently opposed, is the same.

Bhāmaha, Rudraṭa and Jayadeva define virodha in a different way. According to Bhāmaha[8] the expression of something contradictory to the quality or action of varṇyavastu, for establishing its excellence is called Virodha. According to Rudraṭa[9] Virodha exists where jāti; dravya, guṇa and kriyā which are completely opposed to each other are present simultaneously. Thus, Rudraṭa does not say anything about ābhāsatva. Jayadeva[10] opines that

---

1. Ekā. example under VIII. 35.
2. *Ibid.* example under VIII. 35.
3. *Ibid.* example under VIII. 35.
4. *Ibid.* example under VIII. 35.
5. *Ibid.* example under VIII. 35.
6. *Ibid.* example under VIII. 35.
7. *Ibid.* example under VIII. 35.
8. KAB. III. 25.
9. KAR. IX. 30.
10. Candrāloka, V. 74.

when there is asaṅgati about jāti, guṇa, dravya and kriyā there is Virodhālaṁkāra.

(2) *Vibhāvanā*

According to Vidyādhara,[1] Vibhāvanā is the manifestation of an effect in the absence of a well-known cause.

Kinds : Vidyādhara accepts four divisions of Vibhāvanā namely mālārupā and kevalā. Either of these may be uktanimittā or anuktanimittā. 'Ayajñaḥ svarlokaḥ...agamaḥ',[2] illustrates mālārupā anuktanimittā Vibhāvanā. Here svarloka, sukṛta, sudhāsāra, phala, sāmrājya and nidhi are respresented as effects that take place without their established causes, such as yajñaḥ, tapaḥ, abhra, kusuma, śaurya and khanana. Rūpaka shows these effects as identical with king Narasiṁha.

'Bhūtyā bhāsaya...bhavānīśvarah'[3] exemplifies kevala uktanimittā Vibhāvanā. Here the effect, viz., the knowledge of Nṛsiṁha as God Śiva is represented as being produced without its well-known causes, viz., putting ashes on the body etc. Another reason for it is that Nṛsiṁha is an extra-ordinary man (lokottuṅga). Moreover, here the two meanings of bhūti etc. conveyed by Śleṣa are identified by Atiśayokti. Thus there is saṁkara of the figures of Vibhāvanā and Atiśayokti, set up by the idea of śleṣa.

(3) *Viśeṣokti*

Like Vibhāvanā, Viśeṣokti is a figure based on Virodhābhāsa in the field of kāryakāraṇabhāva. The word 'Viśeṣokti' means a statement made to point out its speciality.[4] According to Vidyādhara[5], if the effect is not produced, even when the causes are stated, this is called Viśeṣokti alaṁkāra.

Kinds : Vidyādhara accepts two varieties of the figure namely uktanimittā or when the reason, for the effect not being produced

1. Ekā. VIII. 36.
2. *Ibid.* example under VIII. 36.
3. *Ibid.* example under VIII. 36.
4. Udyota on KP. X. 108.
5. Ekā. VIII. 36.

is expressed and anuktanimittā or when it is not expressed. In 'Avaṁ sa te vīra......nayanāmbujebhyaḥ',[1] though the sun of Nṛsiṁha's glory rises, the lotuses of the eyes of the wives of enemies do not expand. The effect is not produced even though there is preparation for it. It is uktanimittā, for the reason why the lotuses of the eyes do not expand even if the sun of Nṛsiṁha's glory rises, is expressed in the word 'ripusundarīṇāṁ'. Here saṁkara of the figures Viśeṣokti and Rūpaka exists, as the former is based upon the latter.

In 'Uttiṣṭha kandakhananāya......ariste',[2] the effect i.e. his going to a forest, does not occur, even though the causes, sending him there and inviting him there, are present. The figure is anuktanimittā Viśeṣokti here because the reason why the effect is not produced even though the necessary causes are present, i.e. the fear of Nṛsiṁha generated by the rememberance of the power of his bow, is not expressed but implied.

As in Vibhāvanā, the absence of a cause may be represented by putting forth an opposite cause, in Viśeṣokti, the failure to produce the effect may be represented by putting forth the accomplishment of an opposite effect; in such a case, a saṁkara of Vibhāvanā and Viśeṣokti alaṁkāras generally occurs, e.g. in 'Ye patanti...amī',[3] there is saṁkara of these two figures, because the drops of rain in svāti constellation are the known cause for the production of pearls. But there the effect, viz., the rise of pearls is represented as occuring in the absence of cause by using an opposite cause, viz. the drops of rain in the hasta constellation which never produce pearls. Thus here arises Vibhāvanā. Viśeṣokti also exists here, for though the rain drops under hasta constellation are the causes for the pearls not being made, this latter effect is not produced. Moreover, the absence of effect is represented by its opposite,[4] i.e. the creation of pearls. As the figures Vibhāvanā and Viśeṣokti are indistinct, there arises a saṁkara of

1. Ekā. example under VIII. 36.
2. *Ibid.* example under VIII. 36.
3. *Ibid.* example under VIII. 36.
4. *Ibid.* vṛtti on VIII. 36.

the two.[1] Asaṅgati alaṁkāra also exists here, for the cause is described as existant in one place and the effect in another. The drops of water fall into the shells in the hands of brāhmaṇas and pearls are produced elsewhere, i.e. on the chest of their wives.

Vāmana,[2] however, understands the figure in an altogether different light. According to him it is based on aupamya, i.e. when the upameya is lacking in some feature of the upamāna. He admits in his vṛtti that this has features of Rūpaka.[3]

Virodha, Vibhāvanā and Viśeṣokti alaṁkāras differ from each other. In Viśeṣokti the absence of effect even in existence of causes is more emphatic than the causes. In Virodha, the objects opposed to each other are bādhya and bādhaka; in Vibhāvanā kāraṇabhāva is bādhaka and kārya is bādhya, while in Viśeṣokti kāryabhāva is bādhaka and kāraṇasattā bādhya.

(4) *Asaṅgati*

Vidyādhara[4] defines Asaṅgati as that where the cause and effect though arising simultaenously are represented as existing in different places.

It is well-known that cause and effect must exist in the same place, as for example a kitchen—fire cannot cause smoke on a mountain. So, when the effect is represented as existing in a different place from the cause there is Asaṅgati alaṁkāra.

In the instances 'Pratibhaṭamukuṭeṣu......paṅkaḥ',[5] and 'Āyodhane...candanapatravallī',[6] the cause i.e. Nṛsiṁha's sword is said to fall on antagonists and on the battle-field, respectively, while its effect i.e. the dropping of sandal is described from the breasts of the enemies-wives.

---

1. Ekā. vṛtti on VIII. 36.
2. KASV. IV-III. 23.
3. *Ibid.* vṛtti on IV-III. 23.
4. Ekā. VIII. 38.
5. *Ibid.* example under VIII. 38.
6. *Ibid.* example under VIII. 38.

Though this figure is based on Virodna, it is rather an exception to it. Asaṅgati is concerned with the opposition of cause and effect in different places while Virodha is the opposition of things existing in the same place.

Bhoja[1] does not accept Asaṅgati alaṁkāra separately but includes it under Vidurakārya, which is a subdivision of Citrahetu. Vidurakārya citrahetu is quite similar to Asaṅgati where kārya and kāraṇa do not exist in the same place.

(5) *Viṣama*

According to Vidyādhara[2] when two dissimilar objects are put together or when the cause produces an opposite or undesirable effect, there exists Viṣama.

Kinds : Vidyādhara accepts the three divisions of Viṣama, namely—

(i) the association between two ill-suited things,
(ii) the disparity between one's expectations and frustration,
(iii) the disparity between the guṇa and kriyā of the kārya with those of the kāraṇa.

In 'Kva tava Nṛsiṁha deva...padacaṅkramaṇaiḥ';[3] two unsuitable things are put together. Nṛsiṁha's glory is transcendent, while poetic powers are ordinary.

Generally the properties of an effect are similar to those of its cause and representation of any other kind produces Viṣama of the second kind. In 'Rākāgarvitaśarvarī...mālinyamudrādaraḥ',[4] the white glory of Nṛsiṁha is represented as darkening (pale-face) the wives of enemies. The two meanings of mālinya viz. blackening and paleness, are identified by Atiśayokti.

If one strives to accomplish an object. but failing to do so meets with an undesirable consequence, there is Viṣama of the

1. SKBh. III. 351.
2. Ekā. VIII. 38.
3. *Ibid.* example under VIII. 38.
4. *Ibid.* example under VIII. 38.

third type. In 'Uditavati pratāpatapane...bhajate',[1] though the sun of Nṛsiṁha's glory rises, the lotuslike faces of the wives of his enemies do not blossom rather become pale enough to meet the sight of the beholders.

(6) *Sama*

Sahatulyatā mīyate iti samaṁ, i.e. to connect two objects owing to their similarity. Śama is 'equal', 'well-suited,' 'well-matched', and the figure consists in the poet's description of combination, i.e. well-matched. Vidyādhara[2] defines it as consisting in the putting together of two incongruous objects. It is, therefore, opposite to the first variety of Viṣama. The other two varieties do not produce charm and so do not constitute a figure.[3]

In 'Kaumudīva......bhūpate',[4] suitable pairs, the moon and moonlight, Śiva and the Gaṅges; and Nṛsiṁha and glory are mentioned.

(7) *Vicitra*

Vidyādhara[5] defines Vicitra as the effect for the attainment of the fruit by opposite means to hetu.

In 'Malinayituṁ khalavadanaṁ......pratāpoapi',[6] whitening is employed as a means to produce the opposite effect, viz., to blacken the faces of rogues and injuring mitra (the sun)as a means to gladden mitra (friends). If Nṛsiṁha's glory wlshes to blacken the faces of rogues, why does it whiten the three worlds ? Thus in this figure the opposite effect is apprehended by rejecting the cause In Viṣama, however, the cause is rejected by the apprehension of the opposite effect in the form 'if the cause is white, how does it produce blackness'.

---

1. Ekā. example under VIII. 38.
3. *Ibid.* VIII. 39.
3. (a) *Ibid.* vṛtti on VIII. 39.
   (b) RG. p. 452.
4. Ekā. example under VIII. 39.
5. *Ibid.* VIII. 39.
6. *Ibid.* example under VIII. 39.

(8) *Adhika*

Adhika means 'whatever is in process of another'. Vidyādhara[1] defines Adhika as when āśraya and the āśrayī, being opposite to each other, do not suit each other.

In 'Yadiha na diśāṁ sīmni...kaviḥ',[2] the āśrayī, glory, is represented to be greater than its āśrayas, ends of directions and operations of speech.

Rudraṭa[3] defines it in two ways, i.e.

(i) where two things arise from one cause it is called Adhika which has two varieties—where both things are contradictory and where both things are well-known through strongly contradictory actions.

(ii) it is also defined as when one thing is ādhāra and another ādheya; ādheya though really smaller than the ādhāra, is practically described as bigger.

(9) *Anyonya*

Vidyādhara[4] defines Anyonya as when there is mutual creation by two things having one karttā by their creation.

In 'Pṛthvī pūrvāpara...vidhātuḥ',[5] the earth is represented as an ornament of the arm and vice versa. They are thus both mentioned as producing each other with reference to the action of ornamentation. Objects can be both causes and effects of each other through producing the same charming action. As the arm and the earth are the cause and effect of each other by mutual adornment, they are implied as upameya and upamāna respectively.

(10) *Viśeṣa*

Vidyādhara[6] defines Viśeṣa accepting its three divisions namely :

1. Ekā. VIII. 40.
2. *Ibid.* example under VIII. 40.
3. KAR. IX. 26 & 28.
4. Ekā. VIII. 40.
5. *Ibid.* example under VIII. 40.
6. *Ibid.* VIII. 41.

(i) when the āśrayī is represented without the āśraya;

(ii) when one thing is represented as being in many places simultaneously; or

(iii) when an object, engaged in doing something, is represented as doing another impossible thing.

In 'Nipītoayaṁ vīra...suhṛdām'[1] sweetness and other qualities in the speech of Nṛsiṁha are represented as existing, even when there is āśraya viz., speech does not exist being 'drunk' by the ears of the hearer.

In 'Raṇadgīrvāṇastrī...arijanaḥ',[2] the same āśrayī Nṛsiṁha is represented as simultaneously existing in different places, viz., paths, forests, mountains and towns.

In 'Mandāramālokayituṁ...pūrṇakāmam',[3] the eye seeing Nṛsiṁha is represented as seeing Mandāra, an impossible perception.

In above instances the disappearance of the āśraya of sweetness is metaphorical. So is the fact of Nṛsiṁha being thought to be omnipresent by his frightened enemies. The sight of Mandāra while seeing Nṛsiṁha is also metaphorical, for Nṛsiṁha is conceived to be like Mandāra.

(11) *Vyāghāta*

Vidyādhara[4] accepts two varieties of Vyāghāta, viz.—

(i) If a certain thing done by a certain man by a certain means, is undone by another man by the same means, the figure is called Vyāghāta.

(ii) There may also be Vyāghāta when a particular cause which can produce a certain effect is represented as easily producing another contrary effect.

---

1. Ekā. example under VIII. 41.
2. *Ibid*. example under VIII. 41.
3. *Ibid*. example under VIII. 41.
4. *Ibid*. VIII. 42-43.

In the instance 'Tejasā jagatastāpaṁ...nirasyati',[1] the heat caused by the sun's lustre is destroyed by Nṛsiṁha (tāpa meaning affliction in the case of Nṛsiṁha) by the same prowess (tejas). This is Vyāghāta, because the work done is frustrated.

In 'Jaṭābandhaṁvalkāvaraṇampi......bhavataḥ',[2] austerity employed as a means of attaining liberality similar to that of Nṛsiṁha is represented as easily bringing about the opposite effcct.

In other instance 'Jayaśriyaṁ...tatste',[3] fighting with Nṛsiṁha to gain victory is represented as easily producing the opposite effect i.e. attaining celestial damsels, instead of glory on the battle field. This illustrates the second kind of Vyāghāta.

(12) *Kāraṇamālā*

After dealing with figures based on opposition or incongruity, Vidyādhara[4] discusses those which are chainlike or where the preceding and the succeeding objects are connected like links of a chain. Kāraṇamālā is considered first. The name Kāraṇamālā may be thus explained—kāraṇānāṁ mālā or a chain of a number of causes. Though there is Kāryamālā also, the name is due to the poet's greater emphasis on kāraṇas.

Vidyādhara[5] has defined Kāraṇamālā thus—where the preceding objects are represented as cause of the succeeding objects. He has not pointed out any of its divisions. In 'Vitaraṇa karuṇā... mahīpate'[6] mercy is represented as the cause of liberality, liberality of merits, merits of glory and glory of everything.

(13) *Ekāvalī*

Ekāvalī is ekapaṅkti, i.e. one line or one chain. According

1. Ekā. example under VIII. 42.
2. *Ibid.* example under VIII. 43.
3. *Ibid.* example under VIII. 43.
4. *Ibid.* VIII. 44.
5. *Ibid.* VIII. 45.
6. *Ibid.* example under VIII. 45.

to Vidyādhara,[1] when each succeeding word is represented (affirmatively or negatively) as an attribute of each preceding word, the figure is called Ekāvalī.

Accepting the two divisions in the definition itself Ekāvalīkāra illustrates the first one only. In 'Rājñāṁ sabhāḥ sakavayaḥ... bhānti',[2] kavi is an attribute of sabhā, kāvya of kavi, carita of kāvya and citra of carita. Here the succeeding words kavi, kāvya and carita are represented affirmately.

(14) *Mālādīpaka*

There must be a chain of padārthas in Mālādīpaka. Vidyādhara,[3] defines Mālādīpaka as where each preceding object successively helps the succeeding one.

This figure is dealt with separately and not with Dīpaka, because it is based on the special charm, there being a series of objects in which each succeeding object is helped on by the preceding object.

In 'Tava kriyante...tvadguṇavarṇanāni',[4] Nṛsiṁha's merciful glances helps forward the wealth of the poets, their wealth helps on the blooming of the mind; the blooming of the mind helps on the complimentary words and these words in their turn help on the description of the merits of Nṛsiṁha. Thus, each preceding thing successively helps the succeeding one.

(15) *Sāra*

Vidyādhara[5] defines Sāra as when each succeeding object is described as more charming than the preceding one, till the last becomes the most charming of all.

In the verse 'Eke candrakalāvacūḍamapare......nṛpaḥ',[6] some consider Svargaṅgā to be more charming than Candrakalāvacūḍa

1. Ekā. VIII. 46.
2. *Ibid.* example under VIII. 46.
3. *Ibid.* VIII. 47.
4. *Ibid.* example under VIII. 47.
5. *Ibid.* VIII. 48.
6. *Ibid.* example under VIII. 48.

(Śaṁkara), while some others describe Lord Viṣṇu as more charming than Svargaṅgā, still others consider Lakṣmī as more charming than Viṣṇu and still others describe Nṛsiṁha as more charming than Lakṣmī. So Śrīmān Nṛsiṁha is described to be the most charming here.

In 'Antarviṣṇoḥ......vibhāti',[1] kīrtti is described as most charming.

(16) *Kāvyaliṅga*

Kāvyaliṅga is a poetical cause. Vidyādhara[2] defines it as when the sense of a sentence or of a word is represented as a cause of something of which it becomes an attribute.

Kinds : Vidyādhara divides Kāvyaliṅga into two in the definition itself, namely vākyārthagata and padārthagata.

In vākāyārthagata Kāvyaliṅga, the meanings of the sentences represent cause and the effect, so words like 'hi' which expresses a cause may produce a paunaruktyadoṣa when used. In padārthagata Kāvyaliṅga the sense of a word is a cause. Here if a word expressing cause is put in the instrumental or ablative case, the figure would not exist. So the word which expresses a cause must be represented as an attribute.

In 'Alaṁ bhoḥ...aviralam',[3] the sense of the sentence viz., the fame of the king of the Kaliṅgas will smear your body, is the cause of the futility of ornamenting breasts by black agāru. So it is vākyārthagata Kāvyalinga.

In 'Tvadvairikṣitipāla...prabhoḥ',[4] the attribute 'slow' is the cause of an obstacle of the movements of the horses of the sun and the sense of the words 'tvadvairikṣitpāla' is the cause of the slowness of the horses. Thus exists padārthagata Kāvyaliṅga here.

---

1. Ekā. example under VIII. 48.
2. *Ibid.* VIII. 49.
3. *Ibid.* example under VIII. 49.
4. *Ibid.* example under VIII. 49.

Difference between Kāvyaliṅga and Arthāntaranyāsa

In both these alaṁkāras something is supported by another. In Arthāntaranygsa the supporter may be sāmānya or viśeṣa and supported, viśeṣa or sāmānya, but in Kāvyaliṅga, supporter should be kārya or kāraṇa while the supported kāraṇa or kārya; sādṛśya may be a dividing line between the two. Vidyādhara accepts Arthāntaranyāsa in sādṛśyamūlakālaṁkāra and Kāvyaliṅga in kāryakāraṇabhāvamūlakālaṁkāras.

Moreover, in Arthāntranyāsa, the sense of the supported sentence is grammatically independent of the sense of a sentence which supports it, while in Kāvyaliṅga the sense of a sentence to be supported is grammaticālly dependent on that of the supporting sentence.

(17) *Anumāna*

Anu+miti means knowledge through lakṣaṇā. Vātsyāyana[1] explains it as 'mitena liṅgena arthasya anupaścāt mānaṁ' but in poetry it has some what different sense. Vidyādhara[2] defines Anumāna as that in which the sādhya and the sādhana are mentioned.

In 'Narasiṁha mahīpāla......anyathā',[3] Nṛsiṁha is to be demonstrated as the God of love. Nṛsiṁha is pakṣa[4] (the minor term) and Makaradhvaja, Sādhya. The sādhana employed to demonstrate Nṛsiṁha as God of love is sumanomārgaṇatva, the state of having learned men as supplicants in the case of Nṛsiṁha and the state of having flowers as arrows in the case of the God of love. This hetu is found in the pakṣa, Nṛsiṁha and also in the sapakṣa,[5] i.e. in places where sādhya exists definitely, viz., another God of love and does not exist in vipakṣa,[6] i.e. where the major term is absent, viz,, other than God of love. The hetu has

1. Vātsyāyana bhāṣya on Nyāyadarśana, I. 1.3.
2. Ekā. VIII. 50.
3. *Ibid.* example under VIII. 50.
4. Tarkasaṅgraha, p. 43,
5. *Ibid.* p. 43.
6. *Ibid.* p. 44.

thus the three well-known characteristics of being found in pakṣa, in places other than pakṣa, and of being absent in places other than the pakṣa. Thus hetu enables us to infer that, Nṛsiṁha is the God of love, This verse 'Narasiṁha mahīpāla...anyathā', illustrates Anumāna set up by the notion of Śleṣa. The figure may similarly be combined with Rūpaka and other alaṁkāras.

In 'Kāryāṇi kāraṇaguṇān......kīrttiḥ',[1] fame is pakṣa, going beyond the top of the Meru mountain, the sādhya and the violation of the effect always possessing the qualities of the cause is the sādhana. Here Anumāna is not mixed with any other alaṁkāra.

Differennce between Anumāna, Arthāntaranyāsa, Utpreksā and Kāvyaliṅga

In Kāvyaliṅga, the relation between something made well-known and that causing it to be so does not subsist as it does in Anumāna. In the latter case what is not apprehended is caused to be apprehended by implied vyāpti. In Kāvyaliṅga, the hetu is kāraka, while in Anumāna it is jñāpaka. In other words, in the former the cause is efficient or one that produces something, as a stick and a wheel of a jar while in the latter it is indicatory or one that enables us to infer something e.g. a lamp enabling us to recognize an object.

It may be said that in Anumāna the poet wishes the reader to know by representing the hetu as characterised by vyāpti etc., that the inference is drawn by him. In Kāvyaliṅga the reader infers by himself.

In both *Anumāna and Arthāntaranyāsa* the hetutva is stated explicitly. But in Anumāna the hetu is jñāpaka, in Arthāntaranyāsa it is samarthaka. In Anumāna, two sentences are related as kāraṇa-kārya, in Arthāntaranyāsa they are related as sāmānya-viśeṣa. Words like manye etc. are used in Anumāna to mark the deduction made while they are not used in Arthāntaranyāsa.

In both *Annmāna and Utprekṣā,* words like manye, ūha are

1. Ekā. example under VIII. 50.

used. But in Anumāna, there is certainty in the deduction. In Utprekṣā, there is uncertainty. In Anumāna, there is no sādṛśya-pratīti but this does not exist in Utprekṣā.

(18) *Yathāsaṁkhya*

The word Yathāsaṁkhya means 'according to some order.' This word is used in Aṣṭādhyāyī of Pāṇini also.[1]

Vidyādhara,[2] defines Yathāsaṁkhya as that where objects mentioned in a certain order are respectively connected with others mentioned in the order.

In 'Āyāmaślāghanīyaṁ...candraḥ',[3] dostambhaḥ, tyāgalīlā, mitavacanaṁ, uraḥ, rājalakṣmīḥ and yaśaḥ are connected with ahiśa, dyuśākhī etc, and also with āyāṁ and aślāghanīyaṁ.

(19) *Paryāya*

Paryāya means 'krama'. Vidyādhara[4] defines it as when many objects are represented as abiding in one object successively or when one object is represented as abiding in many objects successi vely. Thus, *Vidyādhara has divided Paryāya into two* namely, one object abiding in many āśrayas or vice versa.

'Kāśmīrapāṁsu......sūtraiḥ',[5] illustrates the first variety of Paryāya. Here different things in succession viz., kuṁkumarājaḥ, gairikapramukha etc. are described as remaining in one āśraya i.e. kucataṭa. The other variety is illustrared in 'Prāgāsīnama-karanda...netrāñcale'.[6] Here, Lakṣmī is described as existing in different āśrayas in succession, i.e. padmagarbha etc.

Difference between Paryāya, Viśeṣa, Parivṛtti and Sāra

In Viśeṣa many objects are represented as abiding simultaneously in one, successively.

1. Aṣṭādhyāyī, I-III. 10.
2. Ekā. VIII. 50.
3. *Ibid.* example under VIII. 50.
4. *Ibid.* VIII. 51.
5. *Ibid.* example under VIII. 51.
6. *Ibid.* example under VIII. 51.

It differs from Parivṛtti too, in that here there is no exchange of object. Paryāya and Sāra are also different from each other. In Ekaviṣayasāra there is a regular āroha in the different positions of one object, but in Paryāya I, the object does not necessarily leave its original position. In Paryāya I the charm lies in the same object shifting its place. In Ekaviṣayasāra, it lies in the gradual ascent leading to the climax. In Paryāya II, poet is concerned merely with the variety of phases through which the object passes, irrespective of regular ascent.

(20) *Parivṛtti*

Parivṛtti means 'exchange' and the poet describes some selected facts in life as if they were barters in the figure. Thus there is poetical bargain here.

Vinimaya in the definition means giving up something and taking up another thing in its stead. However, this interchange must not be real but only conceived by the poet, in order to be charming.

Kinds : Vidyādhara accepts three divisions of Parivṛtti namely adhikaparivṛtti, nyūnaparivṛtti and samaparivṛtti. The verse 'Narasiṁha mahīpāla...bhuvam',[1] illustrates adhikaparivṛtti. Here the earth, which is nyūna, is taken and the sky, adhika, is given up. In 'Tanau dattvā...śriyampi',[2] the beauty of śarapāṇḍurā, which is nyūna is exchanged with tāṭaṅkaprabhā etc. adhika. Nyūnaparivṛtti is exemplified here. The śloka 'Pratibhaṭadharaṇipatibhyo...kaṭākṣaparipāṭīḥ',[3] illustrates samaparivṛtti. Here by giving up nārācaparamparā, the same guṇas kaṭākṣaparipāṭī are accepted.

It can be noted that the definition of Parivṛtti alaṁkāra changed many times during its development. Bhāmaha[4] thought it to be the interchange of inferior with superior Arthāntaranyasa

1. Ekā. example under VIII. 52.
2. *Ibid.* example under VIII. 52.
3. *Ibid.* example under VIII. 52.
4. KAB. III. 41.

being existent there; in Daṇḍin's[1] opinion it did not exist. Udbhaṭa and Vāmana accept the exchange with equals or unequals while according to Rudraṭa,[2] the change may be based on upacāra or prasiddhi. Bhoja[3] and Hemacandra[4] did not mention these as the basis of such change.

(21) *Parisaṁkhyā*

Parisaṁkhyā is explained by the Mīmāṁsakas, 'pari' as varjana and saṁkhyā as 'buddhi'.[5] Parisaṁkhyā is the vidhi where the idea of exclusion is stressed. Parisaṁkhyālaṁkāra also derives its charm from its suggestion of exclusion. The word 'parisaṁkhyā' means 'restriction' and the figure is so designated significantly.[6]

According to Vidyādhara,[7] when the existence of an object, which is possible in a number of places is restricted one, there is Parisaṁkhyālaṁkāra.

Kinds : Vidyādhara accepts four kinds of Parisaṁkhyā, namely, praśnapūrvikā, apraśnapūrvikā, the thing excluded may be suggested (ārthī) or expressed (śābdī).

The verse 'Āyāmaślaghnīyaṁ...na candraḥ',[8] is an instance of praśnapūrvikāśābdī. Here the qualities āyāṁ aślāghyatva etc. are found in dostambhādi and ahīśvarādi. It is Parisaṁkhyā because the existance of these qualities is restricted to dostambhādi only. The exclusion is only due to words like nāhīśa etc.

'Aṅgeṣvābharaṇaṁ...ripukṣmābhujaḥ',[9] illustrates praśnapūr-

1. KD. II. 355.
2. KAR. VII. 77.
3. SKBh. III. 103.
4. KAnu. VI. 22.
5. Aṣṭādhyāyī, VIII. I. 5.
6. (a) Tika on Kāvyapradīpa, X. 34.
   (b) AS. vṛtti on 63.
7. Ekā. VIII. 53.
8. supra IX. 3 on p. 170.
9. Ekā. example under VIII. 54.

vikā ārthī Parisaṁkhyā. Here aṅgābharaṇatva is possibe in bhagavaccaraṇayugala and mukuṭa but is restricted to caraṇayugala etc. and there is implied niṣedha of mukuṭa.

The śloka 'Loke asmin...vākpatiḥ',[1] is an instance of apraśnapūrvikā sābdī Parisaṁkhyā. Here the qualities dātṛtva etc. are possible in both kalpadruma and king Nṛsiṁha both, but they are restricted to one only i.e. king. The niṣedha of kalpadruma etc. is expressed.

The stanza 'Vidyāsu tṛṣṇā,...deva',[2] illustrates apraśnapūrvikā ārthī Parisaṁyhyā. Here tṛṣṇā, vyasana and other qualities are restricted to vidyā, kalā etc. So niṣedha of dhana and dyūta is implied.

(22) *Arthāpatti*

'Arthasya āpatti', i.e. coming in of meaning. Arthāpatti was accepted as Pramāṇa by philosophers--Mīmāṁsakas and Vedāntins but Naiyāyikas and Sāṁkhyavādis include it under Anumāna. When something is suggested by some particular stated circumstances there is Arthāpatti e.g. Devadatta does not take meals during the daytime but he is fat. This means that he eats at night compulsorily (pīno Devadatto divā na bhuṅkte cet rātrau bhuṅkte). Here eating at night is known through Arthāpatti.

According to Vidyādhara,[3] the inference of another idea is called Arthāpatti alaṁkāra, e.g. when a stick is bitten by a mouse, the biting of apūpa attached is implied.

Kinds : Vidyādhara divides the figure into two namely an aprakṛta fact may follow from a prakṛta one or vice versa.

In the verse 'Akalaṅkamapi...indumaṇḍalam',[4] dviṣadvadhūvadanendu—prākaraṇika is accomplished from aprākaraṇika indumaṇḍalavṛttānta. Thus this examplifies the first variety of Arthāpatti.

1. Ekā. example under VIII. 54.
2. *Ibid.* example under VIII. 54.
3. *Ibid.* VIII. 55.
4. *Ibid.* example under VIII. 55.

The second variety is illustrated in 'Āpātālaṁ...kṣitīndra'.[1] Here sthāvarabhūbhṛdvṛttānta aprakāraṇika is accomplished from jaṅgamabhūbhṛdvṛttānta prākaraṇika.

First of all Bharata discussed Arthāpatti in thirty-six kāvyalakṣaṇas. The same Arthāpatti was accepted afterwards as an alaṁkāra.

Arthāpatti differs from Anumāna as in Anumāna samānanyāya (i.e. tbe same cause establishing two facts) takes the form of vyāpti, an invariable connection between what is to be established and what establishes it. In Arthāpatti it does not take the form of vyāpti e.g. when a mouse bites a stick to which a cake is attached the biting of cake need not necessarily follow from the same cause.

(23) *Vikalpa*

The word 'Vikalpa' was used by grammarians in the sense of optional.[2] Ācārya Pāṇini used 'vibhāṣā' for this sense. The word Vikalpa is found in one of the five vṛttis in Yogadarśana also, but conveys a different idea.[3]

Vidyādhara[4] defines the figure as that when in a certain case the simultaneity of two equivalent acts though based on equally strong testimony, is impossible on account of their being opposed to each other.

In the verse 'Tvadviprayoge...śarīram',[5] going to the Himālayas and resorting to a bed of leaves are represented as equally powerful remedies for curing the unbearable fever of love—grief. Their simultaneity therefore is impossible and their alteration constitutes Vikalpālaṁkāra.

(24) *Samuccaya*

According to Vidyādhara[6] the simultaneity of properties and

1. Ekā. example under VIII 55.
2. Aṣṭādhyāyī. I. 1.43.
3. Yogadarśana, I.5.6 & 42.
4. Ekā. VIII. 56.
5. *Ibid.* example under VIII. 56.
6. *Ibid.* VIII. 57-58.

actions constitutes the figure Samuccaya. He accepts another variety of this figure, too. So, the figure also arises when a certain cause has begun to produce an effect and another operates rivals to produce the same effect. This second variety is named Tatkara. The term Tatkara is significant as all the causes conjointly bring about the same effect.

Kinds : Ekāvalīkāra points out its two varieties on the basis of guṇa and kriyā. The second variety Tatkara has two subdivisions since many causes that conspire to bring about the effect may be good or bad. In the śloka 'Abhūdyaśo...turaṅgamaiḥ',[1] the whiteness of Nṛsiṁha's glory and the blackness of the disgrace of his enemies are simultaneous.

In 'Svaḥsindhau...hāranti ca',[2] the actions, Moonrays, flood of the heavenly Ganges and garlands are represented as simultaneous.

In 'Mūrttiḥ......jṛmbhayante',[3] though the form of Nṛsiṁha alone is sufficient to produce pride, many other causes, such as fame and wealth are represented as bringing about the same effect. The causes strive with one another and are all good as they are connected with good attributes, like the figure of Nṛsiṁha with beauty. Moreover, here exists Saṁkara of two alaṁkāras viz. Samuccaya (or Tatkara) and Viśeṣokti as the effect, pride is represented as absent even though its causes exist.

In 'Kārpaṇyaikaniketanaṁ...samunmīlitāḥ',[4] kings who are full of meanness, are a sufficient cause to bring about the effect i.e. the miseries of poets, but many causes are represented as striving with one another in bringing about the same end. So, the figure is Tatkara. The causes are bad here as they are linked to bad attributes, viz., kings with meanness and so on.

(25) *Samādhi*

'Samyak ādhiḥ ādhānaṁ, utpādanaṁ', Samādhi.[5] The proper

---

1. Ekā. example under VIII. 57.
2. *Ibid.* example under VIII. 57.
3. *Ibid.* example under VIII. 58.
4. Ekā. example under VIII. 58.
5. Skt. commentary Bālabodhinī on KP. X. 125.

application is called Samādhi. Here the characteristic of an object is applicable to another object. Thus this alaṁkāra is similar to Samuccaya and hence is treated after Samuccayālaṁkāra.[1]

Vidyādhara[2] defines it as an effect rendered easy to accomplish by the occurence of another cause. In 'Lāvaṇyameva sahajam...kokilakūjitānī'[3] the cetaḥ prasādanaṁ of Nṛsiṁhadeva which is caused by the lāvaṇya of māninī, becomes easier with the help 'cooing of a cuckoo'.

Calling it Samāhita Daṇḍin[4] defines Samādhi as that where at the commencement of some work, a person gets an additional ally to accomplish it by virtue of good fortune. It is accepted as a kāvyaguṇa also i.e. Samādhi is that where the properties of onething are beautifully ascribed to some other thing with regard to worldly usage.[5] Udbhata[6] has given a completely different definition. According to him, Samāhita exists where the praśama of Rasābhāsa and Bhāvābhāsa are composed. Calling it Samāhita, Vāmana[7] says that when the similarity of onething becomes the property of another thing is called Samāhita. In Vāmana's view, the emphasis on Sādṛśya is its speciality and this emphasis is found in other alaṁkāras also like Vakrokti and Ākṣepa. Bhoja[8] calls the superimposition of quality of onething on another Samāhita.

Samādhi is different from Samuccya for in Samuccya rival causes go to produce the same effect. In Samādhi though one of the causes is competent to bring about an effect independently, yet another accidently facilitates its accomplishment e.g. the fruit of a palm-tree may fall accidently on the head of a crow perched on the tree and kills it.

1. Ekā. vṛtti on VIII. 59.
2. *Ibid.* VIII. 59.
3. *Ibid.* example under VIII. 59.
4. KD. II. 298.
5. *Ibid.* I. 93.
6. KASS. IV. 7.
7. KASV. IV-III. 29.
8. SKBh. III. 132.

(26) *Pratyanīka*

Having dealt with alaṁkāras based on the maxims of reasoning (Kāvyaliṅga and Anumāna based upon Tarkanyāya) and on the maxims of sentences (Yathāsaṁkhya, Paryāya, Parivṛtti, Parisaṁkhyā, Arthāpatti, Vikalpa, Samuccaya and Samādhi), Ekāvalīkāra discusses the figures based on popular maxims.[1]

In Pratyanīka, anīka means an army and Pratyanīka, an antagonist[2] and the figure is called Pratyanīka in the secondary sense. The object of resorting to lakṣaṇā is to show the greatness of the enemy's might.

Vidyādhara,[3] defines Pratyanīkālaṁkāra as when one unable to conquer a powerful enemy is represented as despising his weak dependent in order to injure his enemy. On the other hand, a man competent to conquer an army does so through ignorance of someone else who represents it.

In 'Sudhākaro......ambujānām',[4] the moon when unable to conquer Nṛsimha is represented as taking away the beauty of sun-lotuses, his weak-friend (being similar to his face) to injure him. The greatness of Nṛsimha is thereby implied.

(27) *Pratīpa* : Pratīpa means-pratikūla.

Ekāvalīkāra,[5] accepts two varieties of Pratīpālaṁkāra. When upameya cannot perform the function of its upamāna through its excellence and upamāna is rejected, i.e. represented as useless, or when upamāna is represented as upameya and thus lowered, the figure is significantly called Pratīpa. In both varieties upameya is opposed to upamāna.

In 'Kāntiḥ svabhāvasubhagaiva...sudhāṁśuḥ',[6] Pratīpa of the first sort is illustrated which is free from any other figure. Here the

1. Ekā. VIII. 60.
2. *Ibid.* vṛtti on VIII. 61.
3. *Ibid.* VIII. 61.
4. *Ibid.* example under VIII. 61.
5. *Ibid.* VIII. 62.
6. *Ibid.* example under VIII. 62.

upameyas kānti and Nṛsiṁha are represented as discharging the functions of the upamānas kuṅkumarasa and Sudhāṁśu and therefore the upamānas are represented as useless.

'Tvaddordaṇḍadhurandharaḥ...tava',[1] illustrates the second type of Pratīpa. Here Śeṣa and other well-known upameyas are represented as upamānas to suggest their inferiority to the arm.

The verse 'Dānaistvayi......anaiṣīt',[2] consists of Saṁkara of Pratīpa of the first kind, Utprekṣā and Apahnuti. If Nṛsiṁha bestows charity as liberally as the heavenly Kalparvṛkṣa, what then is the use of this tree ? Thus upamāna, Kalpavṛkṣa, is represented as useless, its function being performed by the upameya, Nṛsiṁha, and Pratīpa exists here; as the Kalpavṛkṣa is useless, the creator draws as it were the circle of erasure round it. Thus Utprekṣā is implied based on Pratīpa. What surrounded the tree at its base was not the water-basin but the circle of erasure made by the creator. Thus Apahnuti is based on Utprekṣā here which again is based on Pratīpa. Thus Apahnuti depends here for its existence upon Utprekṣā brought about by the notion of Pratīpa.

Though Vidyādhara has mentioned two divisions of Pratīpa, he has illustrated another too, i.e. based on the combination of other alaṁkāras.

In both Pratīpa and Vyatireka, the poet's aim is to establish the upameya as superior to upamāna but the way in which this is achieved is different in both figures. In Pratīpa, the upamāna is declared as superfluous, in Vyatireka there is no such challenge to the upamāna. Pratīpa is not in the form of Upamā, Vyatireka is in the form of Upamā though in favour of the upameya.

(28) *Mīlita*

Mīlita means obscured or concealed. Vidyādhara[3] defines Mīlita as when a natural adventitious object is concealed by an object of another type, the natural by the adventitious and vice versa.

1. Ekā. example under VIII. 62.
2. *Ibid.* example under VIII. 62.
3. *Ibid.*. VIII. 63.

Kinds : Vidyādhara, while defining it, gives two divisions based on whether the object concealed is natural or adventitious.

In 'Viśrāṇanaiḥ...paritoṣalīlāḥ'[1] the adventitious generosity arising from satisfaction is represented as concealed by the superior natural generosity of Nṛsiṁha.

'Āliṅgyamāṇasya......bhīḥ'[2] exemplifies the second sort of Mīlita. In it the tremor arising from inborn fear is concealed by a greater tremor which is adventitious as it arises from the embrace of a beloved.

(29) *Sāmānya*

'Samānasya bhāvaḥ Sāmānyamiti', Sāmānya is whatever is assimliated with another and merge into it.

Vidyādhara[3] defines Sāmānya as that when the object described is represented as identical with and indistinguishable from the object not described on account of their possession of a common property.

In the example 'Dharādhipa Śrī Narasiṁha...vainateyaḥ',[4] the moon and Śeṣa which are aprakṛta objects are considered as similarly to the prakṛta object, i.e. the glory of Nṛsiṁha, on account of their common quality, whiteness. Thus, Sāmānyalaṁkāra exists here.

Sāmānyālaṁkāra is different from Mīlita. In both, the similarity of attributes leads to the lack of apprehension of one of the two circumstances. In Sāmānya this is due to assimilation, while in Mīlita, it is due to domination. In Sāmānya both the circumstances are equally powerful, while in Mīlita one is more powerful than the other. In Sāmānya the distinction between two things becomes imperceptible but in Mīlita one of the two things is obscured.

---

1. Ekā. example under VIII. 63.
2. *Ibid.* example under VIII. 63.
3. *Ibid.* VIII. 64.
4. *Ibid.* example under VIII. 64.

Sāmānya is different from Apahnuti, too, because here one object is not denied and another is not superimposed on it. It differs from Atiśayokti also, due to the absence of upameya as upamānatāvacchedaka.

It differs from Bharāntimān also, because Bhrāntimān proceeds from a man's mistaking onething for another, owing to the remememberance of a similar object.

(30) *Tadguṇa*

Ekāvalīkāra[1] opines that when an object gives up its property and assumes that of another superior object, it is called Tadguṇālaṁkāra. So here prakṛta object is represented acquiring the property of an aprakṛta object of excellent quality.

In the śloka, 'Vīra tvad ripuramaṇī......pāṇḍupatradhiyā',[2] red leaves are represented as having given up their redness and taken up the whiteness of nails. Bhrāntimat also exists in 'pāṇḍupatradhiyā', the leaves being mistaken for white leaves. As this bhrānti is based on the leaves acquiring the whiteness of the nails, there is saṁkāra of two alaṁkāras.

In 'Nṛtyad bhargāṭṭahāsa......avabodhaḥ',[3] Śrīkṛṣṇa is represented as having given up his blackness and taken up whiteness by contact with the glory of Nṛsiṁha. Moreover, as the contact is not real, but conceived, there is asambandhe sambandhātiśayokti, based on Tadguṇa. Thus there is again Saṁkara of two figures.

In both *Tadguṇa and Mīlita* one contiguous thing influences another and the stronger obscures the weaker one. But in Tadguṇa one property obscures another and takes its place. In Mīlita, one dharmin obscures another and becomes conspicuous. In Tadguṇa, the quality obscuring another must be dissimilar to it, otherwise there cannot be replacement. In Mīlita, the attributes of both the dharmin must be similar.

In both *Tadguṇa and Sāmānya,* there is imperception of the

1. Ekā. VIII. 65.
2. *Ibid.* example under VIII. 65.
3. *Ibid.* example under VIII. 65.

actual fact but in Tadguṇa, the lack of perception relates to the guṇa of an object ousted by the stronger guṇa of another object. In Sāmānya, such imperception relates to the thing itself, assimilated with another. In Tadguṇa, the guṇas of the two continuous things are dissimilar. In Sāmānya, they are similar. In Tadguṇa, the guṇa of one is stronger than that of another. In Sāmānya the guṇas of the two contiguous things are of the same intensity.

(31) *Atadguṇa*

As the name indicates, the figure consists in the failure of an object to get tinged by the stronger quality of another contiguous object (na vidyate tasya prakṛtasya aprakṛtasyavā guṇāḥ atra). According to Vidyādhara,[1] when the object under description is of excellent qualities and does not take up the qualities of an undesired object, though nearness exists between the two, it is called Atadguṇa. The figure is significanlly designated Atadguṇa as the prakṛta object does not take up the qualities of the aprakrta one.

In 'Gaṇḍābhoge......Śrī Nṛsiṁha'[2] though Nṛsiṁha's glory contacts the ichoral juice of the temples of direction elephants and the collyrium of the eyes of the wives of his enemies, it does not take up their blackness. The figure is, therefore, Atadguna.

Both *Viśeṣokti and Atadguṇa* appear similar because the effect is not achieved even in the presence of the cause. But the difference is that, in Viśeṣokti, the charm depends on kāryakāraṇa while in Atadguṇa it depends on the failure to achieve qualities. Kāryakāraṇabhāva is not emphasized in Atadguṇa.

(32) *Uttara*

Uttara is a reply, retort, or rejoinder and the figure derives its name from the reply(s) it embodies by it. According to Vidyādhara,[3] the figure Uttara arises when questions and answers are represented in a certain poem more than once but where the answers are not conceived at once. When the question is not given

1. Ekā. VIII. 65.
2. *Ibid.* example under VIII. 65.
. *Ibid.* VIII. 66.

but inferred from the answer it constitutes the second variety of Uttara.[1]

In the example 'Kā viṣamā......lokaḥ',[2] the intended reply is incomprehensible, i.e. daivagatiḥ and not the exclusion of something as āpattiḥ and so with other questions.

In 'Tāvat kutaḥ...mukheṣu',[3] the question 'where one will get evening (pradoṣa) with moonlight', is expressed through the answer. So this illustrates the second variety of Ūttara.

Uttarālaṁkāra is different from Praśnaparisaṁkhyā, because here there is no exclusion of another object in the reply, as in Parisaṁkhyā. The charm here consists in what is expressed and not in what is conceived (as in Parisaṁkhyā where it consists in what is excluded).

(33) *Praśnottarika*

According to Vidyādhara,[4] when questions and answers between two persons are represented, the figure is called Praśnottarikā.

In 'Pītaḥ kenāsi ratnākara...pravāhāḥ',[5] there are questions and answers between the sea and Kālindī, Kālindī employs 'pītaḥ' in the sense of 'yellow', while the sea under-stands it as 'drunk'. So the whole sentence gives a different sense and the sea gets angry and answers the question by a counter-question, 'by whom are you drawn forcibly on the head ?' Yamunā understands this and pacifies him by saying, 'do not be angry, I express my curiosity with regard to your yellow-colour'. Then the sea answers with 'Vadāmi dhāvantyete...pravāhāḥ'. The śloka contains another alaṁkāra asambandhe api sambandhātiśayokti also, for the contact of the sea with streams of Meru, is not real, but brought about by poetic conception.

1. Ekā. VIII. 67.
2. *Ibid.* example under VIII. 66.
3. *Ibid.* example under VIII. 67.
4. *Ibid.* VIII. 68.
5. *Ibid.* example under VIII. 68.

(34) *Sūkṣma*

The figures based on the apprehension of deep or incomprehensible sense, are discussed here. According to Vidyādhara,[1] if a certain thing which cannot be comprehended by dullards is perceived by an intellectual through some gesture and is made known to another intelligent person it is called Sūkṣmālaṁkāra.

In 'Naveṣu kānteṣu...svabimbam',[2] the sun is represented as knowing the deep desire of celestial damsels of securing new-lovers through their gestures. He shows it to them by shaking his own disk, in fear of the warriors slain by Nṛsiṁha on the battlefield. It is believed that those who fall on battle-fields, pierce the disk of the sun and go to heaven where their love is sought by celestial damsels.

(35) *Vyājokti*

Vyājoki is a statement based on pretext. According to Vidyādhara[3] if a certain hidden thing is revealed from some cause and is again concealed by putting in another circumstance, it is called Vyājokti alaṁkāra.

In 'Akarṇyotkalabhūpate......Śakādhīśvaraḥ',[4] the fear of Nṛsiṁha's enemies caused by mistaking, thunder for the sound of war-drums, is concealed by embracing their beloveds. Here both love and fear cause tremor and are, therefore, similar.

Between Vyājokti and Apahnuti two points are common—

(i) Intentional concealment of real fact and

(ii) Similarity between the fact desired to be withheld and one established.

(i) But in Vyājokti, something is concealed by the speaker's silence, in Apahnuti it is concealed by actual denial.

(ii) In Vyājokti, the speaker's aim is practical, viz. to keep

1. Ekā. VIII. 69.
2. *Ibid.* example under VIII. 69.
3. *Ibid.* VIII. 70.
4. *Ibid.* example under VIII. 70.

the hearer in the dark about the real issue. In Apahnuti, it is poetical viz. to drive at the sādṛśya between the thing denied and the one affirmed and thus to exalt it.

(36) *Vakrokti*

Vakra+ukti, i.e. twisted statement. In Sanskrit poetics, Vakrokti is given much importance. According to Vidyādhara[1] Vakrokti is the statement of one purporting onething, but taken by another to mean differently through pun i.e. usually double meaning or change of tone kāku or into-nation.

Kinds : Vidādhara accepts two kinds of Vakrokti in the definition itself. These are through change of tone, i.e. Kāku or Śleṣa, pun. In 'Sarvārthinām......Pārijātaḥ',[2] the speaker means to say that Pārijāta is not ashamed, but on account of his peculiar intonation the hearer takes 'na lajjate' in the sense of 'does not Pārijāta feel shame ? It does not feel shame'. In the verse 'Kiṁ me roṣaṁ karoṣi...Śrī Nṛsiṁha',[3] Śiva uses 'me', in the sense of 'towards me', but Pārvatī understands it to mean 'oh lakṣmī', 'me' by 'Śleṣa' conveying these two senses. Then Śiva says, 'it is not proper for you to be angry', meaning 'na' and 'krodhaḥ' as two separate words. Pārvatī misunderstands this as narkaḥ adhaḥ. Here nakrodhaḥ conveys two meanings by Sabhaṅga or Śabda-śleṣa.

(37) *Svabhāvokti*

Svabhāvokti means literally the description of some trait of an object. The figure consists in the faithful portrayal of some object, bringing into prominence, poetically charming traits.

Vidyādhara[4] defines Svabhāvokti as the faithful description of the very minute nature of an object like its movements, colour and disposition of limbs.

The instance 'Ūrdhvaṁ bhujābhyāṁ···tāvakīnaḥ',[5] describes

1. Ekā. VIII. 71.
2. *Ibid.* example under VIII. 71.
3. *Ibid.* example under VIII. 71.
4. *Ibid.* VIII. 72.
5. *Ibid.* example under VIII. 72.

the development and helpless condition of Nṛsiṁha's enemies, their movements and disposition of their limbs.

(38) *Bhāvika*

According to Vidyādhara,[1] when past/future things are so well represented that they appear actually before our eyes, the figure is called Bhāvika.

Kinds: Vidyādhara speaks of a past and future things visualised by the poet in Bhāvikālaṁkāra and both are cited in one verse, i.e. in, 'Vāmaṁbāhuṁ vidhāya...Śrī Nṛsiṁha'.[2] Nṛsiṁha is so well described as being of extraordinary strength and imposing personality that those saw or will see him experience fear, though this is really in past or future.

In both *Svabhāvokti and Bhāvika* alaṁkāras, there is a faithful portrayal of an accerting theme. But in Bhāvika the charm consists in visualising a past or future event as a fact of the present. In Svabhāvokti, this element of visualization is conspicuously absent. In Svabhāvokti the object is not transferred from the past or future to the present. In Bhāvika the poet presents to us a past or future thing as though it were present. One is likely to mistake it for Gamyotprekṣā due to the absence of Sambhāvanāpratipādakas like iva, manye etc. In Utprekṣā adhyavasāya is connected by 'as if', 'as though'. In Bhāvika, there is no adhyavasāya because when the poet transfers the past or the future to the present, both, he and the reader regard it as of the present, on account of the high emotion.

In Atiśayokti there is adhyavasāya while in Bhāvika it does not exist. Adhyavasāya is always intentional. There is no adhyavasāya when the apratyakṣa is visualised as the pratyakṣa. Like a Yogī, a kavi actually gets the vision of the past or the future.

In both *Bhāvika and Bhrāntimān*, there is a cognition of a thing, which is not there. But whereas in Bhrāntimān the cognition is wrong, in Bhāvika the poet pictures it exactly as it had

1. Ekā. VIII. 73.
2. *Ibid.* example under VIII. 73.

been before. In Bhrāntimān, the poet drives at Sādṛśya, while in Bhāvika, he drives at bhāvanāprakarṣa.

(39) *Udātta*

Udātta is a super-abundance[1] of only good things. According to Vidyādhara[2] Udātta is defined as the description of an object adorned by inconceivable prosperity set up by poetic imagination, and as that when actions of the great are described as subordinate to prakṛta.

Kinds : Vidyādhara accepts two divisions of the figure Udātta. In 'Dāsībhiḥ pratisāritāni...sthitim',[3] the prosperity of Nṛsiṁha is described as so great that the pearls, put in auspicious square-marks on the ground of the court-yard on his way, are removed by maid-servants when they clean the way. These are taken away by merchants who sell them to kings in different categories and the queens wear them as if they were Nṛsiṁha's glory incorporated in the necklaces round their throats.

In 'Velākānanamagrataḥ......saṁkramaḥ'[4] the sea-shore is prakṛta and it is made great by the subordinate description of the greatness of Nṛsiṁha. Nṛsiṁha's bravery is here subordinate to the greatness of the sea-shore. Though there is Vīrarasa here, it is subordinate. If it were principal, the instance would have caused dhvani.

(40) *Ubhayālaṁkāra : Saṁkara and Saṁsṛṣṭi*

As the name suggests, Saṁkara and Saṁsṛṣṭi are the combination or aggregation of two or more figures. The older ālaṁkārikas generally give only one name to every kind of combination which may be either like tilataṇḍula or nīrakṣīra.

Accepting Saṁsṛṣṭi and Saṁkara as independent alaṁkāras Vidyādhara[5] defines Saṁsṛṣṭi as a mixture of figures which exist

1. Skt. Commentary Bālabodhinī on KP. X. 115.
2. Ekā. VIII. 74.
3. *Ibid.* example under VIII. 74.
4. *Ibid.* example under VIII. 74.
5. *Ibid.* VIII. 75-76.

independently. The different figures are united by the maxim of tila-taṇḍula which exist separately. When a number of figures are inseparably connected by intimate relation (Sāmānya) or by the maxim of nīra-kṣīra, the mixture is called Saṁkara.[1] Thus the figures are quite clear and definite in Saṁsṛṣṭi while they are doubtful and not at all clear in Saṁkara.

Kinds : Saṁsṛṣṭi is divided by Vidyādhara into two viz. Sajātīya—Saṁsṛṣṭi or the mixture of figures of same sorts; and Vijātiya-Saṁsṛti or the mixture of figures of different sorts. Saṁkara is divided by him into three classes—(i) the figure may exist in the relation of principal and subordinate and is then called Aṅgāṅgibhāva Saṁkara or (ii) a doubt may arise as of the two or more alaṁkāras which should be accepted and which should be rejected, (i.e. Sandehasaṁkara) no testimony being there either in favour or against the figures, (iii) or a number of alaṁkāras are conveyed by the same expression, the Saṁkara being then called Ekavācakānupraveśasaṁkara.

In 'Uttuṅgā girirājavat......proddāmakīrttikramāḥ',[2] Ārthī Pūrṇopamās are combined. It is sajātīyasaṁsṛṣṭi as there is a combination of one group of alaṁkāras. In 'Mandārasya...dhātrā kṛtam'[3] Śabdālaṁkāra Vṛttyanuprāsa and arthālaṁkāra Viśeṣa are combined. It is now vijatīya Saṁsṛṣṭi as two different groups of alaṁkāras are combined.

In 'Etāvantamanehasaṁ...Saudhād bahiḥ',.[4] Rūpakālaṁkāra (Puṣpekṣaṇa) causes Pratīyamānotprekṣā which results in Aṅgāṅgibhāva Saṁkara.

In 'Eṣa cintāmaṇiḥ......kimīdṛśaḥ',[5] Sandeha Saṁkara is illustrated. There is doubt between Rūpaka and Atiśayokti alaṁkāras. Both the alaṁkāras depend on the same word Eṣa cintāmaṇiḥ, Ayaṁ-Kalpa-pādapaḥ and asau kāmadhenuḥ. Here

1. Ekā. VIII. 76.
2. *Ibid.* example under VIII. 76.
3. *Ibid.* example under VIII. 76.
4. *Ibid.* example under VIII. 76.
5. *Ibid.* example under VIII. 76.

sādhaka or bādhaka pramāṇas for any one of the two are not found.

In 'Pratibhaṭakāntā......jayati',[1] there is mixture of both-Lāṭānuprāsa and Ananvaya and it is Ekavācakānupraveśa, both being conveyed by the same expression.

Bhāmaha, Daṇḍin, Vāmana, Rudraṭa, Bhoja and Hemacandra consider all kinds of combination as one. Bhāmaha, Daṇḍin, Vāmana and Bhoja name this combination as Saṁsṛṣṭi while Rudraṭa and Hemacandra call it Saṁkara. Udbhaṭa and Mammaṭa consider the two alaṁkāras separately. In the divisions also it may be noted that Udbhaṭa counts the combination of Śabdālaṁkāras and arthālaṁkāras in Saṁkara.

In studying these alaṁkāras it is seen that the alaṁkāras based not on sādṛśya, also give charm to the reader. Such basis may be opposition, like in Virodha, Vibhāvanā, and Viśeṣokti or chain like in Kāraṇamālā, Ekāvalī, Mālādīpaka and Sāra or maxims of reasoning as in Kāvyaliṅga and Anumāna. There is also similar charm in alaṁkāras based on maxims of sentence like Yathāsaṁkhya and Paryāya and also in those based on popular maxims like Pratyanīka.

As in the practical world, the curiosity to know the unknown also creates charm in poetry. This is found in Sūkṣma and Vyājokti alaṁkāras.

Sometimes poetry gives charm through the combination of alaṁkāras. Combination of two or more alaṁkāras creates special charm which is different from that which appears through other alaṁkāras. The combination may be of similar or dissimilar alaṁkāras or like tilataṇḍula or nīrakṣīra. In Saṁsṛṣṭi the combination of two alaṁkāras appear like tilataṇḍula and in Saṁkara this appears as nīrakṣīra.

---

1. Ekā. example under VIII. 76.

CHAPTER X

CONCLUSION : CONTRIBUTIONS

After examining the views of Vidyādhara, in connection with poetry and its various constituents, it is said that all the principles were established before Vidyādhara and some minor changes were being made in his time. As a result of the present study the following conclusions are arrived at :—

Traditionally popular six purposes of Kāvya are accepted in the Ekāvalī namely world-wide fame, immense-wealth, relief from evils due to worries, cherishing of sentiments, aesthetic pleasure and expansion of peace by removing mental-fickleness.

Śabdārtha and kavikarma are given importance by Vidyādhara while defining poetry. One should be very careful while composing poetry, for, the properly used words fulfil all desires, but even a single word improperly used, is an offence. Bad composition is called death itself. So, it is better to refrain from poetry than composing bad poetry.

Pratibhā, vyutpatti and abhyāsa, all three conjointly cause poetry. Here Vidyādhara has no new grounds to break.

Vidyādhara, being a staunch follower of dhvani-school, accepts dhvani as the soul of kāvya. He has refuted logically the ideas of anti-dhvani-school. Vidyādhara is the only person after Ruyyaka who has defended dhvani-theory.

Though there is no doubt that he follows Ānandavardhana and has no new grounds to break yet he elaborates his opinions with the force of solid logic in his individualistic way. Ānandavardhana simply uses 'apare' for 'abhāvavādins', while Vidyādhara specifically mentions Bhāmaha.

Vidyādhara stands singular in dividing lakṣaṇā into seven kinds. No other poetician has accepted the jahadajahatsvārthā kind of lakṣaṇā.

Actually, by giving seven kinds of lakṣaṇā, Vidyādhara seems to have committed a mistake. The first three divisions namely jahatsvārthā, ajahatsvārthā and jahadajahatsvārthā should have four subdivisions, two of which are sāropā and sādhyavasānā. Each of the latter should be again subdivided into śuddhā and gauṇī. With three kinds of Saṁkara and one kind of Saṁsṛṣṭi, these twelve kinds total forty-eight. With twelve more kinds not so divided, (i.e. with śuddhabhedas) the total number goes to sixty. Actually, Vidyādhara seems to accept this number.

It may be noted that by following Mammaṭa he adds the kinds instead of multiplying them. So, even according to Mammaṭa, the number of divisions of lakṣaṇā should be eight and not six. Another point to be noted in connection with lakṣaṇā is that Vidyādhara does not consider it only as śabdaśākti but regards it as an element that creates charm. He considers various kinds of *lakṣaṇā as the originators of various alaṁkāras* e.g. jahatsvārthā is the basis of Aprastuta-praśaṁsā and so on.

Three Śabdas and their corresponding arthas are accepted by Vidyādhara just in the manner of Mammaṭa.

As far as the divisions of Dhvanikāvya are concerned Vidyādhara follows the Dhvani-tradition yet he has his own style. While discussing rasa a kind of asaṁlakṣyakramavyaṅgyadhvani, Vidyādhara defines each rasa individually which is not done even by the ancient ācārya Bharata and also by Mammaṭa. While dealing with the ābhāsa of rasa, Vidyādhara has not agreed with Bhoja, who believes Śṛṅgārābhāsa in animals. Vidyādhara says that lower animals, too, can become vibhāvas and, are, therefore, entitled to the expression of rasa. In dividing guṇībhūtavyaṅgya kāvya also, into eight kinds, Vidyādhara completely follows the tradition and has nothing new to say.

Guṇa is discussed in three ways :

(i) as doṣābhāva i.e. absence of doṣa;

(ii) as doṣaviparyaya i.e. the opposite of doṣa; and

(iii) in connection with rasa.

Vidyādhara, like Ānandavardhana and Mammaṭa, accepts

guṇa as connected with rasa. He believes in the existence of three guṇas only and ten guṇas of śabda and artha are included in these three.

Three rītis viz. Vaidarbhī, Gauḍīyā and Pāñcālī are also discussed but in accordance with Mammaṭa. Three corresponding vṛttis namely Madhurā, Madhyamā and Paruṣā are also mentioned.

Although in the treatment of guṇa, rīti and vṛtti and in the acceptance of only three guṇas, Vidyāhara has no new grounds to break, his treatment of rīti differs from that of Bhoja. He has not kept it either under guṇas or under alaṁkāras but has discussed it independently.

While dealing with doṣas Vidyādhara does not define a doṣa which shows that he accepts its general nature i.e. Doṣāstasyāpakarṣakāḥ. Inspite of having full faith in dhvani, Ānandavardhana and Mammaṭa, a diversion is evident regarding the treatment of doṣas. Discussing only four principal doṣas Vidyādhara deviates from tradition. By this it may be concluded that these four doṣas should be avoided completely. However, these should never be overlooked. Moreover, all the doṣas discussed by the previous ācāryas, may be included in these four alone.

A special feature of the Ekāvalī requires particular mention. Avimṛṣṭavidheyāṁśadoṣa is a grammatical one. It has not been discussed in as great a detail by others as by Vidyādhara. Mahimabhaṭṭa accepts five doṣas taking Vācyāvacana and Avācyavacan as two separate, but Vidyādhara accepts these as one because if one is present, the other is naturally present, too. Thus, there is no need of accepting the two separately.

While discussing Punaruktvadābhāsa along with śabdālaṁkāras, Vidyādhara exhibits deep thinking as the opposite of the Paunaruktyadoṣa constitutes a figure namely Punaruktavadābhāsa.

Being a follower of Dhvani-school, Vidyādhara discusses only five śabdālaṁkāras all of which are based on repetition.

In the beginning the śabdālaṁkāras occupied an important

place and were discussed elaborately. Daṇḍin, Vāmana, Rudraṭa and Bhoja have discussed the śabdālaṁkāras elaborately but the number of śabdālaṁkāras had already started to decrease before Vidyādhara. This can be proved by the fact that Appayya Dīkṣita does not deal with even a single śabdālaṁkāra in either of his two great works namely, Citramīmāṁsā and Kuvalayānanda. Similarly, Jagannātha also exempted himself cautiously from their discussion.

The arthālaṁkāras are discussed here under three heads namely Vācyasādṛśyamūlaka, Gamyasādṛśyamūlaka and Sādṛśyetaramūlaka.

Though in the discussion of Vācyasādṛśyamūlaka arthālaṁkāras Vidyādhara has nothing to add yet he cannot be called a blind follower of his predecessors. In dealing with the figures, no doubt, he is greatly influenced by Mammaṭa and Ruyyaka, however, he adopts his own style. He discusses the Upameyopamālaṁkāra prior to Ananvaya, may be because in Upameyopamā, the difference between Upamāna and upameya is more than it is in Ananvaya. Upameyopamā has separate upamāna and upameya while in Ananvaya the same thing is treated as both. This order seems to be quite appropriate.

Grossness was being gradually replaced by subtlity. Moreover, in these alaṁkāras, i.e. from Upamā to Atiśayokti the difference between upamāna and upameya decresses gradually i.e. abheda between the two increases. In Upamā, upameya and upamāna are linked on the basis of similarity. In Rūpaka, two different things appear as similar through super-imposition. So, in Rūpaka, Pariṇāma, Sandeha and Ullekha āropaviṣaya is not concealed while it is concealed in Apahnuti. This different upameya is called upamāna, denying its own characteristics by words signifying falsity, such as chala, vyāja, kapaṭa, miṣa etc. In Utprekṣā, abheda becomes deeper and the poet wants to say that āropaviṣaya is āropyamāṇa. The way of adhyavasāna (certainty) is proved by using the words Sambhāvana, abhimāna, tarka, ūha, manye, śaṅke, nūnaṁ, dhruvaṁ, iva and vā; while in Atiśayokti prominence of adhyavasāna comes with its perfection. Thus the difference between prakṛta and aprakṛta totally disappears in Atiśayokti.

In this way, difference between upamāna and upameya, which exists in its full form in Upamālaṁkāra goes on decreasing slowly in these alaṁkāras. In Atiśayokti, it disappears totally.

The names Tulyayogitā, Dīpaka, Prativastūpamā, Dṛṣṭānta and Nidarśanā are synonymous with Sādṛśya. Being suggested Sādṛśya appears clearly. Ih Vyatireka, the upamāna is changed into upameya and vice-versa. The Sādṛśya does not disappear but the idea that upameya is similar to upamāna, is suggested and not expressed. Due to the opposite use of upamāna and upameya, the similarity becomes more concealed here than in the previous alaṁkāras.

In Sahokti, similarity with others is suggested through the word 'saha'. In ordinary sentences, when it is said that 'Devadatta goes with his brother', there is no sense of similarity. But in poetry, with the word 'saha', the poet conveys the idea of similarity between the two, although this is more concealed than in previous alaṁkāras.

In Samāsokti, there is not a single sign for similarity between prakṛta and aprakṛta but to only adjectives (that have double meaning) readers have a shadow of aprakṛta and then upamānopameyabhāva arises. In Arthāntaranyāsa, the use of adjectives with double meaning also disappears. Only similarity is suggested by the use of two sentences—in one of which the general idea is expressed and in the other, the particular one—connected with Sāmarthyasamarthakabhāva. In Paryāyokti, Vyājastuti and Ākṣepa, similarity is totally concealed and the charm of these alaṁkāras depends only on suggestion.

In this way, in these alaṁkāras, the concealment of the suggested similarity is increasing gradually and in Arthāntaranyāsa, it becomes more and more concealed. In other alaṁkāras like Paryāyokti, Vyājastuti and Ākṣepa the similarity is so concealed that it is not possible for a reader of general poetry to find it but it may only be inferred.

Some alaṁkāras are completely devoid of Sādṛśya and depend on some other basis than sādṛśya. They may be based on opposition as Virodha, Vibhāvanā, and Viśeṣokti; or may be chain like as Kāraṇamālā, Ekāvalī, Mālādīpaka and Sāra : or based on maxims of reasoning as Kāvyaliṅga and Anumāna; or maxims of sentence as Yathāsaṁkhya and Paryāya and also on popular maxims like Pratyanīka etc. These alaṁkāras generally create charm even if they are devoid of sādṛśya. Charm does exist even in those which may be the combinations of various alaṁkāras. The combination may be either of similar or dissimilar alaṁkāras but all these alaṁkāras enhance the beauty of the body of poetry. In the treatment of these alaṁkāras Vidyādhara is greatly influenced by Ruyyaka.

In his Ekāvalī, Vidyādhara has tried to re-establish dhvani by criticising various antidhvani views on one hand and all the poetic principles as dhvani, rasa, guṇa, rīti, doṣa and alaṁkāra, are also discussed in details, on the other hand.

The necessity of writing the Ekāvalī is seen because Vidyādhara must have felt that the king like Narasiṁha of Utkala should not remain unknown for long. So he composed all the illustrations in praise of that king. Narasiṁha was a great king of south India. All the illustrative verses of the Ekāvalī panegyrise king Narasiṁha. Thus, Vidyādhara is an originator of this tradition and this tradition was followed by Vidyānātha (Pratāparudrayaśobhūṣaṇa), Narasiṁhakavi (Nañrājayaśobhūṣaṇa), Kṛṣṇadīkṣita (Raghunātha-Bhūpālīya) and Devaśaṁkarabhaṭṭa (Alaṁkāramañjuṣā). Appayya Dīkṣita and Jagannātha have quoted Vidyādhara many times.

Appendix

INTRODUCTION

Page 2 1. (i) हितेन सह-सहितम् तस्य भावः ।

(ii) सहितयोः (शब्दार्थयोः) भावः ।

(iii) साहित्यपाथोनिधिमन्थनोत्थं कर्णामृतं रक्षत हे कवीन्द्राः ।
यदस्य दैत्या इव लुण्ठनाय काव्यार्थचौराः प्रगुणीभवन्ति ॥

—Vikramāṅkadevacarita. I. 11.

2. साहित्यसङ्गीतकलाविहीनः साक्षात्पशुः पुच्छविषाणहीनः ।
तृणं न खादन्नपि जीवमानस्तद्भागधेयं परमं पशूनाम् ॥

—Nītiśataka. 12.

3. कीदृशे बन्धे, 'वक्रकविव्यापारशालिनि' । वक्रो योऽसौ शास्त्रादि-प्रसिद्धशब्दार्थोपनिबन्धव्यतिरेकी...

—VJ-vṛtti on I. 7.

4. काव्यस्यात्मा स एवार्थस्तथा चादिकवेः पुरा ।
क्रौञ्चद्वन्द्ववियोगोत्थः शोकः श्लोकत्वमागतः ॥ —DhL. I. 5.

Page 3 1. रसैः शृङ्गारकरुणहास्यरौद्रभयानकैः ।
वीरादिभिश्च संयुक्तं काव्यमेतदगायताम् ॥

—Bālakāṇḍa of Rāmāyaṇa, IV. 9.

2. अप्युपमार्थेऽपि कर्मोपसंग्रहार्थेऽपि पदपूरणाः ।

तेषामेते चत्वार उपमार्थे भवन्ति । इवेति भाषायाञ्च ।...नेति प्रतिषेधार्थीयो भाषायाम् ।...चिदित्येषोऽनेककर्मा ।...नु इत्येषोऽनेक-कर्मा ।... —Nirukta I. 2.

3. (i) उपमानानि सामान्यवचनैः ।

(ii) उपमितं व्याघ्रादिभिः सामान्याप्रयोगे ॥

—Aṣṭādhyāyī II-1.55 and 56.

4. (a) सैषा सर्वैव वक्रोक्तिरनयार्थो विभाव्यते ।
यत्नोऽस्यां कविना कार्यः कोऽलङ्कारोऽनया विना ॥

—KAB II. 85.

(b) अलङ्कारान्तराणामप्येकमाहुः परायणम् ।
वागीशमहितामुक्तिमिमामतिशयाह्वयाम् ।। —KD. II.220.

5. विशिष्टा पदरचना रीतिः —KASV. I. 2. 7.

Page 5 1. प्रालेयाचलकन्यकाकुचतटीपत्रावलीशिल्पिनः
प्रेङ्खद्भालविलोचनानलशिखानिष्पीतचेतोभुवः ।
देवस्येन्दुविभूषणस्य सुचिरं पादारविन्दद्वयं
युष्मान्पातु सुरासुरेश्वर शिरोरत्नांशुकिञ्जल्कितम् ।।—EKā. I. 1.

2. As given in the foot notes of the chapter.

Page 6 1. कृत्वा काव्यमवाप विश्वमहितां कीर्त्ति कविग्रामणीः
श्रीहर्षः श्रियमद्भुतां हरिहरो लेभेऽर्जुनक्ष्माभुजः ।
मृत्योस्त्रासमपाचकार मलयक्ष्मामण्डलाखण्डल-
स्तत् किञ्चिन्न विलोक्यते न किल यत्काव्यात्समुन्मीलति ।।
—Ekā. I. 11.

2. Introduction to Ekā.

3. OHRJ, 1954, Vol. IV.

'Date of Vidyādhara, the author of Ekāvalī,'
Śrī Satyanārāyaṇa Rājaguru, pp. 89-98.

4. (a) साहित्यार्णवकर्णधार करुणापीयूषपाथोनिधे
विद्वच्चातकवारिवाह कमलापर्यङ्कपङ्केरुह ।
... ...
—Ekā. example under VIII. 2.

(b) वाहिनीश्वरता लक्ष्मीशालिता भूरिसत्त्वता
... ...
—*Ibid.* example under VIII. 2.

(c) ... ...
सर्वे तन्मनसि स्थितां श्रियमनुध्यायन्ति सैषापि यद्-
भ्रूभङ्गैकवशंवदा स जयति श्रीमान् नृसिंहो नृपः ।।
—Ekā. example under VIII. 48. etc.

5. OHRJ-1959, Vol. 8. 'King Narasiṁha eulogised in the Ekāvalī of Vidyādhara,' Śrī Kedāranātha Mahāpātra, p. 118.

Page 7 1. पृथुलकुचभारमुत्कटमदनं तरलाक्षमाकुलश्वसनम् ।
अन्तः पुरीयति वनं यवनावनिवल्लभो नृसिंह नृप ॥
—Ekā. exemple under VIII. 2.

2. Reports on Sanskrit Mss., 1887-91, pp. LXV-LXIX (Dr. Bhandarkar)

3. JASB-Vol. 72-73 'Chronology of Eastern Gaṅga Kings of Orissa', Babu MM. Cakravarti, p. 97.

4. History of Sanskrit Poetics, p. 282.

5. Descriptive Catalogue of the Sanskrit Mss. in the collection of the ASB, Vol. VI, Preface, pp. ccxciii-ccxciv.

6. PO-1936, I, p. 13. Royal Patronage and Sanskrit Poetics, Baladeva Upādhyāya.

Page 8 1. JASB, 1903, p. 49.

Page 9 1. एष विद्याधरस्तेषु कान्तासंमितलक्षणम् ।
करोमि नरसिंहस्य चाटुश्लोकानुदाहरन् ॥ —Ekā. I. 7.

2. OHRJ-April 1959, Vol. 8, p. 118. King Narasiṁha eulogised in the Ekāvalī of Vidyādhara Mahāpatra (Śrī Kedāranātha)

CHAPTER I

Page 11 1. विश्वोल्लङ्घन-जाङ्घिकीं वितनुते कीर्त्ति विधत्ते श्रियम्
हेलाधिक्कृतयक्षराजविभवां चिन्ताकरं हन्त्यधम् ।
दुग्धे स्वादुतरान् रसान् वितरति स्फारं कलाकौशलम् ।
काव्यं निवृतिमावहत्यपि परिस्पन्दापहं चेतसः ॥ —Ekā. I. 9.

2. धर्मार्थकाममोक्षेषु वैचक्षण्यं कलासु च ।
प्रीतिं करोति कीर्त्तिं च साधुकाव्यनिबन्धनम् ॥ —KAB I. 2.

3. काव्यं यशसेऽर्थकृते व्यवहारविदे शिवेतरक्षतये ।
सद्यः परनिर्वृतये कान्तासम्मिततयोपदेशयुजे ॥ —KP. I. 2.

4. उत्तमाधममध्यानां नराणां कर्मसंश्रयम् ।
हितोपदेशजननं धृतिक्रीडासुखादिकृत् ॥
एतद्रसेषु भावेषु सर्वकर्मक्रियास्वथ ।
सर्वोपजननं नाट्यमेतद्भविष्यति ॥
दुःखार्तानां श्रमार्तानां शोकार्तानां तपस्विनाम् ।
विश्रान्तिजननं लोके नाट्यमेतन्मयाकृतम् ॥
धर्म्यं यशस्यमायुष्यं हित बुद्धिविवर्धनम् ।
लोकोपदेशजननं नाट्यमेतद्भविष्यति ॥ —NS. I. 113-115.

5. द्वे ब्रह्मणी वेदितव्ये शब्दब्रह्म परं च यत् ।
शब्दब्रह्मणि निष्णातः परं ब्रह्माधिगच्छति ॥

—Viṣṇupurāṇa, 6. 5. 54.

6. सहृदयहृदयाह्लादि शब्दार्थमयत्वमेव काव्यलक्षणम् ।

—DhL. vṛtti on I. 1.

7. काव्यं सद्दृष्टादृष्टार्थं प्रातिकीर्तिहेतुत्वात् । —KASV. I. 1.5.

8. निर्दोषं गुणवत्काव्यमलङ्कारैरलङ्कृतम् ।
रसान्वितं कविः कुर्वन् कार्त्तिप्रीतिं च विन्दति ॥ —SKBh. I. 2.

9. कृत्वा काव्यभवाप विश्वमहितां कीर्त्ति कविग्रामणीः
श्रीहर्षः श्रियमद्भुतां हरिहरो लेभेऽर्जुनक्ष्माभुजः ।
मृत्योस्त्रासमणाचकार मलयक्ष्मामण्डलाखण्डलः… —Ekā. I. 11.

Page 12 1. ध्वनिप्रधान काव्य तु कान्तासम्मतमीरितम् ।
शब्दार्थौ गुणतां नीत्वा व्यञ्जनप्रवणं यतः ॥ —Ekā. I. 6.

2. शब्दप्रधानं वेदाख्यानं प्रभुसम्मितमुच्यते ।
ईषत्पाठान्यथापाठे प्रत्यवायस्य दर्शनात् ॥ —*Ibid.* I. 4.

3. इतिहासादिकं शास्त्रं मित्रसम्मितमुच्यते ।
अस्यार्थवादरूपत्वात् कथ्यतेऽर्थप्रधानतः ॥ —*Ibid.* I. 5.

4. कवयत इति कविस्तस्य (कवेः) कर्म काव्यम्…
—*Ibid.* vṛtti on I. 9.

5. शाणोत्कीर्णमिवोज्वलद्युतिपदं बन्धोऽर्धनारीश्वर-
श्लाघालङ्घनजाङ्घिको दिवि लतोद्भिन्नेव चार्थोद्गतिः ।
किञ्चित्पीडितचन्द्रमण्डलगलत्पीयूषहृद्यो रसः
तत् किञ्चित् कविकर्म मर्म न पुनर्वाग्डिण्डिमाडम्बरः ॥
—*Ibid* I. 10.

6. गौर्गौः कामदुघा सम्यक् प्रयुक्ता स्मर्यते बुधैः ।
दुष्प्रयुक्ता पुनर्गोत्वं प्रयोक्तुः सैव शंसति ॥ —KD. I. 6.

Page 13 1. (i) शब्दार्थौ सहितौ काव्यम्… —KAB. I. 16.
(ii) काव्यशब्दोऽय गुणालङ्कारसंस्कृतयोः शब्दार्थयोर्वर्तते ।
—KASV. on I. 1. 1.
(iii) ननु शब्दार्थौ काव्यम्…—KAR. II. 1.
(iv) गुणवदलङ्कृतञ्च वाक्यमेव काव्यम्, —KM. p. 24.
(v) शब्दार्थौ सहितौ वक्रकविव्यापारशालिनि ।
बन्धे व्यवस्थितौ काव्यं तद्विदाह्लादकारिणि ॥ —VJ I. 7.
(vi) तददोषौ शब्दार्थौ सगुणावनलंकृती पुनः क्वापि ।—KP. I. 4
(vii) अदोषौ सगुणौ सालङ्कारौ च शब्दार्थौ काव्यम् ॥
—KAnu. I. 11.

2. वाक्यमिष्टार्थव्यवच्छिन्ना पदावली ॥
काव्य स्फुटदलङ्कारं गुणवद्दोषवर्जितम् ।
योनिर्वेद लोकश्च सिद्धमन्नादयोनिजं ॥
—Agnipurāṇā 337-6-7.

3. …शरीरं तावदिष्टार्थ व्यवच्छिन्ना पदावली ॥ —KD. I. 10.

4. Supra I. 6 on p. 11.

5. Supra I. 8 on p. 11.

6. प्रतिभा बहुशास्त्रदर्शिता, बहुधा काव्यविदां च शिक्षया ।
मुहुरभ्यसनं मनीषिभिः, कथितं कारणमस्य संभवे ।। —Ekā. I.12

7. नैसर्गिकी च प्रतिभा श्रुतं च बहुनिर्मलम् ।
अमन्दश्चाभियोगोऽस्या कारणं काव्यसम्पदः ।। —KD. I.103.

8. ···त्रितयमिदं व्याप्रियते शक्तिर्व्युत्पत्तिरभ्यासः ।। —KAR. I.14

9. शक्तिर्निपुणता लोकशास्त्रकाव्याद्यवेक्षणात् ।
काव्यज्ञशिक्षयाभ्यास इति हेतुस्तदुद्भवे । —KP. I. 3.

Page 14 1. अकवितैव वरं कुकवितायाः ।
कुकविता हि कायानपेतमनस्कं मरणम् ।
—Ekā. vṛtti on I. 12.

2. नाकवित्वमधर्माय व्याधये दण्डनाय वा ।
कुकवित्वं पुनः साक्षान्मृतिमाहुर्मनीषिणः ।। —KAB. I. 12.

3. प्रतिभायाः प्रागुपादानं व्युत्पत्त्यपेक्षया प्राधान्यद्योतनाय व्युत्पत्ति-
मान्द्याविर्भूतदोषापाकरणाय प्रभविष्णुत्वात् प्रतिभायाः ।
—Ekā. vṛtti on I. 12.

4. अव्युत्पत्तिकृतो दोषः शक्त्या संव्रियते कवेः ।
यस्त्वशक्तिकृतस्तस्य स झटित्यवभासते ।।
—DhL. Parikara śloka under III. 6.

5. प्रज्ञा नवनवोल्लेखशालिनी प्रतिभा मता···
—(Kāvyakautuka) quoted by Hemacandra in KAnu under I. 3. and also by Dr. Kane in History of Sanskrit Poetics, p. 335.

6. कवित्वबीजं प्रतिभानम्··· —KASV. I. 3. 16.

7. मनसि सदा सुसमाधिनि विस्फुरणमनेकधाभिधेयस्य ।
अक्लिष्टानि पदानि च विभान्ति यस्यामसौ शक्तिः ।।
—KAR. I. 15.

8. प्रतिभेत्यपरैरुदिता सहजोत्पाद्या च सा द्विधा भवति ।
पुंसा सह जातत्वादनयोस्तु ज्यायसी सहजा ।। —KAR. I.16.

9. प्रतिभास्य हेतुः ।। प्रतिभा नवनवोल्लेखशालिनी प्रज्ञा । अस्य काव्यस्येदं प्रधानं कारणम् । व्युत्पत्यभ्यासौ तु प्रतिभाया एव संस्कारकाविति वक्ष्यते । सा च सहजौपाधिकी चेति द्विधा ।

—KAnu—I.4 and its vṛtti.

10. तेषां हि शिक्षया काव्यकरणविचारयोरविच्छेदेन परिशीलनमभ्यासः ।

—Ekā. vṛtti on I.12.

11. काव्यं कर्त्तुं विचारयितुं च ये जानन्ति तदुपदेशेन करणे योजने च पौनः पुन्येन प्रवृत्तिः ।

—KP. vṛtti on I.3.

12. 'सा केवलं काव्ये हेतुः' इति यायावरीयः । —KM. P.21.

13. प्रतिभैव च कवीनां काव्यकरणम् ।
व्युत्पत्यभ्यासौ तस्या एव संस्कारकारकौ न तु काव्यहेतू ।।
(Alaṁkāratilaka of Vāgbhaṭṭa II), Quoted by Dr. Kane in History of Sanskrit Poetics, p. 334.

Page 15 1. तस्य च कारणं कविगता केवला प्रतिभा । —Rg. p.8.

2. शब्दार्थौ वपुरस्य तत्र विबुधैरात्माभ्यधायि ध्वनि,
इचार्वाकैरिव कैश्चिदस्य न पुनः सत्तापि संभाव्यते ।
कर्तुं लक्षणमक्षमैरयमनिर्वाच्यः परैरुच्यते,
भाक्तोऽन्यैः समुदीर्यतेऽस्य हि ततो ब्रूमः स्वरूपं वयम् ।।

—Ekā. I.13.

3. यत्रार्थः शब्दो वा तमर्थमुपसर्जनीकृतस्वार्थौ ।
व्यङ्क्तः काव्यविशेषः स ध्वनिरिति सूरिभिः कथितः ।।

—DhL I.13.

4. प्रालेयाचलकन्यकाकुचतटी पत्रावली शिल्पिनः
प्रेङ्खद्भालविलोचनानलशिखानिष्पीतचेतोभुवः ।
देवस्येन्दुविभूषणस्य सुचिरं पादारविन्दद्वयं
युष्मान्पातु सुरासुरेश्वर शिरोरत्नांशुकिञ्जलिकतम् ।।

—Ekā. I.1.

Page 16. 1. रसान्तरसमावेशः प्रस्तुतस्य रसस्य यः ।
नोपहन्त्यङ्गितां सोऽस्य स्थायित्वेनावभासिनः ।।

—DhL. III. 22.

2. Supra, I. 2 on p. 15.

3. काव्यस्यात्मा ध्वनिरिति बुधैर्यः समाम्नातपूर्व-
स्तस्याभावं जगदुरपरे भाक्तमाहुस्तमन्ये ।
केचिद्वाचां स्थितमविषये तत्वमूचुस्तदीयं,
तेन ब्रूमः सहृदयमनः प्रीतये तत्स्वरूपम् ।।

—DhL. I.1.

4. तस्य (ध्वनेः) चाभावं मन्यमाना लोकायतिका इव केचन नास्ति ध्वनिरित्याचक्षते ।

···Ekā. vṛtti on I. 13.

Page 17. 1. ···ध्वनिर्गुणालङ्कारेभ्यो न व्यतिरिच्यते ।

—Ekā. vṛtti on I. 13.

2. ···गुणेषु तावन्न ध्वनेरन्तर्भावो रसधर्मत्वात्तेषाम् न हि धर्मे धर्मिणोऽन्तर्भावः । नाप्यलङ्कारेषु, वाच्यमात्रविश्रान्तेषु श्लेषादिषु व्यभिचारात्···

—*Ibid.* vṛtti on I.13.

3. शब्दस्यैकाभिधाशक्तिरर्थस्यैकैव लिङ्गता ।
न व्यञ्जकत्वमनयोः समस्तीत्युपपादितम् ।। —VV I. 27.

4. तदेवं वाच्यप्रतीयमानयोर्वक्ष्यमाण क्रमेण लिङ्गलिङ्गिभावस्य समर्थनात् सर्वस्यैव ध्वनेरनुमानान्तर्भावः समन्वितो भवति ।

—*Ibid.* vṛtti on I.20.

Page 18. 1. यत्पुनरनुमानतो नातिरिच्यते ध्वनिरित्यत्राचष्ट महिमभट्टस्तदपि पलालायमानम्...प्रकृते ध्वनिः साध्यसामान्यं शब्दार्थौ च साधन-सामान्यं । तत्र च ध्वनेरनुपलब्धिर्वा शब्दार्थयोस्तादात्म्यं वा तदुत्पत्तिर्वा साधिका, न तावदनुपलब्धिः साध्यं बोधयतीति··· न हि वयं ध्वन्युपलम्भेन ध्वन्यभावं साधयामः···न हि शब्दोऽर्थो वा गमकत्वेन योऽभ्युपगम्यते तस्य प्रतीयमानेन साध्येन सह गम्यगमक-भावस्तादात्म्येन व्यवस्थितः, प्रत्युत शब्दार्थन्यक्कारेणेव तस्य प्रवर्त्तमानत्वात्, तर्हि···तदुत्पत्तिरेव···न प्रतिष्ठामधिष्ठास्यति··· न च प्रस्तुते शब्दार्थयोरनुमानवादिना लिङ्गत्वेनाङ्गीकृतयोः प्रतीय-मानाज्जायमानत्वमनुमतम् । आत्मजन्मनः प्राचिकाले स्वसामग्री संनिधानादेव तयोराविर्भावदर्शनात् ।

—Ekā. vṛtti on I. 13.

2. (a) अभिहितानां च पदार्थानां तेषामाकाङ्क्षायोग्यतासंनिधिवशादन्योन्यमन्वये जातेऽननुभूतपूर्वः कोऽप्यभूतपूर्वः पदानभिधेयो विशिष्टरूपो वाक्यार्थः परिस्फुरति !

—*Ibid.* vṛtti on I.13.

(b) ननु वाच्यादसंबद्धं तावन्न प्रतीयते यतः कुतश्चित् यस्य कस्यचिदर्थस्य प्रतीतेः प्रसङ्गात् ।—इति व्यक्तिवादिनः पुनस्तत् अदूषणम् ।

—KP. vṛtti on v. 13.

3. यत्र स्वस्वपदार्थमात्राभिधानाय जागरूकव्यापाराण्यपि पदानि स्वैः-स्वैः पदार्थैराब्धमपि न वाक्यार्थमभिधातुमीशते तत्रार्थान्तरभूतो ध्वनिरभिधामवगाहिष्यत इति का नाम वः प्रत्याशा ।

—Ekā. vṛtti on I. 13.

Page 19 1. …वाक्यान्तर्वर्त्तिनामेव पदानामितरेतरमाकाङ्क्षासंनिधियोग्यतावशादन्वितैः पदार्थैरन्वयं गतानामेव संकेतविषयत्वमिति विशेषणविशेष्यभावापन्नः कृत्युद्देशविशिष्टः पदार्थसार्थ एव वाक्यार्थः । अन्वितानामेव पदार्थानां विशिष्टत्वमित्यमिदधानैरन्विताभिधानवादिभिः… ।

—Ekā. vṛtti on I. 13.

2. यत्र संकेतनिकेतनीकृतविशिष्टरूपवाक्यार्थाभिधायिनो वाक्यस्य स्ववाच्यानतिरिक्तासंकेतिताविशेषभूतपदार्थाभिधानेऽपि न सामर्थ्यं तत्रार्थान्तरभूतः प्रतीयमानः कथमिवावतरिष्यति वचनीयताम्।… अपि च यदि न व्यापारान्तरमभिधातः स्वीक्रियते तर्हि कृतं लक्षणया ।

—*Ibid.* vṛtti on I. 13.

3. अपि च नास्ति यदि यङ्ग्यव्यञ्जकभाव इत्युच्यते तर्हि च्युतसंस्कृतिप्रमुखानां दोषाणां नित्यत्वं श्रुतिकटुप्रभृतीनां त्वनित्यत्वमिति विभागकरणस्य कैमर्थ्यं प्रसज्यते ।

—*Ibid.* vṛtti on I.13.

Page 20 1. (a) अपि च यदि प्रतीयमानोऽर्थो नाभविष्यत् तर्हि काव्यान्तर्निविष्टस्यासभ्यस्मृतिहेतोः पदार्थान्तरान्वयविरहिणः पदस्य हेयत्वं न समपत्स्यत ।

—Ekā. vṛtti on 1.13.

(b) किं च 'कुरु रुचिम्' इति पदयोर्वैपरीत्ये काव्यान्तर्वर्तिनि कथं दुष्टत्वम् । न ह्यत्रासभ्योऽर्थः पदार्थान्तरैरन्वितः इत्यनभिधेय एवेति एवमादि अपरित्याज्यं स्यात् ।

—KP. vṛtti on V. 47.

2. अपि च विद्यमानेऽपि विरुद्धधर्माध्यासे कारणभेदे वाच्यव्यङ्ग्ययोर्भेदो नाभ्युपेयते तर्हि क्वचिदपि न भक्तिव्यं भेदेन ।

Ekā. vṛtti on I. 13.

3. कस्स व ण होइ रोसोदट्ठण पिआए सव्वणं अहरं ।
सभमरपदुमग्घायिणि वारिअ अवामे सहसु एण्हिम् ।।

—*Ibid* example under I. 13.

4. 'कस्स व ण···एण्हिम् ।।' इत्यादौ सखीतत्कान्तादिगतत्वेन विषयस्य च भेदेऽपि यद्येकत्वम् तत् क्वचिदपि नीलपीतादौ भेदो न स्यात् ।

—KP. example V. 135 & vṛtti on V. 47.

5. तथापि यदि तस्यानाख्येयत्वं तदा सर्वेष्वपि वस्तुषु तदतिप्रसज्यमानमनिवार्यं स्यात्, अथानयातिशयोक्त्या लोकोत्वरमस्या निरूप्यते, तदा सिद्धं नः समीहितम् ।

—Ekā. vṛtti on I. 13.

6. अथ भक्तेरूपचारादागतोऽयमिति ये भाक्तमभिदधते···

—*Ibid*. vṛtti on I.13.

7. भक्तिर्व्यक्तिश्चेति न तत्वान्तरमिति···न···उभयोरप्यनयोः ··· परस्परविरुद्धाणां धर्माणामुपलम्भसंभवात्, तथाहि मुख्यार्थबाधाद्यनुसंधानप्रवृत्तत्वं भक्तेः । वक्तृबोद्धव्यादिवैशिष्ट्यानुसंधानप्रवृतत्वं तु व्यक्तेः । ··· विवक्षितान्यपरवाच्ये ध्वनौ भक्त्युपलक्षितत्वाभावादुपलक्षणत्वाभ्युपगऽमेपि भक्तिव्यक्त्योरभिन्नत्वासंभवाच्च ।

—*Ibid*. vṛtti on I. 13.

8. (a) वक्तृबोद्धव्यकाकूनां वाक्यवाच्यान्यसंनिधेः ।।
प्रस्तावदेशकालादेर्वैशिष्ट्यात् प्रतिभाजुषाम् ।
योऽर्थस्यान्यार्थधीहेतुर्व्यापारो व्यक्तिरेव सा ।।

—KP. III. 21. 22.

(b) बोद्धृस्वरूपसङ्ख्यानिमित्तकार्य्यप्रतीतिकालानाम् ।
आश्रयविषयादीनां भेदादिभिन्नोऽभिधेयतो व्यङ्ग्यः ।।

—SD. V.2.

CHAPTER II

Page 22 1. मुख्यं तमर्थमाहुः साक्षाद्यत्रास्य संकेतः ।
व्यापारोऽपि च मुख्योऽभिधीयतेऽस्याभिधा रूपः ॥

—Ekā. II. 2.

2. स मुख्योऽर्थस्तत्र मुख्यो व्यापारोऽस्याभिधोच्यते ॥ —KP- II. 8.

3. The PrimaryMeaning of a Word, p. 72.

4. ···यद्यप्यर्थक्रियाकारितया व्यक्तेरेव प्रवृत्तिनिवृत्तियोग्यता तथापि व्यक्तीनामानन्त्याद्व्यभिचाराच्च प्रतिव्यक्ति न शक्यते संकेतः कर्त्तुमिति जातिरेव विषयः संकेतस्य ॥

—Ekā. vṛtti on II. 1.

5. (a) ···प्रतिव्यक्ति न शक्यते संकेतः कर्त्तुमिति···

—*Ibid.* vṛtti on II. 1.

(b) यद्यप्यर्थक्रियाकारितया प्रवृत्तिनिवृत्तियोग्या व्यक्तिरेव तथाप्यानन्त्याद्व्यभिचाराच्च तत्र संकेतः कर्त्तुं न युज्यते ।

KP. vṛtti on II. 7.

Page 24 1. मुख्यार्थानुपपत्तौ तद्योगेरूढितोऽथवापि फलात् ।
अन्योऽर्थो यदि लक्ष्यो भवति तदा लक्षणाभिमता ॥

—Ekā. II.5.

2. मुख्यार्थबाधे तद्योगे रूढितोऽथ प्रयोजनात् ।
अन्योऽर्थो लक्ष्यते यत्सा लक्षणारोपिता क्रिया ॥ —KP. II. 9.

3. कर्मणि कुशल इत्यादौ कुशोपादानरूपावयवार्थासंभवाद्विवेकिनि रूढितो लक्षणा । अन्यत्रद्योषगतपवित्रत्वादिज्ञानफलत्वात् फलतो लक्षणेत्यर्थः । इह रूढितो लक्षणैकविधेव । फलतो लक्षणा तु प्रथमं शुद्धा ।···

—Taralā Sanskrit Commentary of Mallinātha on Ekā. II. 5.

Page 25 1. इत्यस्माभिर्भिदाः सप्त लक्षणायाः प्रदर्शिताः ।
संकरेण त्रिरूपेण संसृष्ट्या चैकरूपया ॥

अस्याः संकलनेऽन्योन्यमष्टाविंशतिरीरिताः ।
पञ्चत्रिंशत् समाख्याताः शुद्धभेदैः समं पुनः ॥

—Ekā. II. 10-11.

2. ···इदं वक्ष्यमाणस्य रूपकालङ्कारस्य बीजम् । ···इदमतिशयोक्ति-प्रथमभेदस्य ।

—KAnu. vṛtti on I. 17.

3. शब्दे पदार्थे वाक्यार्थे संख्यायां कारके तथा ।
लिङ्गे चेयमलङ्काराङ्कुरबीजतया स्थिता ॥

—Candrāloka, IX. 16.

Page 26 1. लक्षणा तेन षड्विधा —KP II. 12.

2. एवमशीतिप्रकारा लक्षणा ।

—SD. vṛtti on II. 23.

3. इयं तावद् द्विविधा निरूढा प्रयोजनवती च । तत्रापि द्वितीया द्विविधा गौणी शुद्धा च । तत्राद्या सारोपा, साध्यवसाना चेति द्विविधा । अन्त्या चतुर्विधा··· —RG. p. 146.

4. लक्षणा त्रिविधा—जहल्लक्षणा, अजहल्लक्षणा, जहदजहल्लक्षणा चेति ।

—Tarkadīpikā, p. 128.

5. प्रकारान्तरेण लक्षणा त्रिविधा—जहल्लक्षणा, अजहल्लक्षणा, जहदजहल्लक्षणा चेति ।

—Vedāntaparibhāṣā, p. 204.

6. शब्दोऽपर्यंति परार्थं यथात्मानं तदा जहत्स्वार्था ।

—Ekā. II.6.

7. ···परार्थं स्वसमर्पणम् ।
···लक्षणं चेत्युक्ता··· ॥ —KP. II. 10.

8. इयं तु लक्षणलक्षणेति परैरभिधीयते ।
इयमेवाप्रस्तुतप्रशंसादेरलंकारस्य बीजम् ॥

—Ekā. vṛtti on II. 6.

9. सा विपरीता यस्यां लक्षयति पदं स्ववाच्यविपरीतम् ॥
···इयमेव व्याजस्तुतेर्बीजम् ॥

—*Ibid.* II. 6 and vṛtti on II. 6 also.

10. त्वत्खड्गधारापयसि प्रवीराः
पतन्ति ये संयति संमुखीनाः ।
वसन्ति ते वीर नृसिंह देव
दुरासदायां सुरदीर्घिकायाम् ॥

—*Ibid*. example under II. 6.

Page 27 1. सिद्धि निजक्रियायाः कर्त्तुंयस्यां परस्य शब्देन ।
आक्षेपः क्रियतेऽसावजहत्स्वार्था समाख्याता ॥ —*Ibid* II. 7.
…इयमेव समासोक्त्यादेर्बीजम् । इयं पुनरुपादानलक्षणेति मतान्तरे गीयते ॥

—vṛtti on II. 7.

2. स्वसिद्धये पराक्षेपः… ।
उपादानं…चेत्युक्ता… ॥ —KP. II. 10.

3. काव्यालंकारमीमांसातर्कव्याकरणागमाः ।
प्रविशन्ति तवास्थानीं नरसिंह नरेश्वर ॥

—Ekā. example under II. 7.

4. अंशेनैकेन पुनर्जहाति न जहाति चान्येन ।
शब्दः स्वार्थं यदि जहदजहत्स्वार्था समाख्याता ॥

—Ekā. II. 8.

5. यत्कर्णतालप्रभवैः समीरैः
प्रतापदीपाः शमिता रिपूणाम्
सोऽयं तव न्यक्कृतदिक्करीन्द्र-
लीलायितो वीर करेणुराजः ॥

—*Ibid*. example under II. 8.

6. विषयी विषयश्च यदा सारोपा स्यात्तदा द्विविधा । —*Ibid* II. 9.

7. ताद्रूप्यप्रतीतिः प्रयोजनम् ।

—ibid. vṛtti on II. 9.

8. …गौणी गुणाध्यारोपरूपात् सादृश्यात् प्रवर्त्तते ।

—*Ibid*, vṛtti on II. 9.

9. वीरश्रीस्वरसाभिसाररजनी निर्माणकर्मान्तिक-
च्छायाकन्दलितान्धकारकलिकातापिच्छिताशाञ्चलः ।
जीयादुत्कलभूमिपाल भवतः खड्गो रणप्राङ्गणे

शत्रुक्षोणिभृतामभर्त्यनगरीयात्रासु कार्त्तान्तिकः ।।

—*Ibid.* example under III. 9.

Page 28 1. शुद्धा पुनरुपचारवती···

—Ekā. vṛtti on II. 9.

2. उपचारश्च कार्यकारणभावादेर्निमित्तस्य पाञ्चविध्यात् पञ्चधा भवति···

—*Ibid.* vṛtti on. II. 9.

3. उपचारश्च अतत्त्वस्य तत्त्वेन व्यपदेश इत्युक्तम् ।

—Taralā on Ekā II. 9.

4. उभयरूपा चेयं शुद्धा । उपचारेण···। क्वचित् तादर्थ्यादुपचारः ।···

K.P. vṛtti on II. 11-12.

5. मदक्षीबक्षोणीपतिपरिषदायोधनमही-
जयाङ्कश्रीशङ्कावहगुणकिणश्रेणिललितः ।
भुवो भारं वोढुं भुजगपतिभोगप्रतिभट-
स्त्रिलोकीकल्याणं जयति तव दोरुत्कलपते ।।

—Ekā. example under II. 9.

6. विषयनिर्गीर्णे विषये साध्यवसाना द्विधा ख्याता ।। —*Ibid. II*. 9.

7. प्रयोजनं च सर्वथैवाभिन्नत्वप्रतीतिः,······इयमेवातिशयोक्तेर्बीजम् ।

—*Ibid.* vṛtti on II. 9.

Page 29 1. आक्रम्य स्मरवैरिशेखरसरित्पूरैकसिंहासनं
राजानं नरसिंह पार्थिव तथाहंकारभारोद्धुरः ।
त्वत्कीर्त्तिप्रसरो हसत्ययमसौ शक्रस्य दन्तावलं
व्यालेन्द्रं मुसलायुधं किमपरं देव्याश्च पञ्चाननम् ।।

—*Ibid.* example under II, 12.

2. एष चिन्तामणिः किं नु किं न्वयं कल्पपादपः ।
किं वासौ कामधेनुर्वा न चेत्त्यागः किमीदृशः ।।

—*Ibid.* example under II.12

3. राकातारकराजमण्डलमहः पाण्डित्यवैतण्डिकी
कीर्त्तिस्ते विदधाति यद्यपि जगच्छ्वेतं समन्तादपि ।
चित्रं वीर नृसिंह देव तदपि प्रत्यर्थिनामानना-
न्यालिङ्गन्ति रुचं शिखावलशिखरिञ्छोलितापिच्छयोः ।।

—*Ibid.* example under II. 12.

Page 30 1. द्विर्भावः पुष्पकेतोर्विबुधविटपिनः पौनरुक्त्यं विकल्प-
श्चिन्तारत्नस्य वीप्सा तपनतनुभुवो वासवस्य द्विरुक्तिः ।
द्वैतं देवस्य दैत्याधिपमथनकलाकेलिकारस्य कुर्व-
न्नानंदं कोविदानां जगति विजयते भूपतिः श्रीनृसिंहः ।।

—Ekā. example under II. 12.

2. आयुर्दानमहोत्सवस्य विनतक्षोणीभृतां मूर्त्तिमान्
विश्वासो नयनोत्सवो मृगदृशां कीर्त्तेः प्रकाशः परः ।
आनन्दः कलिकाकृतिः सुमनसां वीरश्रियो जीवितं
धर्मस्यैव महोदयो विजयते वीरः कलिङ्गेश्वरः ।।

—*Ibid.* example under II. 12.

3. संयोगादिभिरभिधा शृङ्खलिता यत्र कुण्ठतामेति ।
अर्थान्तरावगमने व्यञ्जनमेव क्षमं तत्र ।। —*Ibid* II. 3.

4. यस्य प्रतीतिमाधातुं लक्षणा समुपास्यते ।।
फले शब्दैकगम्येऽत्र व्यञ्जनान्नापरा क्रिया । —KP. II. 14-15.

5. संसर्गो विप्रयोगश्च साहचर्यं विरोधिता ।
अर्थः प्रकरणं लिङ्गं शब्दस्यान्यस्य सन्निधिः ।।
सामर्थ्यमौचिती देशः कालो व्यक्तिः स्वरादयः ।
शब्दार्थस्यानवच्छेदे विशेषस्मृतिहेतवः ।।

—Vākyapadīya, II. 315-316.

Page 31 1. आच्छादितायतदिगम्बरमुच्चकैर्गा-
माक्रम्य संस्थितमुदग्रविशालशृङ्गम् ।
मूर्ध्नि स्फुरत्तुहिनदीधितिकोटिमेन-
मुद्वीक्ष्य को भुवि न विस्मयते नगेशम् ।।

—Ekā. example under II. 3.

Page 32 1. अत्र तावन्न श्लेषः । केवलप्राकरणिकगतत्वेन केवलाप्राकरणिकगत-
त्वेन च तस्य भावात् ।

—*Ibid.* vṛtti on II. 3.

2. नेयं तुल्ययोगिता ।...नापि समासोक्तिः ।...नापि श्लेषः ।
...तस्मात्प्राकरणिकार्थमात्रपर्यवसिनाभिधाव्यापारेणापि शब्देनार्था-
न्तरधीकृद्ध्वनिरित्याहुः ।

—Vyākhyāna of Mallinātha on Śiśupālavadha, IV. 19.

3. वक्तृबोद्धव्यकाकूनां वाक्यवाच्यान्यसंनिधेः ।।
प्रस्तावदेशकालादेर्वैशिष्ट्यात् प्रतिभाजुषाम् ।
योऽर्थस्यान्यार्थधी हेतुर्व्यापारो व्यक्तिरेव सा ।।

—KP. III. 21-22. also quoted in *Ibid.* under II. 13.

Page 33. 1. यः संकेतितमर्थं साक्षाद्ब्रूते स वाचकः शब्दः ।—Ekā. II. 1.

2. वाच्यो लक्ष्यो व्यङ्ग्यस्तेषामर्थो यथाक्रमं वेद्यः ।। —*ibid.* II. 13.

3 वाच्योऽर्थोऽभिधया बोध्यो लक्ष्यो लक्षणया मतः ।
व्यङ्ग्यो व्यञ्जनया ताः स्युस्तिस्रः शब्दस्य शक्तयः ।।—SD, II. 11

4. मुख्यगौणलक्ष्यव्यङ्ग्यार्थभेदात् मुख्यगौणलक्षकव्यञ्जकाः शब्दाः ।।

—KAnu. I. 15.

5. क्रीडासौधं कलानां शरणगतरिपुक्ष्मापविश्रम्मपात्रं
जायेत त्वां नृसिंह क्षितिप कवयितुं को न कण्डूलजिह्वः ।
स्वान्तः सन्तोषगौरीपतिविधुतशिरश्चन्द्रिकाचुम्बितोर्मि-
स्फारस्वः सिन्धुबन्धुः सुरयुवतिगणैर्गीयते यस्य कीर्त्तिः ।।

—Ekā. example under II. 13.

6. भग्नद्वारा लुलितपरिघाश्चूर्णिताट्टाः प्रनष्ट-
स्तम्भा दूरीकृतवलभयः प्रोषितालेख्यलीलाः ।
तास्ताः क्रीडाशिखरपतनान्मोटिताक्रीडभागा-
स्त्वद्विक्रान्तिं रिपुवसतयः श्रीनृसिंह ब्रुवन्ति ।।

—*Ibid.* example under II. 13.

Page 34 1. (a) अनुवाद्यानामर्थानां विधेयार्थपरत्वं तात्पर्यमिति व्यापारान्तरं परैरभ्युपगतम् । यथा···तदेव चात्र विधेयं तत्परत्वमेव तात्पर्यम् ।

—*Ibid.* vṛtti on II.2.

(b) ···तात्पर्यार्थो वाच्याद्यर्थविलक्षणशरीर आकाङ्क्षायोग्यतासत्तिवशादपदार्थोऽपि प्रतीयते । न चापदार्थप्रतीतावतिप्रसङ्गः । स्वरूपसतः शक्यान्वयत्वस्य नियामकत्वात् इत्यभिहितान्वयवादिनां मतम् ।

—Kāvyapradīpa on KP. II. 1.

2. ···तात्पर्यमिति व्यापारान्तरं परैरभ्युपगतम् ।

—Ekā. vṛtti on II. 2.

3. वाच्य एव वाक्यार्थ इत्यन्विताभिधानवादिनः ॥

—KP. vṛtti on II.6.

4. त्रयो ह्यत्र व्यापाराः संवेद्यन्ते-पदार्थेषु सामान्यात्मस्वभिधाव्यापारः, समयापेक्षयार्थावगमनशक्तिर्ह्यभिधा । समयश्च तावत्येव न विशेषांशे, आनन्त्याद्व्यभिचाराच्चैकस्य । ततो विशेषरूपे वाक्यार्थे तात्पर्य-शक्तिः परस्परान्विते 'सामान्यान्यन्यथासिद्धेर्विशेषं गमयन्ति हि' इति न्यायात् ।...भक्तिर्हि लक्षणाव्यापारस्तृतीयकक्ष्यानिवेशी । चतुर्थ्यां तु कक्ष्यायां ध्वननव्यापारः ।

—DhL. Locana on DhL. I. 4.

5. Tātparya : 3 kinds : Abhidhīyamānā, Pratīyamānā and Dhvanirūpa.

Dr. Raghavan in Śṛṅgāraprakāśa of Bhoja, p. 19.

6. तात्पर्यार्थोऽपि केषुचित् ॥ —KP II. 6.

7. उमां स पश्यन्नृजुनेव चक्षुषा प्रचक्रमे वक्तुमनुज्झितक्रमः ।

—Ekā. example under II. 2.

———

CHAPTER III

Page 36. 1. अभिधामूलोऽपि तथा विवक्षितान्यपरवाच्य इत्युक्तः ।।

—Ekā. III. 1.

2. लक्षणामूलगूढव्यङ्ग्यप्राधान्ये सत्यविवक्षितमप्रधानीकृतं वाच्यं यत्र स तथा । येन चाविवक्षितेन सता वाच्येनाविवक्षितवाच्य इति ध्वनिमाचक्षते । —*Ibid.* vṛtti on III. 1.

3. तत्र योऽर्थं उपपद्यमानोऽप्यनुपयोगाद्‌बाधितोऽर्थान्तरे परिणमति सोऽर्थान्तरसंक्रमितस्तादृशो वाच्यो यत्र सोऽर्थान्तरसंक्रमितवाच्य उच्यते । —*Ibid.* vṛtti on III. 1.

4. अयं च पदवाक्यप्रकाश्यत्वेन भवन् न द्वैविध्यं परिहरति ।

—*Ibid.* vṛtti on III. 1.

5. श्रीरमणः श्रीरमणः सुधांशमौलिः सुधांशुमौलिरसौ ।
नरसिंहो नरसिंहः प्रभवति जगतामपि त्रितये ।।

—*Ibid.* example under III. 1.

6. एषा ते कथयामि सांप्रतमहं तिष्ठन्त्वमी मन्त्रिणः
सर्वे यत् प्रतिभाति तत् कुरु रुचिं बुद्धया विमृश्य स्वयम् ।
इत्युक्तः प्रियया रिपुक्षितिपतिस्त्वज्जैत्रयात्रोत्सवे
स्तैमित्यं कलयन् नृसिंहपनृपते तूष्णीमभूदानतः ।।

—*Ibid.* example under III. 1.

Page 37. 1. यः पुनरनुपपद्यमानतयैव बाधितोऽर्थान्तरप्रतिपत्तिं कृत्वा पलायित इव सोऽत्यन्ततिरस्कृतस्तादृशो वाच्यो यत्र सोऽत्यन्ततिरस्कृतवाच्यः ।

—*Ibid.* vṛtti on III.1.

2. असावपि पूर्ववद्‌द्विविधः । —*Ibid.* vṛtti on III. 1.

3. जायेत त्वां नृसिंह क्षितिप कवयितुं को न कण्डूलजिह्वः ।

—*Ibid.* example under III. 1.

4. बाणैः पञ्जरिता गजाः कति कति क्षुण्णा रथामुद्गरै-
र्जीवग्राहमरातयः कति हयैः सार्धं गृहीतास्त्वया ।।

मुक्ता: प्राञ्जलय: कतीति निभृतामर्षस्मिता: स्वप्रियान्
संग्रामापसृतान् नृसिंह नृपते पृच्छन्ति वैरिस्त्रियः ॥

—Ekā. example under III. 1.

5. विवक्षितमन्यपरं व्यङ्ग्यनिष्ठं वाच्यं यत्र स विवक्षितान्यपरवाच्यो ध्वनि: । —*Ibid.* vṛtti on III. 1.

6. क्रमस्यासंलक्ष्यत्वे तु न विप्रतिपत्तिः । न खलु विभावानुभाव-व्यभिचारिण एव रस: । अपितु तेभ्य एव रस इति सतोऽपि क्रमस्यो-त्पलदलशतव्यतिभेदवद्विभावादिप्रतीतावाशुभावित्वेनासंलक्ष्यमाणत्वा-दसंलक्ष्यक्रमव्यङ्ग्य इत्यन्वर्थतामप्यसावाश्रयति ।

—*Ibid.* vṛtti on. III. 1.

Page 38. 1. (a) तेष्वेकोऽपि यत्र प्राधान्यमवलम्बते तत्रालंकार्य एव ।
यत्र पुनरप्राधान्यं तत्र रसवदादिरलंकार: ।।

—*Ibid.* vṛtti on III.1.

(b) प्रधानेऽन्यत्र वाक्यार्थे यत्राङ्गं तु रसादय: ।
काव्ये तस्मिन्नलङ्कारो रसादिरिति मे मति: ॥

—DhL. II. 5.

(c) यत्र प्रधानं रसादिस्तत्र ध्वनि:, यत्र त्वप्रधानं तत्रालंकार इति भाव: । —Kāvyapradīpa on KP. IV. 3.

2. (a) विभावैर्ललनादिभिरालम्बनकारणैरङ्कुरित:···उद्दीपनकारणैः··· अनुभावै:···व्यभिचारिभि:···स्थायी रत्यादिको भाव एव··· श्रृङ्गारिको रसोऽभिधीयते । —Ekā. vṛtti on III. 1.

(b) विभावानुभावव्यभिचारिसंयोगाद्रसनिष्पत्तिः ॥

—NS. vṛtti on VI.32.

3. रतिहासश्चशोकश्च क्रोधोत्साहौ भयं तथा ।
जुगुप्सा विस्मयश्चेति स्थायिभावा: प्रकीर्त्तिता ।। —NS. VI. 18.

4. निर्वेद-ग्लानिशङ्काख्यास्तथासूया मद: श्रम: ।
आलस्यं चैव दैन्यं च चिन्ता मोहः स्मृतिर्धृति: ।।
व्रीडा चपलता हर्षं आवेगो जडता तथा ।
गर्वो विषाद औत्सुक्यं निद्रापस्मार एव च ।।
सुप्तं विबोधो मर्षश्चाप्यवहित्थमथोग्रता ।
मतिर्व्याधिस्तथोन्मादस्तथा मरणमेव च ।।

त्रासश्चैव वितर्कश्च विज्ञेया व्यभिचारिणः ।
त्रयस्त्रिंशदमी भावाः समाख्यातास्तु नामतः ॥ —NS. VI.19-22.

5. स्तम्भः स्वेदोऽथ रोमाञ्चः स्वरभङ्गोऽथ वेपथुः ।
वैवर्ण्यमश्रुप्रलय इत्यष्टौ सात्विकाः स्मृताः ॥ —*Ibid.* VI. 23.

Page 39. 1. …कदाचिदपि नानुभूतोऽभिधया, न कर्णातिथीकृतस्तात्पर्येण, न लक्ष्यीकृतो लक्षणया, न स्वविषयं प्रापितः प्रत्यक्षेण, नात्मनः सीमानमानीतोऽनुमानेनापरिशीलितसरणिः स्मरणेन, नाक्रान्तः कार्यतया, न ज्ञातो ज्ञाप्यतया,…सामाजिकानां वासनात्मतया स्थितः स्थायी रत्यादिको भाव एव विभावादिजीवितावधिः पानकरसन्यासेन चर्व्यमाणश्चर्व्यमाणतैकप्राणः सम्मुलसन् ब्रह्मास्वादसब्रह्मचारी लोकोत्तरचमत्कारकारी शृङ्गारादिको रसोऽभिधीयते ॥

—Ekā. vṛtti on III. 1.

2. अयं च स्वप्नेऽपि परिहरति वाच्यताम् । तथा हि वाच्यो भवन्नयं स्वशब्देनोच्यतां शृङ्गारादिशब्देन वा । इदमुभयमपि न संभवास्पदम् । रसादिशब्दाप्रयोगेऽपि विभावादिप्रतिपादनद्वारैव तस्य प्रतीतिपथपथिकत्वात् । रसादिशब्दप्रयोगेऽपि विभावाद्यप्रयोगे तस्य प्रतीतिपथानधिरोहाच्चेत्यन्वयव्यतिरेकाभ्यां विभावाद्यभिधानद्वारैव प्रतीतिपद्धतिमध्यास्त इति प्रतीयमानतामेवार्हति ॥

—*Ibid.* vṛtti on III. 1.

3. उत यदि तात्पर्यगोचरतामवतरति रस इति भवन्मनसि निविशते तदपि न विचारचारु । रसस्याभिधेयत्वानधिकरणत्वादभिहिते च तात्पर्यस्य प्रगल्भनात् । विधेयानुवाद्यसमभिव्याहारेण विधेयार्थमनुवाद्यमुपादीयते । अप्राप्तं तु विधेयम् । यथा लोहितोष्णीषा ऋत्विजः प्रचरन्तीत्यत्र ऋत्विक्प्रचरणे प्रमाणान्तरतः प्राप्ते लोहितोष्णीषत्वमप्राप्तं विधेयम् । एवमन्यत्रापि यावदप्राप्तमभिहितं च तावति शब्दस्यार्थे तात्पर्यं नाम व्यापारः प्रगल्भते । न पुनः प्रतीतिमात्रे । यदि प्रतीतिमात्रेऽपि तात्पर्यं प्रभविष्णुतामासादयति तदा पूर्वो धावतीत्यादावपराद्यर्थे तात्पर्यं पर्यवस्येत । अपरोऽपि धावतु वा न वा, न तत्र तात्पर्यम् । —*Ibid.* vṛtti on III. 1.

4. अथ यदि लक्षणीयो रसस्तदपि न क्षोदक्षमम् । मुख्यार्थबाधादिरहितैरेव विभावादिभिरस्याभिव्यज्यमानत्वात् ।

—*Ibid.* vṛtti on III. 1.

Page 40. 1. प्रत्यक्षाप्रमाणग्राह्यो रस इति चेत्तर्हि प्रत्यक्षेण गृह्यमाणो रसः किं निर्विकल्पेन गृह्यते सविकल्पेन वा । न तावन्निर्विकल्पकज्ञानगोचरः । विभावाद्यनुसंधानेनैवास्य सत्तासाधनसमर्थत्वात् । अशेषविशेषणरहितवस्तुमात्रपरिच्छेदरूपं हि निर्विकल्पकम् । तर्हि सविकल्पकज्ञानविषय इति चेन्न । निर्विकल्पकस्यानन्तरमुपजायमानत्वात् सविकल्पकस्य । यदि च कारणाभावेऽपि कार्यस्य जन्म तदा कारणानुसंधानप्रयासः क्वचिदपि नानुभूयेत ।। —Ekā. vṛtti on III. 1.

2. ननु सीतादिसंयोगवियोगजनितसुखदुःखवशंवदरामादिभावनटनपटु - नटप्रकटिततद्भावदिलोकनाविर्भूतानुभूततत्तत्स्वगतभावानुचिन्तनानुमितया तयारामादिस्थयावस्थयात्मानं सामाजिकः सुखाकरोति दुःखाकरोति वेत्यनुमेयोऽस्तु रस इति चेत् तदपि न ।

—*Ibid.* vṛtti on III. 1.

3. स्मरणगोचरत्वमपि रसस्य कथमस्तु,…रसस्यानुभूयमानत्वाभ्युपगमे व्यङ्ग्यत्वविरोधः । तस्मादनुभवाभावे स्मृतेरप्यभाव इति स्मृतिविषयो न रसः किं तु व्यङ्ग्य एव ।। —*Ibid.* vṛtti on III. 1.

4. यत् पुनरिहाकार्यत्वमुक्तं रसस्य तन्नटगतविभावाद्यनुत्पाद्यत्वमभिसंधाय । यदपि रसस्याज्ञाप्यत्वाभिधानं तदपि रामस्य रतेरतीतत्वात् संनिहितदेशवर्त्तमानकालेन्द्रियसंनिकर्षाद्यज्ञाप्यत्वाभिप्रायेण ।।

—*Ibid.* vṛtti on III. 1.

Page 41. 1. अतः कारकत्वज्ञापकत्वव्यावृत्तो विभावादिश्चर्वणोपयोगित्वमात्रेण हेतुरलौकिको भवन्नलौकिकत्वमेव रसस्याभिव्यनक्ति ।

—*Ibid.* vṛtti on III.1.

2. 'यो लौकिकोऽप्यतिजनः कारकसिद्धोऽप्यकार्यभूतश्च ।
सविकल्पकोऽप्यविकल्पकः स रसः केनोपमीयते ।।
…अलौकिकसुखास्वादो रस इत्यभिधीयते ।।'

—quoted in the Ekā. in vṛtti on III. 1.

3. स च न कार्यः । विभावादिविनाशेऽपि तस्य संभवप्रसङ्गात् । नापि ज्ञाप्यः सिद्धस्य तस्यासंभवात् । अपि तु विभावादिभिर्व्यञ्जितश्चर्वणीयः ।…लोकोत्तरमेव गमयति न तु विरोधमिति श्रीमदाचार्याभिनवगुप्तपादाः । —KP. vṛtti on IV. 28.

4. ततश्च करुणादीनां दुःखरूपत्वात् कथंकारमुपपद्यते रसत्वमिति चेन्न । विगलितवेद्यान्तरत्वमानन्दस्य रूपम् । तद्यदि विभावानुभाव-व्यभिचारियथोचितोपनिबन्धमहिम्ना काव्यश्रवणसमसमयमेव समुल्लसति तर्हि करुणादावपि कुतस्त्यं दुःखसंवेदनम् ।।

—Ekā. vṛtti on III.1.

5. (a) स्वादः काव्यार्थसंभेदादात्मानन्दसमुद्भवः ।
विकासविस्तरक्षोभविक्षेपैः स चतुर्विधः ।।

—quoted in the Ekā. in vṛtti on III. 1.

(b) स्वादः काव्यार्थसंभेदात्···चतुर्विधः ।। —DR. IV. 43.

6. विकासः कुसुमस्येव पादपस्येव विस्तरः ।
क्षोभोऽब्धेरिव विक्षेपो मारुतस्येव चेतसः ।।

—quoted in the Ekā. in vṛtti on III. 1.

Page 42. 1. निर्वेदग्लानिशङ्का··· —NS. VI. 19.

2. अमङ्गलरूपस्यापि निर्वेदस्य शान्तरसस्थायित्वप्रकाशनायैव मुनिना व्यभिचारिषु प्रथमं निर्दिष्टत्वात् ।···इति स्थायिव्यभिचारिमध्येऽस्य पठनादुभयरूपत्वमस्याभिमतमिति मुनेराशयस्य लक्ष्यमाणत्वाच्च ।

—Ekā. vṛtti on III. 1.

3. एवमेते रसा ज्ञेया नव लक्षणलक्षिताः ।··· —NS. VI. 84.

4. अतश्च नवैव रसा इति नः संमतम् ।। —Ekā. vṛtti on III. 1.

5. निर्वेदस्थायिभावोऽस्ति शान्तोऽपि नवमो रसः । —KP. IV. 35.

6. केचित्तु—'शान्तस्य शमसाध्यत्वान्नटे च तदसंभवात् । अष्टावेव रसा नाट्ये न शान्तस्तत्र युज्यते ।।' इत्याहुः । तच्चापरे न क्षमन्ते ।··· नाट्येऽपि शान्तो रसोऽस्तीति व्यवस्थापितम् । —RG. pp.29-30.

7. रसोऽभिमानोऽहङ्कारः शृङ्गार इति गीयते ।
योऽर्थस्तस्यान्वयात् काव्य कमनीयत्वमश्नुते ।।

....

शृङ्गारी चेत् कविः काव्ये जातं रसमयं जगत् ।
स एव चेदशृङ्गारी नीरसं सर्वमेव तत् ।। —SKBh. V. 1 & 3.

8. निर्वेदादिरतद्रूप्यादस्थायी स्वदते कथम् ।
वैरस्यायैव तत्पोषस्तेनाष्टौ स्थायिनो मताः ।। — DR. IV. 36.

9. ममासनार्धे भव मण्डनं ततः
प्रिये मदुत्सङ्गविभूषणं भव ।
भ्रमाद्भ्रमादालपमङ्ग मृष्यतां
विना ममोरः कतरत्तवासनम् ।।

—Ekā. example under III. 1.

10. वीर नरसिंह नृपते तव विरहे भाति पाण्डुता वपुषि भृशम् ।
तस्या हृदयगतस्य त्वन्मुखचन्द्रस्य चन्द्रिकाभरमधुरा ।।

—*Ibid.* example under III. 1.

Page 43. 1. उत्कासे कण्ठदाहः प्रचुरघृतपयः पानमामज्वरार्त्ते
रक्ताकृष्टिः कृशानामुदरभयहरा कर्कटी सक्तुमिश्रा ।
पथ्या पथ्याऽतिसारे दृशि सरुजि पुनः क्षारचूर्णप्रयोग-
स्तत्तत्पथ्योपचारैस्तरुणयति यमाडम्बरं जन्तुकेतुः ।।

—*Ibid.* example under III. 1.

2. हृदये वसतीति मत्प्रियं
यदवोचस्तदवैमि कैतवम् ।
उपचारपदं न चेदिदं
त्वमनङ्गः कथमक्षता रतिः ।।—*Ibid.* example under III.1.

3. केयं माता पिशाची क इव स जनको भ्रातरः केऽत्र कीटाः
वध्योऽयं बन्धुवर्गः कुटिलविटसुहृच्चेष्टिता ज्ञातयोऽपि ।
(हस्तौनिष्पीड्य) आगर्भंयावदेषां कुलमिदमखिलं नैव निश्शेषयामि
स्फूर्जन्तः क्रोधवह्नेर्दधति न विरतिं तावदङ्गे स्फुलिङ्गाः ।।

—*Ibid.* example under III. 1.

4. क्षुद्राः संत्रासमेनं विजहत हरयः क्षुण्णशक्रेभकुम्भाः
युष्मद्गात्रेषु लज्जां दधति परममी सायका निष्पतन्तः ।
सौमित्रे तिष्ठ पात्रं त्वमसि न हि रुषां नन्वहं मेघनादः
किञ्चिद्भ्रूभङ्गलीलानियमितजलधिं राममन्वेषयामि ।।

—*Ibid.* example under III. 1.

5. ग्रीवाभङ्गाभिरामं मुहुरनुपतति स्यन्दने दत्तदृष्टिः
पश्चादर्धेन प्रविष्टः शरपतनभयाद्भूयसा पूर्वकायम् ।

दर्भैरर्धावलीढैः श्रमविवृतमुखभ्रंशिभिः कीर्णवर्त्मा
पश्योदग्रप्लुतत्वाद्वियति बहुतरं स्तोकमुर्व्यां प्रयाति ॥

—Ekā. example under III. 1.

6. दसमाणुसमांसभालके
कुंभसहस्सवशाहिं शंचिदे ।
अणिसं च पिबामि सोणिदं
बलिशशदं समले भवीयदु ॥

—*Ibid.* example under III. 1.

7. पश्य कञ्चन चकोरलोचने
लोचनाविषयमैन्द्रजालिकम् ।
इक्षुरिष्वसनमङ्कुराः शराः
लक्ष्यमेतदखिलं चराचरम् ॥

—*Ibid.* example under III. 1.

Page 44. 1. कदा वाराणस्याममरतटिनीरोधसि वसन्
वसानः कौपीनं शिरसि निदधानोऽञ्जलिपुटम् ।
अयं गौरीनाथ त्रिपुरहर शम्भो त्रिनयन
प्रसीदेत्याक्रोशन्निमिषमिव नेष्यामि दिवसान् ॥

—*Ibid.* example under III. 1.

2. शृङ्गारादिरसभेदाः पुनः शास्त्रान्तरसुलभनिरूपणा इति नेह प्रपञ्चिताः ॥ —*Ibid.* vṛtti on III. 1.

3. छिन्ते ब्रह्मशिरो यदि प्रथयति प्रेतेषु सख्यं यदि
क्षीबः क्रीडति मातृभिर्यदि रतिं धत्ते श्मशाने यदि ।
सृष्ट्वा संहरति प्रजाः यदि तथाप्याधाय भक्त्या मन-
स्तं सेवे करवाणि किं त्रिजगती शून्या स एवेश्वरः ॥

—*Ibid.* example under III. 1.

Page 45. 1. किमसुभिर्गलितैर्जड मन्यसे
मयि निमज्जतु भीमसुतामनः ।
मम किल श्रुतिमाह तदर्थिकां
नलमुखेन्दुपरां विबुधः स्मरः ॥

—*Ibid.* example under III. 1.

2. (a) यत्र पुनरेकतरानुरागस्तत्र स्थायिनोऽनौचित्येन प्रवृत्तत्वात्
तदाभास एव। —Ekā vṛtti on III. 1.

(b) तदाभास अनौचित्यप्रवर्तिताः। —KP. IV. 36.

3. हीनपात्रेणु तिर्यक्षु नायकप्रतियोगिषु।
गौणेष्वेव पदार्थेषु तमाभासं विजानते ।। —SKBh. V. 30.

4. ...शृङ्गारस्य म्लेच्छादिविषयत्वे त्वाभासत्वम्। तथा चोक्तम्—
'एकत्रैवानुरागश्चेत् तिर्यङ्म्लेच्छागतोऽपि वा।
योषितो बहुसक्तिश्चेद्रसाभासस्त्रिधा मतः ।।'
—Pratāparudrayaśobhūṣaṇa, Rasaprakaraṇa, pp. 162-63.

5. प्रतिनायकनिष्ठत्वे तद्वदधमपात्रतिर्य्यगादिगते।
शृङ्गारेऽनौचित्यं रौद्रे गुर्वादिगतकोपे ।। —SD. III. 219-220.

6. अपरे तु रसाभासं तिर्यक्षु प्रचक्षते तन्न परीक्षाक्षमम्। तेष्वपि विभावादि संभवात्। विभावादिज्ञानशून्यास्तिर्यञ्चो न भाजन भवितुमर्हन्ति रसस्येति चेन्न। मनुष्येष्वपि केषुचित्तथाभूतेषु रस-विषयभावाभावप्रसङ्गात्। विभावादिसंभवो हि रसं प्रति प्रयोजको न विभावादिज्ञानम्। ततश्च तिरश्चामप्यस्त्येव रसः।
—Ekā. vṛtti on III. 1.

7. ददौ सरः पङ्कजरेणुगन्धि
गजाय गण्डूषजलं करेणुः।
अर्धोपभुक्तेन बिसेन जायां
संभावयामास रथाङ्गनामा ।।
—*Ibid.* example under III. 1.

8. ब्रह्मन्नध्ययनस्य नैष समयस्तूष्णीं बहिः स्थीयतां
स्वल्पं जल्प बृहस्पते जडमते नैषा सभा वज्रिणः।
वीणां संहर नारद स्तुतिकथालापैरलं तुम्बरो
सीतायल्लकभल्लभग्नहृदयः स्वस्थो न लङ्केश्वरः ।।
—*Ibid.* example under III. 1.

9. अस्मद्विक्रमचेष्टितानि निखिलत्रैलोक्यहेलाजय-
प्रह्वीभूतसुरासुराणि भवतो भूमेः सुता शृण्वती।

पत्यौ द्वेषकषायितेन मनसा स्निग्धा मयि स्थास्यति
स्त्रीणां प्रेम यदुत्तरोत्तरगुणग्रामस्पृहाचञ्चलम् ॥
—Ekā. example under III. 1.

10. पश्यामः किमियं प्रपद्यत इति स्थैर्यं मयालम्बितं
किं मां नालपतीत्ययं खलु शठः कोपस्तयाप्याश्रितः।
इत्यन्योन्यविलोलदृष्टिचतुरे तस्मिन्नवस्थान्तरे
स व्याजं हसितं मया धृतिहरो वाष्पस्तु मुक्तस्तया ॥
—*Ibid.* example under III. 1.

11. तदद्य विश्रम्य दयालुरेधि मे
दिनं निनीषामि भवद्विलोकिनी।
अदर्शि पादेन विलिख्य पत्रिणा
तदैव रूपेण समः स मत्प्रियः ॥
—*Ibid.* example under III. 1.

Page 46. 1. अर्धे चेतसि जानकी न विरमत्यर्धे च लङ्केश्वरः
किं चार्धं विरहानलः कवलयत्यर्धं च रोषानलः।
इत्थं दुर्विधिवैशसव्यतिकराद्दाहे समेऽप्यर्धयो-
रेकं वेद्मि तुषाग्निदग्धमपरं दग्धं करीषाग्निना ॥
—*Ibid.* example under III. 1.

2. (a) बहूनां भावानां पूर्वपूर्वोपमर्देनोपनिबन्धो भावशावल्यम्।
—*Ibid.* vṛtti on III. 1.

(b) भावशबलत्वं भावानां बाध्यबाधकभावमापन्नानामुदासी-
नानां वा व्यामिश्रणम् ॥ —RG. p. 103.

3. क्वाकार्यं शशलक्ष्मणः क्व च कुलं भूयोऽपि दृश्यते सा
दोषाणामुपशान्तये श्रुतमहो कोपेऽपि कान्तं मुखम्।
किं वक्ष्यन्त्यपकल्पषाः कृतधियः स्वप्नेऽपि सा दुर्लभा
चेतः स्वास्थ्यमुपैहि कः खलु युवा धन्योऽधरं धास्यति ॥
—Ekā. example under III. 1.

4. अस्य विवक्षितान्यपरवाच्यस्य ध्वनेः संलक्ष्यक्रमव्यङ्ग्यत्वादनुरणन-
प्रख्यो य आत्मा··· —DhL. vṛtti on II. 20.

5. (a) संलक्ष्यक्रमव्यङ्ग्यस्तु त्रिधा, शब्दशक्तिमूलानुरणनरूपव्यङ्ग्योऽर्थशक्तिमूलानुरणनरूपव्यङ्ग्य उभयशक्तिमूलानुरणनरूपव्यङ्ग्यश्चेति । —Ekā. vṛtti on III. 1.

(b) अनुस्वानामसंलक्ष्यक्रमव्यङ्ग्यस्थितिस्तु यः ।।
शब्दार्थोभयशक्त्युत्थस्त्रिधा स कथितो ध्वनिः ।
—KP. IV. 37-38.

(c) शब्दार्थशक्तिमूलत्वात्सोऽपि द्विधा व्यवस्थितः ।।
—DhL. II. 20.

Page 47. 1. नरसिंह धरापाल के वयं तव वर्णने ।
अपि राजानमाक्रम्य यशो यस्य विजृम्भते ।।
—Ekā. example under III. 1.

2. आक्रम्य स्मरवैरिशेखरसरित्पूरैकसिंहासनं
राजानं नरसिंह पार्थिव तथाहंकारभारोद्धुरः ।
त्वत्कीर्त्तिप्रसरो हसत्ययमसौ शक्रस्य दन्तावलं
व्यालेन्द्रं मुसलायुधं किमपरं देव्याश्च पञ्चाननम् ।।
—*Ibid.* example under III. 1.

3. हिरण्यकशिपुक्षेत्रदानदर्शितविस्मयः ।
न कस्य श्लाघनीयोऽसि नरसिंह जगत्पते ।।
—*Ibid.* example under III. 1.

4. (a) अत्र राजनि प्राकरणिकत्वेनाभिधाया नियन्त्रितत्वादप्राकरणिकनृसिंह-लक्षणद्वितीयार्थाभिधाने कुतः शक्तिः । सकृदुच्चारितस्य शब्दस्यैकार्थाभिधान एव सामर्थ्यं न द्वितीयार्थाभिधाने । अथानेकार्थोऽयं शब्दस्तावन्न विरमति यावन्न द्वितीयमर्थमभिधत्त इति चेन्न । अनेकार्थस्य शब्दस्यैवाभावात् ।
—*Ibid.* vṛtti on III. 1.

(b) एषूदाहरणेषु शब्दशक्त्या प्रकाशमाने सत्यप्राकरणिकेऽर्थान्तरे वाक्यस्यासम्बद्धार्थाभिधायित्वं मा प्रसाङ्क्षीदित्यप्राकरणिकप्राकरणिकार्थयोरुपमानोपमेयभावः कल्पयितव्यः ।
—DhL. vṛtti on II. 21.

5. गौडगुर्जरकर्णाटलाटमालवसेवणाः ।
नरसिंहनृपे दृष्टे भवन्ति करहाटकाः ।।
—Ekā. example under III. 1.

6. सत्त्वसागर नृसिंह भूपते
तावकैरलममीभिराशुगैः ।
वैरिणामसव एव यद्भव—
न्त्याशुगाः कलितकार्मुके त्वयि ॥

—Ekā. example under. III.1.

Page 48. 1. एकावयवगते भूषणेन कामिनीव पदप्रकाश्येनापि व्यङ्ग्येन भारती भवति चमत्काराय सहृदयानाम् ।

—*Ibid.* vṛtti on III. 1.

2. नृसिंह वसुधाधिप त्वयि रणोन्मुखे धावतः
प्रतीपपृथिवीपतेः पथि पथि प्रदीप्तक्षुधः ।
चिरादगुरवन्ध्यतां दुरवगाहविन्ध्याटवी—
पलाशिविटपाञ्चलाहृतफलार्पणेन द्विपाः ।

—*Ibid.* example under III. 1.

3. नृसिंह क्ष्मापाल त्रिदशतटिनीवीचितुलिते
यशःपूरे दूरात्तव जगदिदं पूरितवति ।
सुमन्मीलत्कालागरुबहुलधूमप्रणयिनी-
स्तमस्तोमस्ताम्यन् विशति कबरीः पक्ष्मलदृशाम् ॥

—*Ibid.* example under III. 1.

4. समरवसुन्धरासु नरसिंह धाराधिपते
रिपुनृपमौलिनीलमणयस्तव पादयुगे ।
सरसविकस्वरारुणसरोरुहलोभलग-
न्मधुकरमण्डलीललितडम्बरमादधते ॥

—*Ibid.* example under III. 1.

5. पूर्वं पयोधरेरुदरे स्थितासि
ततः सुधे त्वं हृदये सुधांशोः ।
मुखे कलिङ्गाधिपतेरिदानीं
यथोत्तरं धाम तवाभिरामम् ॥

—*Ibid.* example under III. 1.

6. हेमाद्रेः कन्दरायां रतिरमणरणाटोपविच्छिन्नहार-
व्यस्तं मुक्ताफलानां तमसि ततः इतः स्तोममन्वेषयन्त्याः ।

कस्याश्चित् स्वस्तरुण्या निकटगतनिजप्राणनाथोपगीता
कीर्तिज्योत्स्ना त्वदीया क्षणमकृत मुदं श्री नृसिंह क्षितान्द्र ॥
—Ekā. example under III. 1.

7. अम्भोजभूचन्द्रकलावतंस—
कंसद्विषः कुत्र पदं लभन्ताम् ।
यशश्रियस्ते महिमा समन्ताद्
व्याप्नोत्ययं वीर नृसिंह देव ॥
Ibid. example under III. 1.

Page 49. 1. तनौ दत्वा पाकोन्मुखशरसखीं कामपि रुचिं
रिपुस्त्रीभ्यस्तासां कलयसि कलिङ्गक्षितिपते ।
प्रभा ताटङ्कानां श्रवणकुसुमानां विलसितं
स्मितानामालोकं स्तनमलयजानां श्रियमपि ॥
—*Ibid.* example undar III.1.

2. भुवः केलीतल्पं जयति नरसिंहक्षितिभुजो
भुजः शौर्यक्रीडाडमरसमरारम्भलटहः ।
नवप्रेयोलाभप्रमुदितसमस्ताम्बरचरी-
विकीर्णैर्मन्दारैर्विततमुपहारं भजति यः ॥
—*Ibid.* example under III. 1.

3. धूर्ताधोरण देव वासव कथं पङ्केन लिप्तः करी
पातुं तोयमुपागतः सुरनदीं तत्रास्ति पङ्कः कुतः ।
सर्वाशा विजयोत्सवं प्रति कृतोद्योगे कलिङ्गेश्वरे
स्फायन्ते करिकर्णतालपवनोद्भूताश्चमूरेणवः ॥
—*Ibid.* example under III. 1.

4. आयोधनेषु रभसादधिरूढवत्या
वीरश्रियः स्तननितम्बभरातिभारात् ।
हन्तुं नृसिंह नृपतेर्न भुजः कथंचित्
पादोपकण्ठपतितान् क्षमते विपक्षान् ॥
—*Ibid.* example under III. 1.

5. बाहुस्ते नरसिंह देव विजयश्रीकेलिसौधध्वज-
स्तत्रापि प्रलयाग्निधूमरुचिना खड्गेन सख्यं गतः ।

निर्मर्यादविशीर्यमाणविशिखप्राग्भारशात्कारिणि
प्राक्रीडत् समरे सपत्नहरिणाक्षीणां ह हा हा विधिम् ।।
—Ekā. example under III. 1.

Page 50. 1. एतास्तारा: समन्ताद्दिशि दिशि नभसि प्राप्य धाम स्वकीयं
निः सापत्न्यप्रकर्षप्रकटनपटुतां नाटयन्त्यः स्फुरन्तु ।
किं चन्द्रः कुत्र तिष्ठत्ययमियमधुना तस्य वार्त्तापि लुप्ता
कीर्त्तौ विस्फूर्त्तिमत्यां शुभचरितनिधेः श्रीनृसिंहस्य राज्ञः ।।
—*Ibid.* example under III. 1.

2. संघर्षोत्कर्षरिङ्खत्प्लवनकपिकुलोन्मूलितोत्तालशैल-
प्राग्भारैः सेतुबन्धो दशवदनशिरश्छेदनाय व्यधायि ।
पूर्वं तावत् त्वयासौ महति जलनिधौ सांप्रतं तत्र सेतुं
कं वा जेतुं नृसिंह क्षितिप रचयसि स्वैर्यशश्चन्द्रकान्तैः ।।
—*Ibid.* example under III. 1.

3. पृथ्वीभारावतारं कृतवति भवतो दोष्णि हर्षेण दूतः
शेषेण प्रोषितोऽसौ निवसति भुजगः कोऽपि संवादहेतोः ।
क्रुध्यत् कालीकटाक्षद्युतिदलनकलाकेलिकारस्त्वदीये
पाणौ नायं कृपाणः शुभचरितनिधे श्रीनृसिंह क्षितीन्द्र ।।
—*Ibid.* example under III. 1.

4. सेना रजोभिस्तव तिग्मभानु-
राच्छादितोऽसौ नरसिंह देव ।
विरोधिशुद्धान्तमृगेक्षणानां
वक्त्रेन्दुरासीन्मलिनप्रकाशः ।।
—*Ibid.* example under III. 1.

5. सुराङ्गनाभ्यो मलये त्वदीयं
श्रुत्वा यशो वीर नृसिंह देव ।
जिह्वाञ्चलान्युल्ललयन्ति दुग्ध-
मृणाललोभादुमयेऽपि नागाः ।।
—*Ibid.* example under III. 1.

6. वियोगिनो बिभ्यति वैरिवीराः
कौतूहलीमश्नुते चकोराः ।

(ii) विरोधिरससम्बन्धिविभावादिपरिग्रहः।
विस्तरेणान्वितस्यापि वस्तुनोऽन्यस्य वर्णनम्॥
अकाण्ड एव विच्छित्तिरकाण्डे च प्रकाशनम्।
परिपोषं गतस्यापि पौनः पुन्येन दीपनम्।
रसस्य स्याद्विरोधाय वृत्यनौचित्यमेव च॥

—*Ibid.* III. 18-19.

3. उचिताभिधानजीवितत्वाद् वाक्यस्याप्येकदेशेऽप्यौचित्यविरहात् तद्विदाह्लादकारित्वहानिः।—प्रबन्धस्यापि कस्यचित् प्रकरणैक-देशेऽप्यौचित्यविरहादेकदेशदाहदूषितदग्धपटप्रायता प्रसज्यते।

—VJ. vṛtti on I. 57.

4. Concepts of Poetic Blemishes in Sanskrit Poetics, Prof. Bechan Jha, p. 124.

———————

CHAPTER VI

Page 92 1. अलंकारास्तु हारादय इव— —Ekā. vṛtti on V.1.

2. काव्यशोभाकरान् धर्मानलंकारान् प्रचक्षते । —KD. II.1.

3. काव्यशोभाया: कर्तारो धर्मा गुणा: ।
तदतिशयहेतवस्त्वलङ्कारा: ।। —KASV. III. 1.1-2.

4. (i) अलङ्कारो हि चारुत्वहेतु: प्रसिद्ध: ।

(ii) अलङ्कारो हि बाह्यालङ्कारसाम्यादङ्गिनश्चारुत्वहेतुरुच्यते ।

—DhL. vṛtti on II. 5 & II. 17.

5. उपकुर्वन्ति तं सन्तं येऽङ्गद्वारेण जातुचित् ।
हारादिवलंकारास्तेऽनुप्रासोपमादय: ।। —KP. VIII. 67.

6. ···यथेति कर्मोपमा।··· मैष इति भूतोपमा।···अग्निरिति रूपोपमा।
···वदिति सिद्धोपमा।···अथ लुप्तोपमान्यार्थोपमानीत्याचक्षते।···

—Nirukta. II-III-14 (pp. 142-149).

7. (i) तुल्यार्थैरतुलोपमाभ्यां तृतीयाऽन्यतरस्याम् ।। – *Ibid.* II-III.72

(ii) उपमानानि सामान्यवचनै: ।। — *Ibid.* II I.55

(iii) उपमितं व्याघ्रादिभि: ।। — *Ibid* II-I.56.

Page 93 1. (i) तथाहि अचेतन शवशरीरं कुण्डलाद्युपेतमपि न भाति ।

—DhL. Locana on II.5.

(ii) अलङ्कारो हि बाह्यालङ्कारसाम्यादङ्गिनश्चारुत्वहेतुरुच्यते ।

—DhL. vṛtti on II. 17.

2. यत्र तु नास्ति रसस्तत्रोक्तिवैचित्र्यमात्रपर्यवसायिन: ।

—KP. vṛtti on VIII. 67

Page 94 1. यत्र हि पर्यायान्तरपरिवृत्तिसहत्वं नास्ति तस्य शब्दगतत्वम्, यत्र तु तत्सहत्वं तत्रार्थगतत्वम् ।

—Kāvya Pradīpa on KP. IX. 8.

5. तत्तद्वीर नृसिंह भूप भवतो दानापदानं मुहुः
श्रुत्वा सिद्धपुरन्ध्रिगीतरचनाशिल्पेषु कल्पद्रुमः ।
नाश्लिष्टो लतया न पल्लवपुटैः पुष्णाति रागोद्गमं
पुष्पैर्नोद्गिरति स्मितं मधुकर ध्वानैर्न चाभाषते ।।
—Ekā. example under IV. 2.

6. साधारणधर्मवशाद्गम्येनाप्रस्तुतेन चारुत्वम् ।
प्रस्तुतमुपैति वाच्यं यस्यामेषा समासोक्तिः ।। —*Ibid.* VIII. 23.

Page 55. 1. नरसिंह देव न वयं कवयो नास्माकमीदृशो धर्मः ।
एष वचसां विलासः केवलमुपहारकुसुमतां व्रजतु ।।
—*Ibid.* example under IV. 2.

2. ब्रूमः किं पद्मनाभं वसति यदुदरे विश्वमेतत् समस्तं
किं वा नागाधिराजं स्वपिति सुखमसौ यत्र लक्ष्म्या समेतः ।
किं वा चन्द्रार्धचूडं यदुपरि भजते सोऽपि हारस्य लक्ष्मी-
माधत्ते सोऽपि चित्ते तव वसति रुचि गाङ्गवंशावतंस ।।
—*Ibid.* example under IV. 2.

3. त्वत्प्रत्यर्थिवसुन्धरेशरमणीः संत्रासतः सत्वरं
यान्तीर्वीर विलुण्ठितुं सरभसा याताः किराताः वने ।
तिष्ठन्ति स्तिमिताः प्ररूढपुलकास्ते विस्मितोपक्रमा-
स्तासामुत्तरलैः स्तनैरतितरां लोलैरपाङ्गैरपि ।।
—*Ibid.* example under IV. 2.

4. त्वयि लोचनगोचरं गते
सफलं जन्म नृसिंह भूपते ।
अजनिष्ट ममेति सादरं
युधि विज्ञापयति द्विषां गणः ।।
—*Ibid.* example under IV. 2.

5. नृसिंह भवतो दानं निशम्य निभृतेक्षणाः ।
विस्रस्तहस्ताः कान्तारेष्वासते राजकुञ्जराः ।।
—*Ibid.* example under IV. 2.

6. समालोक्यालेख्यस्थितमपि मृगाक्ष्यः फणाभृतं
प्रकम्पन्ते धैर्यं त्वदरितरुणीनां त्वनुपमम् ।
यदेतास्त्वद्घाट्यामधिरजनि यान्त्यः फणभृतां
फणारत्नं हस्तैः पिदधति दृढं वीर विपिने ॥

—Ekā. example under IV. 2.

7. एकाभूत् कुसुमायुधेषुधिरिव प्रव्यक्त पुङ्खावलि-
र्जेतुं मङ्गलपालिकेव पुलकैरन्या कपोलस्थली ।
लोलाक्षीं क्षणमात्रभाविविरहक्लेशासहां पश्यतो
द्रागाकर्णयतश्च वीर भवतः प्रौढाहवाडम्बरम् ॥

—*Ibid.* example under IV. 2.

8. सौभाग्यं तस्य चित्रं तदधिचपलता कापि मद्वीरलक्ष्म्याः
पश्यत्सु श्लाघते या रणभुवि नृपतिष्वद्भुतं तद्भुजाय ।
धिग्धातुः प्रातिकूल्यं मयि बलमतुलं तस्यं कस्य ब्रबीमी-
त्याचक्षणो विरोधी श्रयति गिरिवनं श्री नृसिंह क्षितीन्द्र ॥

—*Ibid.* example under IV. 2.

Page 56. 1. प्रधानेऽन्यत्र वाक्यार्थे यत्राङ्गं तु रसादयः ।
काव्ये तस्मिन्नलङ्कारो रसादिरिति मे मतिः ॥ —DhL. II. 5.

2 (a) एत एव रसादयोऽलङ्काराः ॥ —Ekā. vṛtti on IV. 2.

(b) यद्यपि रसवदलङ्कारस्यान्यैर्दर्शितो विषयस्तथापि यस्मिन् काव्ये प्रधानतयाऽन्योऽर्थो वाक्यार्थीभूतस्तस्य चाङ्गभूता ये रसादयस्ते रसादेरलङ्कारस्य विषया इति मामकीन पक्षः ।

—DhL. vṛtti on II. 5.

3. वाच्यस्य सिद्धिहेतुं कृतिनः कथयन्ति वाच्यसिद्ध्यङ्गम् ।

—Ekā. IV. 3.

4. पत्रावली कवलनान्यरिभूमिपाल-
लीलावतीस्तनतटेष्वलमादधाना ।
गङ्गातरङ्गधवलानि यशः पयांसि
दुग्धे धरातिलक वीर तवासिधेनुः ॥

—*Ibid.* example under IV. 3.

5. धाराविषं त्वदसिकालभुजङ्गमस्य
दृस्ट्वा सुदुःसहतरं समरे नरेन्द्राः ।
मूर्च्छां भजन्ति नरसिंह वसुन्धरेश
किं चोद्वहन्ति वपुराश्रितवर्णभेदम् ।।

—Ekā. example under IV. 3.

Page 57. 1. यत्र न सदपि व्यङ्ग्यं स्फुटतां भजते तदस्फुटाभिख्यम् ।।

—*Ibid.* IV. 3.

2. नृसिंह भूप भवतः संख्यामत्सरिणो गुणाः ।
त्रिविक्रमपदैरेव मितमेतज्जगत्त्रयम् ।।

—*Ibid.* example under IV. 3.

3. यदि वाच्यं व्यङ्ग्यं वा मुख्यतया निश्चितं न भवेत्
संदिग्धप्राधान्यं तत्तु सुधीभिर्विनिर्दिष्टम् ।। —*Ibid.* IV. 4.

4. त्वामारूढं मदगजपतिस्कन्धमाधूतखड्ग-
च्छायाविद्युद्वलयितभुजं वीक्ष्य युद्धे नृसिंह ।
दूरोदञ्चत्पुलकपटलीवर्मिताङ्गस्तुरङ्गे
दत्ते दृष्टिं विदितरभसे न्यक्कृतेभः सपत्नः ।।

—*Ibid.* example under IV. 4.

5. यस्मिन्ननयोः साम्यं तुल्यप्राधान्यमिष्यते तदिदम् । —*Ibid.* IV. 5.

6. अस्पृण्टाञ्जनसपंदः स्मृतिपथावस्थायिलीलास्मिताः
प्रत्याख्यातवतंसदामरचनास्त्यक्ताङ्गरागश्रियः ।
दूरोद्धूतकुरङ्गनाभिमकरीभङ्गास्तरङ्गभ्रुवः
संजाता नरसिंह पार्थिव भवत्प्रत्यर्थिपृथ्वी भुजाम् ।।

—*Ibid.* example under IV. 5.

7. आक्षिप्तं यत् काक्वा काक्वाक्षिप्तं तदाख्यातम् ।। —*Ibid.* IV. 5.

8. सर्वार्थिनामर्थितपूरणार्थं
परिस्फुरत्त्यागमहोत्सवेऽत्र ।
त्वयि स्थिते वीर नृसिंह भूप
न लज्जते संप्रति पारिजातः ।।

—*Ibid.* example under IV. 5.

9. यद्भजति न सौन्दर्यं तदसुन्दरमीरितं सद्भिः ।
इत्थममुष्य भिदाष्टकमुट्टङ्कितमेतदस्माभिः ।।
—Ekā. example under IV. 6.

10. अयज्ञः स्वर्लोकः सुकृतमतपः क्लेशसुभगं
सुधासारोऽनभ्रः फलमकुसुमश्रीसहचरम् ।
अशौर्यं साम्राज्यं निविरखननायाससुलभो
नृसिंहः क्षोणीन्द्रो नयनपथमस्माकमगमत् ।।
—*Ibid.* example under IV. 6.

Page 58. 1. उत्तिष्ठ कन्दरवननाय गृहाण चापं
गाहस्व काननमिति प्रहितोऽपि वध्वा ।
आकारितोऽपि सहकेलिसखैः किरातै-
रद्वैनं वीर विजहाति दरीमरिस्ते ।। —*Ibid.* IV. 6.

2. अगूढमपरस्याङ्गं वाच्यसिद्ध्यङ्गमस्फुटम् ।
संदिग्धतुल्यप्राधान्ये काक्वाक्षिप्तमसुन्दरम् ।।
व्यङ्ग्यमेवं गुणीभूतव्यङ्ग्यस्याष्टौ भिदाः स्मृताः ।।
—KP. V. 45-46.

3. रसभावादि तात्पर्यरहितं व्यङ्ग्यार्थविशेषप्रकाशनशक्तिशून्यं च काव्यं केवलवाच्यवाचकवैचित्र्यमात्राश्रयेणोपनिबद्धमालेख्यप्रख्यं यदाभासते तच्चित्रम् । न तन्मुख्यं काव्यम् । काव्यानुकरो ह्यसौ ।
—DhL. vṛtti on III. 24.

4. केचित् चित्राख्यं तृतीयं काव्यभेदमिच्छन्ति । तदाहुः—
'शब्दचित्रं वाच्यचित्रमव्यङ्ग्यं त्ववरं स्मृतम् ।'
इति । तन्न, यदि हि अव्यङ्ग्यत्वे न व्यङ्ग्याभावस्तदा तस्य काव्यत्वमपि नास्तीति । — SD. vṛtti on IV. 17.

5. ...परिपाकवतां कवीनां रसादितात्पर्यविरहे व्यापार एव न शोभते । रसादितात्पर्ये च नास्त्येव तद्वस्तु यदभिमतरसाङ्गतां नीयमानं न प्रगुणीभवति ।...तस्मान्नास्त्येव तद्वस्तु यत्सर्वात्मना रसतात्पर्यवतः कवेस्तदिच्छया तदाभिमतरसाङ्गतां न धत्ते । तथोपनिबध्यमानं वा न चारुत्वातिशयं पुष्णाति । —DhL. vṛtti on III. 42.

———

CHAPTER IV

Page 59. 1. अङ्गिनि रसे स्थिता ये बिभ्रत्युत्कर्षहेतुतां सततम् ।
आत्मनि शौर्यादय इव ते नामैते गुणाः कथिताः ॥ —Ekā. V. 1.

2. ये तमर्थं रसादिलक्षणमङ्गिनं सन्तमवलम्बन्ते ते गुणाः शौर्यादिवत् ।
—DhL. vṛtti on II. 6.

3. ये रसस्याङ्गिनो धर्माः शौर्यादय इवात्मनः ।
उत्कर्षहेतवस्ते स्युरचलस्थितयो गुणाः ॥ —KP. VIII. 66.

4. ···गुणा विपर्ययादेषां माधुर्यौदार्यलक्षणाः ॥ —NS. 16.96.

5. व्यालवन्तो दुरारोहा रत्नवन्तः फलान्विताः ।
विषमा भूभृतस्तेभ्यो भूयमाशु प्रमादिनाम् ॥ —KAB. IV. 19.

6. श्रुतेः सामान्यधर्माणां विशेषस्यानुदाहृतेः ।
अप्रतिष्ठं यदत्रैतज्ज्ञानं तत्संशयं विदुः ॥
ससंशयमिति प्राहुस्ततस्तज्जननं वचः ।
इष्टं निश्चितये वाक्यं न दोलायेत तद्यथा ॥ —*Ibid.* IV. 17-18.

7. 'व्यालवन्तो दुरारोहा···प्रमादिनाम्' ॥···ससन्देहालङ्कारस्य विषयोऽवगन्तव्यः ।

—Skt. commentary Viveka of Hemacandra on KAnu. VI. 20.

8. Concepts of Rīti and Guṇa in Sanskrit Poetics, Dr. P. C. Lahiri, p. 48.

Page 60. 1. श्लेषः प्रसादः समता माधुर्यं सुकुमारता ।
अर्थव्यक्तिरुदारत्वमोजः कान्तिसमाधयः ॥

इति वैदर्भमार्गस्य प्राणा दश गुणाः स्मृताः । —KD. I. 41-42.

2. काव्यशोभायाः कर्त्तारो धर्मा गुणाः ॥ —KASV. III. 1. 1.

3. पूर्वे (गुणाः) नित्याः ॥ —*Ibid.* III. 1. 3.

4. ···दोषहानात्··· । —KASV. vṛtti on I. 1. 3.

5. ···गुणालङ्कारदानात्··· । —*Ibid.* vṛtti on I. 1. 3.

6. अलङ्कृतमपि श्राव्यं न काव्यं गुणवर्जितम् ।।
गुणयोगस्तयोर्मुख्यो गुणालङ्कारयोगयोः ।। —SKBh. I. 72.

7. यः काव्ये महतीं छायामनुगृह्णात्यसौ गुणः ।
—Agnipurāṇa. 346-3.

Page 61. 1. अलङ्कारास्तु हारादय इव कण्ठादीनां संयोगवृत्या वाच्यवाचकरूपाणामङ्गानामतिशयमादधाना रसमुपकुर्वन्ति ।
—Ekā. vṛtti on V. 1.

2. (a) 'समवायवृत्या शौर्यादयः संयोगवृत्या तु हारादय इत्यस्तु गुणालङ्काराणां भेदः ओजः प्रभृतीनामनुप्रासोपमादीनां चोभयेषामपि समवायवृत्या स्थितिरिति गड्डलिकाप्रवाहेणैवैषां भेदः' इत्यभिधानमसत् ।। —KP. vṛtti on VIII. 67.

(b) Bhāmahavivaraṇa-Bhaṭṭodbhaṭṭa, quoted by ācārya Viśveśvara in KP. dīpikā on KP. VIII Chapter (introduction) (p. 378).

Also quoted by late Jhalakīkara in KP. commentary on VIII. 67 (p. 470).

3. वस्तुतस्तु रसस्य धर्मा गुणा गुणालङ्काराणां समावायवृत्या स्थितिरिति गड्डुरिकाप्रवाहेण । —Ekā. vṛtti on V. 1.

Page 62. 1. 'युवतेरिव रूपमङ्ग काव्यं
स्वदते शुद्धगुणं तदप्यतीव ।
विहितप्रणयं निरन्तराभिः
सदलङ्कारविकल्पकल्पनाभिः ।।
यदि भवति वचश्च्युतं गुणेभ्यो
वपुरिव यौवनबन्ध्यमङ्गनायाः ।
अपि जनदयितानि दुर्भगत्वं
नियतमलङ्करणानि संश्रयन्ते ।।' —SKBh. I. 193-194.

2. 'युवतेरिव रूपमङ्ग । काव्यं···संश्रयन्ते ।।'
—KASV. examples 1. 2. under III. 1. 2.

3. तमर्थमवलम्बन्ते येऽङ्गिनं ते गुणाः स्मृताः ।
अङ्गाश्रितास्त्वलंकारा मन्तव्याः कटकादिवत् ॥ —DhL. II. 7.

4. तस्मादलंकार एव काव्यव्यवहारप्रयोजकः । गुणस्तु वस्तुतोऽस्त्येव तस्य रसधर्मत्वात् ॥ किन्त्वलङ्कारास्तं नोपक्षते ततस्तत्कृता शोभैव नास्ति कुतस्तरां तदतिशयोऽलङ्कारजन्य इति ॥
—Ekā. vṛtti on V. 1.

Page 63. 1. आनन्दस्यन्दिता तज्ज्ञैर्माधुर्यमभिधीयते ॥
संभोगे करुणे विप्रलम्भे शान्ते च तत् क्रमात् ।
काष्ठां पुष्यति चित्तस्य विलीनत्वमिवार्पयत् ॥ —*Ibid.* V. 2-3.

2. शृङ्गारे विप्रलम्भाख्ये करुणे च प्रकर्षवत् ।
माधुर्यमार्द्रतां याति यतस्तत्राधिकं मनः ॥ —DhL. II. 8.

3. आह्लादकत्वं माधुर्यं शृङ्गारे द्रुतिकारणम् ॥
करुणे विप्रलम्भे तच्छान्ते चातिशयान्वितम् ।—KP. VIII. 68-69.

4. बहुशो यत्कृतं काव्यमुक्तं वापि पुनः पुनः ।
नोद्वेजयति तस्माद्धि तन्माधुर्यमुदाहृतम् ॥ —NS. 16. 103.

5. ओजो दीप्त्यात्मविस्तारकारणं परिकीर्त्तितम् ।
क्रमेण वीरबीभत्सरौद्रेष्वेतत् प्रकर्षति ॥

किं च भग्नमनोवृत्तिस्वभावेऽपि भयानके ।
दीप्तत्वेन विभावस्य भजत्योजः परां भुवम् ॥ —Ekā. V. 4-5.

6. दीप्त्यात्मविस्तृतेर्हेतुरोजो वीररसस्थितिः ॥
बीभत्सरौद्ररसयोस्तस्याधिक्यं क्रमेण च । —KP. VIII. 69-70.

7. यश्चित्तं व्यश्नुतेऽह्लाय शुष्केन्धनमिवानलः ।
स प्रसादो मतः सर्वरससाधारणस्थितिः ॥ —Ekā. V. 6.

8. श्रव्यं नातिसमस्तार्थं काव्यं मधुरमिष्यते । —KAB. II. 3.

9. बन्धस्य पृथक् पदत्वं यत् तत् माधुर्यम् ।···समासदैर्घ्यविनिवृत्तिपरञ्च एतत् । —KASV. vṛtti on III. 1. 21.

10. असमस्तानि समासवर्जितानि मनोहराणि हृदयाह्लादकानि श्रुति रम्यत्वेनार्थरमणीयत्वेन च यानि पदानि सुप्तिङन्तानि तेषां विन्यासः

सन्निवेशवैचित्र्यं, जीवितं सर्वस्वं यस्य तत्तथोक्तम्। माधुर्यं नाम सुकुमारलक्षणस्य मार्गस्य प्रथमः प्रधानभूतो गुणः ।

—VJ. vṛtti on I. 30.

11. समासवद्भिर्विविधैर्विचित्रैश्च पदैर्युतम् ।
सा तु स्वरैरुदारैश्च तदोजः परिकीर्त्यते ॥ —NS. 16. 104.

Page 64. 1. ओजः समासभूयस्त्वमेतद्गद्यस्य जीवितम् ।
पद्येप्यदाक्षिणात्यानामिदमेकं परायणम् ॥ —KD. I. 80.

2. गाढबन्धत्वमोजः ॥ —KASV. III. 1. 5.

3. (a) गूढार्थमर्थान्तरमर्थहीनं भिन्नार्थमेकार्थमभिप्लुतार्थम् ।
न्यायादपेतं विषमं विसंधि शब्दच्युतं वै दश काव्यदोषाः ॥

—NS. 16. 89.

(b) श्लेषः प्रसादः समता समाधिर्माधुर्यमोजः पदसौकुमार्यम् ।
अर्थस्य च व्यक्तिरुदारता च कान्तिश्च काव्यार्थगुणा दशैते ॥

—*Ibid.* 16. 97.

4. ···समः प्रसन्नो मधुर उदार ओजस्वी चासि । —KM. p. 6.

5. ···लक्ष्मीरिव विना त्यागान्न वाणी भाति नीरसा ॥

—Agnipurāṇa 339. 9.

6. यः काव्ये महतीं छायामनुगृह्णात्यसौ गुणः ।
सम्भवत्येष सामान्यो वैशेषिक इति द्विधा ॥

सर्व्वसाधारणीभूतः सामान्य इति मन्यते ।
शब्दमर्थमुभौ प्राप्तः सामान्यो भवति त्रिधा ॥

शब्दमाश्रयते काव्यं शरीरं यः स तद्गुणः ।
श्लेषो लालित्यगाम्भीर्यसौकुमार्य्यमुदारता ॥

सत्यैवयौगिकी चेति गुणाः शब्दस्य सप्तधा । —*Ibid.* 346. 3-7.

7. भाविकत्वमिति प्राहुः प्रबन्धविषयं गुणम् ।
प्रत्यक्षा इव दृश्यन्ते यत्रार्था भूतभाविनः ॥

चित्तोदात्तादभूतार्थत्वं कथायाः स्वाभिनीतता ।
शब्दानाकुलता चेति तस्य हेतुं प्रचक्षते ॥ —KAB. III. 53-54.

Page 65. 1. त्रिविधाश्च गुणाः काव्ये भवन्ति कविसम्मताः ।
बाह्याश्चाभ्यन्तराश्चैव ये च वैशेषिका इति ॥
वैशेषिकास्तु ते नूनं दोषत्वेऽपि हि ये गुणाः ॥
चतुर्विंशतिराख्यातास्तेषु ये शब्दसंश्रयाः ।
... ...
श्लेषः प्रसादः समता माधुर्यं सुकुमारता ।
... ...
रीतिरुक्तिस्तथा प्रौढिस्थैषां लक्ष्यलक्षणे ॥ —SKBh. I. 72.

2. केचिदन्तर्भवन्त्येषु दोषत्यागात्परे श्रिताः ।
अन्ये भजन्ति दोषत्वं कुत्रचित् नततो दश ॥ —KP. VIII. 72.

3. पदानामेकपदवद्‌मासमानत्वं श्लेषः । —Ekā. vṛtti on V. 8.
4. आरोहावरोहक्रमरूपः समाधिः । —*Ibid.* vṛtti on V. 8.

Page 66. 1. विकृत्वमौदार्य्यम् । —*Ibid.* vṛtti on V. 8.

2. विशिष्टा पदरचना रीतिः । —KASV. I. 2. 7.

3. अस्त्यनेको गिरां मार्गः सूक्ष्मभेदः परस्परम् ।
तत्र वैदर्भगौडीयौ वर्ण्यते प्रस्फुटान्तरौ ॥ —KD. I. 40.

4. असमासा समासेन मध्यमेन च भूषिता ।
तथा दीर्घसमासेति त्रिधा सङ्घटनोदिता ॥
गुणानाश्रित्य तिष्ठन्ती माधुर्यादीन्व्यनक्ति सा ।
रसान् ... ... —DhL. III. 5-6.

5. ...वयमधुना रीतीः प्रचक्ष्महे तिस्त्रः ।
वैदर्भीपाञ्चालीगौडीयेत्यत्र संक्षेपात् ॥ —Ekā. V. 9.

6. अकृतसमासस्पर्शा समग्रगुणगुम्फितादिमा तत्र ।
एकेव जयति रीतिर्विदलितवीणाभिमानसर्वस्वा ॥ —*Ibid* V. 10.

7. ...वैदर्भीरीतिरेकैव शस्यते ।
यतः समाससंस्पर्शस्तत्र नैवोपपद्यते ॥ —VV. II. 16.

8. अनभ्रवृष्टिः श्रवणामृतस्य सरस्वतीविभ्रमजन्मभूमिः ।
वैदर्भरीतिः कृतिनामुदेति सौभाग्यलाभप्रतिभूः पदानाम् ॥
—Vikramāṅkadevacarita, I. 9.

9. सुकुमारस्वभावस्य कवेस्तथाविधैव सहजा शक्तिः समुद्भवति, शक्तिशक्तिमतोरभेदात् । तया च तथाविधसौकुमार्यरमणीयां व्युत्पत्तिमाबध्नाति । ताभ्याञ्च सुकुमारवर्त्मनाभ्यासतत्परः क्रियते ।

—VJ. vṛtti on I. 24.

10. ···The Gauḍīyā rīti in Theory and Practice, Prof. S. P. Bhaṭṭācārya, The Indian Historical Quarterly Journal, June, 1927.

11. ओजःकान्तिविहीनामाहुः श्लथसंधिबंधुरां कवयः ।
पञ्चषपदसमुदञ्चल्ललितसमासां च पाञ्चालीम् ॥ —Ekā.V. 11.

Page 67. 1. माधुर्य्यसौकुमार्य्योपपन्ना पाञ्चाली । —KASV. I. 2. 13.

2. समस्तपञ्चषपदामोजः कान्तिविवर्जिताम् ।
मधुरां सुकुमाराञ्च पाञ्चालीं कवयो विदुः ॥ —SKBh. II. 54.

3. ओजः कान्तिकरम्बितसकलोद्धतपदविराजितां वृत्तिम् ।
बिभ्राणा रीतिज्ञैर्गौडीया रीतिराम्नाता ॥

—Ekā. V. 12.

4. ओजः कान्तिमती गौडीया ॥

—KASV. I.2.12.

5. समस्तात्युद्भटपदामोजः कान्तिगुणान्विताम् ।
गौडीयेति विजानन्ति रीतिं रीतिविचक्षणाः ॥ —SKBh. II·55.

6. (a) एतासामेव साङ्कर्य्याद्भवन्त्यावन्तिकादयः ।
पार्थक्येन ततोऽस्माभिर्नाम्यधीयंत ताः पुनः ॥

—Ekā. V. 13.

(b) अन्तराले तु पाञ्चालीवैदर्भ्योर्याऽवतिष्ठते ।
सावन्तिका समस्तैः स्याद्द्वित्रैस्त्रिचतुरैः पदैः ॥

समस्तरीतिर्व्यामिश्रा लाटीया रीतिरिष्यते ।
पूर्वरीतेरनिर्वाहे खण्डरीतिस्तु मागधी ॥ —SKBh. II 56-57.

7. प्रतिभाप्रथमोद्भेदसमये यत्र वक्रता ।
शब्दाभिधेययोरन्तः स्फुरतीव विभाव्यते ॥
....

विचित्रो यत्र वक्रोक्तिवैचित्र्यं जीवितायते ।
परिस्फुरति यस्यान्तः सा काप्यतिशयाभिधा ।।

सोऽतिदुःखचरो येन विदग्धकवयो गताः ।
खड्गधारापथेनेव सुभटानां मनोरथाः ।। —VJ. I. 34-43.

8. एवं विचित्रमभिधाय मध्यममुपक्रमते—

वैचित्र्यं सौकुमार्यञ्च यत्र सङ्कीर्णतां गते ।
भ्राजेते सहजाहार्यशोभातिशयशालिनी ।।

माधुर्यादिगुणग्रामो वृत्तिमाश्रित्य मध्यमाम् ।
यत्र कामपि पुष्णाति बन्धच्छायातिरिक्तताम् ।। —*Ibid.* I. 49-50.

9. Concepts of Rīti and Guṇa, P.C. Lahiri, p. 235.

Page 68. 1. तासां पूर्वा (वैदर्भी) ग्राह्या—गुणसाकल्यात् ।।
न पुनरितरे,—स्तोकगुणत्वात् ।। —KASV. I. 2. 14-15

2. नाम्ना वृत्तिर्द्वेधा भवति समासासमासभेदेन ।
....

पाञ्चाली लाटीया गौडीया चेति नामतोऽभिहिताः ।
लघुमध्यायतविरचनसमासभेदादिमास्तत्र ।।

....

वृत्तेरसमासाया वैदर्भी रीतिरेकैव ।। —KAR II. 3,4 and 6.

3. वाग्विधासम्प्रतिज्ञाने रीतिः सापि चतुर्विधा ।
पाञ्चाली गौडदेशीया वैदर्भी लाटजा तथा ।।

उपचारयुता मृद्वी पाञ्चाली ह्रस्वविग्रहा ।
अनवस्थितसन्दर्भा गौडीया दीर्घविग्रहा ।।

उपचारैर्न बहुभिरुपचारैर्विवर्जिता ।
नातिकोमलसन्दर्भा वैदर्भीयुक्तविग्रहा ।।

लाटीया स्फुटसन्दर्भा नाति विस्फुरविग्रहा ।
परित्यक्तापि भूयोभिरुपचारैरुदाहृता ।। —Agnipurāṇa 340-1-4.

4. पदसङ्घटना रीतिरङ्गसंस्थाविशेषवत् ।
उपकर्त्री रसादीनाम् ।।
सा पुनः स्याच्चतुर्विधा ।
वैदर्भी चाथ गौडी पाञ्चाली लाटिका तथा ।। —SD. IX. 1-2.

5. वैदर्भादिकृतः पन्थाः काव्ये मार्ग इति स्मृतः ।
रीङ्गताविति धातोः सा व्युत्पत्त्या रीतिरुच्यते ।।

तत्रासमासा निःशेषश्लेषादिगुणगुम्फिता ।
विपञ्चीस्वरसौभाग्या वैदर्भी रीतिरिष्यते ।।

—SKBh. II.51 and 53.

6. (a) माधुर्यव्यञ्जकैर्वर्णैरुपनागरिकोच्यते ।
ओजः प्रकाशकैस्तैस्तु परुषा ।
कोमला परैः ।। —KP. IX. 80.

(b) (i) एषेव (उपनागरिका) केषांचिन्मते वैदर्भी रीतिरिति वक्ष्यते ।

(ii एषेव (परुषा) केषांचिन्मते गौडी रीतिरिति वक्ष्यते ।

(iii) एषेव (कोमला) केषांचिन्मते पाञ्चालीरीतिरिति वक्ष्यते ।

—Vāmanācārya Jhalakīkara on KP. IX. 80.

Page 69. 1. (a) दर्शनान्तरे त्वेता वैदर्भीपाञ्चालीगौडीया चेति तिस्त्रो रीतयो मधुरमध्यमपरुषवर्णारब्धत्वान्मधुरा मध्यमा परुषा चेति वृत्तयो रसविषयव्यापारत्वेन कथ्यन्ते । —Ekā vṛtti on V. 13.

(b) वृत्तिस्तु रसविषयो व्यापारः । ···सा च परुषकोमलमध्यम-वर्णारब्धत्वात्त्रिधा । —AS. vṛtti on 5.

2. (i) शषाभ्यां रेफसंयोगेष्टवर्गेण च योजिता ।।
परुषा नाम वृत्तिः स्यात् ह्लह्वह्याद्यैश्च संयुता ।।

(ii) सरुपसंयोगयुतां मूर्ध्नि वर्गान्त्ययोगिभिः ।
स्पर्शैर्युता च मन्यन्ते उपनागरिका बुधाः ।।

(iii) शेषैर्वर्णैर्यथायोगं कथितां कोमलाख्यया ।
ग्राम्यां वृत्तिं प्रशंसन्ति काव्येष्वाहतबुद्धयः ।। —KASS. I.4.

3. शृङ्गारे चैव हास्ये च वृत्तिः स्यात् कैशिकीतिसा ।
सात्वती नाम सा ज्ञेया वीररौद्राद्भुताश्रया ।।
भयानके च बीभत्से रौद्रे चारभटी भवेत् ।
भारती चापि विज्ञेया करुणाद्भुतसंश्रया ।। —NS. 20. 62-63.

4. शृंगारे कैशिकी, वीरे सात्वत्यारभटी पुनः ।
रसे रौद्रे च बीभत्से, वृत्तिः सर्वत्र भारती ॥ —DR. II. 62.

5. मधुरा प्रौढा परुषा ललिता भद्रेति वृत्तयः पञ्च ।
वर्णानां नानात्वादस्येति यथार्थनामफलाः ॥ —KAR. II 19.

Page 70 1. रसाद्यनुगुणत्वेन व्यवहारोऽर्थशब्दयोः ।
औचित्यवान्यस्ता एता वृत्तयो द्विविधाः स्थिताः ॥

—DhL. III. 33.

2. वाच्याश्रयो यो व्यवहारस्ता एताः कैशिक्याद्या वृत्तयः ।
वाचकाश्रयाश्चोपनागरिकाद्याः ।

—*Ibid.* vṛtti on III. 33.

3. जातिर्गती रीतिवृत्ति··· ।
चतुर्विंशतिरित्युक्ताः शब्दालङ्कारजातयः ॥ —SKBh. II. 3-5.

4. एतास्तिस्रो वृत्तयः वामनादीनां मते वैदर्भीगौडीपाञ्चाल्याख्या रीतयो मताः ॥ —KP. vṛtti on IX. 81.

———

CHAPTER V

Page 72. 1. तत्र काव्यापकर्षहेतवो दोषा इति सामान्यलक्षणम् ।
—Taralā Skt. Commentary on Ekā. beginning of VI Unmeṣa

2. एतस्य च (दोषस्य) विवक्षितरसादिप्रतीतिविघ्नविधायित्वं नाम-सामान्यलक्षणम् । —VV. beginning of II Vimarśa.

3. अनौचित्यादृते नान्यद्रसभङ्गस्य कारणम् ।
प्रसिद्धौचित्यबन्धस्तु रसस्योपनिषत्परा ॥
—DhL. under vṛtti on III. 14.

4. मुख्यार्थहतिर्दोषो··· —KP. VIII. 49.

5. (a) दोषास्तस्यापकर्षकाः ॥ श्रुतिदुष्टापुष्टार्थत्वादयः काणत्वखञ्जत्वादय इव—काव्यस्यात्मभूतं रसमपकर्षयन्तः काव्यस्यापकर्षकाः···।
—SD. I. 4 and vṛtti on it.

(b) रसापकर्षका दोषाः ।
—*Ibid.* VII. 1.

6. एते दोषास्तु विज्ञेयाः सूरिभिर्नाटकाश्रयाः ।
गुणाः विपर्ययादेषां— ॥ —NS. II. 96.

7. सर्वथा पदमप्येकं न निगाद्यमवद्यवत् ।
विलक्ष्मणा हि काव्येन दुःसुतेनेव निन्द्यते ॥ —KAB. I. 11.

8. स दोषगुणालङ्कारहानादानाभ्याम् ॥
—KASV. I. 1.3.

9. अन्यूनाधिकवाचकसुक्रमपुष्टार्थशब्दचारुपदम् ।
क्षोदक्षममक्षूणं सुमतिर्वाक्यं प्रयुञ्जीत ॥ —KAR. II. 8.

Page 73. 1.—एको हि दोषो गुणसंनिपाते निमज्जतीन्दोः किरणेष्विवाङ्कः ॥
—Kumārasambhava (Kālidāsa), I. 3.

2. तत्सादृश्यं तदन्यत्वं तदल्पत्वं विरोधिता ।
अप्राशस्त्यमभावश्च नञर्थाः षट् प्रकीर्तिताः ॥
—Jhalakīkara on KP. I. 4.

3. न हि कीटानुवेद्यादयो रत्नस्य रत्नत्वं व्याहन्तुमीशाः किन्तु उपादेय-तारतम्यमेव कर्तुम्, तद्वदत्रापि श्रुतिदुष्टादयोऽपि काव्यस्य । उक्तञ्च

'कीटानुविद्धरत्नादिसाधारण्येन काव्यता ।
दुष्टेष्वपि मता यत्र रसाद्यनुगमः स्फुटः ॥' इति ।

—SD. vṛtti on I. 2.

4. नाकवित्वमधर्माय व्याधये दण्डनाय वा ।
कुकवित्वं पुनः साक्षान्मृतिमाहुर्मनीषिणः ॥ —KAB. I. 12.

5. तदल्पमपि नोपेक्ष्यं काव्ये दुष्टं कथंचन ।
स्याद्वपुः सुन्दरमपि श्वित्रेणैकेन दुर्भगम् ॥ —KD. I. 7.

6. ···यत्पुनरनलंकारं निर्दोषं चेति तन्मध्यम् ॥ —KAR. VI. 40.

7. —उचिताभिधानजीवितत्वाद् वाक्यस्याप्येकदेशेऽप्यौचित्यविरहात् तद्विदाह्लादकारित्वहानिः । ···प्रबन्धस्यापि कस्यचित् प्रकरणैक-देशेऽप्यौचित्यविरहादेकदेशदाहदूषितदग्धपटप्रायता प्रसज्यते ।···

—VJ.vṛtti on I. 57.

8. दोषः सर्वात्मना त्याज्यो रसहानिकरो हि सः । ···

—Alaṁkāraśekhara (Keśavamiśra), p.14.

9. न विधेयप्राधान्यं वृत्तिर्वक्तुं प्रगल्भते यस्मात् ।
अविमृष्टविधेयांशस्तस्मादस्यामुदीर्यते दोषः ॥

—Ekā. VI. 1.

Page 74. 1. जाते वीर नृसिंह भूप चलतस्त्वत्सैन्यपाथोनिधे-
र्न्यञ्चद्भूतलभारभङ्गुरफणोत्सङ्गोरगाधीश्वरे ।
वाष्पोत्सङ्गितलोचनं कुचतटीविन्यस्तहस्ताञ्चलं
तस्यान्तः पुरसुभ्रुवामुदचरन् हाकारगर्भागिरः ॥

—*Ibid.* example under VI. 1.

2. विधुन्तुद ममाधुना बत करिष्यते किं भवा-
निति स्फुरदहंकृतिस्तुहिनदीधितिर्निर्भयम् ।
विधाय तव कीर्तिभिर्निजवपुः सहस्राण्यसौ
कलिङ्गवसुधाधिप त्रिषु जगत्सु विद्योतते ॥

—*Ibid.* example under VI. 1.

3. यदिह ककुभां सीम्नि व्योम्नः स्थलेऽप्यमितं यश-
स्तव कथमपि ज्योत्स्नागौरं नृसिंह नरेश्वर ।

तदिदमखिलं चित्रं पञ्चाशता परमक्षरैः
कृतपरिकरे वाग्व्यापारे निवेशयते कविः ।।

—Ekā. example under VI. 1.

4. आक्रम्य स्मरवैरिशेखरसरित्पूरैकसिंहासनं
राजानं नरसिंह पार्थिव तथाहंकारभारोद्धुरः ।
त्वत्कीर्त्तिप्रसरो हसत्ययमसौ शक्रस्य दन्तावलं
व्यालेन्द्रं मुसलायुधं किमपरं देव्याश्च पञ्चाननम् ।।

—*Ibid.* example under VI. 1.

Page 75. 1. सर्वंकषति न केषामेषां समरेषु विद्विषां गर्वम् ।
कालीव दानवानां वीर कृपाणो तव स्थिता पाणौ ।।

—*Ibid.* example under VI. 1.

2. न कस्य कर्णयोर्हर्षमेषा वर्षति भारती ।
कवित्वतत्त्वनिष्ठस्य नरसिंहस्य भूपतेः ।।

—*Ibid.* example under VI. 1.

3. नाथः काकोदराणां कथयति लिखति क्ष्मापतिः कार्त्तवीर्यो
मेलानन्दो जलानां निधिरचलपतिलेखनीं व्योमपत्रम् ।
संख्या पारेपरार्घं यदि भवति पुनः किं चवैरिञ्चमायुः
संख्येयत्वं तदानीं दधति तव गुणाः श्रीनृसिंह क्षितीन्द्र ! ।।

—*Ibid.* example under VI. 1.

4. गर्जद्दुर्जयशत्रुसैन्यजलधेर्मन्थाय विद्वज्जना-
भीष्टानां परिपूरणाय वसुधावष्टम्भदानाय च ।
राजन् वीर नृसिंह देव भवतः सृष्टे भुजे वेधसा
व्यर्थः संप्रति मन्दरः सुरतरुः सर्वाधिपश्चाभवत् ।।

—*Ibid.* example under VI. 1.

Page 76. 1. त्यागश्रीहसितेन्द्रकेलिविपिनक्षोणीरुहाहंकृतिः
कीर्तिव्रीडित कार्तिकेन्दुमहिषीगण्डस्थलीपाण्डिमा ।
हेलाताण्डवितप्रतापलहरी निर्धूतकल्पानलः
केषामेष न वर्णनीयमहिमा वीरः कलिङ्गेश्वरः ।।

—*Ibid.* example under VI. 1.

2. त्यागेनोपहसन्महेन्द्रविपिनक्षोणीरुहाहंकृतिं
कीर्त्यापत्रपयन् सुधांशु महिषीगण्डस्थली पाण्डुताम् ।

निर्धुन्वन् प्रबलप्रतापलहरीनृत्येन कल्पानलम्
इति निरवद्यः पाठः । —Ekā. example under VI. 1.

3. अनुवाद्यविधेयांशावुक्तौ स्यातां विपर्ययेण यदा ।
अविमृष्टविधेयांशो भवति तदानीं तु वाक्यगतः ॥ —*Ibid*. VI. 2.

4. कलानिधे वीर कलिङ्गनाथ
प्रायस्त्वमिन्दोरपरावतारः ।

त्वां पश्यतामेव मुदः स्फुरन्ति
यदुत्तरङ्गाः कविकैरवाणाम् ॥
—*Ibid*. example under VI. 2

5. उत्कण्ठाभारताम्यत् कुवलयनयनामानसाम्भोजभानु-
श्चिन्तासंतापमीलत्कविकुलकुमुदव्यूहनक्षत्रनाथः ।

ईर्ष्यासंवर्धमानप्रतिनृपतिकुलाम्भोधिकुम्भोद्भवश्च
ख्यातः सर्वत्र योऽसौ जगति विजयते श्रीनृसिंहः क्षितीन्द्रः ॥
—*Ibid*. example under VI. 2.

Page 77. 1. स पुनरुपक्रमोपसंहारक्रमो द्विविधः शाब्दश्चार्थश्चेति । तत्र द्वयोरुपा-
दाने शाब्दः ।···एकतरोपादाने त्वार्थः । तदितरस्य सामर्थ्येनावसीय-
मानत्वात् ।
—*Ibid*. vṛtti on VI. 2.

2. हिमकरकलामौलिः कृष्णः सरोरुहसंभवः
फणधरकुलं नालं बोद्धुं नृसिंह नरेश्वर ।
यदमरधुनीं दुग्धाम्भोधिं मरालमहीश्वरं
स खलु महिमा विश्वाख्यातस्तवैव यशः श्रियः ॥
—*Ibid*. example under VI. 2.

3. (a) एकतरोपादाने त्वार्थः । तदितरस्य सामर्थ्येनावसीयमानत्वात् ।
—*Ibid*. vṛtti on VI. 2.

(b) एकतरस्योपादाने सत्यार्थः तदितरस्यार्थसामर्थ्येनाक्षेपात् ।
—VV. vṛtti on II. 5.

4. (a) तत्र केवलस्य तद उपादाने सत्यार्थो न त्रैविध्यमतिक्रामति ।
प्रक्रान्तप्रसिद्धानुभूतविषयतयोपकल्पितसंनिधिना यच्छब्देन
तच्छब्दस्याभिसंबन्धात् । —Ekā. vṛtti on VI. 2.

(b) तत्र तदः केवलस्योपादाने सत्यार्थस्त्रिविधः प्रसिद्धानुभूतप्रक्रान्त-
वस्तु विषयतयोपकल्पितसन्निधिना यदा तस्याभिसम्बन्धात् ।

—VV. vṛtti on II. 5.

(c) प्रक्रान्तप्रसिद्धानुभूतार्थविषयस्तच्छब्दो यच्छब्दोपादानं नापेक्षते ।

—KP. vṛtti on VII. 52.

5. लोकेऽस्मिन् नरसिंहदेवनृपतिर्दाता न कल्पद्रुम-
स्तेजस्वी स न पद्मिनीसहचरः कान्तः स नो चन्द्रमाः ।
गम्भीरः स न वाहिनीपरिवृढस्तुङ्गः स नो मन्दरः ।
शिल्पज्ञः स न पद्मभूः किमपरं वाग्मी स नो वाक्पतिः ।।

—Ekā. example under VI. 2.

6. सा किं दत्तवती कदा बत शिला कस्मै स शाली पुनः
कस्यालोकपथं गतो निविशते कस्यान्तिके सा पशुः ।
पर्यायो नरसिंह पार्थिव तव प्रख्यातचिन्तामणि-
र्मन्दारो दिविषद्गवी त्रिभुवनश्लाध्याः समस्ता अमी ।।

—*Ibid.* example under VI. 2.

7. त्वत्प्रत्यर्थी गिरिचरगजस्याङ्कके दत्तदृष्टि-
स्तस्मिंस्तस्मिन् मधुरं तत्तदङ्गे प्रियायाः ।
कुम्भाभोगे गुरुकुचतटं दन्तयोर्गण्डलक्ष्मी-
मुरू हस्ते गतिषु च गतिं श्रीनृसिंह क्षितीन्द्र ।।

—*Ibid.* example under VI. 2.

Page 78. 1. यच्छब्दस्तूत्तरवाक्यगतत्वेनोपात्तः सामर्थ्यात् पूर्ववाक्यगत तच्छब्द-
स्योपादानं नापेक्षते । —*Ibid.* vṛtti on VI. 2.

2. श्रीमन्नृसिंह नृपते कविकाव्यशय्यां
त्वत्कीर्त्तिरेति भुवनत्रयगर्भभारात् ।
यस्याः प्रभा भजति दौर्हृदपाण्डुभावं
प्रौढीभवत्यसिमिषेण च रोमराजिः ।।

—*Ibid.* example under VI. 2.

3. यत्र द्वीपस्तुषारक्षितिभृदुडुगणो मौक्तिकानां निकायः
शैवालं व्योमशङ्खः कुमुदकुलगुरुर्धाम सान्ध्यं प्रवालः ।

यूथं दिक्कुञ्जराणां करिमकरकुलं किं च कृष्णः कृपाण-

स्त्वत्कीर्त्तिक्षीरवार्द्धि स जयति जगति श्रीनृसिंह क्षितीन्द्र ॥

—Ekā. example under VI. 2.

4. यासामम्बुधिरालवालवलयं चक्राचलेन्द्रो वृतिः

कुल्याः सह्यकलिन्दविन्ध्यतनया मुख्याः महानिम्नगाः ।

मेरुः संत्रयभूरुहो मधुकरालापाः कवीनां गिर-

स्ताः प्रीतिं जगतां नृसिंह दधति त्वत्कीर्त्तयोः वीरुधः ॥

—*Ibid.* example under VI. 2.

5. (a) क्वचित्पुनरुपात्तवस्तुविषयतयोऽकल्पितयोरुभयोरपि सामर्थ्या-
दाक्षेपः । —*Ibid.* vṛtti on VI. 2.

(b) केचित् पुनरुपात्तवस्तुविषयतयोपकल्पितयोर्द्वयोरप्याक्षे-पादस्य
चतुर्थमपि प्रकारमिच्छन्ति । —VV. vṛtti on II. 5.

6. न भवसि कथकारं श्लाघ्यः कलिङ्गपुरन्दर

स्मर इति वरारोहाः साक्षान्मुकुन्द इतीन्दिरा ।

सुरतरुरिति त्वां सेवन्ते निरन्तरमर्थिनो

भरतमुनिरित्याचार्यास्तौर्यत्रयी निपुणा अपि ॥

—Ekā. example under VI. 2.

7. कविकुवलयप्रालेयांशुर्जगत्त्रयपावनै-

र्भवसि न गुणैः कस्य श्लाघ्यः कलिङ्गपुरन्दर ! ।

हिमरुचिरसौ कीर्त्या यस्य प्रकामपराजितः

स्मरहरशिरः स्त्रोतस्विन्यां निमज्जति लज्जितः ॥

—*Ibid.* example under VI. 2.

8 कति कति भुवः कोणे कोणे क्वचित्क्वचिदूर्जितै-

र्वितरणगुणैः प्राप्ताः ख्यातिं न सन्ति नराधिपाः ।

अलमधरयन्नेतानिन्दुश्रिया स्वयशः श्रिया

स जयति महीमन्दारोऽसौ नृसिंहनरेश्वरः ॥

—*Ibid.* example under VI. 2.

9. तच्छब्दस्य यच्छब्दसांनिध्यमध्यासीनस्य प्रसिद्धपरामर्शित्वात् ।

—*Ibid.* vṛtti on VI. 2.

10. यत्तदुत्तीर्णमर्यादं नरसिंह नभस्तलम् ।
कीर्त्तेस्तव तदप्यासीत् कस्तूरीतिलकं मुखे ।।

—Ekā. exampie under VI. 2.

11. यत्तद्वैरि वसुन्धरेशरमणी ताटङ्कलीलायित-
स्तेयारम्भनिरङ्कुशं तव धनुस्तत् केन न श्लाघ्यते ।
मौर्वीचुम्बितकोटिना जलनिधि व्यालोलकाञ्चीगुणा
जाता येन नृसिंह देव समरे सभ्रूविलासा मही ।।

—*Ibid.* example under VI. 2.

Page 79. 1. शब्दशास्त्रविरुद्धं यत् तदसाधु प्रचक्षते ।।
उच्यते शब्दहीनं तद्वाक्यं यदपशब्दवत् ।।
व्यर्थमाहुर्गतार्थंयद् यच्च स्यान्निष्प्रयोजकम् ।।

—SKBh. I. 4, 25, 49.

2. (a) भवति प्रक्रमभङ्गः प्रक्रान्तं यत्र भज्यते वस्तु । —Ekā VI. 3.

(b) 'यश्च यथा प्रक्रान्तोऽभिधातुमर्थंस्तथैव तस्य न चेत् ।
निर्वाहः स प्रक्रमभेदो··· ··· ।। —Quoted in VV. II. 31.

3. (a) अयं च प्रकृतिप्रत्ययोपसर्गविभक्तिवचनकालकारकलिङ्गसर्वनाम-विशेषणपर्यायवाक्यसमासालंकारगतत्वेन भवन्ननेकधा भवति ।

— Ekā. vṛtti on VI. 3.

(b) स चायमनन्तप्रकारः सम्भवति प्रकृतिप्रत्ययपर्यायादीनां तद्विषय-भावाभिमतानामानन्त्यात् । —VV. vṛtti on II. 29.

Page 80. 1. जीयात् पार्वणरोहिणीशकिरणश्रेणीसमालिङ्गित-
क्षीराम्भोधितरङ्गलङ्घितयशोराशिः कलिङ्गेश्वरः ।
आश्चर्यं समरे निमज्य सहसा यत्खड्ग धाराम्भसि
प्रोन्मज्जन्ति समन्ततः प्रतिभटाः स्वर्वाहिनीस्रोतसि ।।

—Ekā. example under VI. 3.

2. लोके विक्रमितुं त्रिविक्रमपदाद्दातुं सुरक्ष्मारुहा-
द्धात्रीं धातुमहीश्वरात् प्रभवितुं पत्युश्च नाकौकसाम् ।
तत्तत्कीर्त्तिविकासवासितनभः सीम्नां गुणानां निधिः
को वा वीर नृसिंह देव नृपतिस्त्वामन्तरेणाधिकः ।।

—*Ibid.* example under VI. 3.

3. दयायै दृक् कर्णः सरसकविसूक्ताय वदनं
सरस्वत्यै पृथ्व्यै भुजशिखरमीशाय हृदयम् ।
इति प्रत्तास्तावत् स्वयमवयवा अप्यविरतं
प्रदेयं किं कस्मै न तव नरसिंह क्षितिपते ॥

—Ekā. example under VI. 3.

4. मदान्धास्त्वन्नागाः प्रतिभटपुरं वीर सहसा
घनाक्रीडं क्रीडाशिखरिकमनीयं जगृहिरे ।
ददुस्तेभ्यः कल्पद्रुमपरिगतोद्यानसुभगं-
भविष्णुभ्राजिष्णुत्रिदशगिरिगीर्वाणनगरम् ॥

—*Ibid*. example under VI. 3.

5. वीर नृसिंह कवित्वं चम्पकसौरभ्यमिन्दुसौन्दर्यम् ।
गङ्गाजलमाधुर्यं कस्य न भुवनेषु सर्वदा मान्यम् ॥

—*Ibid*. example under VI. 3.

6. सूत्रामा गोत्रभेदं रचयति भजते दृष्टिवैषम्यमीशोऽ
हीनं कृष्णोऽधिशेते क्षिपति सुमनसो मार्गणान् पुष्पचापः ।
इन्दुर्दोषाकरत्वं कलयति कुमुदं मन्दयत्यंशुमाली
पश्यामस्ते नृसिंह क्षितितलतिलक क्वापि नैवोपमानम् ॥

—*Ibid*. example under VI 3.

7. कर्तृकरणयोस्तृतीया । —Aṣṭādhyāyī, 2. 3. 18.

8. तव क्रियन्ते करुणाकटाक्षैः
श्रियः कवीनां नरसिंह देव ।
ताभिर्विकासा मनसः पुनस्तैः
सूक्तानि तैस्त्वद्गुणवर्णनानि ॥

—Ekā. example under VI. 3.

Page 81. 1. बिम्बं चन्द्रमसः कलङ्कमयते धत्ते विकारं पयः
कुन्दं म्लानिमुपैति किं न कुरुते मैत्रीं मृणालं जलैः ।
मालिन्यं भजते हरित्करिमदस्यन्देन मन्दाकिनी-
स्रोतो वीर नृसिंह भूप भवतः केनोपमेयं यशः ॥

—*Ibid*. example under VI. 3.

2. प्रागासीन्मकरन्दपिच्छिलदले पद्मस्य गर्भे ततः
शौरेः कौस्तुभकान्तिपूरसुभगाभोगे भुजाभ्यन्तरे ।
आवासस्तव लक्ष्मि संप्रति पुनर्निव्याजमूर्च्छत्कृपा-
स्रोतः शीतलिते नृसिंह वसुधानाथस्य नेत्राञ्चले ।।

—Ekā. example under VI. 3.

3. किमेतासामन्तः पुरपरिसरे केवलमभू-
दसूर्यंपश्यत्वं त्वदरिसुदृशामुत्कलपते ।
इदानीमप्येता गिरिगहनगेह प्रणयिनी-
रसूर्यंपश्यत्वं सततमुपबध्नाति किमिदम् ।।

—*Ibid.* example under VI. 3.

4. संत्यज्य पुष्पसमयं कुसुमाभिवृद्धि
ज्योत्स्नाविजृम्भितमपास्य तुषारभानुम् ।
मुक्ताफलोल्लसितमम्बुनिधिं विहाय
कीर्त्तिस्तव स्फुरति वीर कलिङ्गनाथ ।।

—*Ibid.* example under VI. 3.

5. काश्मीरपांसु रुचिरांशुकचारुहारै-
र्या प्राग्बभौ कुचतटी रिपुसुन्दरीणाम् ।
सैवाद्य भाति कुपिते त्वयि वीर भूभृद्-
धातुच्छटातरुणपल्लवरक्तसूत्रैः ।।

—*Ibid.* example under VI. 3.

6. त्यागस्तावत् सुरतरुयशः कौमुदीकालमेघः
शौर्यं कुन्तीतनयचरितश्रुत्यनध्यायपर्व ।
कान्तिः पुष्पायुधवपुरहंभावरुद्रावलोकः
कस्ते वक्तुं प्रभवति गुणान् श्रीनृसिंह क्षितीन्द्र ।।

—*Ibid.* example under VI. 3.

Page 82. 1. यदवाच्यस्य वचः स्यादवाच्यवचनं तु तद्गदितम् ।। —*Ibid.* VI.3.

2. कारणाधारसंबन्धैर्व्यभिचारो न दृश्यते ।
यत्र तस्य प्रयोगे स्यादवाच्यवचनं यथा ।। —*Ibid.* VI. 4.

3. यद्वाच्यस्यावचनं वाच्यावचनं तदुच्यते चतुरैः —*Ibid.* VI. 5.

4. अभवन् मतः (इष्टः) योगः (संबन्धः) यत्र तत् ।

—KP. vṛtti on VII. 54.

5. अनेन च वाच्यावचनेन सामर्थ्यादवाच्यवचनमपि सङ्गृहीतं वेदितव्यम् ।

तस्यापीष्टार्थविपर्ययात्मकत्वात् । —VV. vṛtti on II. 99.

6. निःशेषनिर्जरनमस्कृतपाददद्मं
यं नीलपूर्वमिह लोहितमामनन्ति ।
देवः स एष भवतः शशिखण्डमौलिः
श्रेयः श्रियं दिशतु वीर नृसिंह देव ॥

—Ekā. example under VI. 3.

7. चमत्कारं गौरीसहचरतनुस्पर्धि नकथं
विधत्ते भूयांसं भुवि तव कलिङ्गेश्वर यशः ।
यदन्तः कालिन्दीतटरुहतमालद्युति नभः
सुधा भानुक्रोडस्थितहरिणकेलिं कलयति ॥

—*Ibid.* example under VI. 3.

Page 83. 1. दिक्कुक्षिं भरिभिः कठोरकरिणीकर्ण प्रभाभासुरै-
श्चित्रं वीरनृसिंह भूप तुरगोत्कीर्णैः परागोत्करैः ।
त्वत्सेनाविजयोत्सवव्यतिकरे व्याप्तं वियन्मण्डलं
हम्मीरक्षितिपालचेतसि परं मालिन्यमुन्मीलितम् ॥

—*Ibid.* example under VI. 4

2. हृदा हृष्यति जानाति ध्यायत्यध्येति खिद्यते ।
विलोकयति नेत्रेण श्रवणेन शृणोति च ॥

—*Ibid.* example under VI. 4.

3. चित्रं चेतसि चिन्तेर्ष्याहर्षेच्छाक्रोधविस्मयाः ।
मनसि प्रमदोत्साहभयज्वरमदात्ययाः ॥

—*Ibid.* example under VI. 4.

4. अत्रातिविततत्वादयोऽनुपादानेऽपि प्रतिपाद्यमानमर्थं न बाधन्त इत्यपुष्टाः नत्वसंगताः पुनरुक्ता वा ॥

—KP. vṛtti on VII. 57.

5. व्यर्थमाहुर्गतार्थं यद्यच्च स्यान्निष्प्रयोजकम् ॥ —SKBh. I. 49.

6. दारिद्र्यस्य दयालुत्वं नृसिंह नृप किं स्तुवे ।
यन्मत्वापि निजं नाशमस्भाभिस्त्वामदर्शयत् ॥
—Ekā. example under VI. 4.

Page 84. 1. (a) तस्मान्नाम पदेभ्यो यः कश्चिदर्थः प्रतीयते ।
न स सत्तामनासाद्य शब्दवाच्यत्वमर्हति ॥ —VV. 1. 18.

(b) प्रयुक्तान्तर्गतैरेव यत्र सोऽर्थः प्रतीयते ।
प्रयोगस्तत्र शेषाणां पदानां पौनरुक्त्यकृत् ॥ —*Ibid*. II. 58.

2. इत्थञ्चास्तिभवत्यादि क्रियासामान्यमुच्यते ॥
नान्तरङ्गतयावश्यं वक्तारस्तत् प्रयुञ्जते ॥ —*Ibid*. I. 19.

3. निजचरणसविधनिपतन परमपि पुर एव वीक्ष्य हम्मीरम् ।
राजन् नृसिंह समरे तिष्ठति तूष्णीमसौ खड्गः ॥
—Ekā. example under VI. 5.

4. (a) अन्यस्यालंकारस्य विषयेऽलंकारान्तरोपनिबन्धो यत्र तत्रापि वाच्यावचनमेव ॥ —*Ibid*. vṛtti on VI. 5.

(b) यत्रान्यस्यालङ्कारस्य विषयेऽलङ्कारान्तरनिबन्धस्सोऽपि वाच्यावचनं दोषः । —VV. vṛtti on II. 72.

5. ... ...
मृग्या परिभवो व्याघ्र्यामित्यवेहि त्वया कृतम् ॥
—Raghuvaṁśa, XII. 37.

6. दृढतरनिबद्धमुष्टेः कोशनिषण्णस्य सहजमलिनस्य ।
कृपणस्य कृपाणस्य च केवलमाकारतो भेदः ॥
—VV. example under II. 102.

7. अत्र कृपणकृपाणयोराकारमात्रतो व्यतिरेक उक्तः ।
—*Ibid*. vṛtti on II. 102.

Page 85. 1. (a) दोषोऽर्थपौनरुक्त्यं प्ररुढमभिधीयते बहुधा ॥ —Ekā. VI. 5.

(b) तत्रार्थपौनरुक्त्थं प्ररूढं दोषः ॥ —AS. 2.

2. पुनरुक्तः शब्देन प्रतिपन्नत्वे सति पुनस्तेनैव प्रतिपादितः ।
यत्तु प्रयोजनं विनेति··· । —Kāvyapradīpa on KP. VII. 57.

3. (a) बहुधा प्रकृत्यादिविषयत्वात्… । —Ekā. vṛtti on VI. 5.

(b) प्रकृतिप्रत्ययार्थोऽस्य पदवाक्यार्थं एव च ।
विषयो बहुधा ज्ञेयः स क्रमेणोपदर्श्यते ॥ —VV. II. 49.

4. करटविलुठद्दानस्रोतस्विनी सुरभीकृत-
त्रिभुवनपुटप्रेङ्खत् पुष्पन्धयध्वनिडिण्डिमः ।
समयकुतुकं दृष्टैः पौरैः कलिङ्गपुरन्दर
प्रथयतितरां कस्यानन्दं न ते गजतागणः ॥
—Ekā. example under VI. 5.

5. अर्धमङ्गमुपगूढवल्लभं
बिभ्रदर्धमपि भस्मभासुरम् ।
एक एव सुहृदिन्दुशेखरो
रागिणामपि विरागिणामपि ॥
—*Ibid*. example under VI. 5.

Page 86. 1. तदस्यास्त्यस्मिन्निति मतुप् ।
—Aṣṭādhyāyī, 5. 2. 94.

2. भूमनिन्दाप्रशंसासु नित्ययोगेऽतिशायने ।
संबन्धेऽस्ति विवक्षायां भवन्ति मतुबादयः ॥
—Vārttika on Aṣṭāhdyāyaī, V. 2. 94.

3. दुर्वारैस्ते यशोभिः सकलमपि मम ध्वान्तमाचान्तमेतत्
तत् किं कुर्यामिदानीमिति तव गदितुं श्रीनृसिंह क्षितीन्द्र ।
लोकालोकेन पाथोधरनिवहनिभाः प्रेषिताः पश्य भान्ति
प्राप्ताः प्रत्यन्तपृथ्वीभृत इव गजता द्वारदेशोपकण्ठम् ॥
—Ekā. example under VI. 5.

4. देवस्यास्य चिराय मत्प्रभुकुलाराध्यस्य गौरीपते-
रेषा नैव कदाप्यनुग्रहकथा लक्ष्मीधुरामर्हति ।
इत्यालोच्य रुषेव केतकदलद्रोणीमियं निन्दति
स्वैरं वीर नृसिंह देव भवतः कीर्तिजगज्जाङ्घिकी ॥
—*Ibid*. example under VI. 5.

5. प्लायनपरस्य मे नियतमन्तरायो महा-
नियं भवति दुर्वहा वसुमती भुजालम्बिनी ।
इतीव विरहय्य तामजनि जैत्रयात्रोत्सवे
विरोधिनृपतिर्लघुस्तव नृसिह पृथ्वीपते ॥

—Ekā example under VI. 5.

6. उत्कण्ठाभारताम्यत् कुवलयनयनामानसाम्भोजभानु-
श्चिन्तासंतापमीलत् कविकुलकुमुदव्यूहनक्षत्रनाथः ।
ईर्ष्यासंवर्धमानप्रतिनृपति कुलाम्भोधिकुम्भोद्भवश्च
ख्यातः सर्वत्र योऽसौ जगति स जयति श्रीनृसिंहक्षितीन्द्रः ॥

—*Ibid.* example under VI. 5.

7. वीरः प्राक् कति नात्र तैरहमसावित्थं न संवार्द्धिता
न त्राता न च लालितेति भवतः प्रत्यायनं कुर्वती ।
त्वत्कीर्त्तिः कलहंसकम्बुरजनी जानिच्छलेन स्पृश-
त्यम्भोजासनकंसशासनपुरारातीन् कलिङ्गेश्वर ॥

—*Ibid.* example under VI. 5.

8. 'द्वन्द्वान्ते श्रूयमाणं पदं प्रत्येकमभिसबंध्यते ।' —Maxin in Skt.

Page. 87 1. मधुरसेषु…टवर्गभयां…असकृत्प्रयोगं नैकट्येन वर्जयेत् ।

—RG. p. 69

2. इवशब्देन यत्रैकेनैव दीपकत्वात् कर्त्तृकर्मादीनामप्युपमानोपमेयभावः
प्रतीयते तत्र द्वितीयस्येवशब्दस्य प्रयोगो न योग्यः ।

—Ekā. vṛtti on VI. 5.

3. ततः प्रतस्थे कौबेरीं भास्वानिव रघुर्दिशम् ।
शरैरुस्त्रैरिवोदीच्यानुद्धरिष्यन् रसानिव ॥

—Raghuvamsa. IV. 66.

4. विशेष्यस्याभिधाने तु सामान्योक्तिर्न युज्यते ।
यथामेरुगिरिः श्वासमरुच्चन्दनपादपः ॥ —Ekā. VI. 6.

5. संगीतादिविचारवार्धितरणे सांयात्रिकः कस्य न
श्लाघ्यो वीर कलिङ्ग पार्थिव भवान् भूलोकचिन्तामणिः ।
रेखा लाञ्छितकैतवेन सुकृती पद्माभिधानो निधिः
साक्षाद्यस्य करे कुबेरनगरीसर्वस्वमुज्जृम्भते ॥

—*Ibid.* example under VI. 8.

Page 88. 1. पारम्पर्येण साक्षाच्च तदेतत् प्रतिपद्यते ।
कवेरजागरूकस्य रसभङ्गनिमित्तताम् ॥
यत्र तच्छब्दविषयं बहुधा परिदृश्यते ।
तस्य प्रक्रमभेदाद्या दोषाः पञ्चैव योनयः ॥ —VV. I. 93-94.

2. विभावानुभावव्यभिचारिणामयथायथं रसेषु यो विनियोगस्तन्मात्रलक्षणमेकमन्तरङ्गम्…' अपरं पुनः बहिरङ्गम् ।…अन्तरङ्गबहिरङ्गभावश्चानयोः साक्षात् पारम्पर्येण च रसभङ्गहेतुत्वादिष्टः ।
—*Ibid.* beginning of II Vimarsa.

3. (a) श्रुतिदुष्टादयो दोषा अनित्या… । —DhL. II. 11.

(b) विरोधः सकलोऽप्येष कदाचित् कविकौशलात् ।
उत्क्रम्य दोषगणनां गुणवीथीं विगाहते ॥ —KD. III, 179.

4. गूढार्थमर्थान्तरमर्थहीनं भिन्नार्थमेकार्थमभिप्लुतार्थम् ।
न्यायादपेतं विषमं विसंधिशब्दच्युतं वै दश काव्यदोषाः ॥
—NS. 16. 89.

5. अपार्थं व्यर्थमेकार्थं ससंशयमपक्रमम् ।
शब्हीनं यतिभ्रष्टं भिन्नवृत्तं विसंधिकम् ।
देशकालकलालोकन्यायागमविरोधि च ।
इति दोषा दशैवैते वर्ज्या काव्येषु सूरिभिः ॥
—KD. III. 125-126.

6. (a) दुष्टं पदमसाधुकष्टं ग्राम्यमप्रतीतमनर्थकञ्च ॥
—KASV. II. 1.4.

(b) अन्यनेयगूढार्थाश्लीलक्लिष्टानि च ॥ —*Ibid.* II. 1.10.

(c) भिन्नवृत्तयतिभ्रष्टविसन्धीनि वाक्यानि ॥ —*Ibid.* II. II. 1.

(d) व्यर्थैकार्थसन्दिग्धायुक्तापक्रमलोकविद्यविरुद्धानि च ॥
—*Ibid.* II. II. 9.

7. (i) अन्यूनाधिकवाचकसुक्रमपुष्टार्थशब्दचारुपदम् ।
क्षोदक्षममक्षूणं सुमतिर्बाक्यं प्रयुञ्जीत ॥ —KAR. II. 9.

पदवाक्यस्थो दोषो वाक्यविशेषप्रयोगनियमेन ।
यः परिहृतस्ततोऽन्यस्तदतिव्याप्तिश्च संह्रियते ।।

असमर्थप्रतीतं विसंधि विपरीतकल्पनं ग्राम्यम् ।
अव्युत्पत्ति च वैश्यं पदमिति सम्यग्भवेद्दुष्टम् ।।

—KAR. VI 1-2.

(ii) वाक्यं भवति तु दुष्टं संकीर्णं गर्भितं गतार्थञ्च ।

—*Ibid.* VI. 40.

....

(iii) अपहेतुरप्रतीतो निरागमो बाधयन्नसंबद्धः ।
ग्राम्यो विरसस्तद्वानतिमात्रश्चेति दुष्टोऽर्थः ।।

—*Ibid.* XI. 2.

(iv) सामान्यशब्दभेदो वैषम्यसंभवोऽप्रसिद्धिश्च ।
इत्येते चत्वारो दोषा नासम्यगुपमायाः ।। —*Ibid.* XI. 24.

8. दोषाः पदानां वाक्यानां वाक्यार्थानां च षोडश ।
हेयाः काव्ये कवीन्द्रैर्ये तानेवादौ प्रचक्ष्महे ।। —SKBh. I. 3.

Page 89. 1. दुष्टं पदं श्रुतिकटुच्युतसंस्कृत्प्रयुक्तमसमर्थम् ।
निहितार्थमनुचितार्थं निरर्थकमवाचकं त्रिधाऽश्लीलम् ।।

संदिग्धमप्रतीतं ग्राम्यं नेयार्थमथ भवेत् क्लिष्टम् ।
अविमृष्टविधेयांशं विरुद्धमतिकृत्—
—वाक्येऽपि दोषाः सन्त्येते पदस्यांशेऽपि केचन ।।

—KP. VI. 50-52.

अर्थदोषानाह
अर्थोऽपुष्टः कष्टो—स्वीकृतोऽश्लीलः ।। —*Ibid.* VII. 55-57.

रसे दोषाः स्युरीदृशाः ।। —*Ibid.* VII. 60-62.

2. (i) अनौचित्यादृते नान्यद्रसभङ्गस्य कारणम् ।
प्रसिद्धौचित्यबन्धस्तु रसस्योपनिषत्परा ।।

—DhL. under vṛtti on III. 14.

(ii) विरोधिरससम्बन्धिविभावादिपरिग्रहः ।
विस्तरेणान्वितस्यापि वस्तुनोऽन्यस्य वर्णनम् ॥
अकाण्ड एव विच्छित्तिरकाण्डे च प्रकाशनम् ।
परिपोषं गतस्यापि पौनः पुन्येन दीपनम् ।
रसस्य स्याद्विरोधाय वृत्यनौचित्यमेव च ॥

—*Ibid.* III. 18-19.

3. उचिताभिधानजीवितत्वाद् वाक्यस्याप्येकदेशेऽप्यौचित्यविरहात् तद्विदाह्लादकारित्वहानिः।—प्रबन्धस्यापि कस्यचित् प्रकरणैकदेशेऽप्यौचित्यविरहादेकदेशदाहदूषितदग्धपटप्रायता प्रसज्यते ।

—VJ. vṛtti on I. 57

4. Concepts of Poetic Blemishes in Sanskrit Poetics, Prof. Bechan Jha, p. 124.

CHAPTER VI

Page 139 1. अलंकारास्तु हारादय इव— —Ekā. vṛtti on V.1.

2. काव्यशोभाकरान् धर्मानलंकारान् प्रचक्षते । —KD II 1.

3. काव्यशोभायाः कर्तारो धर्मा गुणाः ।
तदतिशयहेतवस्त्वलङ्कारा: ॥ —KASV, III. 1.1-2.

4. (i) अलङ्कारो हि चारुत्वहेतुः प्रसिद्धः ।

(ii) अलङ्कारो हि बाह्यालङ्कारसाम्यादङ्गिनश्चारुत्वहेतुरुच्यते ।
—DhL. vrtti on II. 5 & I. 17.

5. उपकुर्वन्ति तं सन्तं येऽङ्गद्वारेण जातुचित् ।
हारादिवदलंकारास्तेऽनुप्रासोपमादयः ॥ —KP. VIII. 67.

6. ··· यथेति कर्मोपमा । ··· मैष इति भूतोपमा । ··· अग्निरिति रूपोपमा । ··· वदिति सिद्धोपमा । ··· अथ लुप्तोपमान्यार्थोपमानीत्याचक्षते । ···
—Nirukta. III-III-14 (pp. 142-149).

Page 140. 1. (i) तुल्यार्थैरतुलोपमाभ्यां तृतीयाऽन्यतरस्याम् ॥
—*Ibid.* II-III. 72.

(ii) उपमानानि सामान्यवचनैः ॥ —*Ibid.* II-I- 25.

(iii) उपमितं व्याघ्रादिभिः ॥ —*Ibid.* II-I. 56.

2. (i) तथाहि अचेतनं शवशरीरं कुण्डलाद्युपेतमपि न भाति ।
—DhL. Locana on II. 5.

(ii) अलङ्कारो हि बाह्यालङ्कारसाम्यादङ्गिनश्चारुत्वहेतुरुच्यते ।
—DhL. vṛtti on II. 17.

3. यत्र तु नास्ति रसस्तत्रोक्तिवैचित्र्यमात्रपर्यवसायिनः ।
—KP. vṛtti on VIII. 67.

Page 141. 1. यत्र हि पर्यायान्तरपरिवृत्तिसहत्वं नास्ति तस्य शब्दगतत्वम्, यत्र तु तत्सहत्वं तत्रार्थगतत्वम् ।
—Kāvya Pradīpa on KP. IX.8.

Page 97. 1. दोषोऽर्थऽपौनरुक्त्यं प्ररूढमभिधीयते बहुधा । —Ekā. VI. 5.

2. पुनरुक्तवदाभासो भवति प्रमुखावभासनं द्वेधा । —*Ibid* VII. 1.

3. पुनरुक्ताभासमभिन्नवस्त्वोद्भाति भिन्नरूपपदम् ।

—KASS. I. 3.

4. पुनरुक्तवदाभासो विभिन्नाकारशब्दगा ।

एकार्थता··· ··· ··· ··· ··· ··· ··· ··· —KP. IX. 86.

5. आमुखावभासनं पुनरुक्तवदाभासम् । —AS. 3.

6. भिन्नाकृते: शब्दस्यैकार्थतैव पुनरुक्ताभासः ।। KAnu. V. 8.

7. पुनरुक्तप्रतीकाशं पुनरुक्तार्थसन्निभम् ।

··· ··· ··· ··· ··· ··· ··· ··· ···

—Candrāloka, V. 7.

8. पुनरुक्तवदाभासं···अर्थैकनिष्ठमपि । —Ekā. VII. 2.

9. अर्थपौनरुक्त्यादेवार्थाश्रितत्वादर्थालङ्कारत्वं ज्ञेयम् ।

—AS. vṛtti on 3.

10. एवकार: शब्दपौनरुक्त्यावच्छेदद्योतका: ।···

—AS. Vimarṣiśinī on 3.

11. ······शब्दस्य······ ।

······तथा शब्दार्थयोरयम् ।। —KP. IX. 86.

Page 98. 1. अभ्यस्ताशेषविद्याभरगुरुधिषणं विद्विषद्रक्तपान-
क्रीडानिस्त्रिंशखड्गं विरचितवसुधा चक्ररक्षाविभूतिम् ।
किं चालोकप्रभावक्षपितबुधविपद्ध्वान्तमुद्गायति त्वां
तुङ्गे शृङ्गे सुमेरोः सुरयुवतिगणः श्रीनृसिंह क्षितीन्द्र ।।

—Ekā. example under VII. 1.

2. तान् निर्माति करोति हस्तिततरिपून् युद्धेषु ते विक्रमान्
यैर्लोको भरते बिभर्त्ति कुतुकं रामेऽपि न प्रस्तुते ।
किं चाभ्यर्थनदुष्कृतानि शमयस्याकर्णयस्येकदा
यद्याकृष्टसुधारसं सुमनसां सूक्तं कलिङ्गेश्वर ।।

—*Ibid*. example under VII. 1.

3. छेका विदग्धास्तै: प्रयुक्तोऽयमनुप्रास इत्यन्वर्थः ।

—*Ibid* vṛtti on VII. 3.

4. द्रेक शब्देन कुलायाभिरतानां पक्षिणामभिधानम् ।

—KASS. vṛiti on I. 4.

5. शब्दस्य पौनरुक्त्यं व्यञ्जनसमुदायमाश्रितं यस्मात् ।
सच्छेकानुप्रासः संख्यानियमे समुल्लसति ।। —Ekā. VII. 3.

6. छेकानुप्रासस्तु द्वयोर्द्वयोः सुसदृशोक्तिकृतो । —KASS. I. 4.

7. ···छेकवृत्तिगतो द्विधा··· । —KP. IX. 79

8. संख्यानियमे पूर्वं छेकानुप्रासः । —AS. 4.

9. स्वरव्यञ्जनसन्दोहव्यूहा मन्दोहृदोहदा ।
गौर्जगज्जाग्रदुत्सेका छेकानुप्राससमासुरा ।। —Candrāloka V. 2.

Page 99. 1. कलाकलापं दधदुज्वलोज्वलं
मुहुस्तमस्तोममपाकरोति यः ।
न कस्य हर्षं वसुधासुधाकरः
करोत्ययं वीरनृसिंह भूपतिः ।।

—Ekā. example under VII. 3.

2. वृत्तिस्तु रसविषयो व्यापारः । तद्वती पुनर्वर्णरचनेह वृत्तिः ।

—AS. vītti on 5.

3. संख्यानियमाभावे भवति पुनर्वृत्त्यनुप्रासः । — Ekā. VII. 4.

4. एकस्याप्यसकृत्परः ।।
एकस्य अपि शब्दादनेकस्य व्यञ्जनस्य द्विर्बहुकृत्वो वा सादृश्यं वृत्यनुप्रासः । — KP. IX. 79 & vṛtti on it.

5. आवृत्तवर्णं सपूर्णं — वृत्यनुप्रासवद्वचः ।
अमन्दानन्दसन्दोहस्वच्छन्दास्पदमन्दिरम् ।।

—Candrāloka, V. 3.

6. सरूपव्यञ्जनन्यासं तिसृष्वेतारसु वृत्तिषु ।
पृथक् पृथगनुप्रासमुशन्ति कवयः सदा ।।

—Laghuvṛtti Ṭīkā on K. A. SS. I. 4.

7. आवृत्तिर्या तु वर्णानां नातिदूरान्तरस्थिता ।
अलङ्कारस्य विद्वद्भिरनुप्रासः प्रदर्श्यते ।।
श्रुतिभिर्वृत्तिभिर्वर्णैः पदे··· । — SKBh. II. 230-231.

8. अन्यथा तु वृत्त्यनुप्रास: ॥
केवलव्यञ्जनसादृश्यमेकधा समुदायसादृश्यं, त्र्यादीनां च परस्पर-
सादृश्यमन्यथाभाव: । —AS. 5 and vṛtti on it also.

9. केवलव्यञ्जनसादृश्यं सकृद्व्यञ्जनसादृश्यं त्र्यादीनां व्यञ्जनाना-
मितरेतरसादृश्यं संख्यानियमाभाव: ।

Ekā vṛtti on VII. 4.

10. श्रीमन्नृसिंह नरनाथ कथं यशस्ते
कृत्तारिकण्ठरुधिरारुणितात् कृपाणात् ।
कैलासकाशकरकाकुमुदेन्दुकुन्द-
मन्दारमौक्तिकमृणालमनोज्ञमासीत् ॥

—*Ibid.* example under VII. 4.

11. युक्ता विपक्षेषु कृपा न कर्त्तु-
मेते विकुर्वन्ति हि कार्यकाले ।
इत्याहवे वीक्ष्य कलिङ्गनाथं
नाथन्त्यमी प्राञ्जलय: सपत्ना: ॥

—*Ibid.* example under VII. 4.

Page 100. 1. जगति गजगतिर्नन्दतु श्रीनृसिंह: ।

—*Ibid.* example under VII. 4.

2. …सविसर्गाविसर्गयो: ॥
सबिन्दुकाबिन्दुकयो: स्यादभेदेन कल्पनम् । —*Ibid.* VII. 6-7.

3. इदमेव स्वरसहितं व्यञ्जनसमुदायमाश्रितं यमकम् ॥

— *Ibid.* VII. 4.

अत्र क्वचिद् भिन्नार्थकत्वं क्वचिदनर्थकत्वं क्वचिदेकस्यानर्थकत्व-
मन्यस्य सार्थकत्वमिति । —vṛtti on VII. 4.

4. अत्यन्तबहवस्तेषां भेदा: संभेदयोनय: ।
सुकरा दुष्कराश्चैव दर्श्यन्ते तत्र केचन ॥ —KD. III. 3.

5. पदमनेकार्थमक्षरं वा वृत्तं स्थाननियमे यमकम् ॥

—KASV. IV. 1. 1.

6. विभिन्नार्थैकरूपाया या वृत्तिर्वर्णसंहतेः ।
अव्यपेतव्यपेतात्मा यमकं तन्निगद्यते ॥ —SKBh. II. 146.

7. अर्थे सत्यर्थभिन्नानां वर्णानां सा पुनः श्रुतिः ।
यमकम्··· ... ... ॥
—KP. IX. 83.

8. सत्यर्थेऽन्यार्थानां वर्णानां श्रुतिक्रमैक्ये यमकम् ॥
—KAnu. V. 3.

9. आवृत्तवर्णस्तबकं स्तबकन्दाङ्कुरं कवेः ।
यमकं प्रथमा धुर्यमाधुर्यवचसो विदुः ॥ —Candrāloka V. 8.

10. शब्दाभ्यासस्तु यमकं··· । —NS. 16. 62.

11. तुल्यश्रुतीनां भिन्नानामभिधेयैः परस्परम् ।
वर्णानां यः पुनर्वादो यमकं तन्निगद्यते ॥ —KAB. II. 17.

12. तुल्य-श्रुति-क्रमाणामन्यार्थानां मिथस्तु वर्णानाम् ।
पुनरावृत्तिर्यमकं प्रायश्छन्दांसि विषयोऽस्य ॥ —KAR. III. 1.

13. स्वरव्यञ्जनसमुदायपौनरुक्त्यं यमकम् ॥ —AS. 6.

Page 101. 1. कलिङ्गनाथ यस्मात् त्वं प्रभवः सर्वसंपदाम् ।
अतस्तव तुलां प्राप्तुं प्रभवः कोऽपि नापरे ॥
—Ekā example under VII. 4.

2. भाग्यसौभाग्यसौजन्यनिधिं नरहरिं स्तुमः ।
चतुरं चतुरम्भोधिमेखलावनिपालने ॥
—*Ibid.* example under VII. 4.

3. (a) अत्र क्वचिद्भिन्नार्थकत्वं क्वचिदनर्थकत्वं क्वचिदेकस्यानर्थकत्वमन्यस्य सार्थकत्वमिति संक्षेपतः प्रकारत्रयम् ।
—*Ibid.* vṛtti on VII. 4.

(b) अत्र क्वचिद्भिनार्थत्वं क्वचिदनर्थकत्वं क्वचिदेकस्यानर्थकत्वमपरस्य सार्थकत्वमिति संक्षेपतः प्रकारत्रयम् ।
—AS. vṛtti on 6.

4. प्रायशो यमके चित्रे रसपुष्टिर्न दृश्यते ।
दुश्करत्वादसाधुत्वमेकमेवात्र दूषणम् ॥ —Ekā. VII. 5.

5. (a) प्रायशो यमके चित्रे रसुपुष्टिर्न दृश्यते । ——*Ibid.* VII. 5.

(b) तदुक्तम्—'प्रायशो यमके चित्रे रसवृद्धिर्न मृग्यते।'

—Commentary of Mallinātha on Kirātārjunīyam, V. 7.

6. (a) यमकं तु विधातव्यं कथंचिदपि न त्रिपात् ॥

—Ekā. VII. 7.

(b) पादत्रययमकं तु न चमत्कारि अतो न प्रयुक्तम्।

—K. Pradīpa on KP. IX. 6.

Page 102. 1. (a) भङ्ग्यन्तरकृततत्क्रमवर्णनिमित्तानि वस्तुरूपाणि।
साङ्कानि विचित्राणि च रच्यन्ते यत्र तच्चित्रम् ॥
तच्चकरवङ्गमुसलैर्बाणासनशक्तिशूलहलैः।
चतुरङ्गपीठविरचितरथतुरगगजादिपद पाठैः ॥
अनुलोमप्रतिलोमैरर्धभ्रममुरजसर्वतोभद्रैः।
इत्यादिभिरन्यैरपि वस्तुविशेषाकृतिप्रभवैः ॥

—KAR. (Rudraṭa), V. 1-3.

(b) ...आश्चर्यकारित्वाद्वा चित्रमित्यन्वर्थबलात्।

—Ekā. vṛtti on VII. 8.

2. (a) वर्णानामाकारोल्लासकत्वात् पद्मादिरूपतयाक्षराणां लिख्यमानत्वेन चित्रसादृश्याच्चित्रमिदमुच्यते।

—*Ibid.* vṛtti on VII. 8.

(b) संनिवेशविशेषेण यत्र न्यस्ता वर्णाः खड्गमुरजपद्माद्याकारमुल्लासयन्ति तच्चित्रं काव्यम्। —KP. vṛtti on IX. 85.

(c) वर्णानां खड्गाद्याकृतिहेतुत्वे चित्रम् ॥ —AS 10.

3. रसभावादितात्पर्यरहितं व्यङ्ग्यार्थविशेषप्रकाशनशक्तिशून्यं च काव्यं केवलवाच्यवाचकवैचित्र्यमात्राश्रयेणोपनिबद्धमालेख्यप्रख्यं यदाभासते तच्चित्रम्। न तन्मुख्यं काव्यम्। काव्यानुकरो ह्यसौ।

—DhL. vṛtti on III. 42.

4. अभिनवपदपदार्थपर्यालोचनेन मन्दबुद्धीनां चितोज्ञानस्य त्राणाद्वा चित्रम्...। —Ekā. vṛtti on VII. 8.

5. ... बन्धचित्रेऽपि वर्णानामाकारोल्लासकत्वात् पद्मादिरूपतयाक्षराणां लिख्यमानत्वेन...। —*Ibid.* vṛtti on VII. 8.

6. तच्चित्रं यत्र वर्णानां खड्गाद्याकृतिहेतुता ।। —KP. IX. 85.

7. वर्णानां खड्गाद्याकृतिहेतुत्वे चित्रम् । —AS. 10.

8. स्वरव्यञ्जनस्थानगत्याकार नियमच्युतगूढादि चित्रम् ।।

—KAnu. V. 4.

9. काव्यवित्प्रवरैश्चित्रं खड्गबन्धादि लक्ष्यते ।

—Candrāloka, V.9.

10. गोष्ठ्यां कुतूहलाध्यायी वाग्बन्धश्चित्रमुच्यते ।

—Agnipurāṇa 343-22.

Page 103. 1. KAR. V. 1-3.

2. अहो येन क्रमेणागता वर्णपङ्क्तिस्तेनैव क्रमेण प्रत्यागतेत्याश्चर्यकारित्वाद्वा चित्रमित्यन्वर्थबलाद्वर्णानामाकारानुल्लासकत्वेनाव्याप्तावपि गतप्रत्यागतार्धभ्रमसर्वतोभद्रधेनुप्रभृतिगतिचित्रमत्र संगृहीतम् ।

—Ekā vṛtti on VII. 8.

3. अभिनवपदपदार्थपर्यालोचनेन मन्दबुद्धीनां चित्तो ज्ञानस्य त्राणाद्वा चित्रमित्यन्वर्थमहिम्ना निष्कण्ठ्यनिरोष्ठ्यनिस्तालव्यादिस्थानचित्रं च स्वीकृतम् ।

—*Ibid.* vṛtti on VII. 8.

4. वर्णशब्देन चात्र स्वराणां पृथक्निर्देशाद् व्यञ्जनान्येव प्रगृह्यन्ते ।

—SKBh. vṛtti on II. 359.

5. यत् पुनः स्वरविरहितव्यञ्जनमात्रसादृश्यप्रयुक्तं वर्णचित्रमपरैरभ्यधायि तदस्मिन् दर्शने वृत्त्यनुप्रास एव ।

—Ekā. vṛtti on VII. 8.

6. (a) वर्णस्थानस्वराकारगतिबन्धान् प्रतीह यः ।
नियमस्तद्बुधैः षोढा चित्रमित्यभिधीयते ।।

....

स्वरचित्रेषु ह्रस्वैकस्वरं यथा,

उरुगुं द्युगुरुं युत्सु चुक्रुशुस्तुष्टुवुः पुरु ।
लुलुभुः पुपुषुर्मुत्सु मुमुहुर्नु मुहुर्मुहुः ।।

—SKBh. II. 359 & 377.

(b) यदाह राजा—

उरुगुं द्युरुगुं युत्सु बुबूधुस्तुष्टुवुः पुरु।
लुलुवुः पुपुषुर्मुत्सु मुमुहुस्तु मुहुर्मुहुः ॥

—Ekā. quoted under VII. 5.

7. स्वरचित्रं तु बन्धशैथिल्यकारितया दोष एवेति नालंकारतया स्वीकृतम्।

—*Ibid.* Vṛtti on VII. 8.

Page 104. 1. समाविनोऽप्यन्ये प्रभेदाः शक्तिमात्रप्रकाशका न तु काव्यरूपतां दधतीति न प्रदर्श्यन्ते ॥ —KP. vṛtti on IX. 85.

2. वर्णानां खड्गाद्याकृतिहेतुत्वे चित्रम् ॥ ··· आदिग्रहणाद्यथाव्युत्पत्तिसंभवं पद्मबन्धादिपरिग्रहः ॥ —AS. 10 and vṛtti on it.

3. एतच्च काव्ये गड्डभूतमिति नेह प्रतायते।

—Ekā. vṛtti on VII. 8.

4. अत्र यद्यपि बन्धचित्रमाकारचित्राद्भिन्नं मन्यमानैरपि चिरन्तनैर्न किञ्चिद्भेदकमुक्तं तथापीश्वरकर्तृकत्वे सत्यपि यदेककर्तृकतया प्रसिद्धं तत् पद्मशैलादिकमाकारचित्रम्। यत्तु द्विकर्तृकं हलमुसलमुरजगोमूत्रिकाचापचक्रादि तद्बन्धचित्रमित्यनयोर्भेदः कल्पयितुं शक्य एवास्माभिः। तथापि न कल्पितः।

—*Ibid.* vṛtti ou VII. 8.

5. ···लाटजनवल्लभत्वाच्च लाटानुप्रासः।

—KP. vṛtti on IX. 81.

6. तात्पर्यभेदयुक्तं लाटानुप्रास इत्यदः कथितम्। —Ekā. VII. 9.

7. स्वरूपार्थाविशेषेऽपि पुनरुक्तिः फलान्तरात्।
शब्दानां वा पदानां वा लाटानुप्रास इष्यते। —KASS. I. 5.

8. यमकानां हि यावन्त्यो वर्ण्यन्ते भेदभक्तयः।
अनुप्रासस्य लाटानां भिदास्तावन्त्य एव हि। —SKBh. II. 355.

9. शाब्दस्तु लाटानुप्रासो भेदे तात्पर्यमात्रतः ॥ —KP. IX.81.

Page 105. 1. तात्पर्यभेदवत्तु लाटानुप्रासः ॥ —AS. 8.

2. तात्पर्यमात्रभेदिनो नाम्नः पदस्य वा लाटानाम्। —KAnuV. 2.

3. लाटानुप्रासभूर्भिन्नाभिप्राया पुनरुक्तता ।

—Candrāloka, V. 4.

4. अन्योन्यापेक्ष-शब्दार्थगतत्वेनार्थमात्रगतत्वेन च व्यवस्थितेर्भिन्न-विषयत्वात् । —AS. vṛtti on 8.

5. लाटीयमप्यनुप्रासमिहेच्छन्त्यपरे··· । —KAB II. 8.

6. तात्पर्यभेद एव ह्यस्य जीवितम्··· ।

—AS. Vimarśinī on AS. 8.

7. ··· तात्पर्यमन्वयभेदः ··· ।

—Kāvyapradīpa on KP. IX. 4.

8. ताला जाअन्ति गुणा जाला दे सहिय एहि घेप्पन्ति ।
रइकिरणणुग्गहिआइहोन्ति कमलाह कमलाह ।।

—Ekā. example under VII. 9.

Skt. version of the above verse is as follows :

तदा जायन्ते गुणा यदा ते सहृदयैर्गृह्यन्ते ।
रविकिरणानुगृहीतानि भवन्ति कमलानि कमलानि ।।

9 तात्पर्यमन्यपरत्वम् । ···

—AS. vṛtti on 8.

10. शब्दार्थपौनरुक्त्यं प्ररूढमभिधीयते दोषः ।। —Ekā. VII. 8.

11. अनुगतिरूपमङ्गानामेकस्मिन्नेव जायते वाक्ये ।
यद्येकस्य तदानीमन्वर्थोऽनन्वयः कथितः ।। —*Ibid.* VIII. 4.

Page 106. 1. ... अनन्वयेन सहास्यैकाभिधानलक्षणो न संकरः । अन्योन्यापेक्ष-शब्दार्थगतत्वेनार्थमात्रगतत्वेन च व्यवस्थितेर्भिन्नविषयत्वात् ।

अनन्वये च शब्दैक्यमौचित्यादानुषङ्गिकम् ।
अस्मिंस्तु लाटानुप्रासे साक्षादेव प्रयोजकम् ।।

—AS. vṛiti on 8.

2. प्रतिभटकान्ताकुचतटमकरीलुण्टाक चापटङ्कारः ।
वीरनृसिंह इवाजौ वीरनृसिंहश्चिरं जयति ।।

—Ekā. example under VII. 9.

———

CHAPTER VII

Page 107. 1. विलसति सति साधर्म्ये स्यादुपमानोपमेययोरुपमा ।

....

······साधर्म्ये सति प्रकारत्रयस्य संभवात्, तथा हि क्वचित् भेद-प्राधान्यं दृष्टं यथा व्यतिरेके । क्वचिदभेदप्राधान्यं यथा रूपके क्वचित् पुनरुभयप्राधान्यं यथास्यामेव ।···

—Ekā. VIII. 2. and vṛtti on it also.

2. साधर्म्यं तु गुणक्रियारूपमनुगतमिह भवेदेकेन श्लिष्टाश्लिष्टेन वा शब्देनोपादानमर्हति । —*Ibid.* vṛtti on VIII. 2.

Page 108. 1. तत्र तस्यैव ।। —Aṣṭādhyāyī V-I. 116.

2. इवादयस्तु यत्पराः शब्दास्तस्यैवोपमानत्वमिति यद्यप्युपमानमेव विशिषन्ति तथापि श्रुतेर्महिम्ना षष्ठीवत् संबन्धं द्योतयन्तीति तत्सद्भावेनान्वितार्था श्रौती । —Ekā. vṛtti on VIII. 2.

3. तुल्यसदृशसनाभिसन्निभसंकाशनीकाशसहचरसोदरादि पदोपादाने सार्थकाभिधानेयमार्थी । —*Ibid.* vṛtti on VIII. 2.

4. तेन तुल्यं क्रिया चेद्वतिः ।। —Aṣṭādhyāyī, V-I. 115.

5. महीमण्डलमन्दार नरसिंह नरेश्वर ।
यशः पीताम्बरं भाति तव विष्णोर्वपुर्यथा ।।

—Ekā. example under VIII. 2.

6. कृपाणस्तव विध्वस्तविश्वामित्रमनोरथः ।
नरसिंह धरानाथ वसिष्ठ इव राजते ।।

—*Ibid.* example under VIII. 2.

7. इवेन समासो विभक्त्यलोपश्च ।।

—Vārttika on Aṣṭādhyāyī, II. I. 4.

Page 109. 1. वाहिनीश्वरता लक्ष्मीशालिता भूरिसत्त्वता ।
अकूपारवदाभाति नृसिंह नृपते तव ।।

—Ekā. example under VIII. 2.

2. नृसिंह भूप भवतः कराय श्लाघते न कः ।
दानवारि स्थितिर्यत्र भाति सागरवत् सदा ।।

—Ekā. example under VIII. 2.

3. हेलयैव विनिर्धूततारापति यशस्तव ।
सदृशं भाति रामेण नरसिंह नरेश्वर ।।

—*Ibid.* example under VIII. 2.

4. नरसिंह महीपाल समस्तोऽपि रिपुस्तव ।
पारावारसमानत्वं दधाति स्वपदच्युतः ।।

—*Ibid.* example under VIII. 2.

5. अयं तव यशोराशिरुच्चैरावणाजित्वरः ।
इह रामवदाभाति नरसिंह महीपते ।।

—*Ibid.* example under VIII. 2.

6. ···एवमियं षोढा ।। —*Ibid.* vṛtti on VIII. 2.

Page 110. 1. तद्धिते त्वेषा न संभवति । इवार्थे संभवतोऽपि धर्मानुपादाने वतेर-संभवात् । कल्पबादेरिवार्थे विधानाभावाच्च ।

—*Ibid.* vṛtti on VIII. 2.

2. खड्गो यथोरगपतिस्तव कौमुदीव
कीर्त्तिर्युगान्ततपनेन समः प्रतापः ।
वाक्यं पचेलिमरसालफलानुकारि
बाहुस्तु वीर नरसिंह सुमेरुकल्पः ।।

—*Ibid.* example under VIII. 2.

3. साहित्यार्णवकर्णधार करुणापीयूषपाथोनिधे
विद्वच्चातकवारिवाह कमलापर्यङ्कपङ्केरुह ।
त्वां केनोपमिमीमहे त्रिजगति प्राप्तप्रकर्षैर्गुणै-
स्तुल्यं ते नरसिंह पार्थिव वयं कुत्रापि न प्राप्नुमः ।।

—*Ibid.* example under VIII. 2.

Page 111. 1. वादेर्लोपे समासे सा कर्माधारक्यचि क्यङि ।
कर्मकर्त्रोर्णमुलि··· ··· ··· —KP. X. 89.

2. समसमयसमुद्यद्द्वादशादित्यशङ्का-
चकित जगदसोढप्रौढतापे प्रतापे ।

शिशिरयितुमशेषं गाङ्गवंशावतंस

प्रभवति तव कीर्त्तिर्दुग्धवीचीसमीची ।।

—Ekā. example under VIII. 2.

3. पृथुलकुचभारमुत्कटमदनं तरलाक्षमाकुलश्वसनम् ।

अन्तःपुरीयति वनं यवनावनिवल्लभो नृसिंह नृप ।।

—*Ibid.* example under VIII. 2.

4. उपमानादाचारे ।।

—Aṣṭādhyāyī III-I.10.

5. तव वीरकलिङ्गेश कृपाणः पन्नगायते ।

पानक्रीडासु यस्याजौ रिपुकीर्त्तिः पयायते ।।

—Ekā. example under VIII. 2.

6. कर्त्तुः क्यङ् सलोपश्च ।।

—Aṣṭādhyāyī-III-I-10.

7. पश्यन्नवघनदर्शंतव वीरनृसिंह निस्त्रिंशम् ।

बङ्गः सङ्गरसीमनि संचरति मरालसञ्चारम् ।।

—Ekā. example under VIII. 2.

8. उपमाने कर्मणि च ।।

—Aṣṭādhyāyī, III-IV. 45.

Page 112. 1. तुलामालम्बते यस्य नृसिंह नृपते भवान् ।

न व्यलोकि न चाश्रावि स कश्चन महीतले ।।

—Ekā. example under VIII. 2.

2. समालोक्यालेख्यस्थितमपि मृगाक्ष्यः फणभृतं

प्रकम्पन्ते धैर्यं त्वदरितरुणीनां त्वनुपमम् ।

यदेतास्त्वद्धाट्यामधिरजनि यान्त्यः फणभृतां

फणारत्नं हस्तैः पिदधति दृढं वीर विपिने ।।

—*Ibid.* example under VIII. 2.

3. अनेकमन्यपदार्थे ।।

—Aṣṭādhyāyī, II-II.24.

4. ···साधारणधर्मस्य क्वचिदनुगामितयैकरुप्येण निर्देशः ।

क्वचिद्वस्तुप्रतिवस्तुभावेन पृथङ्निर्देशः ।

पृथङ्निर्देशे च सम्बन्धिभेदमात्रं प्रतिवस्तूपमावत् ।

बिम्बप्रतिबिम्बभावो वा दृष्टान्तवत् । —AS. vṛtti on 11.

5. एकस्यैव धर्मस्य वारद्वयमुपादानं वस्तुप्रतिवस्तुभाव:

—Ekā. vṛtti on VIII. 2.

6. भिन्नयोरेव धर्मयोर्द्विरुपादानं बिम्बप्रतिबिम्बभाव: ॥

—*Ibid.* vṛtti on VIII. 2.

7. परार्ध्यमणिकेयूरस्तव वीर भुजार्गल: ।
धत्ते फणामणिश्लाघ्यां फणिनामीशितु: श्रियम् ॥

—*Ibid.* example under VIII. 2.

Page 113. 1. वक्षस्थली तव नृसिंह धराधिनाथ
विन्यस्तनिस्तल तरङ्गिततारहारा ।
चामीकरक्षितिधरस्य तटीव भाति
मन्दाकिनीसलिलवेणीविटङ्कितश्री: ॥

—*Ibid.* example under VIII. 2.

2. यत्रोपमानगतानेकधर्मसंबन्ध उपमेयस्याभिधातुमभिमतस्तत्र साधारण-मुपभावाचकं पदं वाच्यमेव कर्त्तव्यं न तु धर्माभिधायिपदोपादानेन प्रतीयमानम् । —*Ibid.* vṛtti on VIII. 2.

3. यत्र शब्दशक्तिमूलानुरणनरूपव्यङ्ग्यमहिम्नैवोपमाप्रतीतिस्तत्र वाच्या न कार्या पौनरुक्त्यप्रसङ्गात् ।

—*Ibid.* vṛtti on VIII. 2

4. उपमा दीपकं चैव रूपकं यमकं तथा ।
काव्यस्यैते ह्यलंकाराश्चत्वार: परिकीर्तिता: ॥ —NS. 16-43.

5. विरुद्धेनोपमानेन देशकालक्रियादिभि: ।
उपमेयस्य यत्साम्यं गुणलेशेन सोपमा ॥ —KAB II. 30.

6. यथा कथंचित् सादृश्यं यत्रोद्भूतं प्रतीयते ।
उपमा नाम सा तस्या: प्रपञ्चोऽयं प्रदर्श्यते ।। —KD. II. 14.

7. यच्चेतोहारि साधर्म्यमुपमानोपमेययो: ।
मिथोविभिन्नकालादिशब्दयोरुपमा तु तत् ॥ —KASS. I. 15.

8. उपमानेनोपमेयस्य गुणलेशत: साम्यमुपमा ॥ —KASV.IV. II.1.

9. उभयो: समानमेकं गुणादिसिद्धं भवेद्यत्रेकत्र ।
अर्थेऽन्यत्र तथा तत्साध्यत इति सोपमा त्रेधा ॥

—KAR. VIII. 4.

10. विवक्षितपरिस्पन्दमनोहारित्वसिद्धये ।
वस्तुनः केनचित् साम्यं तदुत्कर्षवतोपमा ॥

तां साधारणधर्मोक्तौ वाक्यार्थं वा तदन्वयात् ।
इवादिरपि विच्छित्या यत्र वक्ति क्रियापदम् ॥

—VJ. III. 30-31.

11. प्रसिद्धेरनुरोधेन यः परस्परमर्थयोः ।
भूयोऽवयवसामान्ययोगः सेहोपमा मता ॥ —SKBh. IV. 5.

12. यद्युभयोः पर्यायात् स्यादुपमानोपमेयत्वम् ।
सन्निहितवाक्येभेदे सत्युपमेयोपमा द्विविधा ॥ —Ekā. 8. 3.

Page 114. 1. (a) द्विविधा धर्मस्य वस्तुप्रतिवस्तुतया निर्देशे साधारण्ये चेति ।

—*Ibid.* vṛtti on 8. 3.

(b) इयं च धर्मस्य साधारण्ये वस्तुप्रतिवस्तुनिर्देशे च द्विधा ।

—AS. vṛtti on 3.

2. लोचनमधुकरमधुरं मधुकरलोचन मनोहरं भवतः ।
कमलमिवाननमाननमिव कमलं भाति वीर नरसिंह ॥

—Ekā. example under 8. 3.

3. अध्यवसिति-सिद्धत्वं प्रकृतस्यान्यत्वकल्पनं यद्वा ।
संबन्धासंबन्धौ तद्वयत्यासे भवेदतिशयोक्तिः ॥ —*Ibid.* 8·13.

4. वीर नरसिंह विभाति क्षितिमण्डलभारभरणहेमाद्रे ।
मन्दाकिनीव भवतः कीर्त्तिर्मन्दाकिनी च कीर्त्तिरिव ॥

—*Ibid.* example under 8. 3.

5. अनुगतिरूपमङ्गानामेकस्मिन्नेव जायते वाक्ये ।
यद्येकस्य तदानीमन्वर्थोऽनन्वयः कथितः ॥ —*Ibid.* VIII. 4.

6. प्रतिभटकान्ताकुचतटमकरी लुण्टाक चापटङ्कारः ।
वीरनृसिंह इवाजौ वीरनृसिंहश्चिरं जयति ॥

—*Ibid.* example under VIII. 4.

Page 115. 1. (a) संस्कारमात्रजन्यं ज्ञानं स्मृतिः ।

—Tarkasangraha, p. 68.

(b) आत्ममनसोः संयोगविशेषात् संस्काराच्च स्मृतिः ।

—Vaiśeṣika Darśana, IX-II. 6.

(c) आत्ममनसोः संयोगविशेषात्···संस्काराद् दृष्टश्रुतानुभूतेष्वर्थेषु ···अतीतविषया स्मृतिः ।

—Praśastapādabhāṣya, p. 128.

2. सदृशं सदृशानुभवाद्यत्र स्मर्येत तत् स्मरणम् । —Ekā. VIII. 5.

3. त्वत्प्रत्यर्थी गिरिचरगजस्याङ्कके दत्तदृष्टि-
स्तस्मिंस्तस्मिन् स्मरति मधुर तत्तदङ्गं प्रियायाः ।
कुम्भाभोगे गुरुकुचतटं दन्तयोर्गण्डलक्ष्मी-
मूरू हस्ते गतिषु च गतिं श्रीनृसिंह क्षितीन्द्र ।।

—*Ibid.* example under VIII. 5.

4. अहो स रणदुन्दुभिः क्व नुगतं तदा तैर्बलै-
रहो स पुरविप्लवः क्व खलु सा कुरङ्गेक्षणा ।
अहो तदपि दुर्दिनं क्व नुगतः कुमारो भवे-
दिति भ्रमति ते रिपुर्गिरिवनं कलिङ्गेश्वर ।।

—*Ibid.* example under VIII. 5.

5. सदृशाद्दृष्टचिन्तादेरनुभूतार्थवेदनम् ।
स्मरणं प्रत्यभिज्ञानस्वप्नावपि न तद्बहिः ।।

गृहीतोयः पूर्वं स एवायं तस्याः पाणिरिति प्रत्यभिज्ञानमपि स्मरणमेव ।। —SKBh. III. 169 and vṛtti on III 175.

Page 116. 1. ··· ··· ··· ··· ··· ··· ··· ··· ···

तद्रूपकमारोपे यत्रापह्नूयते न तद्विषयः ।। —Ekā. VIII. 6.

2. इदं तु निरयवं सावयवं परम्परित चेति प्रथमं त्रिधा । तत्राद्यं केवलं मालया चेति द्विधा । द्वितीयमपि समस्तवस्तुविषयमेकदेशविवर्त्ति चेति द्विधा । तृतीयं तु श्लिष्टाश्लिष्टशब्दनिबन्धत्वेन द्विविधम् । तत्तु प्रत्येकं केवलं मालया चेति चतुर्विधम् । तदेवमिह भेदाष्टकमेवोट्टङ्कितम् । —*Ibid.* vṛtti on VIII. 6.

3. अवयवतो निष्क्रान्तं निरवयवं केवलं··· —*Ibid.* vṛtti on VIII.6

4. हेमाद्रेः कन्दरायां रतिरमणरणाटोपविच्छिन्नहार-
व्यस्तं मुक्ताफलानां तमसि ततः इतः स्तोममन्वेषयन्त्याः ।

कस्याश्चित् स्वस्तरुण्या निकटगतनिजप्राणनाथोपगीता
कीर्त्तिज्योत्स्ना त्वदीया क्षणमकृत मुदं श्रीनृसिंह क्षितीन्द्र ॥
—Ekā. example under VIII. 6.

5 कलानामालम्बः कुसुमविशिखस्य प्रतिकृतिः
क्षितेः क्षेमं लक्ष्म्याः शरणमरणिः क्षात्रमहसः ।
बिलासो भारत्याः सुकृतपरिपाकः प्रणयिनां
खलूरी सौख्यानां जयति नरसिंहक्षितिपतिः ॥
—*Ibid.* example under VIII. 6.

6. समस्तानि वस्तूनि विषयो यस्येति समस्तवस्तुविषयं सावयवं⋯।
—*Ibid.* vṛtti on VIII. 6.

Page 117. 1. यत्र द्वीपस्तुषारक्षितिभृदुडुगुणो मौक्तिकानां निकायः
शैवालं व्योम शङ्खः कुमुदकुलगुरुर्धाम सान्ध्यं प्रवालः ।
यूथं दिक्कुञ्जराणां करिमकरकुलं किं च कृष्णः कृपाण-
स्त्वत्कीर्त्तिक्षीरवार्धिः स जयति जगति श्रीनृसिंह क्षितीन्द्र ॥
—*Ibid.* example under VIII. 6.

2. एकदेशे विशेषेण वर्त्तत इत्येकदेशविवर्त्ति सावयवं यत्रैकं रूपकं कृतं सदकृतमपि रूपकान्तरं सामर्थ्यादगमयति ।
—*Ibid.* vṛtti on VIII. 6.

3. परम्परा जातास्येति परम्परितं श्लिष्टशब्दनिबन्धनं केवलं⋯।
—*Ibid.* vṛtti on VIII. 6.

4. किं वर्ण्यसे वीर कलिङ्ग भूप
विलासिनी मानसराजहंस ।
भवन्ति यत्कान्तिसुधापयोधेः
पयो मनुष्या नलकूबराद्याः ॥
—*Ibid.* example under VIII. 6.

5. रविः पद्मोल्लासे कुवलयविकासे हिमकरः
क्षमाभृत् पक्षालीदलनपरिहासे हरिहयः ।
अशाम्यद्दानाम्भः प्रसरणावलासे करिपति-
र्न केषामासेव्यः स भवति कलिङ्गेश्वर भवान् ॥
—*Ibid.* example under VIII. 6.

Page 118. 1. वीर नरसिंह भूप प्रतिभटविषधरगरुत्मता भवता ।
एष कसलासहायश्चित्रं हृदयेन धार्यते भगवान् ।।

—Ekā. example under VIII. 6.

2. यशस्त्रिदशवाहिनी हिमगिरि: प्रतापातप-
प्रथाप्रथमभूधर: प्रतिबलाब्धिमन्थाचल: ।
पराक्रममहामदद्विरदकेलिविन्ध्यश्चिरं
गुणौघमणिरोहणो विजयते कलिङ्गेश्वर: ।।

—*Ibid.* example under VIII. 6.

3. त्यागस्तावत् सुरतरुयश: कौमुदी कालमेघ:
शौर्यंकुन्तीतनयचरितश्रुत्यनध्यायपर्व ।
कान्ति: पुष्पायुधवपुरहं भावरुद्रावलोक:
कस्ते वक्तुं प्रभवति गुणान् श्रीनृसिंह क्षितीन्द्र ।।

—*Ibid.* example under VIII. 6.

Page 119. 1. शरासनमिदं नमत्तव विलोक्य लोकोत्तरं
पिनाकमिव दानवास्तुहिनरश्मि चूडामणे: ।
अमी निपुमहीभृतो युधि कलिङ्ग पृथ्वीपते
सरत्नविरुदाङ्कदं तव नमन्ति पादाम्बुजम् ।।

—*Ibid.* example under VIII. 6.

2. शोषिताशेषदुर्वारवैरिस्त्रीजनमानस: ।
नृसिंह भूपते भाति प्रतापतपनस्तव ।।

—*Ibid.* example under VI. 6.

3. यस्यानिशं दिविषदश्चरणारविन्द-
मुत्तंसयन्त्यमितभक्तिभरावनम्रा: ।
देव: सुधाकरकिशोरक चारुचूड:,
स श्रेयसेऽस्तु भवतो नरसिंह देव ।।

—*Ibid.* example under VIII. 6.

4. श्रुत्यासंबंधविरहात् यत्पदेन पदान्तरम् ।
गुणवृत्तिप्रधानेन युज्यते रूपकं तु तत् ।। —KASS. I. 11.

5. उपचारैकसर्वस्वं यत्र (वस्तु) तत् साम्यमुद्वहत् ।
यदर्पयति रूपं स्वयं वस्तु तद् रूपकं विदु: ।।

—VJ. III. 20.

6. यदोपमानशब्दानां गौणवृत्तिव्याश्रयात् ।
उपमेये भवेद्वृत्तिस्तदा तद्रूपकं विदुः ।। —SKBh. IV. 48.

7. यत्रोपमानचित्रेण सर्वथाप्युपरज्यते ।
उपमेयमयी भित्तिस्तत्र रूपकमिष्यते ।।
—Candrāloka, V.18.

8. तं परिणामं द्विविधं कथयन्त्यारोप्यमाणरूपतया ।
परिणमति यत्र विषयः प्रस्तुतकार्योपयोगाय ।।

9. आरोप्यमाणस्य प्रकृतोपरञ्जकत्वे रूपकस्य जागरूकत्वात् । यत्रा-
रोपविषयः प्रकृतकार्यसिद्ध्यर्थमारोप्यमाणात्मतया परिणमति तत्र
यथार्थाभिधानः परिणामः ।
—Ekā. vrtti on VIII. 7.

10. (a) तस्य समानाधिकरण्यवैयाधिकरण्य प्रयोगाद् द्वैविध्यम् ।
—AS. vṛtti on 16.

(b) समानाधिकरण्यवैयधिकरण्याभ्यां भवन्न द्वैविध्यमतिक्रामति ।
—Ekā. vṛtti on VIII. 7.

11. अमरनगरीसौधोत्सङ्गाधिरोह-महोत्सव-
व्यतिकरधुराधौरेयाणामरातिमहीभुजाम् ।
मरकतमयी निश्रेणिस्त्वत्कृपाणलता कवीन्
कति न कुरुते श्लाघाव्यग्रान् कलिङ्गपुरन्दर ।।
—*Ibid.* example under VIII. 7.

Page 120. 1. राजन् नृसिह भवतः समरोत्सवेषु
धूलीभिरन्धतमसं सपदि व्यधायि ।
निस्त्रिंशकृत्तशिरसाममरत्वभाजां
स्वर्गाङ्गनासुरतकेलिषु शात्रवाणाम् ।।
—*Ibid.* example under VIII. 7.

2. (a) समानानेकधर्मोपपते विप्रतिपत्तेरूपलब्ध्यनुपलब्ध्यव्यवस्थातश्च
विशेषापेक्षो विमर्शः संशयः ।
—Vātsyāyanasūtra, I. 1. 23.

(b) समानधर्मोपपत्तेर्विशेषापेक्षोविमर्शः संशय इति ।
—Bhāṣya on Vātsyāyanasūtra, I. 1. 23.

3. किसलयति कविः प्रतिभावशतः प्रकृतार्थभित्तिकं यत्र ।
संशयमप्रकृतेऽर्थे संदेहोऽयं समाख्यातः ।। —Ekā. VIII 8.

4. न तु स्थाणुर्वा स्यात् पुरुषोवा स्यादितिवत् स्वरसप्रवृत्ते संदेहे इत्याशयेनाभिहितं प्रतिभावशत इति ।

—Ekā. vṛttī on VIII. 8.

5. कान्तः किं कैरविण्याः कलयति कमलोल्लासने नैष शक्तिं
नाथः कि वासराणामुदयति कुमुदे नैष लक्ष्मीं वितन्वन् ।
किं कृष्णो न द्विजानामधरयति पतिं भूयसोक्तेन किं वा
जातः पश्चान्नृसिंहक्षितितलतिलक त्वं विचित्रैश्चरित्रैः ।।

—*Ibid.* example under VIII. 8.

Page 121. 1. वस्त्वन्तरप्रतीतिर्विलसति सादृश्यहेतुका यत्र ।
तं भ्रान्तिमन्तमेत ब्रुवतेऽलंकारपारदृश्वानः ।। —*Ibid.* VIII. 9.

2. सुराङ्गनाभ्यो मलये त्वदीयं
श्रुत्वा यशो वीर नृसिंह भूप ।
जिह्वाञ्चलान्युल्लयन्ति दुग्ध-
मृणाललोभादुभयेऽपि नागाः ।।

—*Ibid.* example under VIII. 9.

3. कल्पान्तक्षुभ्यदम्भोभरतरलतरोदन्वदुत्तुङ्गरिङ्खत्-
कल्लोलश्रेणिहल्लीसकवलितमिव प्रेक्ष्यते क्षोणिचक्रम् ।
त्वत्खड्गोत्कृत्तवक्षः स्थलविवरवलत्प्राणवायुप्रयाण-
भ्राम्यच्चेतोभिराजौ प्रतिभटसुभटैः श्रीनृसिंह क्षितीन्द्र ।।

—*Ibid.* example under VIII. 9.

Page 122. 1. तत्तन्निमित्तभेदादेकमनेकैरनेकधा यत्र ।
उल्लिख्यते स धीरैरुल्लेखः कथ्यतेऽन्वर्थ ।। —*Ibid.* VIII. 10.

2. न भवसि कथंकारं श्लाध्यः कलिङ्गपुरन्दर
स्मर इति वरारोहाः साक्षान्मुकुन्द इतीन्दिरा ।
सुरतरुरिति त्वां सेवन्ते निरन्तरमर्थिनो
भरतमुनिरित्यार्यास्तौर्यत्रयी निपुणा अपि ।।

—*Ibid.* example under VIII. 10.

3. कलयति विषयेऽपह्नवमारोप्यं यत्र भासते सुतराम् ।
आहुरपह्नुतिमेतां बन्धच्छाया त्रयी चास्याः ।।

—*Ibid.* VIII. 11.

4 अस्याश्च त्रयी बन्धच्छाया। तथाहि क्वचिदारोपविषयमपह्नुत्या-
रोप्यते विषयी। क्वचिद्विषयिणमारोप्यारोपस्यापह्नूयते विषयः।
क्वचित् पुनरसत्यत्वाभिधायिभिश्छलादिभिः शब्दैरपह्नवो निर्दिश्यते।
तत्राद्यं भेदद्वयं वाक्यभेद एव संभवति। तृतीयभेदे त्वेकवाक्यत्वम्।

—Ekā. vṛtti on VIII. 11.

Page 123. 1. आद्यंभेदद्वयं वाक्यभेद एव संभवति। तृतीयभेदे त्वेकवाक्यत्वम्।

—*Ibid*. vṛtti on VIII. 11.

2. अश्रान्तस्यन्दमानोद्धुरमदलहरीसौरभोन्मेषहर्ष-
प्रेङ्खोलच्चञ्चरीकप्रकरपरिकरं दिग्गजाः किं वहन्ति।
किं तूदग्रं कलिङ्गेश्वर तव भुजयोश्चण्डिमानं विलोक्य
व्रीडाचिन्तावनम्रान् स्फुटमसितपटैश्छादयन्ति स्वहस्तान्॥

—*Ibid*. example under VIII. 11.

3. पृथ्वीभारावतारं कृतवति भवतो दोष्णि हर्षेण दूतः
शेषेण प्रेषितोऽसौ निवसति भुजगः कोऽपि संवादहेतोः।
क्रुध्यत् कालीकटाक्षद्युतिदलनकलाकेलिकारस्वदीये
पाणौ नायं कृपाणः सकलगुणनिधे श्रीनृसिंह क्षितीन्द्र॥

—*Ibid*. example under VIII. 11.

4 वीरश्रीसिंह कान्ताविहरणकनकक्ष्माधराकारबाहो
कीर्त्ति ज्योत्स्नासुधांशो गुणमणि जलधे श्रीनृसिंह क्षितीन्द्र।
प्रत्यग्रोदग्रजाग्रद्दवदहनघनज्वालमालापदेशा-
द्देशाः शोकं वहन्ते निजपतिविरहाद्दुःखितास्त्वद्रिपूणाम्॥

—*Ibid*. example under VIII. 11.

5. एवं चोत्कटोपमानकोटिक प्रकृतविषयकसंभावनमुत्प्रेक्षेत्यर्थः।

—Udyota on KP. X. 92.

6. अप्रकृतत्वेन स्यादध्यवसायो गुणाभिसंबन्धात्।
साध्यः प्रकृतस्य यदा कथितोत्प्रेक्षा तदा तज्ज्ञैः॥

—Ekā. VIII. 12.

7. आरोपादध्यवसायस्य प्रकृष्यमाणत्वादत्र निरूपणं समुचितमेतस्याः।

—*Ibid*. vṛtti on VIII. 12.

8. (a) अभिन्नत्वेन प्रतिभासनमध्यवसायः।

—*Ibid*. vṛtti on VIII. 12.

(b) विषयनिगरणाभेदप्रतिपत्तिर्विषयिणोऽध्यवसायः ।

—AS. vṛtti on 21.

Page 124. 1. यत्र लक्ष्यमाणगुणसंबन्धाद् विषयिणो विषयगतत्वेनारोप्यमाणत्वाद्भिन्नस्यापि विषयिणो विषयक्रोडीकारेण प्रवृत्तत्वादभिन्नत्वेन प्रतीतिस्तत्राध्यवसायः सिद्धः।···यत्र पुनरुपात्तविषयत्वाद्विषयिणो भिन्नत्वेन प्रतिभानं तत्र व्यञ्जनव्यापारेणाभिन्नत्वप्रतीतेः साध्यमानत्वात् साध्यः ।

—Ekā vṛtti on VIII. 12.

2. (a) एतदवलम्बनेन प्रवर्त्तमानायाः पुनरस्याः संभावनमभिमानस्तर्क ऊहश्चेति पर्यायाः ।

—*Ibid.* vṛtti on VIII. 12.

(b)···साध्यत्वप्रतीतौ व्यापारप्राधान्येऽध्यवसायः सभावनमभिमानस्तर्क ऊह उत्प्रेक्षेत्यादिशब्दैरुच्यते ।

—AS. vṛtti on 21.

3. श्रीमन्नृसिंह नृपते भवतो यशोभिः
क्षीरार्णवं स्वपितरं परिभूयमानम् ।
उत्पश्यतः सितकरस्य कुरङ्ग एष
शोकाग्निधूम इव भाति तदात्मजस्य ॥

—Ekā. example under VIII. 12.

Page 125. 1. कैलासान् कीर्त्तिरेषा सृजति कति न ते दत्ततिग्मांशुयात्राभङ्गास्त्यागस्तु शृङ्गाञ्चलदलितनभः पर्वणः स्वर्णशैलान् ।
इत्थं मन्दाक्षचिन्ताप्रसरविधुरधीरात्मभूरात्मगुप्त्यै
लीनो वैकुण्ठनाभीसरसिज कुहरे श्रीनृसिंह क्षितीन्द्र ॥

—*Ibid.* example under VIII. 12.

2. त्वत्तः कोऽप्यपरः कदापि पुरुषश्चित्तेऽपि न स्थापितस्त्वच्चिन्तापरया मयेति भवतः प्रत्यायनां कुर्वती ।
तन्वी दुःसहपञ्चबाणदहनोत्सङ्गं प्रविष्टा सती
पाण्डिम्ना विरहोत्थितेन सुभगा व्याख्याति शुद्धिं निजाम् ॥

—*Ibid.* example under VIII. 12.

3. त्रैलोक्यप्रथमानवीर परिषद्व्यावृत्तवीरायितं
श्रीमन् वीर नृसिंह देव भवतः कर्त्तुं वतंसं यशः ।

यत् पूर्वं श्रवणावतंस पदवीं नीतं धरित्रीभुजां
तत्कम्पेन निरन्तरेण शिरसः प्रभ्रंशयन्ते बुधाः ॥

—Ekā. example under VIII 12

4. ननु मृगाङ्कमृगस्य तृणैर्विना
कथममुष्य भविष्यति जीवितम् ।
इति मृगाङ्करुचः कुरुते तृणं
तव कृपालु कलिङ्गपते यशः ॥

—*Ibid.* example under VIII. 12.

Page 126. 1. कान्त्यानया तव तुलातपनीयराशि-
मन्दीकृतद्युतिरिवाञ्चति लज्जमानः ।
किं चामुनार्थिभवनेषु निधीकृतेन
जाता नृसिंह नृपते वसुधा यथार्था ॥

—*Ibid.* example under VIII. 12.

2. मरुत्पाथोवह्निव्यतिकरसुतीक्ष्णेन तपसा
तुलामध्यारूढं तव तदपि कान्त्या जितमहः ।
इति स्नात्वा दानाम्भसि तव नृसिंह क्षितिपते
सुवर्णं निर्विण्णं विरचयति तीर्थेषु वसतिम् ॥

—*Ibid.* example under VIII. 12.

3. दिङ्मातङ्गैः सह स्पर्शं भ्रान्तितः प्राप्य शुद्धये ।
पुष्करं गाहते कीर्त्तिर्नृसिंह नृपते तव ॥

—*Ibid.* example under VIII. 12.

4. स्वः सिन्धौ विबुधेन्द्रबिभ्रभवने खे हाटकाद्रौ दिशां
कण्ठे वीर नृसिंहदेव भवतः कीर्त्तेः परिस्फूर्त्तयः ।
डिण्डीरप्रकरन्ति फुल्लकलिकाभारन्ति तारावधू-
नाथांशु प्रसरन्ति निर्झरसरित्पूरन्ति हारन्ति च ॥

—*Ibid.* example under VIII. 12.

Page 127. 1. अतिशयिता प्रसिद्धिमतिक्रान्ता लोकातीता उक्तिः अतिशयोक्तिः···।

—Jhalakīkara on KP. X. 100.

2. अध्यवसितिसिद्धत्वं प्रकृतस्यान्यत्वकल्पनं यद्वा ।
संबन्धासंबन्धौ तद्व्यत्यासे भवेदतिशयोक्तिः ॥

अनयो: समसमयत्वे पौर्वापर्यस्य वा विपर्य्यासे ।
कार्याशुभावगमिका द्विविधातिशयोक्तिराख्याता ॥

—Ekā. VIII. 13 and 37.

3. पल्लवत: कल्पतरोरेष विशेष: करस्य ते वीर ।
भूषयति कर्णमेक: परस्तुकर्णं तिरस्कुरुते ॥

—*Ibid.* example under VIII. 13.

Page 128. 1. अशेषभोगाधारं त्वामक्रमात्तबलिश्रियम् ।
कलिङ्गेश्वर जानामि नूतन पुरुषोत्तमम् ॥

—*Ibid.* example under VIII. 13.

2. इदमन्यत् सारस्वतमन्यद्गाम्भीर्यमन्यदौदार्यम् ।
त्वं नरसिंह नरेश्वर न भवसि पैतामही सृष्टि: ॥

—*Ibid.* example under VIII. 13.

3. स्थाने स्थाने कुलशिखरिषु त्वद्यशो गीयमानं
सिद्धद्वन्द्वैस्तटतरुलताकेलिदोलाधिरूढै: ।
श्रुत्वा हर्षात् प्रमुषितगतावौपवाह्ये कुरङ्गे
मन्दायन्ते मलयमरुत: श्रीनृसिंह क्षितीन्द्र ॥

—*Ibid.* example under VIII. 13.

4. त्वयीत्थ सर्वेभ्यो वितरति कलिङ्गेश्वर सदा
न दानप्रस्तावो दिविचरतरुणां समजनि ।
यदि स्यादेतेषामपि विषकण्डू विनयन-
क्षणारम्भेष्वैरावणकरटकाषव्यतिकरै. ॥

—*Ibid.* example under VIII. 13.

5. कोशगृहचिरनिषण्णा रिपुनृप-लक्ष्मीर्निजासिलतिका च ।
उत्कलभूपाल कथं युगपद् भवता समाकृष्टा ॥

—*Ibid.* example under VIII. 37.

6. कवीन्द्राणामासन् प्रथमतरमेवाङ्गणभुव-
श्चलद्भृङ्गासङ्गाकुलकरिमदामोदमधुरा: ।
अमी पश्चात्तेषामुपरि पतिता वीर भवत:
कटाक्षा: क्षीरोदप्रसरदुरुवीचीसहचरा: ॥

—*Ibid.* example under VIII. 37.

CHAPTER VIII

Page 130. 1. ... ...

अधुनालंकृतिवर्गं गम्यौपम्याश्रयं ब्रूमः ।। —Ekā. VIII. 14.

2. तुल्यधर्मेण योगो जातोऽस्यामित्यन्वर्थनामा तुल्ययोगिता ।

—*Ibid*. vṛtti on VIII. 15.

3. ···सादृश्यप्रतीत्येव चमत्कारात् । —Udyota on KP. X. 104.

4. औपम्यगम्यतायां प्रकृतानां तुल्यधर्मसंबन्धे ।
अप्रकृतानामथवा चतुर्विधा तुल्ययोगिता ज्ञेया ।।— Ekā. VIII.15.

5. प्रत्यर्थिपृथ्वीपतिमानमर्दनं
सेवासमायातनृपालपालनम् ।
कात्यायनीपादसरोजपूजनं
नैसर्गिकं ते नरसिंह भूपते ।।

—*Ibid*. example under VIII. 15.

Page 131. 1. गर्जद्दुर्जयशत्रुसैन्यजलधेर्मन्थाय विद्वज्जना-
भीष्टानां परिपूरणाय वसुधावष्टम्भदानाय च ।
श्रीमन्नुत्कलभूमिपाल भवतः सृष्टे भुजे वेधसा
व्यर्थः संप्रति मन्दरः सुरतरुः सर्पाधिपश्चाभवत् ।।

—*Ibid*. example under VIII. 15.

2 अलंकारावबद्धानि काव्यान्यरिकुलान्यपि ।
नरसिंह महीपाल कीर्त्ति पल्लवयन्ति ते ।।

—*Ibid*. example under VIII. 15.

3. नियतानां प्राकरणिकानामेव अप्राकरणिकानामेव वा ।

—KP. vṛtti on X. 104.

4. विवक्षितगुणोत्कृष्टैर्यत् समीकृत्य कस्यचित् ।
कीर्त्तनं स्तुतिनिन्दार्थं सा मता तुल्ययोगिता ।। —KD. II. 330.

5. विवक्षितगुणोत्कृष्ट्ये यत् समीकृत्य कस्यचित् ।
कीर्त्तनं स्तुतिनिन्दार्थं सा मता तुल्ययोगिता ।। —SKBh. IV.166.

6. (a) एकस्थस्यैव सर्ववाक्यदीपकत्वेन प्रदीपसाम्यात् ।

—K. Pradīpa on KP. X. 103.

(b) ···दीपनरूपादुपकाराद् दीपसदृशोऽयमिति कृत्वा दीपकालङ्कारः ।

—Sanjīvinī on AS. 24.

(c) ···दीपसाम्यात् दीपकमित्यर्थः ।

—Jhalakīkara on KP. X. 103.

Page 132. 1. मिलितानां तु तथैषां दीपकमित्युच्यते षोढा ।
एतदलंकृतियुगलं कथितं तावत् पदार्थगत्वेन ॥ —Ekā. VIII.16.

2. साधर्म्यस्य तु वाक्यादिमध्यान्तगमित्वादेतत् षट्प्रकारम् ।

—*Ibid.* vrtti on VIII. 16.

3. करोति न मुदं कस्य नरसिंह नरेश्वर ।
राकाचन्द्रमसो बिम्बं पुण्डरीकं यशस्तव ॥

—*Ibid.* example under VIII. 16.

4. क्षीरोदवीची कमलासखेन
प्रकाशते भानुमता दिनश्रीः ।
द्यौः पारिजातेन कलिङ्गनाथ
निशा शशाङ्केन मही त्वया च ॥

—*Ibid.* example under VIII. 16.

5. वीर नृसिंह कवित्वं चम्पकसौरभ्यमिन्दुसौन्दर्यम् ।
गङ्गाजलमाधुर्यं कस्य न भुवनेषु सर्वदा मान्यम् ॥

—*Ibid.* example under VIII. 16.

Page 133. 1. जातिक्रियागुणद्रव्यवाचिनैकत्र वर्त्तिना ।
सर्ववाक्योपकारश्चेत् तमाहुर्दीपकं यथा ॥ —KD. II. 97.

2. क्रियाजातिगुणद्रव्यवाचिनैकत्रवर्त्तिना ।
सर्ववाक्योपकारश्चेद्दीपकं तन्निगद्यते ॥
अर्थावृत्तिः पदावृत्तिरुभयावृत्तिरावली ।
सम्पुटं रसना माला चक्रवालश्च तद्भिदाः ॥ —SKBh. VI.264.

3. यत्रैकमनेकेषां वाक्यार्थानां क्रियापदं भवति ।
तद्वत्कारकपदमपि तदेतदिति दीपकं द्वेधा ॥ —KAR. VII. 64.

4. औचित्यावहमम्लानं तद्विदाह्लादकारणम् ।
अशक्तं धर्ममर्थानां दीपयेद् वस्तु दीपकम् ।। —VJ. III. 17.

5. सकृद् वृत्तिस्तु धर्मस्य प्रकृताप्रकृतात्मनाम् ।
सैव क्रियासु बह्वीषु कारकस्येति दीपकम् ।। —KP. X.103.

6. प्रकृताप्रकृतानां धर्मैक्यं दीपकम् ।। —KAnu. VI. 7.

7. प्रस्तुताप्रस्तुतानां च तुल्यत्वे दीपकं मतम् ।
... ... // —Candrāloka, V. 53.

8. (a) वस्तुशब्दस्य वाक्यार्थाभिधायित्वात् प्रतिवाक्यार्थमुपैति सार्थकताभिधानेयं... । —Ekā. vṛtti on VIII. 17.

(b) वस्तुशब्दस्य वाक्यार्थवाचित्वे प्रतिवाक्यार्थमुपमा साम्यमित्यन्वर्थाश्रयणात् । —AS. vṛtti on 25.

9. वाक्यार्थगतत्वेन स्यात् सामान्यं पृथग्विनिर्दिष्टम् ।
यस्यां द्वेधा तज्ज्ञैः सा प्रतिवस्तूपमा समाम्नाता ।।
—Ekā. VIII. 17.

Page 134. 1. इयं द्विधा । साधर्म्येण वैधर्म्येण च ।
—*Ibid.* vṛtti on VIII. 17.

2. दातारः कति न प्रभाकरकरक्रीडासखीनां दिशां
चक्र किंतु नृसिंह पार्थिवतुलामेकोऽपि नारोहति ।
अध्यास्ते न परोऽपि कश्चन मणिश्चिन्तामणिप्रक्रिया-
मब्धिः क्षीरपयोधिभङ्गिमचलः कैलासहेलामपि ।।
—*Ibid.* example under VIII. 17.

3. याञ्चादैन्यपराङ्मुखी भवतु वो जिह्वा नृपेष्वर्थिनः
सर्वस्यापि कलिङ्गभूपतिरिह क्षेमङ्करः सेव्यताम् ।
तत्तादृक्फलभारवैभवनमन्नीरन्ध्रशाखाभरे
मन्दारे पुरतः स्थिते किमपरैर्लक्षेण वृक्षैरपि ।।
—*Ibid.* example under VIII. 17.

4. संतोषकरणनिपुणो नरसिंह नरेश्वर त्वमखिलस्य ।
नानन्ददानचतुरश्चिन्तामणिमन्तरेण कोऽप्यस्ति ।।
—*Ibid.* example under VIII. 17.

Page 135. 1. (a) दृष्टोऽन्तो निश्चयो यत्रेति यथार्थाभिधानम् ।

—Ekā. vṛtti on VIII. 18.

(b) दृष्टोऽन्तः निश्चयो यत्र स दृष्टान्तः ।

—KP. vṛtti on X. 102.

(c) दृष्टांतवाक्यार्थे गृहीतसहचारेण दार्ष्टांतिकार्थप्रामाण्यनिश्चयात् ।

—Udyota on KP. X. 102.

2. बिम्बप्रतिबिम्बत्वं यद्युपमानोपमेययोर्भवति ।
धर्मस्यापि तदानीं दृष्टान्तः कथ्यते द्विविधः ॥ —Ekā. VIII. 18.

3. साधर्म्यवैधर्म्याभ्यां भवन्नुभयथा भवति ।

—*Ibid.* vṛtti on VIII. 18.

4. त्वमसि रिपुनराधिनाथमाथ
प्रकटभुजार्गलविक्रमो नृसिंहः ।
मदकरटिकठोरकुम्भपीठी-
दलनदुरन्तनखाङ्कुरो मृगेन्द्रः ॥

—*Ibid.* example under VIII. 18.

5. अपि सहज मनोहरं कवित्वं
भवति नृसिंहगुणान्वितं मनोज्ञम् ।
अकुचकलशसंगतं तरुण्याः
कलयति मौक्तिकदाम दुर्भगत्वम् ॥

—*Ibid.* example under VIII. 18.

Page 136. 1. निदर्शनं दृष्टान्तकरणम् । —KP vṛtti on X 97.

2. प्रतिबिम्बनस्य करणं संभवता यत्र वस्तुयोगेन ।
गम्यमसंभवता वा निदर्शना सा द्विधाभिमता ॥ —Ekā.VIII.19.

3. द्विधा संभवद्वस्तुसंबन्धासंभवद्वस्तुसंबन्धा च ।

—*Ibid.* vṛtti on VIII. 19.

4. यदप्येकाकिन्यो यदपि रमणीया युवतय-
स्तथापि स्वच्छाश्चेद्दधति जगति श्लाघनधुराम् ।
इहार्थे प्रामाण्यप्रकटनपरा कीर्त्तिरनिशं
भुजङ्गानां लोके चरति नरसिंह क्षितिपते ॥

—*Ibid.* example under VIII. 19.

5. दृप्यद्दुर्वारवैरिक्षितिपतिवनितालोचनाम्भोरुहेन्दुः
क्रीडासौधं कलानां जगति गजगतिर्नन्दतु श्रीनृसिंहः ।
यत्कीर्त्तिक्रोडलीनं कलयति गगनं क्षीरनीराकरान्त-
र्निद्राणस्य स्रवन्ती सहचरदुहितुः प्राणनाथस्य लीलाम् ॥
—Ekā. exampie under VIII. 19.

Page 137. 1. वीरनरसिंहहतेजः स्तुतिवर्त्मनि यः प्रणेतुमभिलषति ।
अभिनवकमलकलाचीकुहरे विनिवेशयेत् स वड्वाग्निम् ॥
—*Ibid.* example under VIII. 19.

2. या चण्डांशुमयूखमण्डलमहाहंकारसर्वङ्कषा
ख्याता वीर नृसिंह देव जगति प्रौढिः प्रतापस्य ते ।
त्वद्धाटीचकिताः पलाय्य विपिने वासं परः कोटयः
कुर्वन्तोऽनुभवन्ति संततमिमां दावानले विद्विषः ॥
—*Ibid.* example under VIII. 19.

3. यः कैलासनिवासधूर्जटिजटाकोटीरतारापति-
ज्योत्स्नाचुम्बितसिद्धसिन्धुलहरागर्भत्विषां विभ्रमः ।
उद्वेलाम्बरचूडकालिमकथानिर्मन्थनोत्कन्धरः
सोऽयं वीर नृसिंह देव नृपते त्वत्कीर्त्तिषु प्रेक्ष्यते ॥
—*Ibid.* example under VIII. 19.

4. क्रिययैव विशिष्टस्य तदर्थस्योपदर्शनात् ।
ज्ञेया निदर्शना नाम यथेववतिभिर्विना ॥ —KAB. III. 33.

5. अर्थान्तरप्रवृत्तेन किंचित् तत्सदृशं फलम् ।
सदसद्वा निदर्श्येत यदि तत् स्यान्निदर्शनम् ॥ —KD. II. 348.

6. क्रिययैव स्वतदर्थान्वयख्यापनं निदर्शनम् ॥—KASV. IV. III. 20.

Page 1:8. 1. दृष्टान्तः प्रोक्तसिद्ध्ये यः सिद्धेऽर्थे तन्निदर्शनम् ।
पूर्वोत्तरसमत्वे तादृशु वक्रञ्च कथ्यते ॥ —SKBh. III. 11!.

2. इष्टार्थसिद्ध्ये दृष्टान्तो निदर्शनम् ॥ —KAnu. VI. 6.

3. (a) दृष्टान्तालंकार··· परस्परनिरपेक्ष वाक्यार्थगतत्वेन तस्य प्रगल्भमानत्वात् ।··· पुनः परस्परसापेक्षत्वं वाक्यार्थयोरिति निदर्शनैव भवितुमर्हति । —Ekā. vṛtti on VIII. 19.

(b) निरपेक्षयोर्वाक्यार्थयोर्हि बिम्बप्रतिबिम्बभावे दृष्टान्तः ।

—AS. vṛtti on 27.

4. उपमानादुपमेयं यत्राधिक्यस्य गोचरी भवति ।
सति भेदप्राधान्ये व्यतिरेकोऽयं समाख्यातः ।। —Ekā. VIII. 20.

5. आधिक्यं चोपमेयस्योत्कर्षं हेतावुपमानस्यापकर्षहेतौ च सति संभवे तत्र द्वयोर्हेत्वोरुक्तौ द्वयोरनुक्तौ एकैकोक्तौ च चत्वारोऽस्य भेदाः । ते पुनरिवादिशब्द-प्रयोगात् सदृशादि शब्दप्रयोगादर्थाक्षेपाच्च शाब्दत्वार्थत्वाक्षिप्तत्वै. सादृश्यत्रैविध्येन त्रैविध्ये द्वादशभेदाः । ते च श्लेषाश्लेषाभ्यां द्वेधेत्येवं चतुर्विशतिरस्य भेदाः ।

—Taralā on Ekā. VIII. 20.

6. श्रीमन्नुत्कलभूमिपाल भवतो दानाम्बुकल्लोलिनी-
मेतां पूरपवित्रितावनितलां दृष्ट्वापगानां पतिः ।
शिप्रां नेच्छति नर्मदां न मनुते गोदावरीं नेक्षते
कालिन्दीं न धिनोति सिद्ध-तटिनीं नाश्लिष्यति प्रागिव ।।

—Ekā. example under VIII. 20.

7. पवित्रसद्गोत्रमुदीरयन्ति
त्वामुत्कलाधीश विडौजसं च
इयान् विशेषो युवयोर्यदेष
नापारिजातस्त्वमपारिजातः ।।

– *Ibid*. example under VIII .20.

Page 139. 1. प्राधान्येन निबद्धं यद्युपमानोपमेययोरेकम् ।
अन्यत् सहार्थसहितं भवति सहोक्तिस्तदा ख्याता ।।

—*Ibid*. VIII. 21.

2. सहयुक्तेऽप्रधाने ।।

—Aṣṭādhyāyī. II-III. 19.

3. संग्रामाङ्गणभूषणस्य भवतः कर्णावतंसीभव-
ज्ज्यावल्लीवलयोद्धुरेण धनुषा मुक्तैः समं मार्गणैः ।
एतैस्तैः प्रतिमल्लभूमिपतिभिः स्पर्शानुबन्धादिव
श्रीमन् वीर नृसिंह देव सहसा दिक्चक्रमुल्लङ्घितम् ।।

—Ekā. example under VIII. 21.

Page 140. 1. रणे वीरनृसिंहस्य सिंहनादेन तर्जिताः ।
मदं मुञ्चन्ति मातङ्गैः सहैव परिपन्थिनः ।।

—*Ibid*. example under VIII. 21.

2. तुल्यकाले क्रिये यत्र वस्तुद्वयसमाश्रये ।
पदेनैकेन कथ्येते सहोक्तिः सा मता यथा ॥

—KAB. III. 39.

3. तुल्यकाले क्रिये यत्र वस्तुद्वयसमाश्रिते ।
पदेनेकेन कथ्येते सा सहोक्तिर्मता सताम् ॥ —KASS. V. 15.

4. वस्तुद्वयक्रिययोस्तुल्यकालयोरेकपदाभिधानं सहोक्तिः ॥

—KASV. IV. III-28.

5. सहोक्तिः सहभावेन कथनं तुल्यधर्म्मिणाम् ।

—Agnipurāṇa. 344. 23.

6. सहोक्तिः सहभावेन कथनं गुणकर्मणाम् ॥
अर्थानां यो विनिमयः परिवृत्तिस्तु सा स्मृता ॥

—KD. II. 351.

7. सहार्थबलाद्धर्मस्यान्वयः सहोक्तिः ॥ —KAnu. VI. 13.

8. भवति यथारूपोऽर्थः कुर्वन्नेवापरं तथाभूतम् ।
उक्तिस्तस्य समाना तेन समं या सहोक्तिः सा ॥

—KAR. VII. 13.

9. सा हि सहोक्तिर्यस्यां प्रसिद्धदूराधिकक्रियो योऽर्थः ।
तस्य समानक्रिय इति कथ्येतान्यः समं तेन ॥

—*Ibid.* VIII. 99.

10. यत्रैककर्तृका स्यादनेककर्माश्रिता क्रिया तत्र ।
कथ्येतापरसहितं कर्मैकं सेयमन्या स्यात् ॥

—*Ibid.* VIII. 101.

11. यत्रैकेनैव वाक्येन वर्णनीयार्थसिद्धये ।
अर्थानां युगपदुक्तिः सा सहोक्तिः सतां मता ॥

—VJ. III. 37.

12. कर्त्रादीनां समावेशः सहान्यैर्यः क्रियादिषु ।
विविक्तश्चाविविक्तश्च सहोक्तिः सा निगद्यते ॥

—SKBh. IV. 181.

13. सा सहोक्तिः सहार्थस्य बलादेकं द्विवाचकम् ॥ —KP. X. 112.

Page 141. 1. सहोक्तिः सहभावश्चेद् भासते जनरञ्जनः ।
.... ॥
—Candrāloka, V. 60

2. ब्रूमोऽधुना सहोक्तिप्रतिभटभूतं विनोक्त्यलंकारम् ।
एकेन विना किञ्चिद्यत्रान्यत् स्यात् सतोऽसतो यद्वा ॥
—Ekā. VIII. 22.

3. न त्वद्वैरिवधूवक्त्रं विना कान्त्या विराजते ।
ज्योत्स्ना न विना चन्द्रमण्डलं क्षितिमण्डन ॥
—*Ibid.* example under VIII. 22.

4. विना पद्माकरो ग्राहैश्चन्दनं भुजगैर्विना ।
विना भाति खलैर्वीर नृसिंह भवतः सभा ॥
—*Ibid.* example under VIII 22.

5. (a)···संक्षेपेणार्थयोः कथनमित्यन्वर्था समासोक्तिः ।
—*Ibid.* vṛtti on VIII. 22.

(b)···समासोक्तिरुदिष्टा संक्षिप्तार्थतया यथा ॥ —KAB II. 79.

(c)···उक्तिः संक्षेपरूपत्वात् सा समासोक्तिरिष्यते ॥
—KD. II. 205.

6. साधारणधर्मवशाद्गम्येनाप्रस्तुतेन चारुत्वम् ।
प्रस्तुतमुपैति वाच्यं यस्यामेषा समासोक्तिः ॥ —Ekā VIII. 23.

7. पुनरारोप्यमाणपदार्थधर्मविशिष्टत्वेन प्रतिभासनादारोपविषयस्य प्राधान्यं तत्रेयम् । अतस्तु प्रस्तुताद्वाच्यादप्रस्तुतस्य प्रतीयमानत्वे संक्षेपेणार्थयोः कथनम्··· । —*Ibid.* vṛtti on VIII. 23.

Page 142. 1. गुणप्रणयिनी मुष्टिग्राह्यमध्या सुवंशजा ।
नरसिंह धनुर्वल्ली करोति भवतो मुदम् ॥
—*Ibid.* example under VIII. 23.

2. विशालवलभीभुजान् लघुविशीर्णलूतागुण-
प्रतानवसनश्रियः सुफुटसुधाविलासस्मितान् ।
नृसिंह वसुधाधिप त्वदरिवीरलीलागृहान् ।
विशङ्कमुपगूहते विपिनपावकज्वालिका ॥
—*Ibid.* example under VIII. 23.

3. विश्राणनैस्तैः परिभूयमानः
कल्पद्रुमो वीर कलिङ्गनाथ ।
लतोपगूढोऽपि न भृङ्गनादै-
राभाषते न स्मयते च पुष्पैः ॥

—Ekā. example under VIII. 23.

4. धाटीं वीर नृसिंह देव भवतः श्रुत्वा वनान्तं भिया
यान्तीनां रभसादरातिसुदृशां शाखाभुजैः शाखिनः ।
आकर्षन्ति कचान् हरन्ति सिचयं मृद्नन्ति गण्डस्थलीः
श्लिष्यन्ति स्तनयोः स्पृशन्ति जघने गृह्णन्ति कण्ठे मुहुः ॥

—*Ibid.* example under VIII. 23.

Page 143. 1. धावन्तीर्नरसिंह देव रभसाद्वीक्ष्य प्रसूनेक्षणै-
स्तासां बाहुलतासहोदरतया वात्सल्यनिघ्ना इव ।
आहारोऽस्तु फलैरिति प्रतिवनं पादे लगन्त्यो लता
याचन्ते त्वदरातिराजरमणीः पुष्पन्धयानां रुतैः ॥

—*Ibid.* example under VIII. 23.

2. विधुरीकुर्वन् कबरीं लुम्पन् मकरीं विसूत्रयन् हारम् ।
वीर विरोधिमृगीदृशि खेलति कामीव ते खड्गः ॥

—*Ibid.* example under VIII. 23.

3. वस्तु किंचिदभिप्रेत्य तत्तुल्यस्यान्यवस्तुनः ।
उक्तिः संक्षेपरूपत्वात् सा समासोक्तिरिष्यते ॥ —KD II. 205.

4 अनुक्तौ समासोक्तिः ॥ —KASV. IV. III 3.

5. यत्रोपमानादेवैतदुपमेयं प्रतीयते ।
अतिप्रसिद्धेस्तामाहुः समासोक्तिं मनीषिणः ॥—SKBh IV. 133.

6. समासोक्तिः परिस्फूर्तिः प्रस्तुतेऽप्रस्तुतस्य चेत् ।
... ... //

—Candrāloka, V. 62.

Page 144. 1. यत्रोक्ते गम्यतेऽन्योर्थस्तत्समानविशेषणः ।
सा समासोक्तिरुद्दिष्टा संक्षिप्तार्थतया यथा ॥

—VJ. III. 147 Antaraśloka.

2. श्लिष्टविशेषणैरुपमानधीः समासोक्तिः ॥ —KAnu. VI. 14.

3. ...रूपके प्रस्तुतोपरञ्जकत्वमेवाप्रस्तुतस्य । यत्रारोप्यमाणपदार्थत्वेनारोपविषयस्य प्रतिभासनादप्राधान्यं तत्र परिणामः । यत्र पुनरारोप्यमाणपदार्थधर्मविशिष्टत्वेन प्रतिभासनादारोपविषयस्य प्राधान्यं तत्रेयम् ।

—Ekā. vṛtti on VIII. 23.

4. विलसति विशेषणानां प्रतीयमानार्थगर्भता यत्र ।
सहृदयहृदयाह्लादी परिकरनामा स निर्दिष्टः ॥

—*Ibid.* VIII. 24.

5. नरसिंह नरेन्द्रेण नन्दनद्रुम-बाहुना ।
धनेशांशावतारेण धन्याः केनार्थिनः कृताः ॥

—*Ibid.* example under VIII. 24.

6. तादृक् किमपि विशेष्यं साभिप्रायत्वमश्नुते यत्र ।
स परिकराङ्कुरनामालंकारः कीर्त्तितः कविभिः ॥

—*Ibid.* VIII. 25.

Page 145. 1. नरसिंह महीपाल कीर्त्तिस्त्रिपथगा तव ।
न कस्य भविता श्लाघ्या पुनाना भुवनत्रयम् ॥

—*Ibid.* example under VIII. 25.

2. नाथः काकोदराणां कथयति लिखति क्ष्मापतिः कार्त्तवीर्यो
मेलानन्दो जलानां निधिरचलपतिर्लेखनी व्योमपत्रम् ।

संख्या दूरे परार्धाद्यदि भवति पुनः किं च वैरिञ्चमायुः
संख्येयत्वं तदानीं दधति तव गुणाः श्रीनृसिंह क्षितीन्द्र ॥

—*Ibid.* example under VIII. 25.

3. श्लेषः प्रसादः समता समाधिर्माधुर्यमोजः पदसौकुमार्यम् ।
अर्थस्य च व्यक्तिरुदारता च कान्तिश्च काव्यस्य गुणा दशैते ॥

—NS. 16. 96.

4 शब्दपरिवर्तनसहिष्णुत्वमर्थश्लेषस्य विषय इति पुनः काव्यप्रकाशकारस्य सिद्धान्तः ॥

—Ekā. vṛtti on VIII. 26.

5. ...काव्ये दोषगुणालङ्काराणां शब्दार्थोभयगतत्वेन व्यवस्थायामन्वयव्यतिरेकावेव प्रभवतः निमित्तान्तरस्याभावात् ततश्च योऽलङ्कारो

यदीयान्वयव्यतिरेकावनुविधत्ते स तदलङ्कारो व्यवस्थाप्यते इति।...
योऽलङ्कारो यदाश्रितः स तदलङ्कार इति कल्पनायां अन्वयव्यति-
रेकावेव समाश्रयितव्यौ। —KP vṛtti on X. 141.

6. यत्र विशेष्यविशेषणसाम्यं स श्लेष एष तु द्वेधा।
किं चास्मिन् वाच्यत्वं विशेष्ययोस्तुल्ययोरेव॥

—Ekā. VIII. 26.

Page 146. 1. कन्दर्पोदयमाश्रयद्भिरलसैः कान्तारसंप्रापितैः
शश्वत्सानुचरैः प्रभूतकनकोतुङ्गक्षयैर्भूषितैः।
राजन् वीर नृसिंह देव भवतोमित्रैः समस्तैरपि
प्राप्यन्ते ननु चित्रमत्र युगपत्तास्ताः पराभूतयः॥

—*Ibid.* example under VIII. 26.

2. निजकरकलितस्वाहं काष्ठाश्लेषोपनीतमाहात्म्यम्।
हम्मीरमानमर्दन भवतस्तेजो विभावसुं जयति॥

—*Ibid.* example under VIII. 26.

3. 'संयोगो विप्रयोगश्च साहचर्यं विरोधिता।
अर्थः प्रकरणं लिङ्गं शब्दस्यान्यस्य संनिधिः॥

सामर्थ्यमौचितीदेशः कालो व्यक्तिः स्वरादयः।
शब्दार्थस्यानवच्छेदे विशेषस्मृतिहेतवः॥'

—(Vākyapadīya of Bhartṛhari) Quoted in K. P. under II. 19.

4. विशेष्यविशेषणसाम्येन पुनर्यत्र प्रकरणादिना प्रकृतार्थ एव शृङ्खलि-
तायामभिधायामप्रकृतार्थाभिधानाय सामर्थ्यविधुरत्वेऽपि शब्दस्या-
प्रकृतार्थोऽपि प्रतीतिसरणिमनुसरति तत्र शब्दशक्तिमूलानुरणनरूप-
व्यङ्ग्यो ध्वनिः। —Ekā. vṛtti on VIII. 26.

5. *Ibid.* example under VIII. 26. (Given in the body of the thesis).

Page 147. 1. यस्मादलङ्कारो, न वस्तुमात्रं यस्मिन् काव्ये शब्दशक्त्या प्रकाशते स
शब्दशक्त्युद्भवो ध्वनिरित्यस्माकं विवक्षितम्। वस्तुद्वये च शब्द-
शक्त्या प्रकाशमाने श्लेषः,...यत्र तु शब्दशक्त्या सामर्थ्याक्षिप्तं
वाच्य व्यतिरिक्तं व्यङ्ग्यमेवालङ्कारान्तरं प्रकाशते स ध्वनेर्विषयः।

—DhL. vṛtti on II. 21.

2. उपमाननेन यत्तत्वमुपमेयस्य साध्यते ।
गुणक्रियाभ्यां नाम्ना च श्लिष्टं तदभिधीयते ।।
लक्षणं रूपकेऽपीदं लक्ष्यते काममत्र तु ।
इष्टः प्रयोगो युगपदुपमानोपमेययोः ।। —KAB. III. 14-15.

3. स धर्मेषु तन्त्रप्रयोगे श्लेषः ।। —KASV. IV-III-7.

4. सामान्यविशेषत्वे सारूप्ये कार्यकारणत्वे च ।
अप्रस्तुतप्रशंसा निर्दिष्टा प्रस्तुतस्य गम्यत्वे ।। —Ekā. VIII. 27.

5. सामान्यविशेषत्वे सामान्याद्विशेषस्य विशेषाद्वा सामान्यस्य प्रतीयमानत्वे द्वैतं कार्यकारणत्वे कार्यात् कारणस्य कारणाद्वा कार्यस्य व्यज्यमानत्वे द्वैविध्यं सारूप्ये त्वेक एव प्रकार इत्यस्याः पञ्च प्रकाराः । —*Ibid.* vṛtti on VIII. 27.

Page 148. 1. दयायै दृक् कर्णः सरसकविसूक्ताय वदनं
सरस्वत्यै पृथ्व्यै भुजशिखरमीशाय हृदयम् ।
इति प्रत्तास्तावत् स्वयमवयवा अप्यविरतं
प्रदेयं किं कस्मै न तव नरसिंह क्षितिपते ।।
—*Ibid.* example under VIII. 27.

2. नृसिंह वसुधाधिप त्वयि रणोन्मुखे धावतः
प्रतीपपृथिवीपतेः पथि पथि प्रदीप्तक्षुधः ।
चिरादगुरवन्ध्यतां दुरवगाहविन्ध्याटवी-
पलाशिविटपाञ्चलाहृतफलार्पणेन द्विपाः ।।
—*Ibid.* example under VIII. 27.

3. क्षीरोदो लवणोदवत् कुमुदिनी नीलोत्पलिन्याकृति-
र्ज्योत्स्ना ध्वान्तमलीमसा मलयजः कालागुरुश्यामलः ।
हंसाः क्रौञ्चसहोदराः किमपरं मुक्ताश्च नीलोपमाः
श्रीमन् वीर नृसिंह देव भवतः कीर्त्तेः स्फुरन्त्यग्रतः ।।
—*Ibid.* example under VIII. 27.

4. बाहुस्ते नरसिंहदेव विजयश्रीकेलिसौधध्वज-
स्तत्रापि प्रलयाग्निधूमरुचिना खड्गेन सख्यं गतः ।
निर्मर्यादविशीर्यमाणविशिखप्राग्भारशात्कारिणि
प्राक्रीडत् समरे सपत्नहरिणाक्षीणां ह हा हा विधिम् ।।
—*Ibid.* example under VIII. 27.

5. एणश्रेणी शशकपरिषच्छल्यकानां कुटुम्बं
केकिव्यूहः श्रयति सुखितां यत्र कुत्रापि कुञ्जे ।
कोऽसौ धन्यः कथय सुकृती पादपोऽभ्रंलिहश्री-
र्यस्य च्छायामयमनुसरत्यातपार्त्तः करीन्द्रः ।।

—Ekā. example under VIII. 27.

Page 149. 1. अप्रस्तुतप्रशंसा स्यादप्रक्रान्तेषु या स्तुतिः ।। —KD. II. 340.

2. किञ्चिदुक्तावप्रस्तुतप्रशंसा ।। —KASV. IV. III. 4.

3. असमानविशेषणमपि यत्र समानेति वृत्तमुपमेयम् ।
उक्तेन गम्यते परमुपमानेनेति साऽन्योक्तिः ।। —KAR VIII. 74

4. अप्रस्तुतोऽपि विच्छित्तिं प्रस्तुतस्यावतारयन् ।
यत्र तत्साम्यमाश्रित्य सम्बन्धान्तरमेव वा ।।
वाक्यार्थो सत्यभूतो वा प्राप्यते वर्णनीयताम् ।
अप्रस्तुतप्रशंसेति कथितासावलंकृतिः ।। —VJ III. 23

5. अप्रस्तुतप्रशंसा स्यादस्तोतव्यस्य या स्तुतिः ।
कुतोऽपि हेतोर्वाच्यिा च प्रत्येतव्या च सोच्यते ।।—SKBh IV 158

6. अप्रस्तुतप्रशंसा या सा सैव प्रस्तुताश्रया ।। —KP. X. 98.

7. अप्रस्तुतप्रशंसायामपि यदा सामान्यविशेषभावान्निमितनिमित्तिभा-
द्वावा अभिधीयमानस्याप्रस्तुतस्य···प्राधान्यम् ।

—DhL. vṛtti on I. 13.

8. सामान्येन विशेषः सामान्यं वा यदा विशेषेण ।
कथितः समर्थ्यतेऽर्थो भवति तदार्थान्तरन्यासः ।— Ekā VIII. 28

Page 150. 1. लक्ष्मीस्ते परिचारिका दश दिशो दास्यस्तवाज्ञापराः
पृथ्वी ते करदायिनी तव गिरांदेवी विनोदास्पदम् ।
गाढं वीर नृसिंह देव निखिलप्रत्यर्थिलक्ष्मीर्मुदा
त्वामालिङ्गति मन्त्रशक्तिमहतां क वा न वश्याः स्त्रियः ।।

—*Ibid.* example under VIII. 28.

2. वीरः सर्वानपि नरपतीञ्छौर्यगाम्भीर्यभाजः
शक्तो जेतुं निशितविशिखैः कार्मुकाणां कदम्बैः ।

एतत् सत्यं भुवनभवनाभोगसाम्राज्यलक्ष्मी-
शिक्षा दक्षो जयति नृपतीनुत्कलक्षोणिपालः ॥
—Ekā. example under VIII. 28.

3. यत्र व्यङ्ग्यस्य सतो हेतोः कार्याभिधानभङ्गीभिः ।
स्यादभिधानं सुधियः पर्यायोक्तं विदुस्तदिदम् ॥ —*Ibid.* VIII. 29.

4. अस्पृष्टाञ्जनसंपदः स्मृतिपथावस्थायिलीलास्मिताः
प्रत्याख्यातवतंसदामरचनास्त्यक्ताङ्गरागश्रियः ।
दूरोद्धतकुरङ्गनाभिमकरीभङ्गास्तरङ्गभ्रुवः
संजाता नरसिंह पार्थिव भवत्प्रत्यर्थिपृथ्वीभुजाम् ॥
—*Ibid.* example under VIII. 29.

Page 151. 1. यद्वाक्यान्तरवक्तव्यं तदन्येन समर्थ्यते ।
येनोपशोभानिष्पत्त्यै पर्यायोक्तं तदुच्यते ॥ — VJ. III. 24.

2. यत्र प्रक्रान्तायां स्तुतौ कथंचित् प्रतीयते निन्दा ।
निन्दायां स्तुतिरथवा सेयं व्याजस्तुतिर्द्विविधा ॥ —Ekā. VIII.30

3. (a) कथंचित् प्रमाणान्तरबाधितत्वेनेति यावत् ।
—*Ibid.* vṛtti on VIII. 30.

(b) प्रमाणान्तरादिति वक्तृवाच्यप्रकरणादिपर्यलोचनात्मनः ।
—AS. Vimarśinī on 37.

4. प्राणेश्वर ! स्वजनतुल्यसुखस्त्वमेवं
त्वय्यभ्युपेतबहुवल्लभताविलासे ।
यन्निर्विवेश रजनीरमणी. सहस्रं
पूर्वेद्युरेष भवदाननबन्धुरिन्दुः ॥
—Ekā. example under VIII. 30.

Page 152. 1. दिङ्मातङ्गाः कनकशिखरी सप्तयः सप्तसप्ते-
श्चिन्तारत्नं दिविचरतरुः श्रीनृसिंह क्षितीन्द्र ।
अद्याप्येतत् सकलमकृथा नार्थिसादित्यपार्थ-
स्तेनायं ते वितरणकलाकौशलेनावलेपः ॥
—*Ibid.* example under VIII. 30.

2. कमपि विशेषं वक्तुं प्रकृतस्योक्तस्य वक्ष्यमाणस्य ।
   यः प्रतिषेधाभासः कथितः सोऽयं द्विधाक्षेपः ॥ —Eka. VIII. 31

3. अपरस्त्वनिष्टविध्याभासस्तस्याभिधीयते भेदः ।
   यत्रानभिमतपिशुनो विधिर्निषेधं प्रकाशयति ॥ —*Ibid.* VIII. 32

Page 153. 1. नाहं दूती भवामि प्रथितपृथुगुण श्रीनृसिंह क्षितीन्द्र
ब्रूमः श्रेयस्करं ते शृणु हरिणदृशो जृम्भमाणेऽङ्गतापे ।
उद्बुद्धं पुण्डरीकैः कुमुदकुवलयैर्मीलित चक्रवाकैः
संतुष्टं किं च जातं ज्वलदनलशिखाभासुरैः सूर्यकान्तैः ॥
—*Ibid.* example under VIII. 31

2. किं त्वां ब्रूमः कृपालुं यदरिमृगदृशां दृष्टयो बाष्पदिग्धाः
किं सद्वृत्तं रमन्ते त्वदुरसि यदरिक्ष्माभुजां वीरलक्ष्म्यः ।
आज्ञां किं ते सुधांशोः श्रियमपहरति त्वद्यशः किं मनस्ते
हिंसाशून्यं त्वयास्मिञ्जगति कृपणतोन्मीलिता श्रीनृसिंह ॥
—*Ibid.* example under VIII. 31

3. क्षणं प्रतीक्षस्व वियोगकातरं
विधाय यावत् प्रिय सुस्थिरं मनः ।
अयं जनः किञ्चिदुदीरयिष्यति
व्रजाथवा तावदुदीरणेन किम् ॥
—*Ibid.* example under VIII. 31

4. कान्तः किं कैरविण्याः कलयति कमलोल्लासने नैष शक्तिं
नाथः किं वासराणामुदयति कुमुदे नैष लक्ष्मीं वितन्वन् ।
किं कृष्णो न द्विजानामधरयति पतिं भूयसोक्तेन किं वा
ज्ञातः पश्चान्नृसिंह क्षितितलतिलक ! त्वं चरित्रैर्विचित्रैः ॥
—*Ibid.* example under VIII. 31

Page 154. 1. त्वं चेद्गच्छसि गच्छ सिध्यतु तवाभीष्टं मृधे वल्लभ
प्रख्यातं तव को न वेद भुजयोरव्याजमोजायितम् ।
किं चैतत् कथनीयमस्ति भुवनोत्तुङ्गः कलिङ्गेश्वरः
संग्रामेऽभिमुखान् निहन्ति न पुनर्वैमुख्यमासेदुषः ॥
—*Ibid.* example under VIII. 32

———

CHAPTER IX

Page 156. 1. विलसद्विरोधगर्भं ब्रूमोऽलंकारवर्गमधुना तु ।
स्फुरति विरोधाभासे भवति विरोधाभिधो दशधा ।।—Ekā. VIII.33

2. जाते जात्यादिभिः साधं चतस्रः प्रथमं भिदाः ।
जायन्ते ताः पुनस्तिस्त्रो गुणस्य च गुणादिभिः ।।
क्रियायाः क्रियया साधं द्रव्येण च भिदा द्वयम् ।
द्रव्यस्य तु भिदैकैव द्रव्येणेति भिदा दश ।। —*Ibid* VIII. 34-35.

3. यशोनिधे वीर नृसिंह देव
करोऽपि कर्णोऽजनि तावकीनः ।
किं चारिनारीजनतापकारी
धराधरस्ते करवाल एषः ।।

—*Ibid*. example under VIII. 35.

4. अश्रान्तविश्राणनकेलिकौतुकः
काम्यो न कस्यैष नृसिंह भूपतिः ।
शौर्योदधेर्यस्य चिराय दन्तिभिः
दिग्दन्तिनोऽष्टावपि वामनीकृताः ।।

—*Ibid*. example under VIII. 35.

Page 157. 1. शैलाः सर्वेऽपि कैलासाः सिन्धवः सुरसिन्धवः ।
नरसिंह महीपाल संजातास्तव कीर्त्तिभिः ।।

—*Ibid*. example under VIII. 35.

2. परदारपरोऽपि त्वं परदारपराङ्मुखः ।
नरसिंह महीपाल विचित्रचरितो भवान् ।।

—*Ibid*. example under VIII. 35.

3. चापस्थितगुणस्यापि गुणैस्तव जगत्त्रयम् ।
व्याप्यतेस्म जगद्वीर नरसिंह नरेश्वर ।।

Ibid. example under VIII. 35.

4. कर्पूरहारनीहारपटीरविशदोऽपि सन् ।
तव वीर यशोराशिः कथं पीताम्बरोऽभवत् ॥

—Ekā. example under VIII. 35.

5. स जयति वीर नृसिंहः प्रतिभटनृपशैलकोटिशतकोटिः ।
यो रञ्जयन्नपि गुणैः सततमुदारं न रञ्जयति ॥

—*Ibid.* example under VIII. 35.

6. विस्मयमसौ नृसिंहः करोति परिपन्थिगन्धगजसिंहः ।
यस्य प्रतापतपनः कुमुदमुदञ्चयति सर्वतोदिक्कम् ॥

—*Ibid.* example under VIII. 35.

7. आयोधनारम्भविजृम्भमाण-
क्षोणीरजोगत्वरशत्रुलोकः ।
उग्रोऽपि कृष्णस्तव खड्ग एष
विराजते वीर नृसिंह देव ॥

—*Ibid.* example under VIII. 35.

8. गुणस्य वा क्रियाया वा विरुद्धान्यक्रियाभिधा ।
या विशेषाभिधानाय विरोधं तं विदुर्बुधाः ॥ —KAB. III 25.

9 यस्मिन्द्रव्यादीनां परस्पर सर्वथा विरुद्धानाम् ।
एकत्रावस्थानं समकालं भवति स विरोधः ॥ —KAR. IX. 30.

10. विरोधोऽनुपपत्तिश्चेद् गुणद्रव्यक्रियादिषु ।
अमन्दचन्दनस्यन्दः स्वच्छन्दं दन्दहीतिमाम् ॥

—Candrāloka, V.74.

Page 158 1. असति प्रसिद्धहेतौ कार्योत्पत्तिर्विभावना भवति । —Ekā VIII.36

2. अयज्ञः स्वर्लोक सुकृतमंतपः क्लेशसुभगं
सुधासारोऽनभ्रः फलमकुसुमश्रीसहचरम् ।
अशौर्यं साम्राज्यं निधिरखननायाससुलभो
नृसिंह क्षोणीन्दो नयनपथमस्माकमगमः ॥

—*Ibid.* example under VIII. 36.

3. भूत्या मासय सर्वतोऽपि विदुषो मुञ्च द्विजिह्वान् वृषं
स्वात्मन्येव निवेशय प्रकटय ज्ञाने तृतीयां दृशम् ।

दुर्गाश्लेषरसं जहीहि जहिहि प्रीतिं च दोषाकरे
लोकोत्तुङ्गकलिङ्गनाथ तदपि ज्ञातो भवानीश्वरः ।.

—Ekā. example under VIII. 36.

4. विशेषोक्तिरिति विशेषं कंचित्प्रतिपादयितुमुक्तिरित्यर्थः ।

—Udyota on KP. X. 108.

5 यदि कारणसाकल्ये कार्यासिद्धिस्तदा विशेषोक्तिः ॥—Ekā.VIII.36.

Page 159. 1. अयं स ते वीर नृसिंह देव
प्रतापभानुः प्रथितोदयश्रीः ।
चित्रं न दत्तेरिपुसुन्दरीणां
विकासलक्ष्मीं नयनाम्बुजेभ्यः ॥

—*Ibid.* example under VIII. 36.

2. उत्तिष्ठ कन्दखननाय गृहाण चापं
गाहस्व काननमिति प्रहितोऽपि वध्वा ।
आकारितोऽपि सहकेलिसखैः किरातै-
रर्दं न वीर विजहाति दरीमरिस्ते ॥

—*Ibid.* example under VIII. 36.

3. ये पतन्ति तव हस्तसीकराः
पाणिशुक्तिविवरे द्विजन्मनाम् ।
उत्कलेन्द्र नवमौक्तिकावली-
स्तत्कलत्रहृदये सृजन्त्यमी ॥

—*Ibid.* example under VIII. 36.

4. हस्ताम्भःकणानां मौक्तिकानुत्पत्तिं प्रति कारणत्वे सत्यपि मौक्तिकानुत्पत्तिर्माभूदिति कारणसद्भावे कार्यानुत्पत्तिरिति विशेषोक्तिरपि । —*Ibid.* vṛtti on VIII. 36.

Page 160 1. उभयोरपि साधकबाधकप्रमाणविरहिण्योः संदेहेन संकरः ।

—*Ibid.* vṛtti on VIII. 36.

2. एकगुणहानिकल्पनायां साम्यदार्ढ्यं विशेषोक्तिः ॥

—KASV. IV-III.-23

3. रूपकं चेदं प्रायेण··· । —*Ibid.* vṛtti on IV-III. 23.

4. एषासङ्गतिरुक्ता हेतोः कार्यस्य भिन्नदेशत्वे ।

—Ekā. VIII. 38.

5. प्रतिभटमुकुटेषु खड्गधारा
परिपतिता भवतो नृसिंह भूप ।
सरभसगलत्तदङ्गनानां
गुरुकुचभारतटी-पटीरपङ्कः ॥

—*Ibid.* example under VIII. 38.

6. आयोधने वीर नृसिंह देव
समुद्धृतेयं भवताऽसिवल्ली ।
म्लाना पुनः शत्रुविलासिनीनां
पयोधरे चन्दनपत्रवल्ली ॥

—*Ibid.* example under VIII. 38.

Page 161. 1. विदूरकार्य्यः सहजः कार्य्यानन्तरजस्तथा ।
युक्तो न युक्त इत्येवमसङ्ख्याश्चित्रहेतवः ॥—SKBh. III. 351.

2. विषमं विरूपघटना विसदृशकार्यानभीष्टयोर्जननम् ॥

—Ekā. VIII. 38.

3. क्व तव नृसिंह देव भुवनत्रयलङ्घि यशः
क्व च कविता मम स्वरसवलितफल्गुपदा ।
इह दिवमारुरुक्षुरहमस्मि तुषारमहः
किरणपरम्परासु रचितैः पदचङ्क्रमणैः ॥

—*Ibid.* example under VIII. 38.

4. राकागर्वितशर्वरी सहचरप्रस्तावसौवस्तिकैः
क्षीराम्भोधितरङ्गकान्तिलहरी वैवर्ण्यकर्णेजपैः ।
चित्रं वीर नृसिंह देव भवतः कीर्तेर्विलासैः कृतः
स्वैरं वैरिवधूमुखे कथमहो मालिन्यमुद्रादरः ॥

—*Ibid.* example under VIII. 38.

Page 162. 1. उदितवति प्रतापतपने तव वैरिवधू
वदनसरोरुहं भवति वीर कलिङ्गपते ।
अपि कलया कयापि न विकासविलासमुपै-
त्यपितु विवर्णतां नयनतापकरीं भजते ॥

—*Ibid.* example under VIII. 38.

2. अस्य प्रथमभिदायाः सममिति कविभिर्विपर्यये कथितम् ।

—Ekā. VIII. 39.

3. (a) इतरभेदद्वयविपर्ययस्य तु तदभावान्नालंकारत्वम् ।

—*Ibid*. vṛtti on VIII. 39.

(b) तद्विपर्ययस्य कारणादनुरूपकार्योत्पत्तिरूपस्य, वाञ्छितार्थ-प्राप्तिरूपस्य च वस्तुसिद्धतया चारुताविरहात् ।···इत्यलङ्कार-सर्वस्वकृतोक्तम् ।

—RG. p. 452.

4. कौमुदीव तुहिनांशुमण्डलं
जाह्नवीव शशिखण्डमण्डनम् ।
पश्य कीर्त्तिरनुरूपमाश्रिता
त्वां विभाति नरसिंह भूपते ॥

—Ekā. example under VIII. 39.

5. कारणविपरीतफलोत्पत्तौ यत्नो विचित्रमित्युक्तम् ।

—*ibid*. VIII 39.

6. मलिनयितुं खलवदनं विमलयति जगन्ति देव कीर्त्तिस्ते ।
मित्राह्लादं कर्त्तुं मित्राय दुह्यति प्रतापोऽपि ॥

—*ibid*. example. under VIII. 39.

Page 163. 1. अधिकमिदं गदितं तद्यत्राननुरूपताश्रयात्रयिणोः ।

—*ibid*. VIII. 40.

2. यदिह न दिशां सीम्नि व्योम्नः स्थलेऽप्यमितं यश-
स्तव कथमपि ज्योत्स्नागौरं नृसिंह नरेश्वर ।
तदिदमखिलं चित्रं पञ्चाशता परमक्षरैः
कृतपरिकरे वाग्व्यापारे निवेशयते कविः

—*ibid*. example under VIII. 40.

3. यत्रान्योन्यविरुद्धं विरुद्धबलवत्क्रियाप्रसिद्धं वा ।
वस्तुद्धयमेकस्माज्जायत इति तद्भवेदधिकम् ॥
यत्राधारे सुमहत्याधेयमवस्थितं तनीयोऽपि ।
अतिरिच्येत कथंचित्तदधिकमपरं परिज्ञेयम् ॥

—KAR. IX. 26, 28.

4. भवति क्रियोपजननं यद्यन्योन्यं तदान्योन्यम् ॥

—Ekā. VIII. 40.

5. पृथ्वी पूर्वापरगिरिधनोतुङ्ग वक्षोजनम्रा
भूषा बाहोरजनि भवत: श्रीनृसिंह क्षितीन्द्र !
बाहुश्चास्या: सुरगजकरस्थूलदीर्घ: समग्रां
कान्तिं पुष्णात्यघटघटनाचातुरीयं विधातु: ।।

—Ekā. example under VIII. 40.

6. आधेयमनधिकरणं युगपद्यद्येकमप्यनेकत्र ।
यदसंभावितवस्त्वन्तरकरणं च त्रिधा विशेषोऽसौ ।।

—*ibid.* VIII. 4I.

Page 164. 1. निपीतोऽयं वीर क्षणमपि विलासस्तव गिरा-
महो यावज्जीवं मनसि विदुषां पल्लवयति ।
रसालानां स्वादं कुवलयदलानां परिमलं
प्रसादं ज्योत्स्नानामपि च शरदारम्भसुहृदाम् ।

—*Ibid.* example under VIII. 41.

2. रणद्गीर्वाणस्त्रीवलयतुमुलोन्नेयसुभट-
स्वयंग्राहोद्ग्राहाद्द्रुतमपगतो वीर समरात् ।
समस्तोऽप्येष त्वां भयविधुर-धीरध्वसु वने
वने शैले शैले पुरि पुरि च पश्यत्यरिजन: ।।

—*ibid.* example under VIII. 41.

3. मन्दारमालोकयितुं गृहीत-
व्रतं मदीयं नयनं यदासीत् ।
तत् साम्प्रतं वीर नृसिंह देव
त्वदीक्षणेनाजनि पूर्णकामम् ।।

—*ibid.* xeample unper VIII, 41.

4. किञ्चित् केनापि यथा विहितं यद्वस्तु तत्ततोऽन्येन ।
क्रियतेऽन्यथा तथैव व्याघातोऽयं समाख्यात: ।।
सौकर्येण निबद्धा कार्यविरुद्धा क्रिया भवेद्यत्र ।
ख्यातोऽभिमतव्याहतिहेतुर्व्याघात एषोऽपि ।।

—*ibid* VIII. 42-43.

Page 165. 1. तेजसा जगतस्तापं कृतं किरणमालिना ।
नरसिंह, महीपाल तेजसैव निरस्यति ।।

—*Ibid.* example under VIII. 42.

2. जटाबन्धं वल्कावरणमपि तीव्रातपकृत-
स्थिति कुर्वन् कल्पद्रुम सुचिरमुग्रं चर तपः :
अथेदं मा चारी: कथमपि कदाचिन्न भविता
नृसिंह क्षोणीन्दोरिव वितरण हन्त भवतः ॥

—Ekā. example under VIII. 43.

3. जयश्रियं प्राप्तुमकामयन्त
नृसिंह युद्धैस्तव वैरिवीराः ।
त्वया तु चक्रीकृतकार्मुकेण
सुरश्रियं सगभितास्ततस्ते ॥

—*ibid.* example under VIII. 43.

4. इत्थं निरूप्य कतिचिद्विरोधगर्भानलङ्कारान् ।
कथयामो वयमधुनालङ्कारान् शृंखलाकारान् ॥

—*Ibid.* VIII. 44.

5. यद्यत्पूर्वं तत्तद्यथोत्तरं चेत् क्रमेण संश्रयति ।
हेतुत्वं, भवति तदा कारणमालेत्यलङ्कारः ॥

—*Ibid.* VIII. 44.

6. वितरणे करुणा तव कारणं
वितरणं सुकृतस्य निबन्धनम् ।
सुकृतहेतु यशो यशसा न किं
भवति वीर नृसिंह महीपते ॥

—*Ibid.* example under VIII. 45.

Page 166. 1. यत्र विशेषणभावं पूर्वं पूर्वं प्रति क्रमेणैव ।
भजति परं परमेषालंकृतिरेकावली कथिता ॥

—*Ibid.* VIII. 46.

2. राज्ञां सभाः सकवयः कवयो निसर्ग-
सारस्वतप्रसरनिर्मितरम्यकाव्याः ।
काव्यानि वर्णितभवच्चरितान्यतीव
चित्राणि वीर भवतश्चरितानि भान्ति ॥

—*Ibid.* example under VIII. 46.

3. यत्रोत्तरोत्तरगुणावहत्वमुल्लसति पूर्वपूर्वस्य ।
तदिदं मालादीपकमित्याम्नातं विपश्चिद्भिः ॥ —Ekā. VIII. 47.

4. तव क्रियन्ते करुणाकटाक्षैः
श्रियः कवीनां नरसिंह भूप ।
ताभिर्विकासा मनसः पुनस्तैः
सूक्तानि तैस्त्वद्गुणवर्णनानि ॥

—*Ibid*. example under VIII. 47.

5. वस्तुस्पृहणीयत्वे विश्रान्ति चेद्यथोत्तरं तनुते ।
सारो नाम तदानीं कथितोऽलङ्कारसारज्ञैः ॥—*Ibid*. VIII. 48.

6. एके चन्द्रकलावचूडमपरे मौलौ तदीये स्थितां
स्वर्गङ्गामितरे तदाश्रितपदाम्भोजं मधुध्वंसिनः ।
सर्वे तन्मनसि स्थितां श्रियमनुध्यायन्ति सैषापि यद्
भ्रूभङ्गैकवशंवदा स जयति श्रीमान् नृसिंहो नृपः ॥

—*Ibid*. example under VIII. 48.

Page 167. 1. अन्तर्विष्णोस्त्रिलोकी निवसति फणिनामीश्वरे सोऽपिशेते
सिन्धोः सोऽप्येकदेशे तमपि चुलुकयां कुम्भयोनिश्चकार ।
धत्ते खद्योतलीलामयमपि गगने श्रीनृसिंह क्षितीन्द्र
त्वत्कीर्त्तेः कर्णनीलोत्पलमिदमपि च प्रेक्षणीयं विभाति ॥

—*Ibid*. example under VIII. 48.

2. वाक्यार्थो यदि हेतुर्भवति पदार्थो विशेषणद्वारा ।
द्विविधं कथयन्ति तदालंकारं काव्यलिङ्गमिति ॥

—*Ibid*. VIII. 49.

3. अलं भोः पौलोमीसहचरपुरीवारमहिलाः
कुचाभोगे कालगुरुभिरफलस्थासकविधिः ।
कलिङ्गेन्दोः कीर्तिस्त्रिदशपरिषद्गीतमहिमा
समन्ताद्गात्रं वः सरसमनुलिम्पत्यविरलम् ॥

—*Ibid*. example under VIII. 49.

4. त्वद्वैरिक्षितिपालसौधवलभी रिञ्छोलिशालामधु-
च्छत्रोड्डीनसरोषघोरसंरघादंशव्यथाव्याकुलाः ।
मन्दाः स्यन्दनवाजिनः प्रतिपथप्रस्थानदौस्थ्य मुहुः
क्षोणीपालनृसिंह देव नितरां कुर्वन्ति भासां प्रभोः ॥

—*Ibid*. example under VIII. 49.

Page 168. 1. Quoted in the body of the thesis.

2. अनुमतमनुमानमिदं यत्र स्तः साध्यसाधने कथिते ।—Ekā. VIII.50

3. नरसिंह महीपाल विश्वस्त्वां मकरध्वजम् ।
मार्गणास्तव संजाताः कथं सुमनसोऽन्यथा ।।

—*Ibid.* example under VIII. 50.

4. सन्दिग्धसाध्यवान् पक्षः ।—Tarakasaṅgraha, p. 43

5. निश्चितसाध्यवान् सपक्षः ।—*Ibid.* p. 43

6. निश्चितसाध्याभाववान् विपक्षः ।—*Ibid.* p. 44

Page 169. 1. कार्याणि कारणगुणान् न परित्यजन्ती-
त्यव्याप्तमाहुरिह वीर नृसिंह देव ।
न्यग्गत्वरेण तव दानजलेन सूता
मेरोः शिखामपि विलङ्घ्य विभाति कीर्त्तिः ।।

—Ekā. example under VIII. 50.

Page 170. 1. यथासंख्यमनुदेशः समानाम् ।।

—Aṣṭādhyāyī, I-III. . 10.

2. प्रथमं निर्दिष्टानां यस्मिन्नर्थान्तराश्रयोऽर्थानाम् ।
अनुनिर्देशो भवति क्रमेण तत् स्याद्यथासंख्यम् ।।—Ekā. VIII.50.

3. आयामश्लाघनीयं किमभिमतफलप्रापकं किं प्रियं किं
विस्तीर्णं किं स्थिरं किं विमलमथ च किं श्रूयतां श्रीनृसिंह ।
दोस्तम्भस्त्यागलीलामितवचनमुरो राजलक्ष्मीर्यशस्ते
नाहीशो न द्युशाखी न मधु न गगनं नाद्रिनाथो न चन्द्रः ।।

—*Ibid.* example under VIII. 50.

4. एकस्मिन् यदनेकं क्रमादनेकत्र वा भवत्येकम् ।
तमलंकारनिरूपणनिपुणाः पर्यायमब्रुवत् ।। —*Ibid.* VIII. 51.

5. काश्मीरपांसुरुचिरांशुकचारुहारै-
र्या प्राग्बभौ कुचतटी रिपुसुन्दरीणाम् ।
सैवाद्य भाति कुपिते त्वयि वीर भूभृ-
द्धातुच्छटातरुपलाशकरक्तसूत्रैः ।।

—*Ibid.* example under VIII. 51.

6. प्रागासीन्मकरन्दपिच्छिलतले पद्मस्य गर्भे ततः
शौरेः कौस्तुभकान्तिपूरसुभगाभोगे भुजाभ्यन्तरे ।

आवासस्तव लक्ष्मि संप्रति पुनर्निव्याजमूर्च्छत्कृपा-
स्त्रोतः शीतलिते नृसिंहवसुधानाथस्य नेत्राञ्चले ॥

—Ekā. example under VIII. 51.

Page 171. 1. नरसिंह महीपाल मदान्धास्तव दन्तिनः ।
दवात्यरिनरेन्द्रेभ्यो दिवमाददते भुवम् ॥

—*Ibid.* example under VIII. 52.

2. तनौ दत्वा पाकोन्मुखशरसखीं कामपि रुचं
रिपुस्त्रीभ्यस्तासां कलयसि कलिङ्गक्षितिपते ।
प्रभां ताटङ्कानां श्रवणकुसुमानां विलसितं
स्मितानामालोकं स्तनमलयजानां श्रियमपि ॥

—*Ibid.* example under VIII. 52.

3. प्रतिभटधरणिपतिभ्यो नाराचपरम्पराः शिताः दत्वा ।
हरसि नृसिंह नरेश्वर तज्जयलक्ष्मीकटाक्षपरिपाटीः ॥

– *Ibid.* example under VIII .52.

4. विशिष्टस्य यदादानमन्यापोहेन वस्तुनः ।
अर्थान्तरन्यासवती परिवृत्तिरसौ यथा ॥—KAB. III.41.

Page 172. 1. क्रियते परिवृत्तेश्च किंचिद्रूपनिदर्शनम् ॥—KD. II. 355.

2. युगपद्दानादाने अन्योन्यं वस्तुनोः क्रियेते यत् ।
क्वचिदुपचर्येते वा प्रसिद्धितः सेति परिवृत्तिः ॥—KAR. VII. 77

3. व्यत्ययो वस्तुनो यस्तु यो वा विनिमयो मिथः ।
परिवृत्तिरिहोक्ता सा काव्यालङ्कारलक्षणे ॥ —SKBh. III. 103.

4. पर्यायविनिमयो परिवृत्तिः ॥—KAnu. VI. 22

5. परेर्वर्जने ॥

—Aṣṭādhyāyī, VIII-I. 5.

6. (a) परिशब्दो वर्जनार्थः । संख्या बुद्धिः । तेन वर्जनबुद्धिरित्यन्वर्था संज्ञा ।

—Kāvyapradīpa Prabhā (Vaidyanātha Bhaṭṭa) on Kāvya Pradīpa, X. 34.

(b) कस्यचित्परिवर्जनेन कुत्रचित्संख्यानं वर्णनीयत्वेन गणनं परिसंख्या । —AS. vṛtti on 63.

7. एकस्यानेकत्र प्राप्तावेकत्र यो भवेन्नियमः ।
ख्याता सा परिसंख्या संख्यावद्भिश्चतुर्भेदा ॥—Ekā. VIII. 53.

8. Supra IX. 3 on p. 170.

9. अङ्गेष्वाभरणं नृसिंह नृपते किं किं त्वयाङ्गीकृतं
मौलौ चन्द्रकलावचूडचरणद्वन्द्वं श्रुतं कर्णयोः ।
वक्त्रे वागधिदेवता मधुरिमा कण्ठे भुजे विक्रमः
कारुण्यं हृदये करे वितरणं पादे रिपुक्ष्माभुजः ॥

—Ekā. example under VIII. 54.

Page 173. 1. लोकेऽस्मिन् नरसिंह देव नृपतिर्दाता न कल्पद्रुम-
स्तेजस्वी स न पद्मिनी सहचरः कान्तः स नो चन्द्रमाः ।
गम्भीरः स न वाहिनी परिवृढस्तुङ्गः स नो मन्दरः
शिल्पज्ञः स न पद्मभूः किमपरं वाग्मी स नो वाक्पतिः ॥

—*Ibid.* example under VIII. 54.

2. विद्यासु तृष्णा व्यसनं कलासु
दाने विनोदः समरे विहारः ।
कीर्त्तौ रतिः काव्यकथासु राग-
स्तवैव जागर्ति नृसिंह देव ॥

—*Ibid.* example under VIII. 54.

3. दण्डापूपिकया यत् स्यादेवार्थान्तरापतनम् ।
अर्थापत्तिरियं सा कथितालंकारपारगैर्द्वेधा ॥—*Ibid.* VIII. 55.

4. अकलङ्कमपि द्विषद्वधू-
वदनेन्दुं मलिनं वितन्वते ।
तव वीर नृसिंह कीर्त्तयः
सकलङ्कं किमुतेन्दुमण्डलम् ॥

—*Ibid.* example under VIII. 55.

Page 174 .1. आपातालं निबिडघटितान् कम्पयत्येतदुच्चै-
र्मूर्च्छल्लम्बापटहरटितं स्थावरानप्यशेषान् ।
एतांस्तूलीसमभुजबलान् जङ्गमान् भूभृतस्तान्
यात्रारम्भे तव किमु पुनः श्रीनृसिंह क्षितीन्द्र ॥

—*Ibid.* example under VIII. 55.

2. न वेति विभाषा ॥

—Aṣṭādhyāyī, I-I-43.

3. (i) वृत्तयः पञ्चतय्यः क्लिष्टाऽक्लिष्टाः ॥

(ii) प्रमाणविपर्ययविकल्पनिद्रास्मृतयः ।।

(iii) तत्र शब्दार्थज्ञानविकल्पैः संकीर्णा सवितर्का समापत्तिः ।।

—**Yoga Darśana, I-5, 6, 42.**

4 तुल्प्रमाणवैशिष्ट्यात् प्राप्तावेकत्र यौगपद्येन ।
उभयोः समानबलयोः स्फुरति विरोधे विकल्प इत्युक्तः ।।

—**Ekā. VIII. 56.**

5. त्वद्विप्रयोगे परितप्यमाना
मृणालमृद्वी मदनज्वरेण ।
इत्थं कथंचिद्बत वेपमाना
ब्रूते सखी वीर नृसिंह देव ॥
अस्त्युत्तरस्यां दिशि देवतात्मा
हिमालयो नाम नगाधिराजः
किमत्र गच्छामि करोमि किंवा
प्रवालशय्याशरणं शरीरम् ।।

—***Ibid.*** **example under VIII. 56.**

6. यद्भवति यौगपद्यं गुणक्रियाणां समुच्चयः स स्यात् ।
एषोऽदर्शि विकल्पप्रतिभटभूतो द्विधास्माभिः ।।
एकेन क्रियमाणं यत्रान्यः स्पर्धयैव तत् कुरुते ।
सोऽपि समुच्चयभेदः कथितोऽन्यस्तत्करो द्वैधम् ।।

—***Ibid.*** **VIII. 57-58.**

Page 175 1. अभूद्यशो वीर तवेन्दुसुन्दरं
द्विषां मषीवर्णमभूच्च दुर्यशः ।
विरुद्धकार्यद्वयकारि कौतुकं
रजः करोति स्म धुतं तुरङ्गमैः ।

—***Ibid.*** **example under VIII. 57.**

2. स्वः सिन्धौ विबुधेन्द्रविभ्रमवने खे हाटकाद्रौ दिशां
कण्ठे वीर नृसिंह देव भवतः कीर्त्तेः परिस्फूर्त्तयः ।
डिण्डीरप्रकरन्ति फुल्लकलिका भारन्ति तारावधू-
नाथांशुप्रसरन्ति निर्जरसरित्पूरन्ति हारन्ति च ।।

—***Ibid.*** **example under VIII. 57.**

3. मूर्त्तिः कन्दर्पदर्पज्वरभरदमनी कीर्त्तिरुन्निद्रचन्द्र-
ज्योत्स्नाहंकारभङ्गव्यसनकुतुकिनी भूपते श्रीनृसिंह ।
लक्ष्मीर्जागर्ति लक्ष्मीपतिमददमनी तासु गर्वाय पुंसा-
मेकापि स्यात्तवैताः किमिदमुपशमारम्भमुज्जृम्भयन्ते ।।
—Ekā. example under VIII. 58.

4. कार्पण्यैकनिकेतनं नृपतयो दौर्जन्यभाजो बुधाः
सन्तः क्षीणधनाः कृपानमिमुखो लोकः कठोरः कलिः ।
शक्यन्ते विपदः किमत्र कविभिः सोढुं भवेयुर्यदि
स्वैरं वीर नृसिंह देव भवता नैताः समुन्मीलिताः ।।
—*Ibid.* example under VIII. 58.

5. सम्यक् आधिः आधानम् उत्पादनम् समाधिरित्यन्वर्थेयं संज्ञा ।
—Skt. Commentary, Bālabodhinī on KP. X. 125.

Page 176. 1. केनचित् कर्त्तुमुपक्रान्तस्य कारणान्तरव्यतिकरतः सौकर्यं सम्यगाधीयते इति यथार्थाभिधानः समाधिनामायमलंकारः समुच्चयसादृश्यात् तदनन्तरं निर्दिष्टः । —Ekā vṛtti on VIII 59.

2. हेत्वन्तरसंबन्धात् स्फूर्जति कार्यस्य यत्र सौकर्यम् ।
स समुच्चयसादृश्यात् समाधिनामात्र निर्दिष्टः ।।—*Ibid.* VIII. 59.

4. लावण्यमेव सहजं तव मानिनीनां
चेतः प्रसादयति वीर नृसिंह देव ।
तन्वन्ति पञ्चमचमत्कृतिकोमलानि
साहायकं किमपि कोकिलकूजितानि ।।
—*Ibid.* example under VIII. 59.

4. किंचिदारभमाणस्य कार्यं दैववशात् पुनः ।
तत्साधनसमापत्तिर्या तदाहुः समाहितम् ।। —KD. II. 298.

5. अन्यधर्मस्ततोऽन्यत्र लोकसीमानुरोधिना ।
सम्यगाधीयते यत्र स समाधिः स्मृतोयथा ।। —*Ibid* I. 93.

6. रसभावतदाभासवृत्तेः प्रशमवर्धनम् ।
अन्यानुभावनिः शून्यरूपं यत्तत्समाहितम् । —KASS. IV. 7.

7. यत्सादृश्यं तत्सम्पत्तिः समाहितम् ।। —KASV. IV-III 29.

8. काय्यरिम्भे सहायाप्तिर्दैवादैवकृतेह या ।
आकस्मिकी बुद्धिपूर्वोभयी वा तत् समाहितम् ॥

—SKBh. III. 132.

Page 177. 1. निर्णयालंकारान् कतिचिदिमांस्तर्कवाक्यनयमूलान् ।
लौकन्यायाश्रयिणः केचिदिदानीं निरूप्यन्ते ॥ —Ekā. VIII. 60.

2. अनीकं सैन्यं तस्य प्रतिनिधिः प्रत्यनीकम् ।

—*Ibid.* vṛtti on VIII. 61.

3. बलिनं जेतुमनीशः काऽपि तदीयं कृशं तिरस्कुरुते ।
अन्यं कमपि जघन्यो यत्राहुः प्रत्यनीकमिदम् ॥ —*Ibid.* VIII. 61.

4. सुधाकरो वीर नृसिंह देव
यशो विलासैर्ग्लपितानुभावः ।
तवाननस्य प्रियबान्धवाना-
मपाकरोति श्रियमम्बुजानाम् ॥

—*Ibid.* example under VIII. 61.

5. उपमानस्याक्षेपः स्यादुपमेत्वकल्पनं यद्वा ।
यत्र प्रतीपमेतद्विबुधैरभिधीयते द्विविधम् ॥ —*Ibid* VIII 62.

6. कान्तिः स्वभावसुभगैव तवाङ्गरागः
प्रत्यग्रकुङ्कुमरसः खलु मङ्गलाय ॥
आसीः कलिङ्गनृपते भुवनोत्सवाय
प्रीणातु कैरवकुलानि परं सुधांशुः ॥

—*Ibid.* example under VIII. 62.

Page 178. 1. त्वद्दोर्दण्डधुरन्धरः फणिपतिस्वन्नेत्रमित्रं श्रियः
क्रीडापङ्करुहं त्वदाननरुचिस्पर्धी सुधादीधितिः ।
त्वद्गाम्भीर्यनिधिः पयोनिधिरसौ त्वत्कीर्त्तितुल्या वियत्
सिन्धुर्वीरं नृसिंह देव महिमा सर्वोपमानं तव ॥

—*Ibid.* example under VIII. 62.

2. दानैस्त्वयि प्रीणित जीवलोके
सुधायमासीन्नरसिंह देव ।

इत्यालवालस्य मिषेण वेधाः
कल्पद्रुमं कुण्डलनामनैषीत् ।।

—Ekā. example under VIII. 62.

3. स्वाभाविकमागन्तुकमथवा वस्त्वन्तरं तिरोधत्ते ।
यस्मिन् किञ्चन वस्तु ज्ञेयं तन्मीलितं द्विविधम् ।।

—*Ibid.* VIII. 63.

Page 179. 1. विश्राणनैः कालकलानभिज्ञै-
विनोद्यमानस्य निसर्गसिद्धैः ।
नृसिंह भूपाल न तेऽधिगन्तुं
पात्रेषु शक्याः परितोषलीलाः ।।

—*Ibid.* example under VIII. 63.

2. आलिङ्ग्यमानस्य वधूजनस्य
प्रतीपभूपस्य नृसिंह देव ।
त्वत्सैन्यघोषश्रवणेन जाता
सवेपथोनैव विभाविता भीः ।।

—*Ibid.* example under VIII. 63.

3. साधारणगुणयोगाद्यत्र प्रकृतस्य वस्तु संवलितम् ।
न विभावयितुं शक्यं तत् सामान्यं समाख्यातम् ।।

—*Ibid.* VIII. 64.

4. धराधिप श्रीनरसिंह देव ।
यशोविलासे तव जृम्भमाणे ।
विधुन्तुदो वेत्ति न शीतभानुं
नागाधिनाथं च न वैनतेयः ।।

—*Ibid.* example under VIII. 64.

Page 180. 1. अधिकगुणाङ्गीकरणं स्वगुणत्यागेन तद्गुणः कथितः ।

—*Ibid.* VIII. 65.

2. वीर त्वद्रिपुरमणी परिधातुं पल्लवानि संस्पृश्य ।
न हरति वनभुवि निजकररुहरुचि खचितानि पाण्डुपत्रधिया ।।

—*Ibid.* example under VIII. 65.

3. नृत्यद्भर्गाट्टहासप्रसरसहचरैस्तावकीनैर्यशोभि-
धर्वल्यं नीयमाने त्रिजगति परितः श्रीनृसिंह क्षितीन्द्र !
नेदृग्यद्येष नाभीकमलपरिमलः प्रौढिमासादयिष्य-
द्देवानां नाभविष्यत् कथमपि कमलाकामुकस्यावबोधः ॥

—Ekā. example under VIII. 65.

Page 181. 1. सति हेतौ तद्रूपाननुहारोऽतद्गुणः कथितः ॥

—*Ibid* VIII.65.

2. गण्डाभोगे विहरति मदैः पिच्छिले दिग्गजानां
वैरिस्त्रीणां नयनकमलेष्वञ्जनानि प्रमार्ष्टि ।
यद्यप्येषा हिमकर कराद्वैतसौवस्तिकी ते
कीर्त्तिदिक्षु स्फुरति तदपि क्ष्मापते श्रीनृसिंह ॥

—*Ibid.* example under VIII. 65.

3. यत्र प्रश्नपुरः सरमेवासंभाव्यमुत्तरं किमपि ।
असकृद्भवति निबद्धं तदुत्तरं तावदत्रैकम् ॥ —*Ibid.* VIII. 66.

Page 182. 1. यत्र त्वनुपनिबद्धः प्रश्नः स्यादुत्तरोन्नेयः ।
कमपि तदीयं भेदं द्वितीयमाचक्षते सुधियः ॥ —*Ibid* VIII. 67.

2. 'का विसमा देव्वगई किं दुल्लहं जं जणो गुणग्गाही ।
किं सोक्खं सुकलत्तं किं दुक्खं जं खलो लोओ ॥'

—*Ibid.* example under VIII. 66.

Skt. version of the above verse :
का विषमा दैवगतिः किं दुर्लभं यज्जनो गुणग्राही ।
किं सौख्यं सुकलत्रं किं दुःखं यत् खलोलोकः ॥

3 तावत् कुतश्चन्द्रमयूरवभूषाः
सौधाङ्गणे प्रेयसि न प्रदोषाः ।
तस्योत्कलक्षोणिपतेः प्रतापो
जागर्त्ति यावत् ककुभां मुखेषु ॥

—*Ibid.* example under VIII. 67.

4. यत्र प्रश्नपुरःसरमुत्तरमुभयोर्मिथः समुल्लसति ।
प्रश्नोत्तरिकासंज्ञं तमलंकारं विदुर्विबुधाः ॥ —*Ibid.* VIII. 68.

5. पीतः केनासि रत्नाकर कथय बलान्मूर्ध्नि कालिन्दि कृष्टा
केन त्वं मा च कोपीः कुतुकमभिदधे वर्णं एवं वदामि ।
धावन्त्येते नृसिंहक्षितिपतिपृतनादग्धविद्वेषिवेश्म-
ज्वालाहेवाकहेलाहतकनकगिरिस्यन्दवारां प्रवाहाः ॥
—Ekā. example under VIII. 68.

Page 183. 1. अथ वत्गद्गूढार्थप्रतीत्यलंकारलक्षणं भावि ।
गदितमिदं मंलक्षितसूक्ष्मार्थस्य प्रकाशनं सूक्ष्मम् ॥—*Ibid.* VIII.69

2. नवेषु कान्तेषु कृताभिलाषाः स्वर्गाङ्गनाः प्रेक्ष्य मरीचिमाली ।
नृसिंह भूपाल तवाहवेषु कम्पाकुलं दर्शयति स्वबिम्बम् ॥
—*Ibid.* example under VIII. 69.

3. यत्रोद्भिन्नं किञ्चिद्वस्तु कुतश्चिन्निगूह्यते भूयः ।
वस्त्वन्तरनिक्षेपाद व्याजोक्तिं तामुशन्त्येताम् ॥—*Ibid.* VIII. 70.

4. आकर्ण्योत्कलभूपते जलमुचां निर्घोषमाकस्मिकं
त्वत्सेनापटहभ्रमेण सहसा संजातकम्पाकुलैः ।
अन्तर्भीतिपराहतोऽपि दयिताकण्ठग्रहक्रीडया
सान्द्रानन्दमयीं दशामभिनयत्यङ्गैः शकाधीश्वरः ॥
—*Ibid.* example under VIII. 70.

Page 184. 1. वाक्यं यदन्यथोक्तं केनाप्यन्येन योज्यतेऽपरथा ।
तत् काकुश्लेषाभ्यां यदि वक्रोक्तिस्तदा स्फुरति ॥—*Ibid.* VIII.71.

2. सर्वार्थिनामर्थितपूरणार्थं
परिस्फुरत्त्यागमहोत्सवेषु ।
त्वयि स्थिते वीर नृसिंह देव
न लज्जते संप्रति पारिजातः ॥
—*Ibid.* example under VIII 71.

3. किं मे रोषं करोषि प्रियतम किमहं तोयराशेस्तनूजा
न क्रोधस्ते विधातुं भवति समुचितः प्राप्यते कुत्र नक्रः ।
इत्थं वक्रोक्तिभङ्ग्या हिमगिरिसुतया लम्भितो मूकभावं
देवश्चन्द्रार्धचूडस्तव दिशतु मुदं भूपते श्रीनृसिंह ॥
—*Ibid.* example under VIII. 71.

4. वस्तुस्वभाव उच्चैर्यः स्यात् सूक्ष्मो यथावदेतस्य ।
यद्वद्यावर्णनमेषा कथिता कविभिः स्वभावोक्ति ॥—Ekā. VIII.72.

5 ऊर्ध्वं भुजाभ्यां परिरभ्य जानु-
द्वयं तदन्तश्चिबुकं निवेश्य ।
नृसिंह झञ्झानिलवेपितः सन्
वने रिपुः सीदति तावकीनः ॥
—*Ibid.* example under VIII. 72.

Page 185. 1. भूतस्य भाविनो वाया प्रत्यक्षायमाणतार्थस्य ।
विलसति सुतरामेतन्निगद्यते भाविकं कविभिः ॥—*Ibid.* VIII. 73

2. वामं बाहुं विधाय द्विगुणितमुरसि स्पष्टमाबद्धमुष्टिं
धृत्वा शङ्कुं करेण स्फुरदधरपुटस्ताम्रनेत्राञ्चलश्रीः ।
क्षिप्त्वा क्षिप्त्वा धरट्टे परुषकटकटत्कारशीर्यत्करोटीन्
छत्रून् पक्षान्निवान्तः स्फुरसि भुजभृतां भूपते श्रीनृसिंह ॥
—*Ibid.* example under VIII. 73.

Page 186. 1. उत्कर्षेणादीयते गृह्यते स्मेत्युदात्तम् ।
—K.P. Sanskrit Commentary Bālabodhinī on KP.X.115.

2. अभिमतमेतदुदात्तं समृद्धिमद्वस्तु वर्णनं यत्र । —Ekā. VIII. 74.

3. दासीभिः प्रतिसारितानि परितस्त्वन्मार्गण प्राङ्गण-
क्षोणिस्वस्तिकमौक्तिकानि वणिजामादाय वृन्दैर्मुदा ।
विक्रीतानि नृसिंह देव तरसा देशेषु देशेषु ते
मूर्त्तानीव यशांसि राजरमणीकण्ठे लभन्ते स्थितिम् ॥
—*Ibid.* example under VIII. 74.

4. वेलाकाननमग्रतः कलयत श्लाघ्यं कलिङ्गेशितुः
प्रौढैर्यत्र चमूभटैः प्रतिभटाहंकारकूलङ्कषैः ।
वीरश्रीपुलकैः शिलीमुखशतैराचान्तरोदस्तटैः
कीर्त्तेरर्णवलङ्घनाय घटितः सान्द्रक्रमः सङ्क्रमः ॥
—*Ibid.* example under VIII. 74.

5. अथ सर्वेषामन्योन्याश्लेषपेशलावधुना ।
कथयामोऽलंकारौ सहृदयचेतश्चमत्कृतये ॥
एषां तिलतण्डुलवन्मिश्रत्वेनाम्यधायि संसृष्टि. ।—*Ibid.*VIII.75-76

Page 187. 1. कथितस्तु संकरोऽयं त्रिविधो यः क्षीरनीर-वद्भवति ॥

—Ekā. VIII. 76.

2. उत्तुङ्गा गिरिराजवत् सुविततः क्ष्माचक्रवत् पावना-
गङ्गावारिवदुज्वला स्फटिकवत्तापच्छिदश्चन्द्रवत् ।
गम्भीराः जलराशिवत् त्रिभुवनव्याप्तिक्षमाः शंभुवद्
राजन्ते नरसिंह देव भवतः प्रोद्दामकीर्त्तिक्रमाः ॥

—*Ibid*. example under VIII. 76.

3. मन्दारस्य मदच्युति दिनमणेरौद्धत्यनिर्मूलनं
मेरोर्मानविमर्दनं रतिपतेरुत्सेकनिष्कासनम् ।
अम्भोभर्त्तुरहंकृतिप्रशमनं शक्रस्य गर्वक्षतिं
सृष्ट्वा त्वां नरसिंह देव गुणिनं किं किं न धात्रा कृतम् ॥

—*Ibid*. example under VIII. 76.

4. एतावन्तमनेहसं सकुतुकं संवधिता यैर्वयं
क्वैते नः प्रभवो गता इति नभश्चूडास्पृशः शाखिनः ।
औत्सुक्यान्मकरन्दवाष्पभरितैः पुष्पेक्षणैस्त्वद्रिपु-
क्षोणीन्द्रान्नरसिंह देव नृपते पश्यन्ति सौधाद्बहिः ॥

—*Ibid*. example under VIII. 76.

5. एष चिन्तामणिः किं नु किन्वयं कल्पपादपः ।
किं न्वसौ कामधेनुर्वा न चेत्त्यागः किमीदृशः ॥

—*Ibid*. example under VIII. 76.

Page 188. 1. प्रतिभटकान्ताकुचतटमकरीलुण्टाकचापटङ्कारः ।
वीर नृसिंह इवाजौ वीरनृसिंहश्चिरं जयति ॥

—*Ibid*. example under VIII. 76.

———

BIBLIOGRAPHY

Sanskrit Original Books

Agnipurāṇa, Kāśī Sanskrit Series, 174, Benaras, 1966.

Alaṁkārasarvasva (Ruyyaka), Motilal Benarsidass, Delhi, 1965

Alaṁkāraśekhara (Keśavamiśra), Haridāsa Granthamālā No 56, VS. 1948.

Arthaśāstra (Kauṭilya), Paṇḍit Pustakālaya, Kāśī, VS. 2016.

Aṣṭādhyāyī (Pāṇini), Aṣṭādhyāyaī Prakāśikā, Samrat Press, Delhi, VS. 2026.

Uttararāmacarita (Bhavabhūti), Motilal Benarsidas, Delhi, 1962.

Ekāvalī (Vidyādhara), Bombay Sanskrit Series, 1903.

Kāvyaprakāśa (Mammaṭa)—

(i) with Sanskrit Commentary of Jhalakīkara, Bhaṇḍārkar Oriental Research Institute, 1950.

(ii) with Hindi Commentary of Viśveśvara, Vārāṇasī, 1969.

Tenth Ullāsa of Kāvyaprakāśa (S. S. Sukthāṅkara)—Publishing House, Bombay, 1941.

Kāvyālaṁkāra (Bhāmaha), Kāśī Sanskṛit Series, 1903.

Kāvyādarśa (Daṇḍin), Bhaṇḍārakara Oriental Research Institute, 1970.

Kāvyālaṁkāra (Rudraṭa), Vidyābhavan Rāṣṭrabhāṣā Granthamālā, 136, Benaras, 1966.

Kāvyālaṁkārasūtravṛttiḥ (Vāmana), Kāśī Sanskrit Series, 209, Benaras, 1971.

Kāvyānuśāsana (Hemacandra), Śrī Mahāvīr Jaina Vidyālaya, Bombay, 1938.

Kāvyāmīmāṁsā (Rājaśekhara), Oriental Institute, Baroda, 1934.

Kirātārjunīyam (Bhāravi), Nirṇayasāgar Press, Bombay, 1954.

Kumārasāmbhava (Kālidāsa), Kālidāsa Granthāvalī, Bhārata Prakāśana Mandir, Aligarh, VS. 2019.

Kāvyālaṁkārasārasaṅgraha (Udbhaṭa), Hindi Sāhitya Sammelan, Prayāga, 1966.

Kāvyapradīpa (Govindaṭhakkura), Nirnaya Sagar, Bombay, 1912.

Gāthāsaptaśati, Prasāda Prakāśana, Pune, 1956.

Candrāloka (Jayadeva), Motilal Benarsidass, Delhi, 1965.

Citramīmāṁsā (Appayya Dīkṣita), Vāṇivihāra, Vārāṇasī, 1965.

Tarkadīpikā (Annamabhaṭṭa) (A Sanskrit Commentary on Tarkasaṅgraha), Sanskrit Pustakālaya, Benaras, 1940.

Daśarūpka (Dhanañjaya), Vidyābhavan Sanskrit Granthamālā, 7, Vārāṇasi, 1967.

Dhvanyāloka (Ānandavardhana) (with Locana of Abhinavagupta), Vidyābhavan Sanskrit Grantha Mālā, 97, Benaras, 1971.

Nāṭyadarpaṇa (Rāmacandra and Guṇacandra), Gaekwad Oriental Series, 48, 1929.

Nyāyasūtra (Gautama) (Nyāyadarśana), Benaras, 1942.

Nirukta (Yāska), Bhāratabharatī Press, Daryaganj, Delhi-6, 1964.

Nītiśataka, Śṛṅgāraśataka & Vairāgyaśataka (Bhartṛharī), Śrī Venketeśvara Press, Bombay, 1914.

Nāṭyaśāstra (Bharata), Kāvyamālā no. 42, Nirṇaya Sāgar Press, Bombay, 1943.

Pratāparudrayaśobhūṣaṇa (Vidyānātha) Bālamanorama Series No. 3, Madras, 1914.

Mahābhārata (Vedavyāsa), Gītā Press, Gorakhapura, VS. 2026.

Yogadarśana (Patañjali), Bhāratīya Vidyā Prakāśana, Vārāṇasī-1, 1971.

Raghuvaṁśa (Kālidāsa), Kālidāsa Granthāvalī, Bhārata Prakāśana Mandir, Aligarh, VS. 2019.

Rasagaṅgādhara (Jagannātha), Kāvyamālā 12, Bombay, 1930.

Rāmāyaṇa (Vālmīki), Pandit Pustakālya, Kāśī, 1951.

Viṣṇupurāṇa, Gītā Press, Gorakhapura, VS. 2009.

Vakroktijīvita (Kuntaka), Ātmā Rām and Sons, Delhi, 1955.

Vyaktiviveka (Mahimabhaṭṭa), Kāśī Sanskrit Series, 121, Benaras, VS. 1993.

Vedāntaparbhāṣā (Dharmarāja Adhvarīndra), Vidyābhavana Sanskrit Granthamālā, 100, Vārāṇasī, 1963.

Vākyapadīya (Bhartṛhari), University of Poonā, Sanskrit and Prākṛta Series, Poonā 1965.

Vikramāṅkadevacarita (Bilhaṇa), Haridāsa Sanskrit Granthamālā 254, Benaras, 1954.

Śiśupālavadha (Māgha), Vidyābhavan Sanskrit Granthamālā, 8, Benaras, 1955.

Sarasvatīkaṇṭhābharaṇa (Bhoja), Nārāyaṇa Press, Calcutta, 1894.

Sāhityadarpaṇa (Viśvanātha), Calcutta, VS. 1834.

Harśacarita (Bāṇa), Calcutta, 1939.

Sanskrit English Books

Concepts of Poetic Blemishes (Bechan Jhā), Vārāṇasī, 1965.

Concepts of Rīti & Guṇa in Sanskrit Poetics (Dr. P.C. Lahiri), The University of Decca, 1937.

Essays in Indian Poetics, Satya Dev Chowdhry, Vasudev Prakashan, Model Town, Delhi, 1965.

History of Sanskrit Poetics (Dr. P.V. Kane), Motilal Banarsidass, Delhi, 1951.

History of Sanskrit Poetics (S. K. De) (in two volumes) Calcutta, 1960.

Indian Theory of Meaning (K. Kunjuni Raja) Madras, 1963.

Problems of Sanskrit Poetics (S.K. De) Calcutta, 1959.

Principles of Literary Criticism in Sanskrit (R. C. Dwivedi), Motilal Banarsidass, Delhi, 1969.

Some Concepts of the Alaṁkāra Śāstra (V. Rāghavan), The Adyar Library, Adyar, 1942.

Śṛṅgāra Prakāśa of Bhoja (Dr. V. Rāghavan), 7 Śrīkṛṣṇa Puram Street, Madras-14, 1963.

The Problem of Meaning in Indian Philosophy, R. C. Pandey, Motilal Banarsidass, Delhi, 1963.

Journals

Annals of Bhandrakar Oriental Research Journal.

Dacca University Bulletin.

A Descriptive Catalogue of Sanskrit Manuscripts of Orissa. Vol. II.

A Descriptive Catalogue of the Sanskrit Manuscripts in the collection of the Asiatic Society of Bengal.

Indian Historical Quarterly Journal.

Journal of the Ganganath Jha Research Institute.

Journal of Oriental Institute, Madras.

Journal of the Asiatic Society, Bengal.

Orissa Historical Research Journal.

Poona Orientalist.
